DATE

The Evolution of Dutch Catholicism, 1958–1974

The
Evolution of
Dutch Catholicism,
1958–1974

John A. *loysius* Coleman

UNIVERSITY OF CALIFORNIA

BERKELEY / LOS ANGELES / LONDON

University of California Press
Berkeley and Los Angeles, California

University of California Press, Ltd.
London, England

Copyright © 1978 by
The Regents of the University of California

ISBN 0-520-02885-6
Library of Congress Catalog Card Number: 74-22958
Printed in the United States of America

1 2 3 4 5 6 7 8 9

Contents

Preface

I have accumulated a debt of gratitude in the years I have been writing this book. I am grateful to Robert N. Bellah, Ivan Vallier, Thomas O'Dea, and Marie Augusta Neal for advice in conceiving the research. I have profited from the suggestions and corrections of those who read earlier versions of the manuscript: Robert N. Bellah, Felix Malmberg, S. J., Peter McAffery, Marie Augusta Neal, Elizabeth Nottingham, Joseph Powers, S. J., Neil J. Smelser, and Peter Smulders, S. J. I am, of course, ultimately responsible for the way in which I have used their suggestions. Peter Wortelboer and Matthieu Kerbosch were of invaluable help in introducing me to the mysteries of the Dutch language. As young men who knew nothing of pre-conciliar Catholicism, they also convinced me of the goodness of the changes that have taken place within Dutch Catholicism. If future generations of Dutch Catholics resemble them, the church will not have to worry about writing its own epitaph.

I wish to express thanks to William van Burgundien of KASKI in the Hague and Jan Rupert of the Catholic Institute for Theology in Amsterdam for invaluable advice and prompt help in gathering library materials. Jan Rupert, especially, saw to it that no current article or book on my subject escaped my attention.

Two sources of support and suggestions throughout the research need special mention. My fellow Jesuit housemates at 47 De Lairesestraat, Amsterdam, provided constant leads, criticism, and encouragement. They also offered hospitality beyond my expectations. In listing their names I record my gratitude and the recognition of how much this book is really theirs: Wim Beuken, Felix Malmberg, Henry Renckens, Joe Reuzer, Jan Rupert, Peter Smulders, and Jack Wrynn. My daily discussions with Jan van Kilsdonk, S. J., over coffee at the Saint Ignatius College community in Amsterdam helped me greatly in bringing issues into focus and gaining a feeling for the personalities and events in Dutch Catholic history. His manuscript-length criticism of my original text saved me from many factual errors and challenged my interpretations. As much as any living Dutchman, van Kilsdonk embodies in his own history the evolution of Dutch Catholicism from a church of the economic minority to open, post-conciliar Catholicism. This is not the book he would have written, but it could not have been written without him.

I should like to dedicate this book to five teachers who have made a permanent impression on my mind: Maurice M. Belval, S. J., James Collins, Robert N. Bellah, Bernard Cardinal Alfrink, and Thomas E. Lasswell. From Alfrink I learned that it was possible for a bishop to be a great teacher in our own time. Tom Lasswell taught me that a teacher always puts his students' interest before his own.

Chapter 1

Strategy, Coalition, and Conflict

It was apparent to anyone attentively following the religious news stories in the 1960s that a genuine revolution was occurring within Dutch Catholicism. Even though many of the stories focused on isolated excesses or fringe phenomena, the prominence of the Dutch in international consciousness about Catholicism was disproportionate to their size and historic role in the world church. The Netherlands seemed the center for new theological, pastoral, liturgical, catechetical, and structural changes taking place within world Catholicism. The use of the vernacular in the liturgy, reception of communion in the hand, the employment of lay ministers within Catholic liturgies, the erection of church councils at the parish, diocesan, and national level, the articulation of a new theology of collegiality, dialogue, ecumenism, priesthood—all these developments either began in the Netherlands or attained their widest implementation there. The Netherlands thus offered obvious advantages for the study of changes in post-Vatican Catholicism.

The Dutch church also played a special role in the post-Vatican II international church as a symbolic alternative to Rome. Dutch Catholics became a positive or negative rallying symbol for progressive or traditionalist groups of Catholics in Germany, France, Great Britain, and the United States. Newspaper reports speculated about the possibility of a schism between the Netherlands and Rome. In the latter part of the 1960s and into the decade of the 1970s, Dutch-Roman conflicts were more frequent and more intense than ever in the recent history of Dutch-Roman relations, or in comparison with similar clashes between the church center and periphery in other countries.

The prominence of Dutch Catholicism becomes more curious when one learns that until the mid-1950s Dutch Catholicism was, by most indices, the most traditional on the continent. It had the highest rates for weekly mass attendance; the lowest rates of defection into the ranks of the unchurched; the strongest opposition to ecumenism with Protestants or socialists; the most faithful adherence to traditionalist birth-control norms; and it was the heaviest per capita exporter of priests, nuns, and religious workers—for though it represented only about 1 percent of world Catholicism, it produced 10 percent of all missionary personnel in the international church.[1] Both Pius XI and Pius XII had singled out Dutch Catholicism as a model church for other nations to follow. As late as 1958, the Roman nuncio, Mgr. Giobbe, when leaving the Hague after twenty-five years, could comment, "there is much for the church to learn from Catholic Netherlands."[2]

STATEMENT OF THE PROBLEM

What had happened between the 1950s and the 1960s to make the dams of Dutch Catholicism break loose? How had the model church of traditionalist pre-Vatican II Catholicism become the avant-garde in the international church? How was such a startling change in roles, norms, and sanctions within the church possible within such a short period of time? It is, intrinsically, a fascinating sociological problem.

A study of Dutch Catholicism might reveal the process of rapid, even revolutionary shifts in religious self-understanding and structures. Again, it offers an example of religious change that is not, for the purposes of sociology, a totally dependent variable.

Throughout my research I kept asking to what extent Dutch Catholicism was "deviant" within world Catholicism, or, conversely, to what extent it might serve as a model for understanding parallel changes which could be seen working, at slower tempos, in other national settings. The question did not yield any simple answers. On the one hand, Dutch Catholicism would not have been singled out as a phenomenon to watch if it were not in some sense deviant, a unique case. Indeed, I assumed that Catholicism would exhibit variations across national borders in response to historical, demographic, and cultural particularities. On the other hand, there did not seem to be any major theological or structural changes in the Netherlands which

1. For evidence of the traditionalism of Dutch Catholics in the 1950s, see Dr. F. Van Heek, *Het Geboorte Niveau der Nederlandse Rooms-Katholieken* (Leiden: H. Stenfert Kroese N.V., 1954).
2. See *Katholiek Archief*, XIII, *42* (October 17, 1958), column 981.

lacked parallels in other national settings. The very responses of progressives and traditionalists in the international church to Dutch Catholicism was a portent for those outside the Netherlands. It seemed reasonable to assume that Dutch Catholicism was not unique.

I decided to focus on structural changes within the church as my dependent variable. Within the structural complex I chose to look at changes in role definition for bishops, priests, and laity and the implementation of these in new institutional arrangements; at changes in the normative system, from hierarchical command-obedience relationships to concepts of collegiality and dialogue; and at changes in the sanction system, from external control through excommunication, suspension, interdicts, and censorship to internal control through ethical codes for sub-groups within the church.

It was clear that in order to do justice to the dramatic changes within Dutch Catholicism I would need to find explanatory devices which would, in principle, allow comparative study across national boundaries. I assumed throughout the study that Dutch Catholicism was a sort of *eglisse pilote*. Hence, I read Dutch "deviance" as largely a question of speed and thoroughness in implementing new strategies.

The problem, then, was to explain structural changes in church constitution as a variable in one national setting where tempo and sequence of change are the main problems. However, openness to comparative study was an important consideration in the selection of theoretical models.

THEORETICAL FRAMEWORK

My aim was to describe structural states for an entire national church unit. I wanted to know how these changes related to redirections in Dutch society, and I was interested in relating these changes to Catholicism as an international organizational unit. I sought greater inclusiveness rather than a narrow focus. The years 1958 and 1974 were chosen as boundary dates. The pontificate of John XXIII, and the subsequent redefinition of Catholic strategies for church-world influence, began in 1958. By that date one begins to see significant shifts in Dutch Catholicism, at least at the level of episcopal action.

I will be employing a theoretical perspective in sociology in which collectivities are regarded as problem-solving entities similar to individuals. Thus, a problem is treated on the prosaic, pragmatic level of adaptive behavior until symptoms of failure or breakdown raise questions about the adequacy of larger frames of reference: the normative role structures, or even the underlying value system.[3]

This theoretical perspective postulates something like a law of social inertia. Collective problem-solving units, like most individuals, usually do not search for problems. When confronted with a problem that bites hard and will not go away, they first recognize the problem and then begin to look for a solution. Most solutions are found by trial and error through collective experimenting. When collective problem-solving units find a solution that works, they tend to lock onto it, and generalize and perpetuate it as long as it works. Social life, however, is inherently dialectic. Any collective solution to a problem has built into it potential new strains, conflicts, and problems. Change is endemic. But collectivities, like individuals, are basically lazy and conservative. They do not discard old solutions as long as they are working. When facing new problems, their first instinct is to apply old solutions. They wait until it is clear that old solutions have failed before disrupting their routine to recognize and define new problems and collectively initiate the process of finding new solutions.

Furthermore, collectivities usually try to restrict the definition of a problem to the lowest level of cybernetic control within the society— to isolate it as a problem of mere technical adaptation, for example— before recognizing that the problem is fundamental or far-reaching enough to demand basic restructuring of the society at the level of norms and roles, or even at the level of fundamental cultural values. Resistance to change is built into collectivities. When change seems imperative, they try to restrict the extent or scope of the change until pressures build up to a point at which fundamental redefinition of the social structure seems justified.[4]

Genuine identity changes at the personal or collective level— changes that involve more than mere coping or adaptive behavior— seem to follow a sequence which includes: (1) detection of the problem through symptoms of failure; (2) communication that there is a problem; (3) analysis; (4) proposal; (5) attempts at the level of action; (6) evaluation on the basis of experimental action; and (7) institutionalization of the solution as the settled way to deal with the

3. See Talcott Parsons, *The Social System* (Glencoe, Illinois: The Free Press, 1951).
4. For a statement of the relation of the components of social action in social systems and the hierarchy of the components in achieving cybernetic control, see Neil J. Smelser, *Theory of Collective Behavior* (New York: The Free Press, 1962), pp. 32–34.

problem.[5] The base work on collectivities as problem-solving units and the sequencing of problem-solving came out of Bales and Slater's work on problem-solving processes in small groups in the 1950s.[6] Neil J. Smelser extended their insights to historical material in his study of role redefinition for the family during the Industrial Revolution in England and his typology for the study of social movements.[7]

THE CAUSES OF CHANGE

I turned to Smelser's work to find the theoretical framework for my research. From Smelser I chose four explanatory (independent) variables to explain the structural changes within Dutch Catholicism. These variables, shown in Table 1, are extraordinarily open and non-deterministic. In principle they allow cross-national comparisons. Whereas structural settings, pressures, and facilities are "objective" factors, the quality of change agents and the action of the social control authorities as variables depend upon some element of subjective intentional choice. Smelser places greatest weight on the fourth of these variables. Thus, he remarks that "if the public authorities in a society are themselves impaired or do not enjoy the cooperation and support of the population, then the assault on the strain inherited by the second phase will be less effective."[8] Again, when referring to the operation of social control, he says, "if authorities firmly put down displays of violence, but react patiently and responsibly to the grievances associated with violence, the probability of the spread of violence is typically low. If, however, authorities prove ineffectual in containing violence and/or remain inflexible in the face of demands for reform, the probability . . . is increased."[9]

I have adopted Smelser's emphasis on the action of social authorities as a key variable. Thus, great emphasis is placed upon the role of the episcopacy to explain Dutch changes and, in contrast, the less far-reaching changes in other national settings. The model is, in no

---

5. For these stages in collective problem-solving, see Robert Cooley Angell, *Free Society and Moral Crisis* (Ann Arbor: University of Michigan Press, 1958), p. 156.

6. See Robert F. Bales and Philip Slater, "Role Differentiation in Small Decision Making Groups," in *Family, Socialization and Interaction Process*, by Talcott Parsons and Robert F. Bales (London: Routledge and Kegan Paul, 1956), pp. 259–306.

7. Neil J. Smelser, *Social Change in the Industrial Revolution* (Chicago: University of Chicago Press, 1959); *Theory of Collective Behavior* (New York: The Free Press, 1962); *Essays in Sociological Explanation* (Englewood Cliffs, New Jersey: Prentice-Hall, Inc., 1968), Chapter VIII.

8. Smelser, *Essays in Sociological Explanation*, p. 272.

9. *Ibid.*, p. 272.

TABLE 1.
Independent Variables

1. Structural setting for change
2. Structural pressures or tensions for change
3. Mobilization resources for change, which includes
   (a) facilities to socialize a public in new role imagery and to mobilize participants for change and
   (b) the quantum and quality of change agents
4. The action of the social authorities

sense, a forecasting model inasmuch as no claims are made about future states of the structure beyond those which apply to the "objective" factors as situational limiting conditions. Its usefulness in the study of Dutch Catholicism is that it allows comparison of church changes with other social processes in politics, economics, and education. Moreover, since the model has rarely been applied to recent history, its testing in this case extends its usefulness.

I also accept Smelser's way of reading the sequence of change in problem-solving collectivities when the problem entails solutions of fundamental identity-change at the level of role or value, and when this new identity becomes institutionalized in an orderly way.

It should be made clear that the scheme set forth in Table 2 allows for empirical alternatives to successful problem-solving or to problem-solving in an orderly way: it allows for repression of symptoms at stage three and violent closure of the problem-solving sequence, and for revolution as an alternative to repression and a way to reopen the repressive closure of the sequence.[10] Smelser's model has been applied mainly to political changes where change agents and social authorities interact at the political level. In modern times, when the church has been a voluntary association, revolution does not seem very likely. But exit or withdrawal of individuals from the organization, collective schism, or the emergence of alternate "underground churches" seem the equivalent to revolution. We will look later at evidence which explains the absence of an underground church in the Netherlands and its presence in other national settings.

In dealing with Catholic material, one must always distinguish between social authorities at the local and national level (the episcopacy or national council) and those at the center of the international

10. I am following Smelser's account in *Essays in Sociological Explanation*, pp. 79–80. See also Talcott Parsons and Neil J. Smelser, *Economy and Society* (Glencoe, Illinois: The Free Press, 1956), Chapter V.

TABLE 2.
Sequence of Change

Stage One: Symptoms of dissatisfaction with the performance of incumbents of an institutionalized role or with the organization of the roles themselves *(detection of the problem)*.

Stage Two: Symptoms of disturbance, protest, or calls for change, reflecting this dissatisfaction *(communication of the problem)*.

Stage Three: Handling and channeling the symptoms of disturbance. The first line of defense of agencies of control is a kind of holding action in attempts to contain the results of dissatisfaction *(holding the problem at bay)*.

Stage Four: The collectivity encourages the new ideas which purport to deal with the supposed source of dissatisfaction *(analysis of the problem)*.

Stage Five: The collectivity attempts to specify the institutional forms that will ease the supposed sources of dissatisfaction *(proposal)*.

Stage Six: The collectivity attempts to establish new institutional forms *(essay and evaluation)*.

Stage Seven: The new institutional forms are consolidated as permanent features *(locking-in and consensus)*.

SOURCE: After Neil J. Smelser, *Essays in Sociological Explanation* (Englewood Clifs, N.J.: Prentice-Hall, Inc., 1968), pp. 79–80.

church in Rome. Because national church units are sub-units within an international church, they can never be treated as purely autonomous. It also is important to remember that Smelser's model assumes that tremendous costs in psychological and social displacement will accompany modes of change which involve a reconstitution of norms or values.

STRUCTURAL DIFFERENTIATION

The seven-sequence model is essentially an explanatory device for the study of structural differentiation. Smelser defines and exemplifies the concept:

Simply defined, differentiation is the evolution from a multi-functional role structure to several more specialized structures. . . . During a society's transition from domestic to factory industry, the division of labor increases, and the economic activities, previously lodged in the family, move to the firm. Formally defined . . . structural differentiation is a process whereby one social role or organization . . . differentiates into two or more roles or organizations which function more effectively in the new historical circumstances. The new social units are

structurally distinct from each other, but taken together are function-
ally equivalent to the original unit.[11]

Structural differentiation occurs under certain conditions of strain
which push the collective unit toward the search for a solution. The
emergence of new structures out of a parent structure which performed fused or diffuse functions alleviates strain. The process may
sound smooth and neat, but that is seldom the case. First, there is
generally a time lag between the recognition of a problem, its
proposed solution, and consensus on a solution which constitutes an
extension of the common culture.[12] In that time lag, the drama of
history takes place. The fact that groups are problem-solving units
does not mean that they are always rational, efficient maximizers of
their utilitarian interest. For social life as well as for personal life,
Freud's metaphor obtains: rationality is the mere tip of the iceberg.
As Smelser states it:

> Differentiation does not happen automatically. It occasions a great
> deal of pain and dislocation for people and it destroys many traditions
> that are likely to be held sacred; consequently, it brings on a flurry of
> protest, uncertainty, groping and experimentation before new, more
> differentiated, units actually appear. Differentiation, therefore, pro-
> duces conflict and social disorganization which is likely to jeopardize
> social stability.[13]

It is clear, then, that the seven sequence model presented in Table
2 predicts conflict. In stages one through three, conflict is predicted
between change agents (the prophets of change who signal symptoms
of disturbance and dissatisfaction) and the social authorities who
engage in a holding action; in stages four through six, conflict is
expected between interest groups with material or ideal interests
supportive or resistant to change.

It will be my contention that the massive changes occurring within
world Catholicism and the especially dramatic shifts within the Dutch
church are best understood through the model of differentiation. In
effect, two very different but related kinds of differentiation have
taken place. The postwar period produced strong evidence of growing
dissatisfaction with the role definitions within the international
church and also the first response of a "holding action" on the part of
the social authorities. The problem was that traditional organization

11. Smelser, *Essays in Sociological Explanation*, p. 129.
12. For evidence of this time lag, see Bales and Slater, "Role Differentiation in Small Decision
Making Groups," p. 301.
13. Smelser, *Essays in Sociological Explanation*, p. 79.

assumed a Catholic-dominated society in which pope, bishop, priest, and laity were organized in a hierarchical fashion. The hierarchical church set its stamp upon the way secular society was organized. Hence, Catholics argued for a fusion of church and secular society. In pluralistic societies in which Catholics were a minority, they organized the sub-units into separately institutionalized confessional organizations—subject to the hierarchical church—in order to influence secular society. The church's aims were diffuse rather than specific.

For a long time Catholicism failed to face the problem of function-loss, as economics, politics, education, and welfare became separated from the church, and the civil religions (based on religious understanding of national identity) became differentiated from Catholicism or from Christianity as a particularist creed.[14] Social differentiation implies both some function-loss for the parent institution and a concomitant functional specialization. The process had not been completed because the church had not yet specialized around religious tasks nor differentiated the church as a community of faith, distinct from separately organized Catholic institutions operating in the secular world. Hence, the Catholic case presents an example of reactive differentiation. The church was catching up with a long process by which the world came of age. As even religious functions, such as the civil religion, moved away from the church, Catholics emerged from their long isolation to seek new partners in the ecumenical movement or in non-Christian milieus. On the other hand, more than a mere reaction to external forces was involved. Internally, the church differentiated itself as a community of faith from its own organizational apparatus.

Such processes of specialization and differentiation do not reduce the significance of institutional spheres—religion, family, education, and so on. They tend to focus and integrate the peculiar competencies of a particular institutional sphere. The given unit no longer has to be all things to all persons. Instead of attempting to provide order to all aspects of society, the specialized unit performs a defined range of tasks within a wider, integrated system.[15]

14. For a treatment of the differentiation of the civil religion from the churches, see Talcott Parsons, "Belief, Unbelief and Disbelief," in *The Culture of Unbelief,* Rocco Caporale and Antonio Grumelli, eds. (Berkeley: University of California Press, 1971), pp. 221–224. Wider treatments of the concept of civil religion can be found in *Beyond Belief* by Robert N. Bellah (New York: Harper and Row, 1970), pp. 168–189, and John A. Coleman, "Civil Religion," *Sociological Analysis,* XXXI, 2 (Summer 1970), 55–67.
15. See Ivan Vallier, *Catholicism, Social Control and Modernization in Latin-America* (Englewood Cliffs, New Jersey: Prentice-Hall, Inc., 1970), p. 154.

The church in France in the postwar period was the main battle-ground for the prophets of change in the 1950s, and French theology became a typical model for others.[16] The rise of the *nouvelle théologie* of Congar, Teilard, de Lubac, and Danielou in France, the worker-priest movement, and the international response to the postwar letters of Cardinal Suhard revealed that the problems raised during the modernist crisis would not go away. The holding-action in the late papacy of Pius XII, symbolized by *Humani Generis* and the revival of the anti-modernist techniques of repression (censorship and removal from office), was similar to that of Pius X and Cardinal Merry del Val during the modernist crisis earlier in the century.[17] The holding action of Pius XII affected Dutch Catholicism and represents its first modern conflict with the papal center. Its public disclosure in the period of Vatican II made Dutch Catholics conscious for the first time of the "myth" of Roman wisdom and justice and the perils of secrecy.

John XXIII, who had lived in France during the crisis of the *nouvelle théologie*, recognized that the growing dissatisfaction with the traditional strategy for church influence would not go away. (The traditional strategy was determined by role norms for priest, laity, and bishop, an authoritarian sanction system, and value foundations in a two-world, two-order society—nature and supernature, clergy and lay.) At Vatican Council II, John XXIII opened a forum to encourage new ideas for dealing with the supposed sources of dissatisfaction. If the years of the council represent stage four in the seven-stage sequence of change, the years since then represent varying stages within the international church. In some settings (England, for example), the national church remains at stage four, with different sub-groups of Catholics fighting over the new ideas which claim to be able to handle the dissatisfaction. In other settings (such as the United States and France), the battles are over the institutional forms which will specify these ideas, since wide-reaching consensus at stage four has been achieved. In still other settings (The Netherlands, Belgium, Scandinavia, Switzerland, and to a lesser extent Germany), the church is already in stages six or seven.

16. Garry Wills, *Bare Ruined Choirs* (Garden City, New York: Doubleday and Company, Inc., 1973), pp. 38–60, relates the influence of French postwar Catholicism upon American Catholics.
17. For a succinct treatment of the modernist crisis, see Thomas O'Dea, *The Catholic Crisis* (Boston: Beacon Press, 1968), pp. 38–39.

A TYPOLOGY OF STRATEGIES
FOR CHURCH INFLUENCE

Granted that new institutional arrangements will vary across national boundaries, is it possible to draw up ideal types of pre- and post-Vatican role structures which display both the church's traditional missionary strategy and its new cultural, pastoral strategy? I turned to the work of Ivan Vallier, one of the few sociologists to study Catholic structures in a comparative, cross-national perspective, for ideal-type hypotheses.[18] Since Vallier's types were not derived from Dutch data, it was less likely that my before-and-after typologies would be ad hoc nominalistic descriptions. In principle, they allow cross-national comparisons. Since they were drawn from a setting long thought to be a bastion of traditional Catholicism, Latin-America, they indicate the extent to which differentiation is occurring internationally. Finally, they allow a measure of "objectivity" to the claim that Dutch Catholics are not deviant in the direction of their change, but only in the speed and thoroughness with which they have implemented new role definitions, norms, and sanctions. Table 3 shows Vallier's types.[19]

FROM A MISSIONARY TO A
CULTURAL-PASTORAL STRATEGY

Reading down and across Table 3 we can see the following patterns:

1. The model of end-points for structural differentiation assumes that the level of church ambitions remains constant for both pre- and post-Vatican strategies. There is a shift from the style of militant missionary strategies toward a cultural-pastoral strategy, with accompanying shifts in the role expectations for bishops, priests, and laity. Under both conditions the church is anxious to extend its influence beyond its own sphere to the wider society and to deepen the level and intensity of commitment within its own membership. Thus the model assumes that church ambitions remain high.

18. Ivan Vallier, *Catholicism, Social Control and Modernization;* see also his "Religious Elites: Differentiations and Developments in Roman Catholicism," in Seymour M. Lipset and Aldo Solari, eds. *Elites in Latin America* (New York: Oxford University Press, 1967), pp. 190–232. For problems of methodology in comparative studies of Catholicism, see Vallier's "Comparative Studies of Roman Catholicism: Dioceses as Strategic Units," *Social Compass*, XVI, 2 (1969), 147–184.
19. Table III is an adaption from Vallier, *Catholicism, Social Control and Modernization*, p. 72.

TABLE 3.
Pre-Vatican and Post-Vatican Structure

Factors	Missionary Strategy	Cultural-Pastoral Strategy
1. Level of church ambition	High	High
2. Church-society relationship	Separation and controlled contact	Integrated autonomy
3. Major base of influence	Differentiated Catholic organizations	Socio-ethical leadership
4. Secondary base of influence	Ideological formation	Local congregation
5. Target group	Workers and middle class within Catholic population; converts	Intellectuals and youth within Catholic population; general "other person" within the society
6. Dominant ideology	Block or overcome secularization	Pluralist participation
7. Religious action principle	Penetration of strategic secular spheres *en bloc*	Secular involvement
8. Priest's primary role	Missionary and militant organizer, political middleman for Catholic economic minority	Pastor and spiritual leader
9. Organizational mode	Grassroots missions and Catholic action cells coupled with decentralized pastoral units	National unit and coordinated micro-units at congregational level
10. Layman's role	Hierarchical auxiliary: agent of the bishop	Christian citizen

2. The relationship between the church and the secular society changes as the church shifts from a missionary to a cultural-pastoral strategy. In traditional pre-Vatican Catholicism a stark separation of the church from the secular is emphasized. The church is not a pure sect because it allows controlled contact between its membership and the secular world. It invests great energies in maintaining controls to see that that contact, insofar as possible, takes place entirely on its own terms. In the post-Vatican strategy the church aims at a condition of integrated autonomy wherein both church and secular world remain independent in an emergent condition of integrated co-operation.

3. In the pre-Vatican missionary strategy, the church sees its major basis for influencing wider society in separate confessional organizations—Catholic labor unions, political parties, school systems, recreational facilities, and so on. Through these the church gains political power in society at large. In the post-Vatican cultural-pastoral strategy, the church attempts to rely more on persuasion and religious authority to reach audiences beyond its membership. In a process of differentiation, the Catholic episcopacy foregoes informal political roles to provide socio-ethical leadership within the wider community. The bishops speak to more than their own faithful when they expand particularist Catholic symbols to cover the rights and duties of citizenship, so as to legitimate not only Catholic positions but also human rights, and when they fight against poverty, war, inequality, dishonesty, and persecution. This is not to say that the bishops learn overnight to transcend their traditionally narrow particularist interests. But the pattern postulated in Table 3 can be seen in several national settings, particularly Brazil, the Netherlands, Chile, and to a lesser extent the United States and Canada, all following the lead set by John XXIII. Bishops acquire a new role, which Vallier describes as follows:

> Instead of using their office and prestige as bases for promoting confessional goals and mobilizing commitments to sacramental participation, the stress has been on the problems of the poor, the importance of human freedom and dignity, and the sacredness of the value of social justice. In these allocutions the "Catholic" elements of religious meaning are subordinated to values and goals that are universally sacred. Political issues are implied in these endorsements, of course. But they do not necessarily politicize the church, first, because the church lays the responsibility for the implementation of changes on members as citizens; second, because these values hold a

charisma and legitimation on many bases other than Christian beliefs or Catholic theology.[20]

4. In traditional Catholicism, the church elites saw their secondary base of influence—their influence upon their own membership—to depend upon strategies of ideological formation within Catholic schools or Catholic action cells. The episcopacy sought to produce "formed" Catholics who might become agents of the church's purpose in the world. In the post-Vatican strategy, the locus for church influence over its own membership is the local congregation. Each congregation begins to specialize in liturgical and pastoral functions, drawing its constituency across traditional parochial boundaries and building a sense of community. Religious choices and conscientious decisions are seen, increasingly, as allowing pluriform outcomes. Vallier notes:

> In addition, the church concentrates on activities at the local level in order to draw the individual into the church as a fully committed and loyal layman. The goal of the control strategy is twofold: the formation of local church units which supply a focus for merging religious and social needs (and, incidentally, the locus for disseminating church influence), and the socialization of a layman able to live in a pluralistic, secular society as a Christian and a citizen simultaneously—the key agent of Catholic influence. At this point, the role of the clergy is essentially that of a teacher-counselor or pastor who aids the members of his congregation without infringing upon their individual autonomy.[21]

5. Factor five in Table 3—target groups for church influence—refers to groups which need special attention or receive special priority from the church elites, either because they are peculiarly receptive to church influence or because they are especially vulnerable to the temptation of defection to the ranks of the non-churched. In the period after the industrial revolution, so disastrous for the church's hold over workers, the traditional church (at least since the papacy of Leo XIII) placed special priority on programs directed toward the workers and the middle class. The church was more interested in preserving its own members than in recruiting converts. In the post-Vatican strategy, the church shifts emphasis to those groups most likely to defect: the Catholic intellectuals and youth. While it has reduced efforts at conversion, the church retains ambitions to

20. *Ibid.*, pp. 85–86.
21. *Ibid.*, p. 76.

influence the moral and ethical persuasions of non-Catholics by initiating dialogue networks and inviting them to cooperate with transconfessional aims. Here we ascertain new strategies for ecumenism and dialogue.

6. The dominant ideology of the pre-Vatican missionary strategy was concerned with blocking or overcoming autonomous secular movements which, generally, were regarded negatively. In the post-Vatican cultural-pastoral strategy, the church accepts a cooperative role in religiously pluralistic societies.

7. The key religious action principle of traditional Catholicism envisioned the penetration of strategic secular spheres (education, politics, the media) by means of Catholic elites or through confessional organizations. The church hoped to use these strategic secular spheres from within for its own purposes. The cultural-pastoral strategy, on the other hand, sees secular involvement by emancipated yet conscientious Catholic laity as the fundamental principle of religious action.

8. In traditional Catholicism the priest's primary role, besides dispensing sacramental rituals and instruments, was that of a missionary and militant organizer forming Catholic action cells or confessional organizations. Much of the priest's diffuse authority and prestige flowed from his role as political middleman and spokesman for Catholic economic minorities. Indeed, despite rhetoric systems of otherworldly piety which exalted his position in the system of spiritual stratification within the church, the priest's energies were diffuse, unspecialized, and frequently expended on non-pastoral tasks within Catholic political, educational, or recreational systems. The post-Vatican strategy foresees a new role for the priest. His primary tasks become the liturgy, the sermon, and spiritual counseling, as well as the formation of a local sense of community. It is assumed that while the priest's message and counseling will have secular, even political import, the priest will not translate that message into partisan politics or engage directly in secular occupations.

9. The mode for internal organization within traditional Catholicism consisted in a strong organization at the international level in areas of doctrine and discipline rather than in pastoral, liturgical, and catechetical planning and coordination. The central bureaucracy of the church was more concerned with controlling orthodoxy than serving as a coordinating and planning administration. At national and diocesan levels, planning and coordination were typically decentralized within territorial pastoral units, the diocese and the parish,

rather than between them. Rather than being an organizational monolith, traditional Catholicism was decentralized, unfocused, and often chaotic. The traditional structure was "ideologically divided, extensively segmented at the national and diocesan levels and generally uncoordinated in its administrative and pastoral efforts . . . flat and decentralized rather than hierarchical and bureaucratic."[22] Besides decentralized territorial pastoral units, church elites organized grassroots missions and Catholic Action cells which were, typically, poorly articulated either with one another or with the territorial pastoral units. Competition between religious orders and the diocesan clergy exacerbated the pre-Vatican lack of coordination.

The post-Vatican cultural-pastoral strategy looks to the emergence of national unity among dioceses within a national coordinating unit. The national episcopal conferences which have emerged since Vatican II entail, further, coordination of the micro-units at the congregational level through central bureaucracies.

10. In traditional Catholicism the lay person's role was either that of passive hearer and doer of the church's word or, in more active phases, the hierarchy's auxiliary who, as agent of the bishop, represented Catholic Action in the secular sphere. In place of this role, the post-Vatican strategy foresees new possibilities of mobilizing independent lay energies within the church and non-church spheres around the role of the Christian citizen. The layman is expected to be a responsible co-participant as a committed Christian within both the church and the political society.

Vallier sums up the new strategy:

> In the cultural-pastoral stage, the church develops a four-fold influence relationship with society. (1) At the cultural level, it assumes the role of *spokesman for a higher moral order,* emphasizing the contemporary needs and relations of men. (2) On the instituational level, it sponsors programs of public assistance and social development in areas and spheres not dealt with by the government. . . . (3) But in addition, the church concentrates on activities *at the local level* in order to draw the individual into the church as a fully committed and loyal layman. (4) The goal of the control strategy is twofold: the formation of local church units, which supply a focus for merging religious and social needs (and, incidentally, the locus for disseminating church influence) and the socialization of a layman able to live in a pluralistic, secular society as a Christian and citizen simultaneously, *the key agent of Catholic influence.*[23]

22. *Ibid.,* p. 24.
23. *Ibid.,* p. 76. Use of numbers and italics in the citation are mine.

Table 3, which compares the pre-Vatican missionary strategy with the post-Vatican cultural-pastoral strategy, helps us fill out the seven-sequence model for structural differentiation. Note, however, that this table is a typology, essentially a series of hypotheses about the ways in which elites will structure church resources and energies—that is, the kind of coalitions they will enter, the roles defined for bishops, priests, and laity, the target groups for church influence, and modes of organization. Only the data from history can flesh out these hypotheses and test their validity. In the attempt to test this typology for Dutch Catholicism, I will go beyond Vallier's categories to discuss norms and sanctions regulating command-obedience relations.

We have, then, all of the theoretical ingredients necessary to undertake a systematic look at historical materials for the years 1958 to 1974: (1) four independent variables to explain the tempo and sequencing of structural change in the Dutch case (Table 1); (2) a model for history which predicts a definite sequencing of the changes in the process of structural differentiation (Table 2); (3) a before-and-after typology as hypotheses for describing the face of the structural change in the Dutch case (Table 3).

One last caveat remains. Both Smelser and Vallier tend to place greater weight upon the structural variables than they are able to support. Structures are never totally autonomous from culture or vice versa. Both are interdependent, if partially autonomous, variables. In a sense, my theoretical model is still too mechanical, reductionist, and mono-causally structuralist. While structural setting, strains, and mobilization resources help plot the pressures which are being responded to or repressed, the model of sequence predicts stages followed in structural differentiation. Vallier's typology provides an ideal-type structural freezing of before-and-after states of differentiation.

What the model does not provide is a clue to why the structural changes take the particular content and direction they do. It seems demonstrably to be the case that the content and direction of change in the church is partially dependent upon the new theological culture legitimized by Vatican Council II around the themes of collegiality, dialogue, democratization, pluralism in theology, free theological inquiry, and free speech in the church. New theologies of creation, salvation, revelation, and grace have undercut rigid nature-super-nature distinctions or too-facile divisions between the sacred and the profane. These new theologies have implications for the way in which the roles of priest and laity are defined in the church, and for the way in which they allow the appeal to experience (instead of to trans-physical fiat) as the basis for the church's understanding of its own symbols and "the signs of the times." What is involved, then, is not only two different structures for the church, but two different theological visions. Depending on which vision one has, one will make either a positive or negative assessment of the structural differentiation.

In Chapters Two and Three, I focus mainly on structural setting for change and pressures for change. In Chapter Two, I present historical material prior to 1958 to show how Catholics and other Dutch groups chose to adapt the peculiarly Dutch solution to the problem of pluralism: *verzuiling,* which literally means "columnization" or "pillarization," referring to a metaphor of separate columns supporting a common arch, which is Dutch society. I relate how the Dutch Catholics were spared the great crises which divided the church elsewhere in Europe, like the crisis over the principle of separation of church and state following the French Revolution; the defection of the working class to socialism; the intellectual crisis of modernism; and the compromise of the church with Fascism in World War II.

In Chapter Two we see how the Catholic minority in the Netherlands achieved economic emancipation. They did so collectively through separate confessional institutions. They did so relatively late in modern history. They entered the period of Vatican II with a *conscious* identity as Catholics who had achieved collective emancipation in a pluralistic country where there was Protestant and socialist air to breathe, yet a world of separatist confessional organizations. Finally, I relate how, in the postwar period, the first symptoms of dissatisfaction and disturbance arose and how the first response of the episcopacy was a repressive holding action: in its 1954 mandatory letter, *Het Mandament,* it ruled that Catholics who joined the socialist labor unions, listened to socialist radio broadcasts, or regularly bought socialist newspapers would be excommunicated.

In Chapter Three, I freeze history in the 1950s to distill Dutch social structure. With the help of extensive statistical material I detail the cost and advantages to Dutch society of columnization. I argue that with economic emancipation for the three underprivileged groups of the nineteenth century (the orthodox Calvinists called the Gereformeerden, the Catholics, the Socialists), the costs of columnization began to outweigh its advantages. The costs led to inter-group conflict, duplication of facilities, low national consensus, a blocked movement of employment opportunity, and smothering organizational life. Columnization was able to work smoothly only at the cost of elitism and internal authoritarianism within each bloc. There were inherent structural strains and contradictions in maintaining a "wider" society which was pluralistic, democratic, and dedicated to free speech when the groups involved were Dutch sub-societies which were unitary, non-democratic, and dogmatic.

I argue, further, that these pressures could not be alleviated unless the Catholic bloc underwent change. Socialist attempts—supported by about one-third of the Dutch Reformed Church and a very small Catholic group—to change confessional columnization in 1945 and the years immediately after the war failed. Columnization increased rather than decreased until the mid-1950s. At 40 percent of the population, the Catholics were the largest single bloc. They were also by far the best organized confessional enclave, because the Protestants were divided into many organizations.

The Catholics had been the middlemen for any dialogue, cooperation, or consensus between the orthodox Protestant and socialist blocs. Catholics were also more vulnerable than the orthodox Protestants to appeals to break out of confessionalism. The Catholics are the structural keystone for the arch which bridges the columns. Culturally, of course, Protestantism is central, a main source of the sober life style of the Dutch; but structurally it is more peripheral. Real power in politics and the media is divided between socialists and Catholics, the two largest blocs.

My controlling argument is that major shifts in Catholics' understanding of their role within wider Dutch society (hence, real shifts toward a more open society) were dependent upon changes within the church. Only a rethinking of the traditional roles of bishop, priest, and laity and the traditional strategy for church influence could remove the tensions which had built up in the 1950s.

Dutch Catholics, receptive to the new ideas emanating from Vatican II, discovered an elective affinity between these ideas and their own structural needs. As Chapters Four and Five relate, they opened up their own column, reduced self-identities based on negative out-group identity, democratized their own internal Catholic world, and distinguished between the church as a community of faith and the confessional apparatus. The confessional apparatus continues in only slightly reduced vigor (really, only politics has been deeply changed), although few people "believe" in separatism any longer. Self-interests will keep the apparatus going for some time. Nevertheless, the decline in belief in the principle of separation should eventually undermine this commitment. At any rate, Dutch Catholics are now on record as supporting the open, deconfessionalized world.

Chapters Two through Five try to capture a threefold set of pressures for change which coalesced to produce the rapid change in Dutch Catholicism in the 1960s. (1) There were pressures from outside Catholicism but from within Dutch society: the socialists, a minority faction of the Dutch Reformed Church, and a tiny group of Catholic elites wished to abandon separatism for an open, neutral society within which pluralism would be respected. These groups put pressure on Catholics to accept new rules for accommodation in Dutch society. (2) There were indigenous pressures from within Catholicism: elite groups of clergy and laity sought democratic freedoms within their closed society, arguing for a "loyal opposition" within the church. (3) There were pressures from Catholicism on the international level: Dutch Catholics responded to the *nouvelle théologie* of the French church in the 1950s, as well as to the legitimations for rethinking Catholic role identifications and strategies proposed during the pontificate of John XXIII. There was an elective affinity between the new ideas of dialogue, pluralist participation, and collegiality and the needs of Dutch society to break away from elitism and internal authoritarianism. In turn, the speed with which these new ideas were given structural embodiment made Dutch Catholicism a symbolic alternate center to Rome for those committed to the new theology of Vatican II.

Chapters Four through Seven focus upon the unequal facilities for mobilizing change within Dutch Catholicism. In these chapters I show how advocates of change gained control of key positions and how others in positions of power changed their attitudes in the period 1958-1974. Laity staffed or headed the confessional organizations. It was to their advantage to champion new role definitions of lay autonomy and co-responsibility for the church. This would give them an active voice in the policy of the church.

Chapters Four through Seven also contain the principal treatment of the Dutch episcopacy. The Dutch bishops were almost unique in world Catholicism in their independence from state and Roman control. Because of a special medieval privilege, they were nominated by members of their own lower clergy, a privilege rescinded unilaterally by Rome in 1971. Again, small numbers discouraged careerism in the episcopacy. Once a man is bishop, he has no place to go. Finally, the Dutch church forms one natural unit: a church province consisting of one archdiocese and its suffragen dioceses.

Because of columnization, the Dutch church had long been organized *ad extra* as a national rather than a diocesan church. The bishops met together frequently, exercising a collegial form of government. Since Vatican II, the church, as such, is organized more and more on a national basis, with the bishops as a sort of collective board of trustees. The Dutch bishops thus had a head start over other national episcopacies in forming an episcopal conference at the end of Vatican Council II.

Chapter Four places great emphasis on the new "style" given to the role of the bishop by the popular "Pope John of the Netherlands," Bishop Willy Bekkers, and on Bernard Alfrink's championing of free inquiry, freedom of the press, open dialogue, and collegiality. Because the Dutch bishops became champions of social reform in the church, the structural changes occurred in the Netherlands with less conflict than elsewhere.

Because Chapters Four through Seven contain the core of the evidence, they are addressed to several tasks. Besides exemplifying the two independent variables of mobilization resources and actions of the social authorities, they test Smelser's hypotheses about sequences of change and Vallier's hypotheses about the end-points of the structural differentiation. I argue in Chapters Four and Five that the period 1958-1965 represents stage four, and in Chapters Six and Seven that the period 1967-1974 represents stages five and six in the structural differentiation.

I have organized Chapters Four through Seven around seven rubrics which provide key themes: (1) National Coordinating units for planning the pastorate, liturgy, catechesis, and preaching. (2) Collegial structures: role definitions of bishop, priest, and laity. (3) Public opinion in the church. (4) Ecumenism and new coalition partners. (5) Congregational form for specialized parishes. (6) Contestation groups. (7) Center-periphery conflicts.

Rubrics 1 through 5 in the above list are topical ways to test my hypotheses about a cultural-pastoral strategy. They include, as they are fleshed out in Chapters Four through Seven, detailed descriptions of the new roles, norms, and sanctions in the church and the organizational mode in which the church coordinates them around a new strategy for influence. Rubrics 6 and 7 are intended to handle the predicted conflicts built into the differentiation model. Rubric 6 treats of conflict at the national level and rubric 7 of conflicts between Rome and the Netherlands.

The action of the Roman social authorities vis-à-vis Dutch developments is not simple to chart. From 1958 to 1966 there was a hands-off attitude toward developments in the Netherlands. John XXIII seemed to have had a special admiration for Alfrink. The Roman curia was busy protecting its own interests during the years of the council. Rome began to dispute Dutch developments only after 1966, and the first intense conflicts occurred in 1968. Until the appointment of two conservative bishops in 1971 and 1972, Rome could not get a real grip on Dutch Catholicism. Neither of the conservative episcopal appointments has been a conspicuous success for Rome's purposes. The first appointment, Mgr. Adrien Simonis, increasingly resembles the other Dutch bishops.

The second conservative, Mgr. Jan Gijsen, has been locked into a sort of ecclesiastical civil war in his diocese, and has had no major success in winning allegiance from his lower clergy and laity. None of the other Dutch bishops has come to his aid. Nor has the collective style of episcopal pronouncement noticeably altered. It is my view that Rome moved too late to stop the structural changes which had been institutionalized by 1970, and that these will not be easily reversed, as the extraordinary difficulties of Mgr. Gijsen in gaining authority in his diocese seem to show. Had Rome wanted to stop the differentiation, the time to have intervened was in 1966, by forbidding the amazing collective enthusiasm connected with the Dutch National Pastoral Council described in Chapter Six.

A description of the impact of the Simonis and Gijsen appointments is given in Chapter Eight. The purpose of studying the episcopal careers of Simonis and Gijsen is to test my assumption that the differentiation described in Chapters Four through Seven has already been institutionalized. If it has, even those who oppose the direction of change in Dutch Catholicism will have to confront the new structures and the new expectations built into role definitions for bishop, priest, and laity. The appointments of Simonis and Gijsen provide an important test of the support for the new structures. They also remind us of the varying power of social structure versus individual personality in processes of social change.

In the final chapter, I attempt a prognosis for the future of the church in the Netherlands on the basis of statistical evidence on decolumnization in the 1960s.

The three terms which form the title of this chapter are a summary way of organizing my analysis:

1. Strategy. The church has shifted from a diffuse strategy for controlling society to a new, cultural-pastoral strategy based on a structural differentiation of church and secular society, a differentiation which entails neither separation nor opposition, but a new integration.

2. Coalition. As a result of the new strategy, the church is open to a new pluralistic coalition as it participates in the secular world. It joins the ecumenical movement and exercises new forms of socio-ethical leadership which address the whole society, and often claim to speak for it, without imperialistic pretensions. As the church itself becomes an open, pluralistic sub-society, it provides opportunities for new intra-church coalitions to emerge. Dutch Catholicism is not particularly "radical" nor does it represent a successful coup carried out by a small cabal of progressives. It consists of a coalition of forces within Catholic society which mirrors forces in Dutch life. Like Dutch political society, the church is a moderately progressive organization based on compromise and practical problem-solving. Perhaps more than any other group of bishops, the Dutch bishops have found ways to allow their collective mind to come to conscious articulation.

3. Conflict. Interlevel lags and leads and an open forum for expression within the church provoked conflict both within the Dutch church and between it and Rome. My theoretical models anticipate conflicts, so they came as no surprise. These models value conflict as part of the dialectic of continuity and change in social existence. Now, let us examine the theory in the light of the drama of history.

Chapter 2

Collective Emancipation and Catholic Power

AN EMBATTLED CHURCH, 1559–1853

On the eve of the Reformation and the eighty-year war for Dutch independence from the Hapsburgs and Spain, the Netherlands was politically and religiously atypical within Catholic Europe. Long a feudal holding of the German emperors, the Netherlands lay too far from the imperial court to have acquired a large nobility. Lacking political centralization, it was divided into seventeen semi-autonomous provinces, each containing cities or local areas, jealously preoccupied with their ancient privileges and local rights. Especially in the north, the constant battle against the sea had necessitated local cooperative units to man the dikes and dams. These units were typically democratic in their constitutional structure.

On the eve of the Reformation, the Dutch church was poorly organized. The diocese of Utrecht was large and unwieldly, covering all of present-day Netherlands except the southern provinces of Limburg and North Brabant. The south—present-day Belgium—was divided into two dioceses.

The revolt of the Netherlands against Philip II was rooted in diverse motives and causes. It was generally a fight against the presence of Spanish troops on Dutch soil, heavy taxation without representation imposed by the Duke of Alba, the introduction of the methods of the Spanish Inquisition, and a proposal for reorganizing the church into twelve dioceses with the right of nomination in the hands of Philip II. It was feared that Philip's nominees would be either Spaniards or their tools. In essence, the Dutch revolt was a conservative revolt for

ancient privileges, "the privileges, the charters and what they contained—the right of local self-government and independence of
social groups."[1]

Prior to the Reformation the Netherlands had undergone a religious reform in which the lower clergy and lay elements turned
toward pietism, biblical sources, and a Christian humanism. At the
upper levels of Catholic life, voices of reform and criticism, such as
those of Gerard Groote and Thomas à Kempis, Erasmus and Agricola, were heard in the church. Only the province of Utrecht sent
clergy to the parliament; in other provinces the clergy was not represented. Similarly, even before the Reformation, "the town councils
forbade by law the transfer of real estate to the church . . . they
limited ecclesiastical jurisdiction over people not directly connected
with the church."[2]

Religious Background of the New Republic

In the course of the eighty-year war for independence the Catholic
south (present-day Belgium) came to terms with Spain. By 1580 the
north had fallen into the control of the Calvinist merchant class.
Nevertheless, it would be a mistake to see the revolt of the Netherlands as primarily a religious war. The leader of the revolt in the
north, William the Silent, insisted on religious toleration and forced
acceptance of it upon a reluctant, Calvinist-controlled states-general,
even in the provinces of Holland and Zealand, which were Calvinist
strongholds. Throughout his life William upheld "the right of the
individual who was peaceful and law-abiding to liberty of opinion
and freedom of religion."[3] The Calvinist William won Catholic
support. "Confidence was expressed by Catholics no less than by
Protestants that only under his leadership could the country be
delivered from Spanish tyranny."[4] The north and the eastern
provinces of the Netherlands where most of the nobility were centered remained Catholic until well into the eighteenth century.[5]

1. See Bernard H. M. Vlekke, "The Dutch Before 1581," in *The Netherlands*, Bartholomew
Landheer, ed. (Berkeley: University of California Press, 1943), p. 36. In my general account of
the first formative years of the Dutch Republic I am following, besides Vlekke, George
Edmundson, *History of Holland* (Cambridge: The University Press, 1922); Charles Wilson, *The
Dutch Republic* (New York: McGraw-Hill and Company, 1968); and Peter Geyl, *Revolt of the
Netherlands* (London: Williams and Norgate, Ltd., 1932).
2. Vlekke, "The Dutch Before 1581," p. 28.
3. Edmundson, *History of Holland*, p. 52.
4. *Ibid.*, p. 68.
5. The classic work on the history of the Protestantizing of North Netherlands is L. J. Rogier,
Geschiedenis van het Katholicisme in Noord-Nederland in de 16e and 17e Eeuw (Amsterdam:

It seems the best historical judgment that the successful revolt of the Netherlands was due more to strategic advantages—the greater ease of defending the provinces north of the rivers Rhine, Maas, Waal, and Lek, from Spanish attack—than to religious factors. Even after William's assassination during the eighty-year war, Dutch Calvinist leaders such as Frederick Henry and the Grand Pensionaries Johan Oldenbarneveldt and John de Witt encouraged religious tolerance toward Catholics or Remonstrant groups. Further, the ruling merchant class in the cities was conspicuously latitudinarian. Willem Banning writes, "It might be argued with some justice that liberalism was closely associated with the national cause even in the sixteenth century: it was to be found primarily in the merchant and regent classes of the trading towns which thought the dogmatism and the theocratic policies of Calvinism pernicious—also for the economy—and advocated tolerance in all fields."[6]

The Calvinist merchants in the cities, "almost Jeffersonian in their belief in decentralization, minimum government, theological liberalism and consistent, if empirical, pacifism in foreign affairs" discouraged excessive religious sanctions.[7] These merchants, "latitudinarian, empirically tolerant, had not fought off the threat of the Inquisition only to find themselves shackled by a persecuting theocracy of Calvinists."[8] The essential meaning of the Dutch revolt was disputed. "The ministers often rebuked the civil magistrates for telling the people that the war had been fought for freedom's sake. The Dutch had fought for religion's sake, they claimed, for the Calvinist religion, to the exclusion of other creeds."[9]

That the merchant class dominated Dutch political and social life in the Golden Age of the seventeenth century is evidenced by the fact that "the Dutch republic because of its determined struggle for independence became a haven of refuge for all who sought freedom of worship or safety from coercion."[10] The Portuguese and Spanish-Jewish refugees from the Inquisition found asylum in Amsterdam.

Urbi et Orbi, 1945); also J. A. de Kok, *Nederland op de Breuklijn Rome-Reformatie* (Assen: Van Gorcum, 1964); J. Visser, "De Plaatselijke Verspreiding der Katholieken in Friesland tot het Begin der 19ᵉ Eeuw," *Social Kompas*, V, 3 (1957–1958), 120–132. Leo Laeyendecker treats the same material in English in "The Netherlands," in *Wetsern Religion: A Country by Country Sociological Inquiry*, Hans Mol, ed. (The Hague: Mouton, 1972), pp. 325–327.

6. Willem Banning, "The Co-Existent Steeples: Religion in the Netherlands," *Delta*, I, 4 (Winter, 1958–1959), 7.

7. Charles Wilson, *The Dutch Republic*, p. 48.

8. *Ibid.*, p. 14.

9. Adriaan J. Barnouw, "The Seventeenth Century: The Golden Age," in *The Netherlands*, p. 54.

10. Barnouw, "The Seventeenth Century: The Golden Age," p. 42.

The French Huguenots fled northward to the Netherlands. Locke, Descartes, and Spinoza enjoyed in Holland a freedom of intellectual inquiry and expression denied them elsewhere. Half of all the books published in Europe in the seventeenth century came from Dutch presses, largely because of the absence of strong censorship.

In 1619 a synod took place in Dordrecht which shaped the course of Calvinist orthodoxy for three centuries. The issues were complex. On the one hand, Arminius and the Remonstrant party argued for some genuine freedom of the will, while the orthodox Calvinists, under the leadership of Gomarus, defended strict predestination. Most interesting for our purposes are the issues raised by the Remonstrant and Contra-Remonstrant parties over the question of church establishment and the relation between church and state.

Arminius and the Remonstrants, calling for the supremacy of each province in religious affairs, opposed a national synod which would impose orthodoxy. In this, they played into deep decentralist sympathies of the merchant-regent class. Secondly, the Remonstrants made a distinction between the public and private church. The private or voluntary church was autonomous. It was a voluntary association with freedom to determine its own forms and purposes so long as these did not conflict with the safety and welfare of the state and the system of law and order which protected the rights of all. Inasmuch as the church was a public organization, it fell directly or indirectly under the control of the ruler. The Remonstrants rejected the orthodox Calvinist theocracy, according to which the ruler was obliged to enforce the one true church and further the aims of religion as outlined for him by his Calvinist minister. While the Arminians accepted the public establishment of Calvinist religion, they argued for freedom inasmuch as the churches were private.[11]

The Contra-Remonstrant party rejected the Arminian theory that the ruler was subject in his actions, even in public religion, only and directly to God and not to the Calvinist ministers. The synod was a pyrrhic victory. The Remonstrants held their own antisynod at Rotterdam. They continued to meet for worship, openly defying the proscriptions passed against them. By the mid-seventeenth century they were once again in power through the Grand Pensionary, John de Witt. In 1662, *The Interest of Holland* (by Pieter de la Court), widely known as *The Maxims of John de Witt,* declared: "Toleration and

---

11. An interesting and thorough discussion of Remonstrant vs. Contra-Remonstrant views on church-state relations is found in Douglas Nobbs, *Theocracy and Toleration: A Study of Disputes in Dutch Calvinism from 1600–1650* (Cambridge: The University Press, 1938).

freedom of religion is not only exceedingly beneficial for our country in general but particularly for the reformed religion which may and ought to depend on its own evidence and veracity.''[12] The availability and partial legitimacy of the Remonstrant position gave Catholics the leeway needed to survive as a group in a predominantly Protestant-controlled nation.

Catholic Organization in the Secret Church Period

By 1580 the Netherlands had become a Catholic missionary territory organized under an apostolic delegate. Large numbers of priests from religious orders, including the Jesuits, were rushed into the territory to save or win back adherents for the Catholic fold. The much-needed reorganization of a loosely structured, often chaotic, church organization proved impossible in the face of hostile Calvinist elements. At the end of the eighty-year war in 1648, with the Treaty of Munster, Catholics in the Netherlands were subjected to distinct religious and economic disadvantages which would continue until late in the nineteenth century.[13]

The two overwhelmingly Catholic southern provinces of Limburg and North Brabant were governed as territorial colonies of the states-general, without the right of representation, until the end of the eighteenth century. Elsewhere Catholics were denied voice in the parliament as well as access to governmental posts and higher education. The laws included placards calling for the extirpation of Catholics and proscribing the public celebration of any form of worship except that of the reformed religion, in accord with the decrees of the Synod of Dordrecht. But they were notoriously not enforced. The location of Catholic "secret" churches in the attics of the homes of wealthy Catholic merchants was an open secret. Anyone who was willing to pay for the dispensation from the placards could obtain it. Catholics were unfairly taxed, however, to support the Calvinist state religion, and thus had to shoulder the double burden of paying for dispensations from the placards as well as the cost of their secret churches. Further, the Catholic south lay heavily burdened by taxes. In the period before 1800, Catholic farming areas paid on the average

12. John de Witt, *The True Interest and Political Maxims of the Republick of Holland* (Amsterdam: No publisher given, 1702), p. 242.
13. My principal sources for the historical information in the following section are: L. J. Rogier, *Katholieke Herleving: Geschiedenis van Kathliek Nederland Sinds, 1853* (The Hague: Pax Publishers, 1956); A. G. Weiler *et al.*, *Geschiedenis van de Kerk in Nederland* (Utrecht: Aula Books, 1962); J. M. G. Thurlings, *De Wankele Zuil* (Amersfoort: De Horstink, 1971).

more than twice the amount in taxation on land holdings as they did in the Calvinist province of Holland.[14]

Each of the apostolic vicars in seventeenth-century Netherlands— Sasbout Vosmeer (1580-1614), Philip Rovenius (1614-1651), and John van Neercassel (1651-1686), tried to bring some order into a disorganized church province. A brief occupation of the Netherlands by Catholic France in 1672-1673 afforded some respite for recovering Catholic forces. The problem was twofold. First, there was an absence of ordinary diocesan structures: bishops, diocesan curias, parishes, and seminaries. Second, a large number of religious order priests claimed to be exempt from the jurisdiction and control of the apostolic vicars. Jealousy between diocesan and religious order priests was exacerbated by the fact that the latter controlled the largest and most prosperous congregations.

Both Rovenius and Neercassel were sympathetic to the teaching of Cornelius Jansen, the bishop of Ypres in Belgium, who developed a doctrine of predestination and grace very similar to the Calvinist doctrine. In 1689 Pope Alexander VII issued a bull condemning the position of the followers of Jansen in France and the Gallican doctrine of Cardinal Pierre de Berulle. The French Jansenists, following the Huguenots, fled to the Netherlands.

Neercassel, while always loyal to Rome, was surprisingly ecumenical and irenic in his dealings with Calvinism. He found ways to make adaptations to the vernacular in the liturgy and to revive the reading of scripture. Further, he warned Catholics against exaggerations in their devotion to Mary. Neercassel openly recognized the legitimacy of Protestant baptisms. The apostolic vicar found a nuanced formula to allow Catholics to be married before civil magistrates, in direct contravention of the Tridentine declaration that only a marriage before a priest and two witnesses was validly consecrated.[15] In his efforts to reorganize the Dutch church province and make pastoral adaptations, Neercassel ran afoul of religious order priests, especially the Jesuits.

The Schism of Utrecht

Neercassel's successor as apostolic vicar, Peter Codde, continued his policies. As a result of complaints from the Jesuits, Codde was

---

14. See Dr. A. Chorus, *De Nederlander Uiterlijk en Innerlijk* (Leiden: A. W. Sijthoff, 1965), p. 133.
15. Thurlings, *De Wankele Zuil,* pp. 64-69, discusses Neercassels' pastoral strategy.

summoned to Rome in 1699 to defend himself against charges of favoring Jansenist positions. Dutch priests gathered a petition in defense of Codde which was signed by 303 priests, 289 diocesan priests, and 14 religious order priests. "All of the leading figures among the diocesan clergy signed."[16] Codde, after consultation with his priests, refused to underwrite the bull condemning the Gallican articles against Jansenism. Summoned a second time to Rome, he received word while there that he had been relieved of office. His successor, a bullheaded and unpopular if unflinchingly papal priest, Theodore de Cock, was unacceptable to a majority of Dutch priests. The appointment of de Cock led to a schism and the establishment of the Old Catholic Church of Utrecht. Only 89 of the 355 diocesan priests accepted the appointment and legitimate authority of de Cock; the 129 religious priests remained outside the struggle, since they considered themselves exempt from de Cock's jurisdiction and directly bound to Rome.

By the time Rome recognized its mistake and rescinded the appointment of de Cock, it was too late. Dissident priests, supported by the states-general of Holland and Utrecht, saw to it that succeeding apostolic vicars were denied a visa. From 1705 to 1723 the Netherlands was without a bishop. Finally in 1723 the Jansenist elements, declaring the bishop's seat vacant, chose Cornelius Steenhoven as Archbishop of Utrecht. Ninety-eight priests, of whom 51 were foreigners, and 51 parishes joined the schismatic Old Catholic Church of Utrecht, while the majority of Dutch priests who had fought the appointment of de Cock remained loyal to Rome.

From 1723 until the restoration of a Dutch hierarchy in 1853 Catholic organization was decentralized and disorganized. Only the diocese of Roermond in the south had a bishop during that period, but he was not allowed to exercise jurisdiction beyond his isolated corner of Limburg in the area above the river Moerdijk, where the majority of Catholics live. Church affairs were handled from Brussels or Antwerp.

The legacy of the Utrecht schism was a lack of authority within the national church, a far-reaching lay control over church properties, and "church tower" politics—with each parish priest or archpriest, jealous of his autonomy, acting as if he were bishop. The religious priests continued to operate completely free of the jurisdiction of

16. L. J. Rogier, "De Katholieke Kerk van 1559 tot 1795," in A. G. Weiler, *Geschiedenis van de Kerk in Nederland,* p. 210. For the account of the Utrecht Schism I am following this work of Rogier, pp. 206–215.

local or diocesan priests, and did not coordinate their work with the diocesan priests' pastoral efforts. The long postponement of a restoration of the Dutch hierarchy, which in the mid-ninetenth century became a scandal to educated Dutch Catholics, was due to three fears. Local pastors feared a loss of autonomy; the religious order priests feared that they would be subject to the new bishops' control; and Rome was haunted for a century with the memory of the Utrecht schism and Dutch clerical independence.

From 1580 until 1795, the period of the secret church, Dutch Catholicism was characterized by disorganization and a gradual but steady loss of members to Calvinism. The Catholics represented an embattled minority whose world "mainly and primarily consisted in fellow believers from whom it was expected and demanded that they should remain true to the Roman cause, and non-Catholics with whom one ought to find some modus-vivendi."[17] Like any embattled minority sect, Catholicism in that period exhibited a high degree of internal intolerance toward deviant tendencies among fellow believers. The strategy open to such a church was predetermined. "To seek enough money to pay for dispensations; to ask for the intervention of Catholic ambassadors in the Hague; to gain tolerance for Protestants in the Austrian controlled lowlands in exchange for tolerance for Catholics in the Republic of the Netherlands; caution and respect in one's behavior toward non-Catholic fellow citizens with a view to diminishing their existing mistrust; and wherever possible taking advantage of political developments which promise greater room for maneuver for a religious minority."[18]

From the Batavian Republic to the Restoration of the Hierarchy, 1795–1853

The Republic of the Netherlands felt the aftershocks of the French Revolution as the party of the Patriots founded the Batavian Republic in 1795, abolishing the established Reformed Church and bringing to Dutch soil the principles of liberty, equality, and fraternity. While Catholics in France were fighting the revolutionary principles of democracy as ungodly, the transplanted revolution in the Netherlands was "greeted by the overwhelming majority of priests and laity with approval."[19]

17. Thurlings, *De Wankele Zuil*, p. 63.
18. *Ibid.*, p. 80.
19. Rogier, *Katholieke Herleving*, p. 10.

With the advent of Napoleon, the Dutch Patriots were confronted with the choice of returning to the House of Orange, then in disfavor, or being annexed by France. Under the government of Louis Bonaparte the Dutch Catholics enjoyed religious freedom. With the fall of Napoleon and the restoration at the Congress of Vienna of the House of Orange, church and state were separated and all groups enjoyed religious freedom.

The union between the Netherlands and Belgium (1815-1830) was an unhappy one. Belgium was given less representation in parliament and fewer ministerial posts than its numbers warranted; most important posts in the military, civil service, and diplomatic corps remained in the hands of the Dutch. William I, highly autocratic, tried to impose Dutch as the national language and force candidates for the priesthood to attend the state-controlled Collegium Philosophicum at Louvain. The government department for Roman Catholic Worship, especially under P. G. van Ghert, was in the hands of anti-Roman, anti-clerical Catholics. William was opposed in his efforts by the papal states and by the relatively well-organized Belgian hierarchical church.

During the period of Dutch-Belgian union some efforts were made to regulate the affairs of Catholic Netherlands. Apostolic vicars were appointed to govern in Breda and Den Bosch in the Catholic province of North Brabant, while elsewhere the governance of the church was left in the hands of seven archpriests, who were never given permission to confirm. Indeed, until 1842 the apostolic vicars were denied any of the ruling privileges of a bishop. Only in 1823 were they allowed to administer the sacrament of confirmation. In 1827 the Dutch government signed a concordat with the Holy See which envisioned two Dutch dioceses, one in Amsterdam and the other in Catholic Den Bosch.

The decade 1840-1850 was for Dutch Catholicism a "time of hesitation, internal division, and renewed anti-papism."[20] Within the Dutch Reformed Church the orthodox Protestant revival movement, the *Reveil,* under the leadership of Groen van Prinsterer, turning to piety, was increasingly anti-Catholic. Politically the decade saw the rise of Dutch liberalism, which became pitted against an alliance of monarchists and reactionaries. Under the lay Catholic convert and journalist Le Sage ten Broek, many Catholic intellectuals followed the spirit of the French Catholic liberal Felicité Lammenais, arguing for a free church in a free state without concordats or establishment.

20. *Ibid.,* p. 17.

Dutch Catholics in the decade 1840-1850 were divided into liberals, such as F. J. van Vree, president of the Catholic seminary in Warmond, and Father Judocus Smits, founder of the first Catholic daily, *De Tijd,* and conservative monarchists, who were centered in Tilburg around the figure of the future bishop, John Zwijsen. The conservatives argued that the best Catholic strategy lay in unswerving loyalty to the king, who exhibited Catholic sentiments and sojourned, by choice, in the Catholic south. Indeed, on November 8, 1840, the king had allowed the return of cloister life to the Netherlands. Religious congregations began to mushroom, each pastor vying with his neighbor to found his own congregation of sisters. On January 14, 1842, the Netherlands finally got indigenous bishops: the two apostolic vicars in Den Bosch, H. den Dubbelden and his coadjutor John Swijsen, and J. van Hooydonk in Breda. Catholic Limburg already had a bishop in Roermond, Mgr. Paredis. Nevertheless, north of the rivers which separated the Catholic south from the heart of the Netherlands there were no bishops. Moreover, the bishops were ordinaries of nonexistent sees in *partibus infidelium.*[21] The Netherlands still lacked a regular diocesan structure.

The Catholic liberals did not wish to entrust their church's fate to the whims of the personal friendship between Bishop John Zwijsen and William II. The Catholic laity, responding to the anti-Catholicism of the Protestant *Reveil,* founded newspapers and journals such as *De Katholiek, De Tijd,* and *De Spektator;* and they turned to the liberal J. R. Thorbecke, who sought a constitutional monarchy, full separation of church and state, and the extension of the franchise. Thus Jan Wep, a Catholic anti-clerical in Breda, wrote an open letter in the *De Noordbrabander* on March 24, 1840, calling for freedom of education and worship. The founders of the liberal papers *The Algemeen Handelsblad* and *Nieuwe Rotterdamse Courant*—to this day the voice in the Netherlands for nineteenth-century liberalism—were Catholics. Leading Catholic laymen, such as J. Alberdingk Thijm and J. W. Cramer, belonged to the party of the liberals. When the apostolic vicar requested that Judocus Smits take a more monarchical position in his paper *De Noordbrabander,* Smits replied, "It is impossible for me to countenance any outside influence upon the editorial policy of the *Noordbrabander.* I am too independent on that point."[22] When he moved the paper, now christened *De Tijd,* to Amsterdam, Smits made clear that although the paper was by and for

21. A bishop who is bishop of a see in *partibus infidelium* is not, in the Catholic structure, an ordinary with jurisdiction over a territorial diocese.
22. Rogier, *Katholieke Herleving,* p. 39.

Catholics, it was no one's house organ. The first issue on June 17, 1845, carried the slogan, "We represent no one."[23]

The Catholics in the Netherlands continued to chafe at the irregularity of church organization. In 1847 a group of laity addressed a petition to the Holy See for a restoration of dioceses. The Bishop of Liege in Belgium, Mgr. van Bommel, asked Pius IX to return to a plan, envisioned in 1559 but never fully realized, whereby Utrecht, Haarlem, Roermond, Breda, and Den Bosch would be the dioceses, with Utrecht as the archdiocesan center of the church province. The Roman apostolic delegates to the government were reluctant to see a restored hierarchy.

In 1848, after revolutions rocked European capitols, William II, sniffing a dangerous trend, became a liberal "overnight" and invited J. R. Thorbecke to form the ministerial government. Recalling that event years later, the Catholic historian Willem Nuyens said of the Catholic lay intellectuals of that period: "We were all liberal—very liberal, indeed."[24]

The following year, 1849, the government of Thorbecke, supported by the Catholic liberals, renounced the concordat with the Holy See. In the first parliamentary elections, based on a district system, all of the Catholic representatives came from the south, although by that time Amsterdam was one-fourth Catholic and Rotterdam, the Hague, Leiden, Haarlem, and Schiedam were almost one-third.

The restoration in 1850 of the Roman Catholic hierarchy in England, a land which numbered only 600,000 Catholics—most of them Irish immigrants—in a population of eighteen million, and which enjoyed in Nicholas Wiseman and William Ullathorne bishops of international repute, made the callous treatment of Dutch Catholicism all the more unbearable. On December 12, 1850, twelve of the fifteen Catholic members of the parliamentary second chamber asked the pope to restore dioceses to the Netherlands, where Catholics represented two-fifths of the population. Again, the Holy See hesitated, demanding as a condition the restoration of the concordat. The Catholic supporters of Thorbecke urged him to refuse to yield.

In the three years which intervened before the actual organization of an indigenous Dutch church, the Holy See, the internuncio, and Dutch Catholic parties skirmished over where the bishoprics should be located. Finally, Utrecht was chosen as the site for the archdiocese.

23. *Ibid.*, p. 42.
24. *Ibid.*, p. 46.

Pius IX is reported as saying: "Utrecht, the seat of St. Willibrord. I will let Europe see that the Catholics of the Netherlands were not born yesterday."[25] Besides Utrecht, dioceses were erected in Breda, Den Bosch, and Haarlem to join the already existing but isolated diocese of Roermond. An ancient medieval privilege was allotted to the cathedral chapters in these five dioceses, a privilege Dutch Catholicism shares only with some dioceses in Switzerland. Cathedral chapters—not the papal internuncio or the secular government—enjoy the right to nominate candidates for vacant sees.

In the papal bull *Ex Qua Die,* dated March 4, 1853, Pius announced the establishment of normal church government in the Netherlands, referring in passing to the need for such regular diocesan structures to oppose "the sword and fury of the Calvinist heresy."[26] Reacting to this lack of diplomacy, Thijm averred that he felt no need to defend the Holy Father's every word. Judocus Smits published the bull in his *De Tijd* only under severe pressure from the nuncio, Mgr. Belgrado. Even Bishop Zwijsen is reported to have informed the pope: "Holy Father, we can achieve a great deal in my land, so long as we do it quietly."[27]

There are several points worth noting here.

1. The long period of abnormal church organization, heightened by the tragedy of the Utrecht schism, led to considerable strains between diocesan and regular clergy, a coolness still evident at the beginning of the 1960s.

2. An established normal church government for Dutch Catholics began relatively late in modern history. This lack of an organized church structure contributed to the continuous defection of Catholics to Protestantism, which was heaviest in the eighteenth century, as well as to the late start of Dutch Catholics toward economic emancipation.

3. The presence in the Dutch church structure of an almost unique method for nominating bishops should be noted, a method which gave it a qualitatively different sort of bishop. The Dutch bishops differed from bishops in other countries on several significant points. First, they were nominated by a cathedral chapter consisting of representatives of their own lower clergy. Second, with only three exceptions since 1853, they were originally resident priests in the diocese in which they became bishop. Third, with only one exception since 1853

25. *Ibid.,* p. 72.
26. *Ibid.,* p. 75.
27. *Ibid.,* p. 76.

(Mgr. Snickers), no Dutch ordinary switched from one diocese to another. This is important because it removed from the Dutch scene the kind of episcopal "careerism" which characterizes the church in other countries, where bishops who seek advancement to more important dioceses must court the good graces of Rome. Careerism in the Dutch episcopate was further reduced by the sparing use of auxiliary bishops; typically, these were appointed as coadjutors with the right to succession or they resigned upon the improved health or death of the ordinary. Finally, at least since the middle of the nineteenth century the Dutch episcopacy has shown greater preference for collective, collegial pastoral letters and decisions.

4. Already in 1853 one notes the beginnings—in laymen such as Thijm, Cramer, and others, and in periodicals such as *De Tijd*—of a tradition in Dutch Catholicism wherein persons and organizations could be spokesmen for Catholicism without necessarily being agents of the bishop.

5. Catholics in the Netherlands, unlike their counterparts in France, Belgium, and Italy, were spared the choice of siding with liberal democracy and thus giving up their religion or accepting conservative monarchism as a necessary part of their Catholic faith. In Holland, those who opposed the spirit of the French revolution were —and are—Protestants, and members of the Anti-Revolutionary Party. The French Benedictine supporter of Lammenais, Dom Pitra, who visited the Netherlands and published a small book entitled *La Hollande Catholique,* could write to his friend Bishop Dupanloup on March 20, 1849, "Holland is the land where the Catholics have most wisely profited from our revolutions."[28]

6. In the Utrecht schism and the negotiations around the restoration of the hierarchy, Dutch Catholics combined a stubborn refusal to accept abjectly Roman curial strategies with a certain loyalty to the institution of the papacy and an acceptance of Rome.

7. Dutch Catholics proved during the revolt against Spain and the secession of Belgium that they were loyal to the Netherlands as embodied in the ruling House of Orange. Catholics in the Netherlands could claim to be as loyal as any other group.

28. Cited in Rogier, *Katholieke Herleving,* p. 119. That Dutch Catholicism was spared the great crises from the French Revolution to the Second World War is the thesis of G. A. Abbink, "Van Isolement Near Openheid—A Comparative Analysis of Catholicism in Holland and Other Western European Countries," in *Bijdragen,* Vol. XXXIII, 4 (December 1970), pp. 350–372.

CATHOLIC DEFENSIVE ORGANIZATIONS, 1853–1910

The response of the orthodox Protestants, especially those who belonged to the *Reveil* party of W. Bilderdijk and Groen van Prinsterer, to the "monster-alliance" between Catholics and liberals, and to the restoration of the hierarchy, was fierce. In April 1853, with its slogan "Better Turkish than Papist," the Protestant April Movement held anti-Catholic rallies. Turning to King William III as a symbol of the Protestant character of the nation, they reminded him of his task to further Protestantism and of the fall of the Stuarts in England when they flirted with Catholicism. William received a delegation of Protestants who gave him a protest petition with 51,000 signatures of anti-Catholics. The Protestants, waving their orange, white, and blue flags as a symbol of anti-papism, called upon the House of Orange to protect their Protestant interests. William gave a subtle reply which pointed to the possibility of a monarchy above confessional divisions. "I shall pray to God . . . that He might spare me yet longer for the welfare not just of one part of my people but for the whole nation."[29]

Just previous to the restoration of the hierarchy, the spirit of the Enlightenment began to infiltrate the upper levels of Catholic liberal intellectualism, especially in the circle of professors in the Catholic seminary in Warmond. Several priests in the diocese of Haarlem, notably F. C. de Groeve, Jacob Vinkers, and Joseph Olivier Josset, had called for an open Catholicism and the abandonment of celibacy. Any misgivings which Rome had about its Dutch Catholics must have been dissipated in 1858, however; in that year, responding to the plea of Pius IX for volunteers to defend the papal states against the Italian patriots, 3,000 Dutch Catholics enlisted to serve the cause, the largest national contingent in Europe.

The Enlightenment had its most profound effect, however, within the Dutch Reformed Church. David Strauss's critical *Leben Jesu* had found a ready audience in the Protestant faculties of theology in Groningen and Leiden. In response to what was felt to be increasing secularization of the Christian message, the orthodox party of Calvinists, centered in the theological faculty of Utrecht, sought to distance themselves from their more humanistic liberal brethren. Although the constitution of 1848 allowed for freedom of education, Prime

29. Rogier, *Katholieke Herleving*, p. 97.

Minister Thorbecke was a strong supporter of neutral public schools, culturally Christian in character yet without a clear denominational base. Groen van Prinsterer, however, spoke for the Protestant pietist *Reveil* when he began to form confessional Protestant schools in 1851. When the question of state recognition and support of confessional schools came before the parliament in 1857—a question which would dominate Dutch political life until the end of World War I—six of the twelve Catholic representatives sided with Thorbecke and the liberals. As one of these representatives, Jhr. C. van Nispen Tot Pannerden, stated it: "separate confessional schools can only lead to diminished tolerance."[30]

Two major causes gradually drove the Catholics away from their liberal, Dutch Reformed, coalition partners. First, the liberal elite in mid-nineteenth century Netherlands was a closed, relatively snobbish group. They offered little room for advancement to the "little" man within Protestantism, let alone to a Catholic. Leading liberals such as J. T. Buys stated publicly that the Catholics were not to be trusted. The liberals looked down their noses at the relatively small nouveau riche Catholic elite, distancing themselves still further from the ordinary Catholic proletariat and farmers whom they dubbed a "nonpeople." Social and university clubs, such as Unitas and Philacterion, requiring oaths of their members to exclude Catholics, circulated address books containing the names of Catholic doctors, lawyers, and business establishments with the injunction that Catholic establishments were to be avoided. With few exceptions, Catholics were informally excluded from the university or important government posts. Second, the rightist reaction of the papacy under Pius IX signaled by the papal encyclical *Quanta Cura* and the papal list of condemnation, the *Syllabus of Errors,* found echoes among Dutch Catholics. The Collective Mandatory Letter of the Dutch Bishops, issued July 22, 1868, decried the errors of modernity and called for a strong Catholic organizational life. The last straw was the dismissal by the liberals of the Netherlands' diplomatic mission to the pope in 1871 in response to the fall of the papal states.

By 1870 the seeds of a new Catholic coalition with the extreme orthodox Calvinists had been sown.[31] The Calvinist small farmers, workers, and shopowners were also excluded from advancement in society. They, too, were denied access to universities and government

30. *Ibid.,* p. 145.
31. My principal sources for the following section are: Willem Banning, *Hedendaagse Sociale Bewegingen* (Arnhem: van Loghum Slaterius, 1950); Hans Daalder, "Parties and Politics in the

posts. While poverty and inequality were everywhere to be seen—especially after a disastrous series of potato famines—the liberals continued to state that the social classes were willed by God. The sons of the rich learned their Heidelburg catechism at the home of the Calvinist minister, but the sons of the poor had to wait outside. The Dutch Reformed church, firmly in the hands of the Groningen school of modernists, mirrored this liberal elitism. The poor sat in the worst seats in the church, which were clearly marked as "seats for those who did not pay." The poor were also herded into groups for collective church weddings.

As early as 1834 some groups of the Protestant proletariat tried to break off from the Dutch Reformed Church. A second attempt was made in 1846. Many of the Protestant proletariat sought relief by migrating to America or South Africa. Finally, the Calvinist "little man" found a voice in Abraham Kuyper. This prodigious Calvinist minister was founder of the Anti-Revolutionary Party, the Gereformeerden church, the Free University in Amsterdam, the first Protestant working man's organization, Patrimonium, and, later, toward the end of his life, was twice prime minister of the Netherlands. Probably more than any man in Dutch history, Kuyper is the chief architect of modern Dutch social structure.[32]

Kuyper's strategy in championing the rights of the little man was "to arouse in them the old Reformation principles of belief but no less to demand on their behalf a solution to their social needs."[33] As early as 1860 Kuyper had started a Union for Christian National Schools. In 1878 he drew up a program for the Anti-Revolutionary

Netherlands," *Political Studies,* III, 1 (February 1955), 1–16; Hans Daalder, "The Netherlands: Opposition in a Segmented Society," in *Political Oppositions in Western Democracies,* Robert A. Dahl, ed. (New Haven: Yale University Press, 1966); Johan Goudsblom, *Dutch Society* (New York: Random House, 1968), Chapters II and IV; J. Hendriks, *De Emancipatie van de Gereformeerden* (Alphen aan den Rijn: Samson, 1971); H. Hoefnagels, *Een Eeuw Sociale Problematick: Van Social Conflict naar Strategische Samenwerking* (Assen: van Gorcum, 1957); A. Hoogewerf, *Protestantisme en Progressititeit* (Meppel: J. A. Boom, 1964); Fr. De Jong, "Verzuiling in Historisch Perspectief," *Socialism en Democratie,* XIV, 1 (January, 1957), 2–10; L. W. Scholten, J. A. Bornewasser, *et al., De Confessionalen: Onstaan en Ontwikkeling van hun Politieken Partijen* (Utrecht: Ambo, 1968); H. Verwey-Jonker, "De Emancipatie Bewegingen," in *Drift en Koers,* A. N. J. den Hollander *et al.* (Assen: van Gorcum, 1968), pp. 105–125.
32. Perhaps one indication of the successful confessionalization of Dutch society since the mid-nineteenth century is that, with the exception of the monarchy, Dutch society lacks great political heroes. Each group has its own—Schaepman, Nolens, and Poels for the Catholics, Troelstra and Nieuwenhuis for the Socialists, and Kuyper for the Gereformeerden Protestants—but they have very few shared heroes.
33. J. Hendriks, *De Emancipatie van de Gereformeerden,* p. 98. Hendriks should be read side-by-side with Thurlings, *De Wankele Zuil,* to see the parallels in developments toward confessional separatism between Catholics and Gereformeerden.

Party, gathering 300,000 signatures to present to the king, demanding state support for a school with the bible. When his petition failed, he turned to organizational power. Seeing the need for a coalition with Catholics if the orthodox Protestants were to win their battle for state support for confessional schools, the old anti-papist Groen van Prinsterer advised Kuyper to name his newspaper *De Standaard* instead of the more provocative *De Geus*.[34] Believing that ''in isolation lies our strength,'' the Gereformeerden proceeded to form their own political party, newspaper network, and church. Their slogan, ''sovereignty in our own circle,'' claimed both that the Calvinist doctrine of the sovereignty of God necessitated separate sovereign areas of social life, outside of the overarching control of the state, and that the sovereignty of God militated against a generally neutral or secular public life.

The Catholics followed the lead of the Gereformeerden. Having finally won a clear intra-church organization with the restoration of the hierarchy—an organization which spared Dutch Catholicism from the effects of the schism which occurred in Germany, Poland, and elsewhere in the aftermath of the proclamation of papal infallibility in 1870—Dutch Catholics began to pursue militant defensive confessionalism. In 1870 the first separate Roman Catholic Election Union was established in North Brabant. In 1883, under the priest-poet Henry Schaepman, the first specifically Roman Catholic political program was drawn up, which eventually led to the founding of the Roman Catholic State Party.

From 1880 to 1917 four questions dominated Dutch political life: (1) state support for confessional schools; (2) the enlargement of the franchise; (3) rescinding the law which allowed the rich to buy a mercenary replacement for military service; (4) the social question of the industrial proletariat. In 1888 a coalition of Catholics and Protestants was able to win partial state subsidy for confessional schools which at that date served almost one-fourth of Dutch school children.

Henry Schaepman hoped that it would be possible to follow the German model of a Christian Democratic Union, which embraced Protestants and Catholics in one interconfessional party. Kuyper was cool to the idea. Similarly, Schaepman was open to changing the law on military service and to enlarging the franchise. As he put it, ''if you don't want any slum dwellers on the electoral rolls you had better

34. *Geus* in Dutch means, literally, beggar. It came to refer to the most militantly anti-Catholic Protestants at the time of the Dutch Revolt and, in general, to anti-papist Calvinism.

clear out the slums.''[35] The Protestant party split on the issue of social welfare, with De Savornin Lohmen leaving Kuyper's Anti-Revolutionary Party in the last decade of the century to form his own Christian Historical Party.

In order to understand developments within Dutch Catholicism during this period it is important to remember that the industrial revolution came to Holland a half century after it came to England and a good twenty-five years after it arrived in France, Germany, and Belgium. The trend toward industrialization and the trek toward the cities began in earnest only after 1870. As late as 1870 there was no Dutch word for strike. The rise of large-scale industry began only in the last decade of the century. Two important events in 1891 coincided. The Philips electrical plant was opened in Eindhoven, and Pope Leo XIII issued his social encyclical *Rerum Novarum,* championing the labor movement.[36]

In the years 1880-1917 three different groups vied for the support of the industrial and farming proletariat: Catholicism, the Gereformeerden, and the new socialist movement. In 1888 the first Roman Catholic People's Union was formed by the priest W. C. Pastoors. Around the same time, the priest Alphonse Ariens, who years earlier had come to know the work of Don Bosco for the working classes in Turin, sought, in Twente and Enschede, to replace this People's Union—a loose bond of workers, small businessmen, and industrialists operating under a corporatist model—with special organizations for the working men, with the twin purpose of warding off socialism and protecting the faith. Ariens founded an interconfessional union of Catholics and Protestants, Unitas, patterned on the German model of interconfessional labor unions. When in 1906 the Dutch bishops forebade interconfessional unions for Catholics, most of the members of Unitas joined the new exclusively Catholic union. Ariens had, nevertheless, won the day for Catholic support for working men's unions.

In response to the great railway strike of 1903—the first Dutch nationwide strike—the Catholics formed a St. Raphael's union of railway workers under the leadership of the priest A. J. Mutsaers. Throughout the land Catholic priests and laymen, such as Ariens in the north, P. J. Aalberse and J. D. Aengenent in the diocese of

---

35. Rogier, *Katholieke Herleving,* p. 365.
36. The best single work focusing on the rise of labor unions and the question of the industrial proletariat is Hoefnagels, *Een Eeuw Sociale Problematiek.*

Haarlem, P. A. Gompertz in Rotterdam, Lambert Poell and Henry Poels in the southern provinces, fought to save the workingman for the church. Ariens was successful in winning episcopal support, especially that of Mgr. Snickers, the bishop of Haarlem, later Archbishop of Utrecht. In the southern provinces of North Brabant and Limburg, the church successfully fought the concentration of industry within any one city, arguing that this would destroy communal ties and pleading instead for the spread of factories in Breda, Eindhoven, Tilburg, and Den Bosch. In the Limburg mine area the priest Henry Poels demanded workers' housing and dormitories for the unmarried under the tutelage of priests and nuns, as a way of avoiding the evils of alcoholism and company control over the miners. The Catholic coal mine area in Limburg is probably the unique instance of the introduction of large-scale mining in modern times without drastic disruption of families, community ties, and religious bonds.[37]

In the first decade of the century a dispute arose between the Leiden school under the leadership of Aengenent and Aalberse, who argued for separate Catholic unions for each diocese, and the Limburg school under Henry Poels, who championed the principle of national organization. In 1909 the national principle won out, with the founding of the Roman Catholic Trade Central. With its founding two other clear principles of Catholic organizations were established. First, the legitimacy of separate interest associations within the Catholic population was recognized. Second, Catholic organizations had legitimate independence from direct episcopal control. As Henry Poels formulated it, "the workers' organizations are properly Catholic but not church organizations."[38] The importance of this victory is that it meant that the bishops had to deal with national organizations, hence collegially.

Neither the Catholics nor the Gereformeerden lost large numbers from the church to socialism. More recruits for the socialist movement came from the Dutch Reformed Church than from any other source. Socialism began in the Netherlands under the leadership of Ferdinand Domela Nieuwenhuis, a former Protestant minister, who organized the Socialist Democratic Union in 1881. Nieuwenhuis was succeeded by "the founding fathers"—significantly dubbed "the twelve apostles"—who established the Social Democratic Anarchist

37. William Petersen, *Planned Migration: The Social Determinants of the Dutch Canadian Movement* (Berkeley: The University of California Press, 1955), treats this material. See p. 23, 95.
38. Rogier, *Katholieke Herleving*, p. 474.

Party in 1894 and the first Dutch national labor union, The National Trade Union, in 1906. The early socialists, especially under the leadership of Pieter Jelles Troelstra, were sectarian, Marxist in ideology and deeply ascetical. Almost all of them were teetotalers and nonsmokers, and some were even vegetarians. They drew to their ranks such leading intellectuals as the poets Henriette Roland Holst van der Schalk and Herman Gorter. Dutch socialism had all the marks of a sectarian religious group until after World War II. Typically, party meetings were held on Sunday mornings at the same time as church services. The socialists also had their own "socialist" football, radio, and music.

With the introduction of the socialist movement we can see the fundamental principle of Dutch social structure. Three economic minorities—all of them, in some sense, religious yet on the ideological level diametrically opposed to each other—represented the overwhelming majority of Dutch society. Kuyper had enunciated a principle they could all accept, "sovereignty in our own circle," and a strategy of "separate organizational division of public life."[39] Organization led to economic emancipation. Each group developed its own political parties, labor unions, newspapers, youth groups, and school systems. Yet socialists, Catholics, and orthodox Calvinists make strange bedfellows. How could they be brought together? Catholics and Protestants agreed on the principle of state support for confessional schools. The socialists in their Groningen school motion of 1902 supported the confessional parties' efforts to obtain full subsidy for elementary and secondary education. In 1901, 1905, and again in 1917 the question of establishing equality between denominational and neutral schools came before parliament. The Protestants, especially Kuyper after the railway strike of 1903, had become opponents of universal suffrage, whereas the Catholic leader in parliament, Mgr. Schaepman, was a consistent supporter of it. Finally, in the Pacification Law of 1917, with the Catholics as brokers between Protestant demands for schools with the bible and socialist pleas for social reform, a compromise was found which joined together the questions of electoral reform and subsidies for schools.

In the period 1853-1910 Catholic confidence grew. The working man had been spared for the church. Dutch Catholic numbers had

---

39. "Sovereignty in our own circle" is not so different from the traditional Catholic social theory of subsidiarity—that voluntary associations take precedence over the state unless and until state intervention is necessary. For this point, see Hoefnagels, *Een Eeuw Sociale Problematiek,* p. 191.

swelled in the first half of the century, when German refugees came from Westphalia, and toward the end of the century, when large numbers of priests and nuns came from France and Germany to escape Bismark's Kulturkampf and the French *legislation laique*. Missionary orders and congregations grew up overnight on Dutch soil.

In 1867 modern Dutch Catholicism got its own patron saints when the pope canonized the martyrs of Gorcum, who had been murdered by the Calvinist Geuzen (or by pirates) during the revolt against Spain in 1567. The location of their death at Den Briel became a place of pilgrimage. Catholic culture blossomed: in the neo-Gothic architecture of Pierre Cuypers, architect of the Rijksmuseum in Amsterdam and numerous public buildings and churches; in the music of composers such as J. J. Verhulst and Alphons Diepenbrock, who raised the level of Dutch church music to new heights; and in the work of Catholic intellectual and social leaders, such as Poels, Schaepman, Willem Nuyens, and the Brom brothers, Gerard and Gilbert. Many new Catholic daily and weekly newspapers and journals appeared: *De Gelderlander, De Maasbode, Het Huisgezin, Het Centrum,* the *Nieuwe Schiedamse Courant,* and *Katholieke Illustratie*— all of them, with the exception of *De Maasbode,* under lay editorial control, being Catholic but not church organizations.

The only troubling area for Catholicism in this period lay in the school question. Although elementary Catholic education began to be widespread, secondary education remained underdeveloped. The first Catholic gymnasium was established in 1905, the first general curriculum secondary school in 1909.[40] The universities remained forbidden territory for Dutch Catholics. In 1904 the Klarenbeekse Club was established by Catholic priests and lay intellectuals to further advance learning among Catholics. In 1904, there was only one Dutch Catholic university professor and no Catholic governmental ministers. Catholic university students were very few, 200 out of a total of 2,800, mainly concentrated in the faculties of medicine and law. If the economic emancipation of the Catholics was to be completed, their education needed to be developed.

Even by 1910 Dutch Catholicism showed clear signs of having adopted the missionary strategy of confessional particularism as defined by the typology in Table 2. Organizational particularism had achieved much for Dutch Catholics by 1910. Not about to give up a

40. For a history of Catholic education, see M. Matthijssen, *De Intellectuele Emancipatie der Katholieken* (Assen: van Gorcum, 1958), which is my source of statistics on the subject in this book.

winning strategy, Dutch Catholics proceeded to organize even more, and with a vengeance.

1910–1940: SELF-CONFIDENCE AND TRIUMPHALISM

If the period 1853-1910 represents one of defensiveness, the establishment of separate confessional organizations, and the adoption of the missionary strategy in Catholic competition with other groups for economic emancipation, the period 1910-1940 ushered in a new sense of self-confidence, even a frontier mentality for a religious-economic minority "on the make."

In the years just before World War I the reaction to modernism exacted heavy costs from international Catholicism. The Dutch, once again, were spared another of the great Catholic crises which split the church elsewhere. Perhaps because the Dutch Catholics lacked institutions of higher learning—except the seminaries, where theology continued according to the scholastic manual tradition—modernism passed the Netherlands by. Dr. Henry Poels, who had been dismissed from the Catholic University in Washington, D.C., because of his advanced ideas in Old Testament studies, returned to his native Netherlands to busy himself organizing the Limburg miners. When the appointment of Mgr. L. Schrijnen as bishop of Roermond raised suspicions in Rome, the Dutch curial cardinal W. van Rossum defended the choice. Throughout the period of anti-modernism, van Rossum and Schrijnen fought the spirit of distrust, secrecy, and integralism in the curial policy of seminary purges. Only the priest M. A. Thompson, editor of the Catholic daily *De Maasbode,* thought that the Netherlands might be infected with the poison of modernism. Among the bishops only Mgr. A. J. Callier, the bishop of Haarlem, showed any traces of the integralist spirt. As the leading Dutch historian of Catholicism has stated it: "Our land seemed . . . as good as completely immune from the infection."[41] At any event, no Dutch priest refused the oath against modernism.

Indeed, on questions other than the integralist tactics of the anti-modernist curia, the Dutch Catholics seemed more Roman than the pope. The Dutch implemented the decrees of Pius X on frequent communion and the lowering of the age for first communion more thoroughly and speedily than any other European country. In 1865,

41. Rogier, *Katholieke Herleving,* p. 434.

anticipating Pius X's call for a liturgical revival, they began the St. Gregorius Association for Gregorian chant. When Pius X revived the chant as the official church music, Dutch Gregorian choirs blossomed in parishes across the land. When Pius XI approved periodic continence—the so-called "rhythm method" of birth control—Catholic preachers had to assure their people that it was a perfectly acceptable practice. After all, one need not be more Roman than the pope.[42]

Between 1910 and 1930 Dutch Catholicism pursued confessional separatism to its logical conclusion. In 1915 the Netherlands Roman Catholic Small Businessman's Association joined the Catholic Labor Union. The same year saw the foundation of the General Roman Catholic Association of Manufacturers. In 1929 the Catholic Union of Dutch Farmers and Truck Gardeners was established. Catholic associations for sport, theater, music, even a Catholic association for the furtherance of Esperanto, appeared. No area of social life lacked its corresponding Catholic, Protestant, or Socialist voluntary association.

In 1920 the Catholic School for Social Work was founded, beginning a pattern by which social welfare activities—hospitals, counseling centers, low-cost insurance companies, neighborhood cultural, recreation, or health centers—were also divided along confessional lines, in later years enjoying handsome state subsidies in proportion to confessional numbers. In the large cities there were alternate Catholic, Protestant, and neutral libraries.

Politically the Catholics also prospered. In 1918 the Netherlands parliament adopted universal suffrage and a system of proportional representation. In the election that year the Catholic party won the largest number of seats in parliament. The priest Willem Nolens, successor to Mgr. Schaepman as titular head of the Roman Catholic State Party, became the first Catholic to form a cabinet and the layman Ruys de Beerenrouck became the first Catholic prime minister. The Catholic party is the only Dutch political party to govern uninterruptedly in every parliamentary majority government since that time.

With the definitive winning of the school conflict, Catholic education spread throughout the land. By the beginning of World War II the Catholics had, for practical purposes, gained their equal share in the secondary school system. Advanced education was slower to develop. It was only in 1923 that the Catholic University at Nijmegen was inaugurated, followed in 1929 by the opening of the Catholic Institute for Advanced Economics in Tilburg. The statistics make

42. See the remarks of A. W. Hoegen, cited in F. Van Heek, *Hat Geboorte-Nivaeu der Nederlandse Rooms-Katholieken* (Leiden: H. E. Stenfert Kroese, 1954), p. 176.

clear that once the Catholics got their own university, the defenses against Catholics attending non-Catholic universities broke down, so that simultaneously with the founding of Nijmegen the proportion of Catholic students attending state universities dramatically increased.

The Catholics began to flex their cultural muscles in the 1920s. Calling for their own literature, they produced in the pages of literary magazines such as *Beiaard, Roeping,* and the influential journal *De Gemeenschap,* and in the work of such authors as Gerard Brom and the poet Anton van Duinkerken, the Dutch Catholic equivalent to Belloc, Chesterton, and Waugh in England. The layman Gerard Brom called for lay Catholic action a full decade before Pope Pius XI, claiming that the church would be committing suicide if it did not accept the laity as full emancipated bearers of Catholic culture. His call was heard, as retreat groups for the laity and militant lay groups such as the Grail and the Crusaders of St. John were established.

At the great international Eucharistic Congress held in Amsterdam in 1924, the leading Dutch Catholic preacher, the Franciscan Borromaeus de Greeve, could refer to "the formerly Protestant Netherlands."[43] On the third of August, 1925, the Catholic daily *De Maasbode* celebrated the third national Dutch Catholic day by looking forward to 1975, when it predicted that the Roman Catholic Church would enjoy a clear majority in the land and be held in honor by the remaining minority. The *Maasbode* foresaw that by 1975 the Protestant Cathedral Church in Utrecht would be once again in Catholic hands. A Dutch cardinal, surrounded by twelve Dutch bishops and twenty abbots, would preside "in all the glory of our liturgy in the Utrecht church."[44] What has come to be known as the "rich Roman life" of the 1920s and 1930s had a definite triumphalist ring, but there were other voices, such as those of Anton van Duinkerken and Gerard Brom, who called for a more open, less confessionally triumphalist Catholicism. Catholic priests such as Joseph Schrijnen and Henry Poels warned against the dangers of the Catholic ghetto and clericalism.

With the introduction of radio to the Netherlands, it seemed natural that this new media should be divided equally between the ideological empires. In 1926 a Dutch Dominican formed the Catholic Radio Broadcasting Company. It is important to note that the leadership of priests in forming radio broadcasting companies, labor unions, political parties, and associations of intellectuals kept the

43. See Rogier, *Katholieke Herleving,* p. 556.
44. Cited in Van Heek, *Het Geboorte-Niveau der Nederlandse Rooms-Katholieken,* p. 150.

clergy close to the Catholic laity. There were no dramatic cleavages in the Netherlands between the clergy and lay intellectuals or working men. Further, most of the priest founders, sharing Henry Poels' conviction that clericalism was the greatest danger for the church, tended to yield the direction and control of the Catholic association to lay hands.

Like most of Western Europe, the Netherlands experienced a severe economic depression during the 1930s. In the troubled times of unemployment and poverty, many of the Dutch looked to the German fascist economic "miracle" with some envy and awe. When Dutch Catholics such as Ernst Michel and Arnold Meyer thought that National Socialism would answer the problems of an unstable economy, the Dutch bishops reacted swiftly, firmly, and unswervingly. In January 1934 they issued a collective letter warning Catholics of the dangers in fascist National Socialism. When a Council of Catholics for National Socialism was set up, the bishops refused to appoint a chaplain for the group. Finally, in a collective episcopal letter issued in 1936 the Dutch bishops forbade Catholics, under penalty of excommunication, to support fascist organizations.

THE SEEDS OF STRUCTURAL DIFFERENTIATION, 1940–1958

By the outbreak of World War II and the fall of the Netherlands to the Nazi occupier in May 1940, the missionary strategy of confessional separatism had been more successfully institutionalized than in any other land, for several reasons. (1) Church ambitions were high. (2) The dominant ideology looked to successful Catholic efforts at blocking or overcoming secularization. (3) The major base of influence upon society lay in differentiated Catholic organizations; the secondary base rested upon the ideological formation of the laity in the Catholic school systems and through Catholic Action cells and retreat movements. (4) The accepted pattern of church-society relations consisted in efforts at maintaining separation and allowing controlled contact with the wider society through the dominant religious action principle of penetration in strategic secular spheres. (5) The primary roles of the priest were that of missionary, militant organizer of Catholic organizations and ideological groups, and political middleman for the Catholic economic minority. Priestly prestige and authority were diffuse. (6) The primary role of the layman was that of a hierarchical auxiliary, the agent of the bishop and the church's purposes in the secular sphere. (7) The primary target groups for Catholic strategy were the workers and the middle class. Although intellectuals were tolerated, and even encouraged, they did not give the tone to Catholic strategy. (8) The organizational mode for the church lay in grassroots missions and Catholic Action cells coupled with decentralized pastoral units, the separate dioceses and parishes. The hypotheses presented in Table 3 about the face of the pre-Vatican structures are strongly confirmed.

World War II introduced unrest and eventual change in the direction of structural differentiation. The occupied Netherlands was governed by a civilian German government under the leadership of the high commissioner, Arthur Seyss-Inquart. The German occupation brought drastic changes. Throughout the war the Dutch confessional groups refused to compromise with the Nazis. The Dutch bishops issued a Lenten pastoral letter condemning Naziism and forbidding, under the strictest sanctions, Catholic cooperation with the Germans. On February 28, 1941, the bishops instructed Catholic parishes, rectories, and seminaries to refuse to supply the German high command with economic and manpower statistics. The following month the bishops told Catholic journals not to comply with the demand that all journals be submitted to Nazi headquarters. When, in the spring of 1942, the Nazis attempted to infiltrate the confessional system by appointing pro-Nazi school officials, the Catholics and the Protestants came to a mutual agreement that they would call a nationwide school strike in retaliation should Nazis be placed in either of their systems. In 1940 the Catholics had suspended their radio operations rather than cooperate with the Nazified radio service. In August 1942, they did likewise with their labor unions.[45]

Against threats from the German high command that converted Catholic Jews would be deported as a retaliatory measure along with other Jews, the Dutch bishops issued a strong letter, to be read at all masses in July 1942, condemning Nazi Jewish policy. Again in 1943 they issued a joint letter exhorting Catholics to practice civil disobedience rather than assist the Nazi hunt for Jews. They forbade Catholic students to sign the oath of loyalty to the Germans, which led to the closing of the Catholic University in Nijmegen.

During the Nazi occupation the House of Orange became a rallying symbol for the diverse ideological groups. The socialists, in their

45. I am following the short sketch in Rogier, *Katholieke Herleving,* pp. 580–604; also the study by Werner Warmbrunn, *The Dutch under German Occupation: 1940-1945* (Palo Alto, Ca.: Stanford University Press, 1963).

underground paper *Het Parool,* reversing prewar anti-monarchical stands, pledged loyalty to the House of Orange and reprinted the speeches of Queen Wilhelmina. Catholics enthusiastically sang the hymn *Domine Salvam fac Reginam Nostram* in their Sunday services. In concentration camps such as the Saint Michael's Camp or in exile in London, Catholics, Protestants, and socialists began to question separatism. Nevertheless, there were three major underground resistance movements—The Order Service, the National Organization for the Assistance of "Divers," and The Council of Resistance; and six major underground papers—*Vrij Nederland, Het Parool, Je Maintiendrai, Trouw, De Waarheid,* and *Christofoor.* Although more mixed in composition of staff than prewar organizations, these still reflected separatism. If the ideology had gone out of confessional politics, the structural reality would remain long after the war was over.[46]

On December 31, 1944, three of the five Catholic bishops, meeting in the already liberated south, declared that postwar Catholicism would continue the strategy of missionary confessionalism. They laid plans for the restoration of the Catholic Labor Union, political party, newspapers, and schools. The personal authority of the Dutch bishops had been enormously enhanced by their courageous anti-Nazi stance during the war. "The people heard week after week the voice of their bishops. They knew in advance that at the appropriate moment a voice of protest would be heard from the pulpits and such protest not just in vague terms."[47]

In the period immediately after the war, three different political visions for postwar Dutch society were available. On the left, the communists, through their newspaper *De Waarheid* and their movement for one federated labor union, sought a deconfessionalized postwar Dutch society along Marxist lines. In the middle, a coalition of socialists, less dogmatic than their prewar predecessors, and liberal progressives from the Dutch Reformed Church, as well as a small minority of Dutch Catholic lay intellectuals, sought a "breakthrough" from prewar confessionalism around a vision of humanism and socialism. Finally, the majority of orthodox Calvinists and Catholics sought the restoration of prewar confessionalism.

46. The metaphor of "divers" refers to people "diving" underwater—that is, going underground. *Vrij Nederland* is progressive Protestant and Socialist; *Het Parool* is Socialist; *Je Maintiendrai* had a mixed staff of Catholics, Protestants, and Socialists; *Trouw* is Protestant; *De Waarheid* is Communist; *Christofoor* was Catholic. Midway during the war *Christofoor* and *Je Maintiendrai* merged. It is significant that only the most confessional underground papers survived the war.
47. Rogier, *Katholieke Herleving,* p. 603.

From one point of view, World War II did little or nothing to change Catholic confessional apartheid. Table 4, showing the percentages of confessional and neutral organizations for five different periods of the first half of the century, makes evident that the degree of confessional separateness increased in the postwar period. It also shows that the relative shift by which the percentage of neutral organizations declined is largely due to Catholic separateness.[48] Again, the percentage of mixed marriages decreased in the postwar period from 23.1 percent in 1946 to 19.9 percent in 1957.[49] The Catholics were the least likely to marry outside their group. The fact that until the beginning of the 1960s the confessional parties enjoyed a majority in the parliament is a further proof that the socialist-Christian humanist "breakthrough" in the postwar period was a failure.

In what sense was there a breakthrough in confessional strategies? First, socialism shed most of its ideological dogmatism, allowing and even inviting Protestant and Catholic participants. A significant group of Dutch Reformed Christians and a smaller number of Catholic intellectuals joined the Socialist Workers' Party. Second, even though the inter-church dialogue in the time of the resistance movement was allowed to lapse, acceptance of confessional separatism had broken down. Economic emancipation had been almost fully achieved.

Third, between 1945 and 1958 there was a growing unrest among Catholic elites with the missionary strategy of triumphal separatism. This unrest was expressed by such Catholic laymen as Geert Ruygers, J. and W. Tans, William Pompe, Ludolf Baas, Daniel de Lange, and Bernard Delfgaauw. They wanted Catholics to distinguish between the community of faith and the church confessional organizations, as they had traditionally distinguished between the national community and the state. In progressive postwar journals such as *Dux* (refounded in 1947), *De Nieuwe Mens* (founded in 1949), *Ter Elfder Ure* (founded in 1953), there were consistent calls for a redefinition of the role of the Catholic layman. Catholic lay voices sought a new style from their bishops, modeled on the open Catholicism of Emmanuel Cardinal Suhard in Paris. In the period 1930-1947 the ratio of lay

48. J. P. Kruyt and Walter Goddijn, "Verzuiling en Ontzuiling als Sociologisch Process," in *Drift en Koers*, den Hollander *et al.*, pp. 244–245. A great source of the increase of confessionalism in postwar Dutch society was the inclusion of confessional social welfare activities under the state subsidy. See William Petersen, "Fertility Trends and Population Policy," *Sociologia Neerlandica*, III, 2 (1965–1966), p. 10.
49. See G. Decker, "Verandering in de Frequentie van het Gemengde Huwelijke," *Mens en Maatschappij*, XXXXIV, I (January–February 1969), 33–37.

TABLE 4.

Degree of Organizational Separateness for Five Different Periods
(Based on eight areas of activity)

Year	Total No. of Organizations		Neutral Non-Confessional Organizations		Roman Catholic		Inter-denominational Protestant		Dutch Reformed		Gereformeerden		Other Religious[a]		External Federations Coordinating Groups
	N	Pct. of Total	N	Pct. of Total	N	Pct. of Total	N	Pct. of Total	N	Pct. of Total	N	Pct. of Total	N	Pct. of Total	N
1914	271	100	154	56.8	37	13.7	48	17.7	1	0.4	15	5.5	16	5.9	8
1925	414	100	229	55.4	61	14.8	79	19.1	3	0.7	20	4.8	22	5.2	9
1932	514	100	272	52.9	89	17.3	94	18.3	5	1.0	27	5.2	27	5.4	14
1939	597	100	306	51.2	108	18.2	105	17.6	8	1.3	33	5.5	36	6.3	17
1956	897	100	424	47.3	193	21.5	132	14.7	31	3.5	50	5.6	67	7.4	28

SOURCE: Adapted from J. P. Kruyt and Walter Goddijn, "Verzuiling en Ontzuiling," in *Drift en Koers*, A.N.J. den Hollander (Assen: van Gorcum, 1968), pp. 244-245. The eight areas of activity are: social welfare, education, non-school youth programs, press, sports, health organizations, cultural organizations, and labor unions.

[a]The Salvation Army, Jewish, Unitarian, and so forth.

Catholic university graduates per 100 priests increased from 71 to 114. Now that economic emancipation had been completed, it was time for the layman to achieve his proper place as a free agent in the wider society, perhaps even in the church.

There were additional symptoms of disturbance among the lower clergy.[50] Many saw a strange pastoral discrepancy in the fact that 20 percent of the Dutch clergy was engaged full time in non-pastoral tasks. In 1947 a group of pastors began meeting to discuss new strategies, publishing their conclusions in 1950 in *Unrest in Pastoral Care*. Priests and laity formed groups to consider problems inherent in the missionary strategy. A small group of Catholic theologians and pastors met to suggest ways in which the bishops could celebrate the hundredth anniversary of the restoration of the hierarchy in a less than triumphalist way. They suggested a joint pastoral letter to be entitled "The Bishop, Witness of Hope," in which the bishops, following the pattern of Cardinal Suhard, would speak to a biblically grounded, humanistic Catholicism open to the best results in Reformation Christianity and non-Christian humanism. They suggested to their episcopal go-between, Mgr. Huybers, Bishop of Haarlem, that the bishops preach tolerance and dialogue. They cautiously intimated that the bishops might break through the Catholic impasse on the question of contraception.[51]

Here we see evidence for the existence of stages one and two in the sequence of structural differentiation (Table 2, Chapter One): a growing dissatisfaction with the performance of incumbents of an institutionalized role, or with the organization of the role itself, and other symptoms of disturbance which were not restricted to dissatisfaction among Catholic laymen and lower clergy. The Catholic proportion within the Dutch population had increased a dramatic 5 percent in the first half of the twentieth century. Dutch Catholics not only outbred their local competitors, but significantly outbred their Catholic confreres in Belgium, Germany, and France.[52] By the beginning of the 1950s Dutch Catholicism was the best organized, most

---

50. The best treatment of symptoms of disturbance in the early 1950s is to be found in O. Schreuder, "Van Kerk naar Denominatie," in *Sociologische Gids*, XV, 4 (June–July 1968), 247–259. See also Martin van Amerongen and Igor Cornelissen, *Tegen de Revolutie: Het Evangelie* (Amsterdam: Paris–Manteau, 1972), pp. 85–97.

51. I am indebted for my information here to an unpublished manuscript by Jan van Kilsdonk. The members of the group which drew up the document read like a Who's Who of theological Catholic Netherlands: J. Willebrands, presently the Cardinal archbishop of Utrecht; Dr. Jan Groot; Piet Schoonenberg, S.J.; Herman Fortman; Hans Weterman; Frs. Pauwels, O.P., and van Kilsdonk, S.J.

52. That the Catholics in the Netherlands in the postwar period outbred every other group as well as fellow Catholics in every European country except Portugal is an established statistical

conservative and observant of traditional Catholic laws, and least ecumenical Catholic population in industrial Europe. The Dutch hierarchy, for example, was the last hierarchy in Western Europe to take advantage in the postwar years of a Vatican privilege allowing bishops to ease the traditional church laws on fast and abstinence. The more triumphal Catholics rested in the assurance that they would outbreed "them," accepting the position of the leader of the Catholic party, Dr. Romme, who could write in the largest Catholic daily in 1951, "full Catholic emancipation can be achieved only when our people will have become Catholic in the vast majority."[53] It was not merely a set of irrational projections when the Synod of the Dutch Reformed Church declared in 1950 that "the Catholic Church is an intolerant Church which cannot change its ways without denying its very essence."[54] Protestant fears were so great that even the relatively irenic Professor Miskotte could state a few years after the war that Protestants must prepare for the inevitable: "Sooner or later we shall realize that there is only one set of choices confronting us: to leave the country or defend our nation from Catholic takeover."[55]

It is apparent that in the early 1950s Dutch Catholicism exhibited a series of symptoms of disturbance and dissatisfaction with the organizational structure of the Catholic missionary strategy. According to the hypotheses about sequences of change (Table 2), the first response of the social control agencies in the face of structural differentiation is a "holding operation," an attempt to contain the disturbance and reaffirm the existing structure.

---

fact. The explanatory cause is debatable. E. W. Hofstee in "De Groei van de Nederlandse Bevolking," in den Hollander et al., Drift en Koers, pp. 13–84, argues that it was due to delayed industrialization in the Catholic South in the Netherlands. Van Heek, Het Geboorte Niveau, argues that the abnormality in postwar Dutch population statistics was due to a religious factor, a peculiarly militant frontier mentality. The key evidence which weights the argument in van Heek's favor is the example of the small town of Tudderen, which before 1949 belonged to Germany but after that date became part of the Netherlands. This border town of 6,300 population, almost entirely Catholic, increased its birthrate from 19.5 in 1949 to 25.0 in 1959 while in the same period the birthrate in neighboring German Catholic villages across the border fell from 16.3 to 12.9. Van Heek attributes this to the assumption that Catholics could breed themselves into the majority. For a survey of the debate in English, which also sides with van Heek, see William Petersen, "Fertility Trends and Population Policy," Sociologia Neerlandica, II, 2 (1965–1966), 2–13.

53. See the article on Romme in De Volkskrant, October 25, 1951, p. 7.
54. Cited in Rogier, Katholieke Herleving, p. 625.
55. Cited in van Heek, Het Geboorte Niveau der Nederlandse Rooms-Katholieken, p. 151. See also, the article in Vrij Nederland, April 26, 1952, p. 8, which refers to "the impressive self-consciousness and even more impressive thrust toward internal unity, which far from falling off grows in proportionate strength to the extent that Catholicism wins, both quantitively and qualitively, a definitive and decisive place in our land."

The Dutch bishops began to read the signs of disturbance. In 1952 the Socialist Workers' Party made significant inroads into the hitherto impenetrable Catholic provinces of North Brabant and Limburg. The Catholic Sociological Census Bureau reported that while the Netherlands enjoyed the highest rate of attendance at weekly mass in Western Europe, the numbers of weekly attendants were declining. The bishops had been submitted a position paper for a bishop's pastoral letter which went far beyond their limits. It was time to restore the shaky unity of Catholic Netherlands. In place of the proposed letter entitled "The Bishop, Witness of Hope," the bishops issued the stern Collective Mandatory Letter of 1954, in which Catholic membership in a socialist union or significant reading of socialist newspapers and listening to socialist radio was to be punished by excommunication. Those who persisted in such action until their death would be denied church burial.

The bishops stopped just short of condemning membership in the socialist party, "because it involves a relatively small group who, furthermore, even without sanctions, can know very clearly what the desires of the bishops are."[56] The Collective Mandatory Letter of 1954 pays lip service to the concept of an open Catholicism, preferring, however, to allow the dialogue to take place at the organizational top layers, in the form of compromises between the elites of the various ideological confessional organizations. The Mandatory Letter speaks the old Catholic language, calling for passive obedience thirty-eight times while only once referring to lay independence in a positive vein, and quoting papal documents in preference to biblical sources.

Although the general Catholic press and the leaders of Catholic organizations accepted the bishops' Mandatory Letter with enthusiasm or at least without unfavorable commentary, there were other signs that the problems would not go away. The press reaction from the socialist and liberal Protestant side was one of shocked indignation, surprise, or confirmation in all their worst fears. It should be remembered that the Dutch socialism which the bishops so roundly condemned represented the least dogmatic branch of socialism on the continent. Besides socialism, the bishops also condemned Catholic participation in the Union for Sexual Reform, taking swipes as well at the Humanist Association ("they effectively deny God") and liberalism ("they privatize religion."). Had Dutch Catholics followed the

---

56. See "Episcopal Mandatory Letter on the Catholic in Public Life at the Present Time," *Katholiek Archief,* IX, 25 (June 18, 1954).

mandatory letter of 1954 they would be left with only the most orthodox Calvinists as coalition partners.

The leadership of the socialist labor union was aghast, pointing out that the Dutch bishops' position was stricter than the stands taken by the hierarchy in Italy, Austria, and Germany. They complained of the unfairness of an attack on a party which had accepted fully the principles of religious freedom and supported legislation to increase state subsidies for confessional universities. They charged the bishops with a dangerous dividing of the Dutch people.[57] The Dutch Reformed Synod the following year issued its own pastoral letter, pointedly taking an opposite tack from the bishops by calling for deconfessionalization. The Catholic members of the socialist party, in a dilemma of conscience, decided that they could remain both Catholic and socialist. One of them, D. M. Delfgaauw, wrote in response to the bishops' Mandatory Letter: "An intellectual, inasmuch as he is an intellectual, seeks the truth. That is his personal task. Present-day Catholic life is entirely determined by organizational schemas, that is, in the last instance, by the exercise of collective power. . . . The Catholic intellectual stands before the painful conflict between personal truth and organized power."

Delfgaauw left little doubt which side he would choose. "Institutional power never avoids dangers in a subtle way but rather smothers every spirit to death."[58] A leading Catholic intellectual, William Pompe, could admit to a friend that with the publication of the Mandatory Letter he felt ashamed to be a Catholic for the first time in his life.[59] As one of the drafters of an alternate pastoral letter puts it, his reaction to the Mandatory Letter was such that "my consciousness of the need to go in opposition dates from that very moment." He goes on to state, "the Mandatory Letter had the significance that it worked to polarize Catholics for the first time in modern history in such a way that its critics felt assured that the future lay with them."[60]

While Archbishop Alfrink traveled the land defending the principles of the Mandatory Letter in and out of season, other forces in Dutch Catholicism recognized that the problems inherent in confessional separatism would not go away once economic emancipation

57. For non-Catholic reactions to the Mandatory Letter, see *Katholiek Archief*, IX, *32* (August 6, 1954).
58. Cited in J. A. van Doorn, "Verzuiling: Een Eigentijds Systeem van Sociale Controle," *Sociologische Gids*, III, *3* (March 1956), 47.
59. Jan van Kilsdonk, unpublished memoria to Igor Cornelissen, p. 9.
60. Van Kilsdonk memoria, p. 8.

had been achieved.[61] The students at the Catholic University of Nijmegen were being exposed to Dutch translations of the new theology in France, which prompted Pius XII to send the Jesuit Sebatian Tromp to visit the university in 1955 to certify its orthodoxy. In 1957, the newly erected Saint Willibrord's Association warned the bishops that confessional separatism was "a continually growing greater danger for Dutch national society."[62]

61. A survey of Alfrink's speeches reprinted in *Katholiek Archief,* 1954–1957, will substantiate the point.
62. See *Katholiek Archief,* XII, *19* (May 9, 1958).

Chapter 3

The Costs of Columnization

It will be my purpose in this chapter to give a picture of traditional Dutch social structure as a way of providing a better view of our first variable, structural setting for change.[1] I will then attempt to draw up a checklist of the advantages and the costs inherent in Dutch social structure, seeing the costs as pressures or tensions toward change, our second variable. At the risk of great simplification, it can be argued that in the 1960s Dutch society was primarily addressing itself to the problematic costs in its structure. Finally, I will look to the Catholic bloc within that structure—whose internal pressures toward change we have already seen—to account for the resources available to it in mobilizing for change, our third independent variable.

It will be useful to begin this chapter by stating the questions we shall seek to answer and the general argument to be pursued. In the 1960s the Dutch Catholic community underwent radical and dramatic changes. While these changes were the most newsworthy events in Dutch society in the 1960s, they were by no means isolated. Rather substantial changes also occurred in other areas of Dutch life—in

1. I am indebted for my understanding of Dutch social structure to, among others, the following sources: P. van Daalen, *Wij Nederlanders* (Utrecht: Aula Books, 1967), Chapter 4, pp. 136–148; J. A. van Doorn, "Verzuiling: Een Eigentijdse Systeem van Sociale Controle," *Sociologische Gids*, III, 3 (March 1956), 41–49; Johan Goudsblom, *Dutch Society* (New York: Random House, 1967); J. P. Kruyt, *Verzuiling* (Zaandijk: Heijnes, 1959); J. P. Kruyt, "Sociologische Beschouwingen Over Zuilen en Verzuiling," *Socialisme en Democratie*, XIV, 1 (January 1957), 11–29; J. P. Kruyt, "The Influence of Denominationalism on Social Life and Organizational Patterns," *Archives de Sociologie des Religions*, IV, 8 (July–December 1959), 105–111; J. P. Kruyt and Walter Goddijn, "Verzuiling en Ontzuiling als Sociologisch Process," in *Drift en Koers*, A. N. J. den Hollander *et al.* (Assen: Van Gorcum, 1968), pp. 227–263; David Moberg, "Social Differentiation in the Netherlands," *Social Forces*, XXX, 4 (May 1961), 333–337; David Moberg, "Religion and Society in the Netherlands and America," *Social Compass*, IX, 1 (Spring 1961), 17–19; J. A. Ponsioen, "Notities voor de Sociologische Bestudering van de Verzuiling," *Sociologische Gids*, III, 3 (March 1965), 50–52; I. Schoffer, "Verzuiling, Een Specifiek Nederlands Probleem," *Sociologische Gids*, III, 4 (April 1956), 121–127.

politics, the military, the university, and the labor unions. The major social changes of the period can be grouped under four rubrics. (1) A decline in ideological solidarity within the constituent sub-groups of Dutch society. (2) The growth of internal democracy within each constituent sub-group or within organizational life. (3) The neutralization of organizational appendages of the sub-groups, and (4) greater flexibility in preferences for political parties or membership in confessional associations. For each of these four points, the Catholic community was the sub-group most strongly affected. Why were the changes focused upon the Catholic community, and why are the changes more far-reaching within the core of the church itself than in the periperhal zones of confessional organization? The following chapter attempts to answer these questions as follows:

1. Traditional Dutch social structure was based on the premise of a balance of power. This balance, in turn, rested upon ideological solidarity within each sub-group of Dutch life. When the solidarity broke down, the balance of power was upset and the structure could not return to balance. The Catholic bloc upset the balance.

2. Anyone interested in redressing the costs and problems inherent in the traditional social structure would need to affect the Catholic bloc. It had become the keystone of the structure.

3. There could be no way to change the position of the Catholic bloc within the Dutch structure without internal changes in the role structures within the church itself, because these roles were based upon post-Tridentine international Catholic models of confessional separatism.

The Catholics, therefore, were the key to social change in the Netherlands.

PILLARS AND CIRCLES

We can begin to understand Dutch social structure if we employ two visual images—the metaphors of the pillars and the circles. The Dutch word *verzuiling*, which refers to the confessionalization of the society into separate, tightly organized, ideological blocs, rests upon a metaphor of separate pillars or columns *(Zuilen)*, each of which is indispensable for maintaining the common roof of Dutch society. In effect, traditional Dutch society looked more like several friendly nations in consort than one homogeneous state.

Lacking a wider neutral public sector, the Dutch fell back upon the protective circle of the family, intimate friends, and like-minded associates for support and meaning. To a foreigner first learning the language, two Dutch words seem much overused: *kring* and *gezelligheid*. Both tell us a great deal about the society. The first word means "circle," as in the expression, "in our circle we do it this way." Dutch social life is centered around the primary units of the family— almost all national holidays are family feasts including the typically Dutch and charming St. Nicolaus feast—and the warm circle of close friends. Thus, "more than 60 percent of the time available for leisure is spent at home . . . and at least 75 percent of the free time spent outside the home is passed in the company of members of the family."[2] *Gezelligheid* is untranslatable. It means something like snug and cozy, conjuring up the image of a familiar surrounding, close friends, and good food and drink. These two metaphors tell us volumes about Dutch social structure. The greatest problems of the society lay in the need to correlate the highly integrated sub-groups (circles) into the segmented national society (separate pillars).

COLUMNIZATION DEFINED

The Dutch sociological literature on *verzuiling* or columnization is voluminous. Since the phenomenon may be unique to Dutch society, it is difficult to sum up in one simple definition. In general, columnization refers to a peculiarly Dutch approach to pluralism whereby there was an almost perfect correlation between membership in a religious or ideological group and other associations. There was a bare minimum of crosscutting interests, group memberships, and alliances. All of the religious or ideological groups had "their own schools, their own political parties, their own press, but, also in general: their own trade unions, farmers' unions, employers' unions, shop keepers' unions, cooperatives, agricultural loan banks, their own institutes for social research and societies for physicians, for lawyers, for teachers, for social workers, for scientists, for employees, for artists, for musicians, for authors; their own music bands, choral societies, sport clubs, theater clubs, travelers' clubs, dance clubs, clubs for adult education, public libraries, broadcasting; their own youth organizations, women's clubs, student clubs or fraternities and sororities . . . their own hospitals, sanatoriums, organizations for all kinds of social work and charitable work, etc."[3]

2. The figures are cited by Goudsblom, *Dutch Society*, p. 135.
3. Kruyt, "The Influence of Denominationalism on Social Life and Organizational Patterns," 108.

Yet it would be a mistake to limit the concept of columnization to the notion of plural, semi-autonomous sub-groups, or *social segmentation*. The concept also includes the metaphor of an arch, and the rules of interaction within the one society, or *social integration*. "The nearest English cognates are the concepts of subcultures, pluralism, unity in diversity, special interest groups, and pressure groups. If somehow all of these were woven together and given, in addition, an ideological twist, we might come near an understanding of the term."[4]

The metaphor of the columns does not perfectly coincide with any received sociological concept. Thus, the sub-groups are not castes, since their isolation is self-chosen, not imposed. Further, they do not form a simple hierarchy. They are not classes since the divisions cut across economic boundaries. They are neither ethnic groups, nor political or religious sects. Finally, since each group forms an indispensable part of the whole fabric of society and tries to wield influence in it, the sub-groups are not ghettoes.

There are three main ways of defining the phenomenon: *"verzuiling* is a situation wherein a large number of social activities which have no direct bearing on ideology or religion are, nevertheless, organized around associations whose foundation is ideological."[5]

How many columns are there in Dutch society? If we take as a starting point the idea that a column is a set of statistical probabilities that members of an association founded upon an ideology will also hold membership in sister associations based on the same ideological principle, we can conclude that there are four major columns in Dutch society: a Catholic column, a Protestant column, a Socialist column, and a laissez-fair Liberal column, each with an overlapping net of political parties, broadcasting companies, newspapers, and so forth.[6] We can see that for two of the columns the founding principle

4. Moberg, "Social Differentiation in the Netherlands," 333.
5. Mady A. Thung and Anneke H. Schipper-van Otterloo, *Kerkelijke Verandering* (Alphen aan den Rijn: Samson, 1972), p. 55.
6. The literature on columnization, starting from different definitions, does not agree on the number of columns. J. P. Kruyt and Walter Goddijn, in "Verzuiling en Ontzuiling," argue that there are three: Catholic, Protestant, and neutral. They reason that the Socialist and Liberal blocs, since they are in principle open to all Dutchmen, do not form separate columns. Other authors, citing smaller clusters—what the Dutch call *hokjes* or compartments to distinguish them from the *Zuilen* or columns—place the number at greater than four, including such constellations as The Humanist Association or splinter Gereformeerden clusters. My own preference for a statistical starting point for definition agrees with Arend Lijphart, *The Politics of Accommodation* (Berkeley: University of California Press, 1968). Lijphart demonstrates that the Socialists and Liberals represent distinct statistical clusters within the "neutral" zone; see pp. 26–58 for the correlations.

is religious confessionalism, and for the other two the basis rests on competing secular ideologies.

One of the major Dutch churches, the Dutch Reformed Church, has very few sister organizations in secular spheres. The majority of its membership belong to either the liberal or socialist column. Since the war, that church has repeatedly deplored the columnization of Dutch society. According to the Dutch usage, the churches as such do not constitute a column. This usage is justified by the fact that there are active members of the Protestant and Catholic churches who belong to the socialist or liberal column, and a small percentage of the non-churched who tend to organize their associational life within the Catholic or the Protestant column. The Protestant column draws from more than one church. Finally, for a proportion of the Catholic or Protestant population, the ties to the church are exclusively through the cluster of sister associations rather than through strictly church activities.

The internal coherence of sister organizations within any cluster of overlapping memberships varied across the columns. Thus, the relationship between the church, as such, and the Catholic column was greater than that between the Protestant churches and the Protestant column. Until recently, for example, the Catholic bishops exercised the prerogative of ratifying the constitution of any ''official'' Catholic organization and providing spiritual advisors for all the organizations. Nevertheless, there were also a large number of ''unofficial'' Catholic organizations free of direct episcopal control. The Protestant column had no direct organizational ties with the churches, although informal ties were real and many. Again, in the Catholic column and to a lesser degree in the Protestant column, the organizational unity of the cluster was formalized in interlocking directorates: for example, a director of the Catholic labor union had a seat within the governing committee of the Catholic People's Party and a director of the Catholic People's Party had a seat on the Board of Directors of the Catholic Radio Broadcasting Company. At least since the end of the war, the unity between sister organizations within the socialist and liberal blocs rested mainly on the fact that these columns catered to a similar clientele. Memberships rather than directors tended to overlap.

Comparison of the four parallel groupings is further complicated by the fact that the organizational activities of the columns do not perfectly coincide. All four columns have their own political parties: (1) Catholic People's Party (K.V.P., Catholic); (2) The Socialist

Workers' Party (P.V.D.A., Socialist); (3) The Party for Freedom and Democracy (V.V.D., Liberal); (4) The Anti-Revolutionary Party (A.R.P., Protestant, mainly Gereformeerden); and (5) The Christian Historical Union (C.H.U., Protestant, mainly Dutch Reformed and other Protestant).

These five parties have dominated Dutch political life since the turn of the century. Before 1960 their only competition came from the small Netherlands Communist Party, The Socialist Pacifist Party, and small splinter parties representing rightist Gereformeerden groups. These smaller parties, together, never represented more than about 5 percent of the vote. Since 1960, however, the political scene has been complicated by the emergence of many new parties. Three important smaller ones are the Farmers' Party, the Middle-Class Party, and the right-wing splinter Roman Catholic Party of the Netherlands; the three larger ones are Democracy '66 (D'66), founded in 1966 on the slogan of breaking through columnization; Democratic-Socialists 1970 (DS '70), a splinter of moderate socialists from the Socialist Workers' Party, and the Political Party of Radicals (P.P.R.), a confessional left-wing splinter drawing its original membership mainly from the Catholic People's Party in 1967. The traditional balance of power politics rested on ideological solidarity within each of the columns. Since this has broken down, the splintering of parties has made it increasingly difficult to find a working majority in the parliament.

All four columns, similarly, maintained a network of national and regional daily newspapers and weekly opinion magazines as well as radio and television broadcasting companies. There were five major broadcasting companies: (1) Catholic Radio Broadcasting Company (K.R.O., Catholic); (2) The Association of Working Class Radio Amateurs (V.A.R.A., Socialist); (3) The General Association of Radio Broadcasting Company (A.V.R.O., Liberal); (4) The Netherlands' Christian Radio Association (N.C.R.V., Protestant); and (5) The Free-thinking Protestant Broadcasting Company (V.P.R.O., Protestant).

These five ruled the field unchallenged until 1965, when a new law was passed which further complicated Dutch broadcasting. An umbrella organization, The Netherlands Broadcasting Institute (N.O.S.), supplies 40 percent of all television and 25 percent of radio time. Each company receives a proportional share from a state tax on television sets and the common funds from radio and television advertisements.

Protestants and Catholics maintain separate, state-supported primary and secondary school systems, but the Socialists and Liberals attend public schools. Socialists, Protestants, and Catholics have their own labor unions, but the Liberals do not. Liberals, Protestants, and Catholics have their own associations of manufacturers, but the Socialists do not. Socialists, Catholics, and Protestants tend to have separate youth organizations, sports clubs, and so on, and the Liberals do not.

A SECOND DEFINITION

"*Verzuiling* is the process by which several ideological groups, together making up one society, are organized around a predominantly organizational social control system, with a tendency toward the displacement of the ideal values of the ideology by the organization and a further ideological justification of organizational power as an end in itself."[7]

Other societies besides the Netherlands have exhibited the phenomenon of ideological pluralism, but the Netherlands' case was unique in three ways:

1. Dutch columnization represented a quadruple structure of sizable minorities whose existence and public right could not be denied without serious danger to the public order. None could ever realistically capture a majority. The columns were relatively balanced in size. Coalitions between the columns shifted. The system was based on balance of power. This differentiates the Netherlands from Belgium, Italy, Austria, and France, where divisions tended to be bipolar, between rightist Catholic groupings and leftist non-churched groups. Where, as in England, the United States, or Australia, Catholics also pursued strategies of confessional separatism, they tended to become isolated in ghettoes, cut off from the dominant secular culture. In the Netherlands there were no ghettoes. As those who opposed columnization—such as the Liberals from the beginning and the Socialists since the end of the war—have put it, "We are in a column because we are against the whole idea of columnization."[8] A series of successive attempts have been made in postwar Dutch political and social life to found "neutral" political parties or television broadcasting companies around the catchword of "breaking through" columnization. Each new organization became, in turn, another compartment.

7. Van Doorn, "Verzuiling: Een Eigentijdse Systeem van Sociale Controle," 42.
8. Kruyt, *Verzuiling*, p. 6.

2. Subsidy politics within the Dutch welfare state have been far-reaching and strictly proportional. Confessional organizations need not compete against better financed or more efficient neutral state-provided services. Besides the relative equality and balance of power in memberships across the columns, there was also equality in efficiency and competence in services rendered by competing organizations. Ideological differences tipped the scales of choice for consumers approaching marginally differentiated commodities, goods, and services.

3. Finally, the metaphor of the arch is important. The Dutch assume that every column or compartment has its inalienable right to public existence—indeed, that each is indispensable to the good functioning of the whole of Dutch society. This assumption is equivalent to the British sense of "fair play." Two examples will bring home the point.

In the mid-1960s a parliamentary proposal to do away with the parcelling of public television into multiple, ideologically founded broadcasting companies foundered on the counter-argument that this would endanger every group's right to free speech and public presentation of its point of view. Similarly, throughout the 1960s repeated proposals for an electoral threshold for eligibility to parliament as a way of reducing the almost unmanageable number of parties in parliament have been defeated on the argument that the small State Gereformeerden Party and the Gereformeerden Union would, thereby, lose representation. Thus a typical and indispensable, if very small, Dutch voice would be deprived of a political forum.

J. A. Van Doorn emphasizes, in his definition of *verzuiling*, that the clusters of ideologically similar organizations functioned as a social control system for the sub-group. Leaving one column for another, which would entail breaking many associations, was psychologically similar to emigration to another land. Van Doorn, moreover, sums up historical process in his definition by reminding us that the columns tended to invert means and ends, so that organizational separatism, which began as a means for furthering special values and the advancement of economically depressed groups, became an end and value in itself.

If Van Doorn places greatest stress upon cleavages between the columns, William Shetter, in a third definition, reminds us of the rules of integration: "In principle, the *Zuilen* are thought of as coordinate and equal, the separate but inviolable pillars on which—to return to the architectural sense—society rests. The chasms between them are bridged over by a highly developed feeling for the necessity of respect for another's views, no matter how strongly one may be opposed to them; if the sanctity of his belief is threatened, one's own is equally vulnerable."[9]

Although columnization was primarily a facet of organizational life, it penetrated deeply into informal relations as well. Marriage and friendship took place within the columns. Informal rules stipulated that Catholics or other groups support only their own milkmen, vegetable and bread stores, and tobacconists, for example. Buying and hiring practices tended to be protectionist. Again, the Catholics were often the most explicit and consistent in this custom. The Dutch bishops, for example, reminded all Catholic parish or diocesan organizations, in 1958, that it was their serious duty to employ only Catholic architects, contractors, and workers affiliated with the Catholic labor union.[10]

Anyone, with a few clues and a keen eye, could upon first meeting place a Dutchman in his proper column. Catholics and Protestants wear their wedding rings on different hands. They have separate vocabularies, such as the different ways to refer to "in the first place" when presenting a list of items. First names are often a clue. Old Germanic names such as Dirk, Barend, Aal are most likely non-Catholic. Latinized names such as Titus, Clemens, Aloysius, Cecilia are almost certainly Catholic. The Dutch sign letters or documents with their first two or three initials and the last name. A large proportion of Catholics have M., standing for Maria, for a middle or third initial. The somberness of clothing style, speech, and even facial expression can give away the Gereformeerden Dutchmen.[11] Thinking in terms of columnization has become such an ingrained Dutch habit that even opponents of the structure tend to be identified as Catholic, Protestant, Socialist, or Liberal *"van huis uit"*—in their origins.

The best starting definition of columnization is a statistical one: the probabilities that members of an association founded upon an ideology will also hold membership in sister organizations based on the same ideology. Such a purely statistical definition says nothing, however, about organizational unity among the sister associations through interlocking directorates, or the rules of interaction providing the arch which joins the columns together.

9. William Shetter, *The Pillars of Society* (The Hague: Martinus Nijhoff, 1971), p. 7.
10. Cited in Kruyt, *Verzuiling*, p. 42.
11. Catholics wear the wedding ring on their left hand. They say *"op* de eerste plaats" whereas Protestants say *"in* de eerste plaats." For further informal clues to each column, see A. Chorus, *De Nederlander: Uiterlijk en Innerlijk* (Leiden: A. W. Sijthoff, 1965), pp. 121ff.

STATISTICS ON COLUMNIZATION
IN THE 1950s

I have chosen the 1950s as a critical period for understanding the structural setting for Roman Catholic changes because outside pressures, connected with columnization, accumulated during that period on the Catholics, inasmuch as they formed the keystone for the system of columns. Table 5 presents a complex diagram showing the relationship between church membership and the church-related cluster. For simplicity's sake, the Socialist and laissez-faire Liberal columns are combined under one rubric, "neutral." The figures in the diagram blocked-in by diagonal or vertical lines or dots represent the columns.[12]

When we compare the neutral with the confessional columns we see that together the confessional ones represented a precarious majority within Dutch society in the 1950s. So long as there was solid support in the churches, any breakthrough was impossible. By reason of its size, at almost 40 percent of the population, and the undivided nature of Catholic sister-organizations (only *one* Catholic party, broadcasting company, and school system versus many Protestant or "neutral" political parties, broadcasting systems, and schools), the Catholic column was, by far, the giant among the columns, the best organized and most coherent.

Table 6 translates the data into statistics, showing what percentage of each religious group was likely to belong to a confessional organization, measured for eight different activities.[13] Note that with the exception of the choice for confessional schools (50 percent), the majority of members of the Dutch Reformed Church did not choose confessional organizations. Thus, while 89 percent of the Catholics subscribed to the Catholic Radio Broadcasting Company and 84.3 percent voted for the Catholic People's Party in the 1950s, only 32 percent of the Dutch Reformed membership chose confessional broadcasting companies or voted for a confessional political party. Table 7 presents the data for confessional versus neutral organizations for nine different activities.[14] This table further demonstrates that confessionalism commanded the allegiance of a majority of Dutchmen through the 1950s for most activities, although the neutral sector was predominant in the fields of newspapers, higher education, and voluntary health organizations. Table 8 reproduces the preferences

12. Adapted from Kruyt and Goddijn, "Verzuiling en Ontzuiling," p. 237.
13. Adapted from Kruyt and Goddijn, "Verzuiling en Ontzuiling," p. 242.
14. *Ibid.*, p. 243.

TABLE 5.

The Structure of Columnization in the 1950s

	Roman Catholic Community	Gereformeerden Community	Dutch Reformed and Other Protestant Community	Unchurched Community
8.	Roman Catholic Voluntary Associations — Ung.	Neutral Assoc. — Ung.	Protestant Associations — Ung.	Neutral Assoc. — Ung.
7.	Catholic Labor Unions — Ung.	Neutral Labor Unions — Ung.	Protestant Labor Unions — Ung.	Neutral Labor Unions — Ung.
6.	Roman Catholic Farmers' Association — Ung.	Neutral Farmers — Ung.	Protestant Farmers Assoc. — Ung.	Neutral Farmers Assoc. — Ung.
5.	Roman Catholic Radio Broadcasting — Ung.	Neutral Broadcasting — Ung.	Protestant Broadcasting — Ung.	Neutral Broadcasting A.V.R.O. — Ung.
4.	Roman Catholic Daily Newspaper	Neutral Papers — Ung.	Protestant Papers — Ung.	Neutral Newspapers
3.	Roman Catholic People's Party	Neutral Parties — Ung.	Protestant Parties — Ung.	Neutral Parties: V.V.D. & P.V.D.A.
2.	Roman Catholic Primary Schools	Neutral Public Schools / Gereformeerden Prim. Sch.	Prot. Ch. Sch. / Dutch Ref. Prim.	Neutral Public School
1.	Roman Catholic Church 40%	Gereformeerden Church 10%	Dutch Reformed and Other Protestant Churches 31%	Unchurched 19%

KEY:

- = Catholic Column
- = Protestant Column
- = Neutral Column
- = Unorganized Column

1. Church Affiliation, 1959
2. Choice of Primary Schools, 1957
3. Party Vote, 1959
4. Newspaper Choice, 1956
5. Subscription to Broadcasting Guide, 1956
6. Membership in Farmers' Association, 1953
7. Membership in Labor Union, 1958
8. Membership in Voluntary Association, 1958

SOURCE: Adapted from J. P. Kruyt and Walter Goddijn, "Verzuiling en Ontzuiling," in *Drift en Koers*, A.N.J. den Hollander (Assen: van Gorcum, 1968), p. 237.

TABLE 6.
Choice of Confessional Organizations for Eight Activities
(Percentages for each religious affiliation where organized)

Choice of Confessional Org. or Inst.	Roman Catholic	Gereformeerden	Dutch Reformed	Other Churches	Un-churched
1. Primary School (1957)	90.0	90.0	50.0		10.0
2. Farmers Assn. (1953)	95.0	90.0	37.0		Near 0
3. Union of Manufacturers (1958)	90.0	90.0	30.0		Near 0
4. Radio Guide Subscription (1959)	89.0	94.0	32.0	18.0	4.0
5. Newspaper Subscription (1955)	79.0	58.0	9.0	8.0	1.0
6. Vote for Second Chamber (1959)	84.3	95.0	32.0	Slight	Slight
7. Active Member, Voluntary Assn. (1955) (a) Exclusively Confessional	71.0	73.0	36.0	33.0	13.0
(b) Some Non-Confessional Membership	77.0	80.0	43.0	40.0	14.0
8. Use of Confessional Library Books (1956)	16.0	39.0	19.0	18.0	15.0

TABLE 7.
Choice of Confessional vs. Neutral Organizations
by Members of Religious Groups

Activity	Year of Survey	Roman Catholic	Protestant	Percent Confessional	Percent Neutral
Members of Farmers' Assn.	1953	48.0	16.0	64.0	36.0
Choice of Primary School	1957	35.0	28.0	63.0	37.0
Vote for Political Party	1959	31.6	20.4	52.0	48.0
Subscription to Radio Guide	1957	25.0	22.0	47.0	53.0
Member of Labor	1960	35.2	18.2	53.4	46.6
Member of Voluntary Health Association (Cross-Assn.)	1957	30.0	12.0	42.0	58.0
Newspaper Subscriptions	1955	—	—	40.0	60.0
Students in Univeristy or Higher Education	1958-1959	9.4	7.4	16.8	83.2
Control of Hospitals	1954	43.0	14.0	57.0	43.0

NOTE: Table 7 gives the percentage of all "organized" members of religious groups—including subscribers, voters, etc.—who choose confessional organizations. Table 8 gives percentage of total number of participants for each activity for the various columns. Table 13 shows relationships between church affiliation and the columns, whereas Table 14 shows relationships between columns themselves.

TABLE 8.
Membership in Voluntary Associations by Church Relationship and by Type of Voluntary Associations

A. Type of Voluntary Association	B. Percent of Members Belonging to Organizations (Total = 100)	C. Percent of Choice for Type of Organization by Church Affiliation			
		Roman Catholic (Total = 100)	Dutch Reformed (Total = 100)	Gereformeerden (Total = 100)	Unchurched (Total = 100)
1. Sport Associations					
Roman Catholic	22	61	0	0	1
Protestant	8	0	18	36	2
Neutral	70	39	82	64	97
2. Women's Clubs					
Roman Catholic	37	97	0	0	0
Protestant	40	0	55	99	12
Neutral	23	3	45	1	88
3. Song, Music, Theatre					
Roman Catholic	25	83	0	0	0
Protestant	29	0	39	84	3
Neutral	46	17	61	16	97
4. Youth Groups and Clubhouses					
Roman Catholic	36	96	0	0	7
Protestant	39	2	72	87	11
Neutral	25	2	28	13	82

NOTE: Column B should be read as follows: "Of all members of sport associations in the Netherlands, 22 percent (etc.) belonged to Catholic, 8 percent to Protestant, and 70 percent to Neutral sport associations. Column C should be read as follows: "Of all Roman Catholics (etc.), 61 percent joined Catholic sport associations and 39 percent joined neutral sport associations."

for Catholic, Protestant, and "neutral" organizations for four activities in the recreational sphere: sport clubs; women's clubs; song-music-theater clubs; youth groups and clubhouses.[15] Once again, we see the strong tendency toward separatism.

POLITICAL LIFE

In Table 9 we present the division of seats in the second chamber of parliament for the postwar period in three sub-tables: 1946-1956, 1956-1963, and 1967-1972.[16] The points worth noting in Table 9 are, first, the preponderance of confessional religious parties over non-confessional parties from 1946 through 1963 and the subsequent decline of the confessional proportion of the vote since 1963. The liberal V.V.D. and the socialist P.V.D.A. have gained at the expense of the confessional parties. Notice also the increased splintering of the old power blocs, registered in the table under the rubrics "other non-religious" and "other religious" parties. These parties have increased their share of the electorate from 6 percent of the total vote in 1956 to 25 percent in 1972, making a "gentlemen's agreement" between the four large blocs more difficult to reach. Note, further, that whereas the Protestant A.R.P. party has remained stable through the years, the greatest victim in the de-confessionalizing process in Dutch political life in the 1960s, the Catholic Party, was nearly halved in less than ten years. A final point worth remembering is that parties within the confessional and non-confessional blocs are not necessarily allies. In particular, the two largest non-confessional parties, V.V.D. and P.V.D.A., are natural opponents.

THE MEDIA

Table 10 reproduces readers' preferences for newspapers in the 1950s.[17] It has been estimated that 76 out of 100 Catholic households in 1955 subscribed to a Catholic daily.[18] We see the connection between church membership and the reading of newspapers in the statistics for the national dailies, the trend-setters within Dutch

15. Adapted from van Daalen, *Wij Nederlanders*, p. 140.
16. Source: Netherlands Central Bureau of Statistics, Election Statistics. The reason for three tables is that in 1956 the number of seats in the second chamber was increased from 100 to 150; after 1963 new parties changed the landscape of the traditional balance of power between the four large columns.
17. Source: M. Rooij, "Is de Nederlandse Pers Verzuild?" in *Pacificatie en de Zuilen*, J. Goelen, ed. (Meppel: J. A. Boom and Son, 1965), p. 87.
18. See G. W. Marsman, *De Katholieke Dagbladpers in Sociologisch Perspectief* (Assen: Van Gorcum, 1967), p. 190.

TABLE 9.
Division of Seats in the Second Chamber of Parliament, 1946–1972

Election Year	VVD (Liberal)	PVDA (Socialist)	Other Non-Religious	KVP (Cath.)	ARP (Prot.)	CHU (Prot.)	Other Religious	Total Non-Confessional	Total Confessional
A. 1946–1956 (Total number of seats = 100)									
1946	6	29	10	32	13	8	2	45	55
1948	8	27	8	32	13	9	3	43	57
1952	9	30	6	30	12	9	4	45	55
1956	9	34	4	33	10	8	2	47	53
B. 1956–1963 (Total number of seats = 150)									
1956	13	50	7	49	15	13	3	70	80
1959	19	50	3	49	14	3	12	72	78
1963	16	47	6	50	13	13	4	70	80
C. 1967–1972 (Splintering of the traditional blocs)									
1967	17	34	21	39	15	12	7	77	73
1971	16	39	30	35	13	10	7	85	65
1972	22	42	24	27	14	7	13	88	62

TABLE 10.
Percentages of Population Which Read Daily Newspapers

Newspaper	Pct. of population which reads
Roman Catholic Daily	26.4
Protestant Daily	8.7
Socialist Daily	19.3
Liberal Daily	5.1
Neutral, Independent Daily	40.5

journalism. Ninety percent of the readership of the two Catholic national dailies were practicing Roman Catholics, and an additional 6 percent of the readership consisted of lapsed or lax Catholics. Ninety percent of the readership of the Protestant dailies consisted of members of the Protestant churches, while an additional 5 percent came from lapsed or lax Protestants. Ninety-four percent of the readers of the two Socialist newspapers belonged to the Socialist or neutral column in Dutch society. The Liberal national papers drew their readership for the most part from the neutral column (76 percent) with a sizable portion from the Protestant column (19 percent).[19]

The situation for the radio and television broadcasting companies was similar to that of the newspapers. Dutch national radio has three channels while television has two. Public time on these channels is divided between a number of autonomous broadcasting companies. Each company is allotted time in proportion to its number of subscribing members. Membership is equivalent to subscribing to the radio-television guide published by the company. Each of the companies must devote a certain proportion of its time to cultural, religious, educational, sport, or entertainment programs, although the rules are flexible. In practice, the five largest companies try to adhere to the principle of a varied schedule. The Catholic Radio Broadcasting Company, however, can devote a fair proportion of its prime time to Catholic news, especially current and controversial topics.

The membership of the Catholic KRO was 99 percent Catholic, for the period under review; that of the Protestant NCRV was 91 percent

19. For these statistics, see Lijphart, *The Politics of Accommodation,* pp. 41ff.

Protestant, and that of the VPRO 65 percent Protestant. The Socialist VARA drew 96 percent of its membership from the neutral column, while the Liberal AVRO drew 86 percent of its members from that column.[20]

Dutch radio and television devote more prime time to religious news, controversies, and discussions than any other national radio and television service. Excluding strict news programs or background, Dutch television devotes on the average three and a half to four hours of prime television time per week to topics related to religion or inter-church affairs. The Dutch have a proverb which runs, "Every Dutch-man is a theologian." It is, at any rate, evident that the average Dutchman is exposed to more religious news than his counterpart in other countries.

CONVIVIUM AND CONNUBIUM

As we might by now expect, religious affiliation and friendship patterns are correlated. Table 11 reproduces this relationship. Each respondent in a nationwide survey conducted in 1955 was asked, "Now, a question about your circle of friends. Here is a list of different groups. To which of these groups do your best friends belong?" The respondent was then presented with a list of a number of well-known religious or political groupings within the Nether-lands. Even though the list did not perfectly correspond with the four columns as we have defined them, the results in Table 11 make clear that friendship patterns often break through the columns. At least a third of all the respondents had close friends who belonged to more than one of the four columns.[21] Nevertheless, convivium across columns was decidedly less probable than within one's own column.

In Table 12 we pursue the question by inquiring into the percen-tage of mixed or heterogeneous marriages for the year 1957. It will help us to see the peculiarity of the situation in the Netherlands if we compare its statistics for Roman Catholic mixed marriages to those in Germany and Switzerland for the same year, which were 24.7 percent and 22.6 percent respectively.[22]

A last piece of evidence for columnization is taken from organiza-tional life. In the beginning of the 1960s there was not one example

20. See *ibid.*, pp. 47–48. Since the 1960s the AVRO has disclaimed the "liberal" label.
21. Adapted from Lijphart, *The Politics of Accommodation*, p. 55.
22. Source for Table 12 and the comparative statistics for Germany and Switzerland: Gouds-blom, *Dutch Society*, p. 56.

TABLE 11.
Religious Affiliation and Friendship Choices
(percentages)

Respondent's Church Affiliation	Friends Are							Total[a]
	Roman Catholic	Gereformeerden	Dutch Reformed	Un-churched	Socialist	Liberal	No Answer Don't Know	
Roman Catholic (Church)	85.0	9.0	14.0	13.0	3.0	6.0	6.0	N = 389 136.0
Roman Catholic (Lapsed)	53.0	7.0	15.0	21.0	14.0	8.0	10.0	N = 105 128.0
Gereformeerden	17.0	78.0	38.0	15.0	8.0	10.0	7.0	N = 157 173.0
Dutch Reformed (Church)	14.0	38.0	85.0	17.0	6.0	9.0	2.0	N = 151 172.0
Dutch Reformed (Lapsed)	23.0	12.0	63.0	23.0	28.0	11.0	8.0	N = 351 167.0
Other Churches	41.0	25.0	39.0	41.0	18.0	16.0	9.0	N = 56 189.0
Nonchurched	19.0	12.0	27.0	53.0	26.0	11.0	7.0	N = 361 156.0

[a]The total percentages are greater than 100 percent because of double counting, owing to choices of friends belonging to more than one religious or political group.

TABLE 12.
Percentage of Mixed Marriages, 1957

Roman Catholic	9.2%
Gereformeerden	23.1%
Dutch Reformed	24.6%
Other Denominations	58.7%
Unchurched	31.9%

SOURCE: Johan Goudsblom, *Dutch Society* (New York: Random House, 1967).

of an interlocking directorate in which two different columns were joined. Thus, for example, not one of the directors of the Protestant labor union was also a director of a Socialist organization or a parliamentary representative for the Socialist Party. No director of a Catholic Businessmen's Association was active in Liberal politics. There was no instance where a full professor was to be found in a "wrong" university.[23]

We would expect that such strictly vertical, ideological pluralism should have given rise to overt and continuous conflict across the columns. Yet, surprisingly, the Netherlands has enjoyed a calm and ordered public and political life throughout this century with a comparatively low rate of serious strife, violence, strikes, or political crises. How was this order and stability possible? In assessing the advantages and costs of columnization we will look more closely at the rules of interaction which provided the arch to join the separate columns together.

ADVANTAGES OF COLUMNIZATION

There were four main advantages in columnization as a way of accommodating to pluralism. First, it guaranteed the institutionalization of genuine pluralism and variety. Every point of view lay under competition in politics, school systems, and public media. The columns gave a mosaic to social life and culture.

Secondly, the structure of separate columns provided the means for collective emancipation for three economically underprivileged

23. See Lijphart, *The Politics of Accommodation*, p. 68. Of the universities in the Netherlands, two are "officially" confessional: The Catholic University in Nijmegen and the Gereformeerden's Free Univesity in Amsterdam. Both are fully subsidized by the state. Two universities are "unofficially" liberal or socialist: The Advanced School of Economics in Rotterdam (since 1973, The Erasmus University of Rotterdam), and the University of Amsterdam, respectively.

groups. In the process, jobs and positions were both multiplied and protected against competition from equally competent members from another column. Socialist journalists did not feel the threat of competition from their Catholic confreres and vice versa. A play of mutually complementary self-interests insured that each group would try to maintain or increase the supply of jobs and privileged opportunities for "its own kind."

A third advantage of columnization was that it proved effective in reducing radicalism, isolation, or withdrawal from the public process by any of the larger columns or smaller compartments. Each column or compartment had its inalienable rights. Every subculture gained considerable recognition for its special claims, and each obtained, for all practical purposes, all that could be gained through state action. Every group was reasonably assured that its future claims would be honored as far as possible through compromise and proportional sharing of state benefits. Each group had learned, through painful experience, that it could not enforce its particularist values upon other groups through state action.[24] No column can govern alone, and coalitions within Dutch political life are unstable. Today's opponent might be tomorrow's ally. It is best, therefore, not to antagonize an opponent too much.

A final advantage of the structure of columns was that it contributed to stability and order. Besides the balance of power principle, there was a system of cross pressures *within* the columns. So long as the ideological solidarity within each group held constant, the proportions of each column remained relatively stable. There were few threats of competitive inroads from other columns and few opportunities for raiding a neighboring column's nest. State subsidy guaranteed equal services for each group for state-supported activities. Competition was limited even in the voluntary sectors.

We are familiar with the concept of cross-pressures, so well documented for the American case, and the way in which membership in several associations tends to reduce radicalism and promote stability. The principle behind cross-pressures is that membership in several cross-cutting interest groups puts the social actor in a situation where pressures cancel each other out. Thus, being Jewish in the United States "pushes" the Jewish vote toward leftist politics. Being a member of a high socio-economic class "pushes" the Jewish voter back in

24. H. Daalder makes this point in "The Netherlands: Opposition in a Segmented Society," in *Political Opposition in Western Democracies*, Robert A. Dahl, ed. (New Haven: Yale University Press, 1966), p. 219.

the direction of conservative politics. The sum of the pressures tend to balance out, yielding moderation. It has been argued that countries which have multiple cross-cutting interest groups and voluntary associations will be more stable politically than countries, such as the Netherlands, where memberships in associations overlap to form a constellation of coherent interests.[25] This argument, while generally true for cases of bipolar columnization, does not apply to the Netherlands, where a quadruple balance-of-power structure introduces cross-pressures at a different level.

Thus, the columns reduced the effects of class cleavages in Dutch society, and thereby minimized economic polarization.[26] Because they needed to maintain the allegiance of their working class members, the Gereformeerden and Catholics were more progressive on economic and political issues than most Christian parties in other countries.[27] On the other hand, as the Socialists gained economic emancipation, their political stance became muted to cater to Socialists from higher economic positions. Just as it is possible to have all of the effects of a two-party system under the wing of what is, formally, one party, so the Netherlands demonstrates that it is possible to have the effects of mutually cancelling cross-pressures within vertically integrated separate columns. These cross pressures are strengthened when, as in the Netherlands, a column's proportionate power varies across activities. Thus in the 1950s the Catholics had the largest political party and governed in coalition with the Socialists. The Socialists had the largest labor union, in opposition to a Catholic-Protestant coalition at the level of union activities. The Liberals had the largest control over the media. An opponent in the battle for power in one activity could, theoretically, be an ally in another activity. In the classical period of Dutch columnization, coalitions were not only unstable; they were also not monolithic in their activities.

Johan Goudsblom reminds us of another unintended way in which columnization helped to promote national integration. In a discussion of the organizational structure of Dutch radio and television he remarks:

25. For one statement of the relation of cross-cutting affiliations and political stability, see S. M. Lipset, *Political Man* (Garden City, New York: Doubleday, 1960), pp. 88–89.

26. Indeed, discussion of social class differences is a sort of Dutch taboo, and there is as yet no comprehensive analysis of social classes in Dutch sociology; see Goudsblom, *Dutch Society*, pp. 62–63.

27. In his survey of political attitudes and religion conducted in Delft in 1962, Hoogewerf found that Catholics were the most progressive on political issues, tied with the non-churched

The very idea of *verzuiling* implies a tacit negation of class difference. Consequently, each broadcasting corporation, in an effort to please the taste of the members of all socio-economic strata, covers the whole range from "highbrow" art to "lowbrow" entertainment. This policy leads to the unintentional consequences that the audience tends to select its programs regardless of the producing corporation. In this way radio and television, while reflecting *verzuiling* in their organizational structures serve to counteract *verzuiling* in their actual effect.[28]

I have more than once alluded to the metaphor of the arch which bridged over the columns. Especially since the end of World War II, there have been many attempts within Dutch society to build organizations which set common policies and coordinate activities for the separate organizations within different columns. Thus, economic development is regulated by a sort of economic parliament, the Commission on Social and Economic Affairs (SER). Its membership consists of fifteen representatives from the unions, fifteen members from the world of employers, and fifteen professors of economics, with an informal quota system of proportional representation for the four columns. Similarly, there are contact and coordinating commissions for the radio and television broadcasting companies, newspapers, social work, voluntary health services, and so on.

Arend Lijphart has suggested seven rules of interaction between the columns which helped to promote unity, order, and stability— the arch—within Dutch political life.[29] His rules apply beyond the field of parliamentary politics. Lijphart's seven rules show that elitism, secrecy, proportionality as an inviolable rule, and balance of power formed the basis for a stable "gentlemen's agreement" between the columns.

COSTS OF COLUMNIZATION

Although the system of columnization had worked for so long and so well, it also had a shadow side which has led in the last decades to

at 71 percent on his measurements of conservatism and progressivism. Protestants followed a U-curve, so that being a Protestant diminished progressivism in income groups averaging fl. 3,000 to fl. 6,000 per year; diminished conservatism in the middle group earning fl. 6,000 to fl. 12,000 a year; strengthened conservatism in the highest income group averaging fl. 12,000 or more. Since the greatest bulk of the Protestants fell in the middle group, Protestantism had a net result in increasing progressivism in the Netherlands. See A. Hoogewerf, *Protestantisme en Progressiviteit* (Meppel: J. A. Boom and Sons, 1963), especially the tables on pp. 144, 152, and 184.

28. Goudsblom, *Dutch Society*, p. 119.

29. For the rules as they appear in Lijphart, see *The Politics of Accommodation*, pp. 122–138.

mounting pressures for change, as the disadvantage of separate columns became more apparent and outweighed the advantages.[30] The majority of commentators on Dutch social structure in the 1950s did not predict major changes for columnization, but those a decade later were looking for explanations of its rapid decline. The explanation can be best found in a view of social structure as a solution to historic problems containing a balance of tendencies which are linked and opposite at the same time. The developments within Dutch society since the 1960s can be seen as attempts to redress the costs of columnization.

There is no dramatic "moment of realization" when everyone in a society suddenly sees with clarity that structures formed to solve old problems will not solve new ones. Nevertheless, changes in structure are first announced by the fact that the accent shifts away from attempts at shoring up the traditional structure toward facing the costs inherent in the structural arrangements. Of course, the past lingers on as a channeling mechanism, providing the framework within which new solutions are thought through. What price did Dutch society pay for stability achieved through separate columns?

1. Columnization reduced national consensus and a sense of conspicuous national identity. Individual religions were strengthened at the cost of the common civil religion. As one Dutch sociologist puts it, "religion, while engulfing the life of the individual from its very prime, causes such a division in the community that the latter can hardly be considered a religious unit any more."[31] In their cross-national study of national identification conducted in 1948, Buchanan and Cantril found that the Netherlands ranked eighth among nine countries, ahead of Italy and tied with Mexico. All the other industrial lands in Western Europe and North America outranked her citizens in a sense of national identity.[32]

2. Dutch stability was bought at the price of elitism and internal authoritarianism within each column. Democracy between the groups was achieved at the expense of democracy within the column. In a

---

30. I have found David Moberg's article, "Social Differentiation in the Netherlands," and S. Miedema, "De Kosten van de Verzuiling," *Socialisme en Democratie*, XIV, 1 (January 1957), 47–48, helpful in formulating the following points.

31. I. Gadourek, *A Dutch Community: Social and Cultural Structure and Process in a Bulb-Growing Region in the Netherlands* (Leiden: H. Stenfert Kroese, 1956), p. 487.

32. William Buchanan and Hadley Cantril, *How Nations See Each Other: A Study in Public Opinion* (Urbana: University of Illinois Press, 1953), p. 18. Some caution is necessary in this and the following citation because of the gross way in which concepts were defined in the surveys.

cross-national survey entitled *The Civic Culture,* which compared the United States, Great Britain, West Germany, Italy, and the Netherlands, Almond and Verba discovered that the Dutch exhibited the highest degree of political passivity and acceptance of authoritarian structures among the nations studied. When asked to rank the qualities which they most admired, the Dutch showed the greatest proclivity to choose this one: "Shows obedience. Knows his place."[33]

Elitism could work well when the Protestant, Catholic, and Socialist blocs consisted of "little fellows" seeking economic advancement through a few educated spokesmen. As education and prosperity were evenly spread across the columns, elitism came under attack. The rise and proliferation of para-political action groups in the late 1960s is an example of one attempt to penetrate and change the elitist system. The institutions of Dutch society have been besieged in the last decade by demands for democracy, freedom of speech, and the right of participatory access to decision makers as a way of redressing the elitist bias. Democratization was the key slogan for changes in the 1960s. It meant opening up a pillar or circle to internal democracy as much as it meant decolumnization. With no real "neutral" world to escape into, members of each column are "neutralizing" their columns.

3. Plural columns involved expensive reduplication of facilities, personnel, and bureaucratic coordination. Besides the economic costs in terms of inefficiency, heavy taxes, and inflation, the country has been organized to death. Separate organizations for each column and spanning organizations to coordinate the columns took their toll in personal liberty. In the last decade many organizations have merged across columns to reduce costs or promote efficiency. The merger of the Catholic, Protestant, and neutral Boy Scouts provides one example of such a move. There are efforts in new suburbs to merge school systems into what the Dutch call the "samenwerkingschool" within which each religious group has their right to present its own confessional viewpoint in special classes.

4. Columnization reduced the consciousness of the working class to their real interests, and lowered the possibilities of solidarity based on similar economic life chances. Despite disparities in income and economic opportunities rather similar to those of other Western European countries, the Netherlands had the lowest strike record in postwar industrial Europe. At least one sociologist has suggested that this

33. See G. A. Almond and S. Verba, *The Civic Culture: Political Attitudes and Democracy in Five Nations* (Princeton: Princeton University Press, 1963), p. 265.

was due less to the fact that the Netherlands is a social paradise than to the fact that "the desire for social peace is everywhere the master."[34] Toward the end of the last decade, the labor unions have shown new-found militancy, occupying factories and refusing to agree to government-set price and wage controls. The three unions have now joined one federation.

5. It was difficult to maintain a perfect fit between supply and demand opportunity structures within each column. One organization, to give an example, might suffer because it could not find enough trained radio technicians, while another would be over-supplied with such technicians. Privileged access to job positions within a column had a reverse side of blocked opportunities for access to available jobs outside the column. In the last decade, for example, the number of Catholic nurses in non-Catholic hospitals, and Protestant social workers in Catholic charities has been on the increase, for the barriers between the columns have crumbled and the Netherlands has achieved a more open job market.

Anyone who has watched the de-confessionalization of Dutch society in the last decade is aware that the Catholic bloc has been the major victim. In the period after the war it had thrown the system out of balance. It was too large, well-organized, and seemingly mono-lithic. As Catholics began in the postwar period to act as if they did not need to work in a coalition, Protestant and Socialist fears increased.

We know now that the words of the KVP leader, Dr. Romme, predicting a Catholic majority, were a last hurrah on a crest of Catholic power. Despite the brave words and organizational monolith in the 1950s, the Catholics have proved more vulnerable ideologically than the orthodox Protestant column. In the mid-fifties Dutch society was divided into a bare majority of supporters of confessionalism—52 percent, versus 48 percent for an open, neutral society. The Socialists, Liberals, and a section of the Dutch Reformed Church had stood up for a change of the rules. So long as the Catholics remained intact, these opponents of columnization would be forced into a column.

There are three main reasons why the Catholics proved more vul-nerable. First, as the largest and best-organized single bloc within Dutch society, it was more difficult for Catholics to sustain an identity as a psychological minority group than it was for the Gereformeerden,

---

34. See H. Hoefnagels, "Nederland Een Sociaal Paradijs?," in *Sociologische Gids*, VIII, 5 (September-October, 1962), 283. For other evidence of reduction of working-class conscious-ness in the Netherlands, see Goudsblom, *Dutch Society*, pp. 61–70.

who represent less than 10 percent of the population. Secondly, Catholic international theology encouraged Dutch Catholics to try to shape national life in their own mold. Traditionally, the Catholic People's Party sought to leave a major imprint upon public life. The Geerformeerden, on the other hand, were much more modest. They were content with a semi-sectarian stance. Their slogan, "sovereignty in our own circle," looked to the protection of their own distinctive minority values much more than to molding Dutch society into their image. Finally, Catholic theology is more open to the positive values of the "natural" or neutral world than is orthodox Gereformeerden theology. It was to this tradition of "open Catholicism" that the Catholic opponents of columnization were appealing. In the 1950s the Socialists had a small Catholic wing but the more orthodox Protestants were not represented. Further, the Socialists made inroads in 1952 into hitherto impenetrable Catholic territory, while the orthodox Protestant voters remained more stable. To get at the traditional social structure, one would have to get at the Catholic bloc. They had become the keystone.

The balance of power depended on ideology, which separated socialism or liberalism from Catholicism *on both sides*. When postwar socialism lost its anti-religious foundations, the socialists became, for the first time, a genuine threat to the Catholic market. The bishops, urged on by politicians from the Catholic party, tried to reinstate the ideological objections from the Catholic side. If one rereads the Dutch bishops' Mandatory Letter of 1954 today, through the lens of our typology for pre-Vatican II missionary strategies, it perfectly mirrors the traditional stance of *international* Catholicism. The position defended by the bishops rested on traditional Catholic role structures for bishop, priests, and laity.

The bishops saw themselves as religious monarchs with a worldly calling. The Dutch bishops declared that their "leading position is not limited only to the apostolic works within the church but extends also to the application of the gospel to secular spheres." This competence led them to impose Catholic organizational unity as a good in itself; the bishops made acceptance of columnization a matter of religious principle, binding upon all Catholics under pain of excommunication. The episcopacy responded to the pressure from without and within Catholicism by remarking: "We have been deeply troubled these last years, beloved faithful, by the fact that there are Catholics in our land who are apparently so filled with the idea of 'break-through' that they seem to have little or no eye for the unity among Catholics." The bishops left little doubt where they stood on the definition of their own role competence: "We intend to speak the decisive word."

The role of priests was defined as "advisors of the Catholic organizations." Priests, as agents of the bishops, should form action cells to carry out the bishops' mission in the world. The test of a true bond between Catholic action and the bishops lay in the acceptance by the laity of their priest advisors. The laity were to show "respect" and "trust" toward their priests and acknowledge their "dignity." Priests, in turn, must recognize that the laity have an active role in Catholic action. The bishops recognized very well that the position they were proposing agreed with the international strategy, best formulated by Pius XI. "We feel confident that we have chosen the right path for the Netherlands because it agrees with the path outlined by the pope."[35]

It was clear, then, that the only way to change the position of the Catholic bloc was through internal changes within the role structures of the church itself. There being no ready-made "neutral" Dutch society to turn to, progressive Catholic energies first turned into the church, and then from within the church neutralized their own column. In a peculiar way, the majority of believers had felt connected with the larger political community only through their collectivity. These believers would respond to the pressures of columnization by trying to bring their whole Catholic column into the neutral world. Only widespread changes from within the church itself could ease the pressures pent up over the years. All these pressures converged upon the Catholic bloc. Although many of the Catholic changes in the 1960s may be seen as efforts at de-columnization, the evidence suggests that the church has changed even more than its confessional apparatus, and indeed that the movement toward de-columnization received its greatest stimulus from within the church itself. De-columnization for the Catholics has meant more than the loss of members. It has also required efforts to render the column more neutral, less a separate enclave within wider Dutch society.

Columnization represented a balance of costs and benefits for the church as well as for the whole society. The Catholic opponents were pointing to the disadvantages for the church. First, there was an unhealthy identification of the church with its confessional organizations. Did the church run the risk of confusing issues, so that those who rejected the Catholic Party, for example, would be led to

---

35. Citations from the Episcopal Mandatory Letter, "The Catholic in Public Life at the Present Time," in *Katholiek Archief,* IX, 25 (June 18, 1954). The citations derive from paragraphs 14, 17 and 18 of the bishops' letter.

reject the church as well? Some of the same reasons why a church could benefit from separation of church and state also apply to the separation of a church from its array of confessional organizations. Too close an identity between the two compromises the religiously transcendent message of the church, which tends to get lost in political and organizational particulars or falls victim to the mixed motives of those who staff confessional organizations and use them to serve personal interests or to gain collective power.[36]

Second, the costs to religious efficiency and specialization incurred by the church were extensive. While the church was splendidly organized *ad extra* in its relations to the world, it was badly organized from within, with little pastoral, liturgical, or catechetical planning and coordination. The church was bound to provide chaplains to all the Catholic organizations, thus squandering valuable religious specialists upon non-religious or dubiously religious tasks, or tasks better left to the laity. Almost a quarter of all priests in the 1950s were employed full time in such profane tasks. Meanwhile, was the church overextending itself, losing valuable energies needed to reinterpret or reformulate the gospel for modern man—which was its primary task?

The church had chosen advanced education to achieve closed, collective emancipation. It invested its capital in training the kind of laymen who could make a Christian impact on his milieu. Ultimately, however, the milieu would make its indelible impact on him as well. In time, such a layman would make his own claims to autonomy within the church. Would it not be better for the church in the Netherlands to do away with clericalism while it still had the good favor of its laity and was free from anti-clericalism?

MOBILIZATION RESOURCES

Dutch Catholicism in the 1950s possessed unique mobilization resources for change. Despite the Mandatory Letter of 1954, its bishops still enjoyed widespread legitimacy and good will. Dutch energy and self-conscious Catholicism were unparalleled anywhere. The church enjoyed all the benefits of an established church with none of its disadvantages: generous financial subsidy from the state for its auxiliary activities in education, charity, health, and recreation; strong social control over the activities of its members; relative freedom from effective ideological competition; and access to political decision

36. For this dilemma, see Thomas O'Dea, *Sociology of Religion* (Englewood Cliffs, New Jersey: Prentice-Hall, Inc., 1966), pp. 91–92.

makers. The Netherlands provided, as a result of columnization, the best Catholic educational system in the world. Ninety percent of the Catholic population attended Catholic elementary schools. Eighty-nine percent subscribed to the Catholic radio company. Seventy-nine percent read Catholic daily newspapers. Seventy-five percent attended weekly mass. The plethora of Catholic organizations meant that a significant number of Catholic laity gained their livelihood by being employed in "Catholic" organizations as journalists, nurses, teachers, union leaders, politicians, psychiatrists, and social workers. The Catholic identity was positively valued and salient. The church had the finances to support a lay church.

Religious pluralism in the Netherlands meant that the Dutch could not take their Catholicism for granted, as an Italian, Spaniard, or Irishman could. In the Netherlands, Catholicism was *conscious*. On the other hand, isolation in a column, the cradle-to-grave Catholic organizational life, and the recent history of successful collective emancipation—all these added up to make that consciousness *Catholic*. If there was ever a church which was strong enough to experiment with change, it was the Catholic church in the Netherlands. Even before Vatican II, that church was marked as a unique example of successful implementation of the missionary strategy of confessional separatism. With the coming of the Council, pressures from within and without the Catholic community on Dutch soil combined with pressures from international Catholicism itself to start a movement for structural changes in the church. If new people with new visions came to control the elaborate apparatus of school systems, unions, newspapers, and radio and television, the same resources which had once supported traditional Dutch Catholicism could be mobilized to provide a unique laboratory, a pilot church for post-Vatican structures.

Because of the rapidity with which the Catholic structure yielded to their pressures, Catholic reformers must have been led to believe that it was a house built on sand. As one of them put it, "Like the walls of Jericho the bastions of tradition fell by the first trumpet blast. This gave to the trumpeters an enormous encouragement to continue their blast."[37]

37. Daniel De Lange, cited in Martin van Amerongen and Igor Cornelissen, *Tegen de Revolutie: Het Evangelie* (Amsterdam: Paris-Manteau, 1972), p. 90.

Chapter 4

Collective Redefinition: Experiment with Ideas, 1958–1965

Some real shifts had already occurred between 1954, the year of the bishops' Mandatory Letter, and 1958. In the spring of 1954, Archbishop Alfrink had defended the bishops' holding action in a speech on the occasion of the thirtieth anniversary of the Thijm fellowship; he appealed to a linear, hierarchical, and one-way chain of command in the church, which saw bishops as agents of the pope, priests as agents of their bishop, and the laity as agents of the will of priests and bishops. Once a higher authority had decided, the matter was settled. *Roma locuta est!* "And when that authority has spoken, then everyone who belongs to the church, no matter what position he holds or what personal opinions he may have in the matter, bows his head in respect."[1] In 1954, the leader of the Catholic People's Party, Dr. Romme, was speaking for the majority of Catholic lay leaders in the confessional organizations when he greeted the Mandatory Letter with the remark that the bishops had a perfect right to do what they did, and that the only right left to ordinary Catholics was to follow their orders.[2]

By the spring of 1959, however, Alfrink and his fellow bishops were proposing a very different view of authority in their Lenten letter to all the faithful: "While the hierarchy claims the teaching role in

---

1. For Alfrink's speech, see *Katholiek Archief* (hereafter cited as *KA*), IX, 43 (October 22, 1954), columns 861–863. For other examples, from the many, of Alfrink's use of this one-way hierarchical model of authority in the church during the years in which he was defending the bishops' Mandatory Letter, see *KA*, X, 51 (December 23, 1955), columns 1323–1336, a speech to his Utrecht priests; XI, 8 (February 24, 1956), columns 195–198, on the occasion of a realignment of boundaries between the diocese of Utrecht and Haarlem; XII, 37 (September 13, 1957), columns 877–882, in a speech in which Alfrink stresses that obedience to *higher* superiors is the *only* compass within which lower agents can discover God's will.
2. See *KA*, XI, 43 (October 22, 1954), columns 915–918.

the church and determines what belongs to the treasure of the faith, *the hierarchy only teaches what is already to be found living within the community of the faithful.''*[3] The bishops proposed a view of differential responsibilities rather than a simple hierarchy of authority in the church.

If in 1954 the bishops ran the risk of exalting organizational life at the expense of the church as a community of faith, by 1959 they gave signs that they wanted to differentiate the two, explicitly stating in the same Lenten letter that the church as a community of faith took precedence over the confessional organizations. Further, the 1959 letter shows the seeds of a dialogic view of authority—authority as a two-way process of command and feedback—which came to predominate within Dutch Catholicism in the period. In this new view, bishops and priests listened as much as they spoke. The bishop, moreover, was not simply an agent of the pope. He had his own responsibilities within his territorial church and within the world church, not the least of which was within the community of the faithful entrusted to him. Without yet specifying what such areas might be, the bishops granted that there were many areas within the church wherein the laity had prime responsibility.

When social structure is understood as the congealed results of collective problem-solving, there will occur, in the growth and evolution of groups, pressures and problems which will not go away. Thus in the mid-fifties, Dutchmen, with many Catholics among them, were shocked and embarrassed by the intolerant actions of a Catholic audience in Roermond during an election campaign: they heckled the Socialist Prime Minister, William Drees, off the stage and cut the wires to his microphone. In many of the mining communities in Catholic South Limburg, the children of Catholic socialists were mocked and ostracized as "outside the circle" because their fathers had not obeyed the bishops' mandate to vote Catholic.[4] Was such treatment the necessary price? The problem of columnization simply would not go away.

The pressures of columnization surfaced again in 1957 over the question of Catholic membership in and support for the Netherlands Organization for International Assistance (Dutch initials, NOVIB), an organization which tried to amalgamate the various columns in an

---

3. *KA*, XIV, 7 (February 13, 1959), column 152. The italics are mine to emphasize a dominant myth which emerges during the period 1958–1965.
4. See Fons Hermans, "Van Katholiek Conformisme Naar Groeiende Openheid," in *Met Betrekking tot Limburg*, H. G. Derks, ed. (Hilversum: Paul Brand, 1966), p. 352.

effort at joint development aid to underdeveloped nations. Catholic participation in NOVIB became a public issue when Professor Zeegers, Director of the Catholic Sociological Research Bureau (Dutch initials, KASKI) resigned from NOVIB on the grounds that Catholic membership in NOVIB violated the bishops' mandatory letter. He thought NOVIB too socialist and too dedicated to the proposition of "break-through" in columnization.

In a speech to a gathering of priests in the Hague, Zeegers explained his resignation. "I am leaving NOVIB because our own Catholic activities, in my opinion, demand all of our effort and attention. Our own Catholic confessional work in building up infrastructures in non-Western societies contributes sufficiently to the social emancipation of the people in the mission territories."

The Catholic Council for Social Work, disagreeing with Zeegers' line of reasoning, urged retention of its NOVIB membership. The issue came to Archbishop Alfrink for mediation. The terms in which Zeegers had couched his resignation from NOVIB made Alfrink's decision on the issue a test case for the viability of the bishops' 1954 position on Catholic separatism. Hence, Alfrink hesitated to give a definitive answer, claiming that he saw many implications for the understanding of the church and its role in society hidden within his choice. Rather than merely repeat the bishops' 1954 decision, Alfrink let it be known in a press communique that "the Archbishop is resolved to entrust this question to a study commission of experts and, thus, come to the desired clarity on the issue."[5] The Archbishop thereby encouraged new proposals for dealing with the dissatisfactions.

The commissioned study group, consisting of representatives of the most important Catholic organizations, began its work in 1958. It issued a series of six volumes entitled *Welfare, Well-Being, and Happiness: A Catholic Viewpoint on Dutch Society*. While Alfrink charged the group with the task of finding new practical applications for the principles laid down in the bishops' Mandatory Letter, in fact, the group shifted the original episcopal emphasis in the direction of a greater Catholic openness. For the first time, for example, it questioned the immutability of the confessional school system, and it pointed to pastoral problems of preaching and catechesis as crisis points within the church, labeling them "the two weakest points in church life in our land."[6]

5. The documents from which this citation of Alfrink and that of Zeegers are taken are available in *KA*, XII, 47 (November 22, 1975), columns 1113–1127.
6. *Welvaart, Welzijn en Geluk: Een Katholiek Uitzicht op de Nederlandse Samenleving* (Hilversum: Paul Brand, 1960), Vol. I, p. 165.

The study group placed great emphasis on a lay church. "Let no one forget that leadership, the assumption of responsibility for others, and the making of far-reaching decisions has more and more become the task of the laity and does not remain as a preserve for the clergy." In pointing to growing criticisms about the role distribution between clergy and laity, the group suggested that it would be better if "the clergy, on the one hand, would concentrate its efforts *in a more pastoral and religious direction* while, on the other hand, the responsibility of the laity for the lay organizations was stimulated by their not leaning on the prop of spiritual advisors."[7]

Welfare, Well-Being and Happiness provides evidence of unrest in the late 1950s over previous speedy appeals to Rome for decisions which might better be left to the national or local church. It pointed out that "a characteristic element of present day life is the growing self-consciousness of the local churches; we could almost have said, the dedication to the local bishop."[8] Moreover, the document gave a revised definition of tolerance. The 1954 bishops' letter had provided fuel for non-Catholic fears that Catholic tolerance was purely opportunistic, the kind of tolerance defined in the Dutch Catholic Encyclopedia in 1951 as "the mere sufferance of an evil which, nevertheless, one has the right and duty to fight against."[9] *Welfare, Well-Being, and Happiness* proposed, instead, that "by tolerance is meant that one person leaves the other alone and supports him in his difference, not for opportunistic reasons, but from fundamental ethical principles: because of the unassailable worth of the person in his being as a person."[10]

This reexamination of the mandatory letter lasted from 1958 through 1965. The commission's task was completed by 1965 when the Dutch bishops publicly rescinded all of the negative sanctions applied to Catholic membership in socialist or other non-Catholic organizations, resolving, in this final act, the conflicts of conscience which arose in reaction to their decision of 1954.[11]

By 1958 a majority of the Dutch bishops were non-signatories to the bishops' letter of 1954. Its principal author, Mgr. Hanssen, was succeeded by the new bishop, Mgr. Moors. In 1956 two new bishops were consecrated for Rotterdam and Groningen, with jurisdictions carved out of existing dioceses, expanding the number of dioceses to

---

7. *Ibid.*, pp. 168–169.
8. *Ibid.*, Vol. II, p. 242.
9. *De Katholieke Encyclopedie* (Amsterdam: Joost van den Vondal, 1951), Vol. XXIII, p 747.
10. *Welvaart, Welzijn en Geluk: Een Katholiek Uitzicht op de Nederlandse Samenleving*, Vol. 1, p. 120.
11. See *KA*, XX, 39 (September 24, 1965), columns 989–990.

its present seven. Mgr. van Dodewaard was appointed in 1958 as coadjutor-bishop to replace the aging Mgr. Huybers of Haarlem. Msgr. William Bekkers had been consecrated coadjutor–bishop in Den Bosch. In such a small church province as the Netherlands, five new bishops could significantly change the tone of the episcopal voice. There are other signs of a changing of the guard in 1958 to justify our choosing it as a cut-off point: Professor Zeegers yielded his directorship of KASKI; Mgr. Giobbe, the papal nuncio, left Holland after almost a quarter-century of service there, full of praise for Dutch Catholicism; the theologian Edward Schillebeeckx came that year to the Catholic University in Nijmegen from his native Belgium.

The cut-off points, 1958 and 1965, lend themselves to several piquant contrasts. In 1958 Archbishop Alfrink could warn his Catholics that "just because something is being done in the Church in some other land does not mean that it has to be done here"; by 1965 many of his confreres in Germany, Belgium, England, and the United States would be saying the same thing to their Catholics about what was occurring in the Netherlands.[12] In their letter on the occasion of the death of Pope Pius XII, the Dutch bishops remarked, in a comment which raised no eyebrows in the Netherlands or Rome or elsewhere, "Catholic Netherlands has always been so truly faithful to Rome and the Pope."[13] By 1965, Italian newspapers were complaining of Dutch anti-Romanism.

EXPERIMENT WITH IDEAS

Stage four in the process of structural differentiation (see Table 2, Chapter One) can be likened to the "brainstorming" phase in a discussion group, the free flow of ideas as a way of groping toward solutions for the problem-solving unit and the emergence, within the group, of the ideas which will function as the group's symbols of identity, the collective representations. To what extent was Dutch Catholicism in the period under study like a discussion group? What was the cue to engage in brainstorming? What myths or collective representations began to emerge as new symbols of collective identity?

12. Cf. *KA*, XIII, 6 (February 7, 1958), column 50.
13. *KA*, XIII, 42 (October 17, 1958), column 980. Leo Laeyendecker has tried to explain the special fidelity of traditional Dutch Catholics to the Roman center by the economic minority position of the Catholics as a culturally deprived group in "Protestant" Holland; he suggests they turned to Rome as a symbol of the existence of a Catholic high culture. See his "Theologische Veranderingen, Sociologisch Beschowd," *Sociologische Gids*, XV, 4 (June–July 1968), 247–259.

It will be helpful at the outset to review the supposed sources of dissatisfaction within Dutch Catholicism:

1. The pressures of columnization had led to the isolation and alienation of the Catholics from their non-Catholic milieu. In the period under study, Catholics turned to new ideas which gave a positive evaluation to secularization. In the theology of "secularization," the theologians distinguish between "secularism" (the decline of religious values within society) and "secularization" (the autonomy of institutional sectors of society from control by the church). Secularization does imply, however, a new way of organizing the articulation between religion and society, so that dialogue and pluralist participation replace external control as the dominant strategy for church influence. Secularization will turn into secularism if the churches, in entering dialogue on an equal footing through pluralist participation, lose their religious identities or cease to generate specifically religious motivations for secular conduct or fail to excite religious commitment by successful recruiting across generations. Secularization as implied by the hypotheses of a post-Vatican cultural-pastoral strategy (see Table 3) need not imply a diminution of the quantum of religious values within society, but it certainly does imply a displacement of the situs where those values are realized—away from church-controlled confessional organizations and toward organizations in the secular sphere.

2. The dissipation of columnization pressures was dependent, for the Catholic bloc, upon a rethinking of international Catholic strategies of confessional separatism. These strategies, in turn, were structurally imbedded in the classic role definitions of bishop, priest, and laity, which saw each as an agent of the corporate purposes of the church and, further, as being dependent in this agency upon the will of higher agents in an hierarchical, one-way traffic of command-obedience relations. In the period under study, Dutch Catholics turned toward a different church model, based on the key concepts of collegiality, dialogue, and member participation in decision-making processes. The Dutch began to revise the role descriptions of bishop, priest, and laity within the church.

3. The internal organization of the church as a community of faith suffered at the expense of the external confessional organizational apparatus. In particular, pastoral tasks such as preaching, the liturgy, and catechesis were in an acute state of crisis, ill-adapted to the needs of a modern industrial society and poorly coordinated across Catholic units (parishes and dioceses; religious-order versus secular-priest activities). In the period under study, Dutch Catholics encouraged ideas

related to parish reorganization, diocesan-wide and inter-diocesan coordination, and efforts to bring together religious-order and diocesan priests.

In Chapters Two and Three I have concentrated on the first two independent variables: (1) the structural setting for change, and (2) the pressures toward change. Here and in Chapter Five I will be employing mainly the two other independent variables: (3) mobilization resources for change, and (4) action of the social authorities. It will be my contention that the unusual configurations of Dutch Catholicism in the post-conciliar period are chiefly attributable to the interplay of the unique mobilization resources available there and the unparalleled way in which the Dutch authorities reacted to the pressures for change.

I will use seven topics in this and the following chapters, as general rubrics to follow the chronological development within Dutch Catholicism. These seven rubrics embody the postulated role changes in post-Vatican cultural-pastoral strategy (see Table 3).

1. National coordinating units for planning the pastorate, liturgy, catechesis, and preaching.
2. Collegial structures: role definitions of bishop-priest and laity.
3. Public opinion within the church.
4. Ecumenism and new coalition partners.
5. Congregational form for specialized parishes.
6. Pressure groups.
7. Center-periphery conflicts.

NATIONAL COORDINATING UNITS

Even prior to 1958, the Dutch bishops had shown a more marked preference for joint consultation, communiques, and letters than their confreres in other nations, who restricted their communiques almost entirely to separately written letters for their own dioceses. The deviant Dutch practice was in part due to the fact that confessional organizations, founded upon a national rather than a diocesan basis, demanded joint episcopal surveillance and decision. In part, the practice was a legacy of the wartime experience of episcopal solidarity against the threat of Nazi German occupation. In part, the size of the unit plays a role. Another factor may be that the Dutch church forms a natural unit as one church province.

The Dutch episcopacy prior to 1958 was not, as yet, an effectively functioning national planning and coordinating unit. In the first place, episcopal conference meetings to discuss joint decisions were relatively infrequent, held only once or twice a year. Secondly, each individual bishop maintained jealous guard over his autonomy on strictly pastoral matters within his own diocese. Hence, such matters of pastoral policy as intermarriage between Catholics and Protestants, confession faculties for priests, the handling of church annulments, ecumenical arrangements, and catechesis varied across the dioceses. Cardinal Alfrink's diocese of Utrecht, for example, was notorious for its refusal to grant permission to Catholics to marry non-Catholics. Such marriages were blessed by the church only when the oldest child from the marriage enrolled in a Catholic school. Inter-marriage policies were more supple in the dioceses of Den Bosch and Breda.

Given the almost rank growth of confessional life in the Netherlands, the seven Dutch bishops were frequently in demand to serve as speakers at meetings of Catholic organizations or to consecrate the buildings and works of Catholic life. Major conflicts came to them for mediation and decision. Freed from serious financial needs because of a generous state subsidy, the Dutch bishops, more than their confreres elsewhere, had frequent contact with their people. They were not, as the American bishops have been, for example, principally fund-raisers. It was almost impossible for the Dutch bishops to be cut off from the pressure points within Dutch life. The country is so small and the communication network so well organized, that, the Dutch often remark, if a bishop sneezes in Roermond, he will be heard in Groningen. The bishops could sense theological changes within the Catholic elite, which were mirrored, for example, at the national congresses of the Thijm fellowship and the Adelbert Association. In the late 1950s these congresses were sponsoring speakers who were transposing the "new theology" of Congar and de Lubac in France to the Dutch setting.[14] This "new theology," which became the theology of Vatican II, gained a national Dutch platform in 1957 with the inauguration of national Catholic study days in Nijmegen.

As early as 1958 and 1959 the Dutch bishops responded to complaints about the need for national planning units by beginning to coordinate some pastoral activities across dioceses. In 1958, for example, they appointed the first joint episcopal delegate for ecumenical work, Mgr. J. G. M. Willebrands, who was entrusted with determining national policies for inter-faith cooperation. In 1959 they set

14. The two most important shifts in the so-called "new theology" in France in the 1950s were in the direction of a this-worldly rather than a "supernatural" emphasis and the championing of lay autonomy in the church. See Yves Congar, *Lay People in the Church*, D. Attwater, translator (Westminster, Maryland: The Newman Press, 1957).

up a bishops' Commission for Church Statistics to aid in national church planning. The same year they inaugurated an inter-diocesan liturgical secretariat and a National Pastoral Institute. This latter organization was expected to report to the bishops its recommendations for handling the major problem first signaled in 1950 in the report entitled *Unrest in the Pastorate:* was the Dutch church employing the most efficient and spiritually efficacious forms of pastorate? Still, these early examples of national planning units lacked real independent authority and remained uncoordinated with each other.

The task of preparing for and participating in the Second Vatican Council gave the Dutch bishops the decided stamp of a governing college for their church province. Collective episcopal gatherings increased in number and frequency. The bishops requested, more than previously, the expert advice of theologians and sociologists. During the Council the small corps of Dutch bishops in Rome, coming from a little country and speaking a non-major language, were thrown in daily contact with each other. One could almost say that they became a college by going to "college" together at the Council. Their joint communiques to Catholics at home increased in frequency and number, averaging ten to fifteen per year and covering a wide range of theological issues and pastoral decisions binding upon all the dioceses.

During these same years, the bishops made further attempts at coordination and pastoral planning in the Netherlands. In 1961 they instituted a Central Episcopal Council for the Industrial Apostolate in the Netherlands. In 1962 they entrusted the national coordination of catechesis for youth and adults to the Advanced Institute of Catechetics in Nijmegen, commissioning the Institute to write a new modern catechism. In December 1963 the bishops inaugurated the Pastoral Institute for the Netherlands Church Province, PINK, which subsumed the work of the Pastoral Institute erected in 1958. PINK, with a full-time staff of sociological experts and canonists, acted as a clearing house for documentation and orientation for pastoral experiments, an information-gathering center, and an advisory board to the collective bishops on pastoral matters. It was already, in embryo, the episcopal executive secretariat which it became in the years 1966-1971.

At first glance, this proliferation of national coordinating units and institutes in the late 1950s and the early 1960s looks like a replay of the process of organizational ramification within Dutch Catholic life between 1880 and 1954. The crucial difference is that the new organizations aimed at planning and coordinating the pastoral tasks of the church as a community of faith rather than organizing the Catholic community into a unified political bloc *ad extra,* a separate "nation" within Dutch society.

The Council put the Dutch church on the map. Bernard Alfrink was made a cardinal in 1960, the second resident cardinal in Dutch history. Moreover, he was appointed as one of the non-curial cardinals on the Council Preparatory Commission which controlled the structures and agenda of the Council. During the Council itself, he acted as one of the four rotating permanent chairmen of the working sessions. At the end of the Council, by reason of his interventions, Alfrink emerged, with Belgium's Leo Cardinal Suenens, as the chief episcopal spokesman for progressive reform in the church. A second Dutch bishop, William Bekkers, who also emerged as an international episcopal figure during these years, was described by Pope John as "a bishop after my own heart."[15] The Dutch hierarchy was the only important national hierarchy at the Council which acted as a unified bloc for progressive positions in their intervention and votes, earning itself the reputation of an avant garde in the world episcopacy. How did the Dutch get progressive bishops of this stripe?

We have already come across enough pre-conciliar citations from Cardinal Alfrink to recognize that he was not always the progressive he came to be. The same judgment holds for the other Dutch bishops, even the remarkable William Bekkers.

A review of Bishop Bekkers' early pre-episcopal career reflects the exaggerated confessional separatism in pre-Vatican Dutch society. Bekkers was, in turn, a chaplain to the Roman Catholic Association of Laundry Owners in Brabant, the Association of Catholic Tobacconists of Den Bosch, the National Association of Catholic Barbers, and the National Dutch Catholic Association of Watchmakers and Dealers in Gold, Silver, and Bronze! When Bekkers was the head of Catholic Charities for the diocese of Den Bosch, he argued in 1947 that the industrialization of the province of North Brabant brought the danger that "many foreigners will come to North Brabant, persons who have little or nothing in common with the Brabant character. From this we cannot expect Catholicism to gain, on the contrary."[16]

15. See Robert Adolfs, "Dutch Catholicism: What the Council has Wrought," in *Jubilee*, XV, 4 (October 1967), 10.
16. William Petersen, *Planned Migration* (Berkeley: University of California Press, 1955), p. 147.

This early Bekkers, the champion of closed Catholicism, was a far cry from the bishop admired by John XXIII.

Dutch progressive theologians are fond of pointing out that they "made" their bishops into reformers. While there is some truth in this statement, it still misses the mark. This was not a simple case of reform-minded bishops making a national church progressive, or progressive theologians schooling their bishops in reform.

There was, to begin with, an interplay of timing: the simultaneity of achieved Catholic economic emancipation in the Netherlands with a period of critical reexamination of Catholicism at the international level. There was also an interplay of pressures, the coincidence of pent-up internal pressures due to columnization and movements within international Catholicism to revise the role structures of the traditional missionary strategy. Finally, a high degree of episcopal autonomy from state or central Roman church control, coupled with a developed infrastructure of church organizations, gave to the Dutch church an uniquely open communication network favorable to structural reform.[17] The Dutch bishops, situated at the nodal points of that network with an unusually high level of information and communication among themselves and with other sectors of the church—theologians, lower clergy, and lay elites—were in a position to be keenly aware of pressure points within their church. On almost every issue which would involve fundamental church change, their first response was a holding action, a reiteration of the old truths. Because channels of communication between the episcopacy and other groups remained open, however, once the bishops recognized that the holding action would not work, they turned to encouraging new ideas which might handle the dissatisfactions.

Neither the bishops nor the mobilization resources alone were the heroes of Dutch reform; it was the interplay of both variables that was responsible. By "mobilization resources" I am referring to (1) resources of persons, movements, and groups which provide leadership in articulating new programs for structural change; and (2) resources within the organizational infrastructure which can be mobilized for new goals and used to socialize the population in new collective imagery and myths. Mobilization resources as a variable, then, refers both to the quantum of change-agents in the population and the

---

17. Ivan Vallier in "Comparative Studies of Roman Catholicism: Dioceses as Strategic Units," *Social Compass*, XVI, 2 (Spring 1969), 154, suggests that we use these two variables—degree of episcopal autonomy and level of relational infrastructure—in plotting comparative structural change across national settings. Dutch episcopal autonomy includes more than autonomy from state control. The Dutch bishops were chosen by a unique nomination system and freed from episcopal careerism.

instruments available to propagate change—people and institutions as resources.

My choice of the action of the social authorities as an explanatory variable needs further justification. It is not fashionable within Dutch Catholic circles to stress the role of the bishops in the post-conciliar developments. The episcopacy is seen more as a tool than as an agent of change. To emphasize the role of the authorities suggests an elitist bias blind to new ideas on the pastorate and church structure which were articulated among the theologians and in Catholic intellectual journals such as *De Bazuin, De Nieuwe Linie, Te Elfder Ure, Dux,* and *G-3* long before they were endorsed by the bishops. Again, there is evidence of the spread of a new biblically based spirituality and a rethinking of the priestly role among the lower clergy and lay elites in the late 1950s, before the bishops' espousal of them. For example, the important reformer Jan Van Kilsdonk, S.J., gave biblical retreats to over 4,000 Dutch priests in the years 1955-1958.

Would it not be better to stress these shifts among the lower clergy and lay elites rather than focus on the hierarchical reaction, which was, after all, an after-the-fact legitimation of changes which had already occurred? As one writer on Dutch Catholicism has put it: ''the changes in the hierarchical attitudes and the rationalizations of the theologians seem to have been forced by a groundswell from the bottom, from the lower clergy, and journalists, the intellectuals and, strangely enough, from the very masses of Catholic youth.''[18]

I have no quarrel with those who point to the mobilization resources within Dutch Catholicism as a factor for explaining structural change. It will help to understand the role of the social authorities if we explicate, for a moment, the comparative perspective. We can begin by considering the variable of mobilization resources as ''an infrastructure which can be mobilized to socialize the wider population in imageries of change''—an infrastructure comprised of the schools, the media, and so on. Dutch mobilization resources in this sense were unparalleled anywhere else in the Catholic world. Nevertheless, a comparative time perspective shows that the same mobilization resources which were employed to socialize toward change within Dutch Catholicism in the 1960s had previously supported traditional Catholicism. Mobilization resources in the sense of institutions cannot alone explain the Dutch development.

Consider, next, mobilization resources in the sense of change-agents and reforming groups within Dutch Catholicism in the late

18. Frederick Franck, *Exploding Church* (New York: Delacorte Press, 1968), p. 3.

1950s. A comparative cross-national perspective suggests evidence of shifts very similar to those registered for the Netherlands among the theologians, lower clergy, and lay elites in the late 1950s and early 1960s in almost every Western industrial country. Thus, in Germany, Belgium, the United States, and France we can find journals parallel to *De Bazuin, Dux,* and the others for the same period. Lay elites and lower clergy in these countries were, similarly, reflecting shifts in the traditional Catholic lay-clergy role definitions.

The church in the Netherlands is unique, however, in post-conciliar Catholicism by virtue of the actions of its body of bishops. By the end of the 1960s the episcopacy in the United States, Germany, and France was undergoing a crisis of credibility and a loss of episcopal authority among its theologians and progressive lower clergy and lay elites. These episcopal bodies were locked in conflict with "leftist" groups of priests and laity or inflicted with an "underground Church."[19] The Dutch bishops, meanwhile, commanded broad support from their clergy and laity, enjoying the unique distinction of spawning at least two "social movement" groupings within the Dutch Church dedicated to supporting the policy of *their* bishops!

The Dutch bishops are a different breed from many of their confreres in the world episcopacy. In his inventory of progressive contestation groups in Europe, Ruud Bunnik notes their absence in the Dutch setting. Of such leftist groups that exist, he says: "Whatever differences of meaning from the official church there might be is restricted actually to the fact that progressive groups sometimes merely differ from their bishops in the best tactic for renewal."[20] A NIPO national public opinion sample of Dutch Catholics in 1969 showed that 88 percent had strong confidence in the leadership qualities of their bishops.[21]

Without a permissive yet decisive episcopacy which holds channels of communication open to dissatisfied parties and tries to guide them

19. For the evidence for the United States, see Paul Philibert, "Verzet en Contestatie in de Amerikaanse Kerk," *Concilium,* VII, *8* (October 1971), 29–37; John Tracy Ellis, "Whence Did They Come, These Uncertain Priests of the 1960s," *American Ecclesiastical Review,* LCVI (November 1970), 165–166; T. Steeman, "The Underground Church: The Forms and Dynamics of Change in Contemporary Catholicism," in *The Religious Situation,* 1969, D. Butler, ed. (Boston: Beacon Press, 1969). For the evidence for Germany and France, see Ruud Bunnik, "Solidaire Groepen in West Europe," *Concilium,* VII, *8,* 18–29; Jean Seguy, "De Innerlijke Dynamiek van de Informele Groepen," and Rene Lourau, "Sociologische Vragen Vooraf over de Informele Groepen," *Alternative Groepen in de Kerk* (Amersfoort: De Hoorstink, 1972), pp. 102–165.
20. See Bunnik, "Solidaire Groepen in West Europa," 24.
21. See *KA,* XXIV, *22* (May 13, 1969), column 536.

along reformist lines, while showing a firm resistance to revolutionary movements, the reforming voice is either dissipated or pushed into rebellious contestation with the authorities. The response of the social authorities to pressures for change is more than window-dressing or public rhetoric. The social authorities help to determine the directions of change.

We can see the interplay of mobilization resources and authorities by looking at the remarkable documentation and information center, DOC, maintained by the Dutch Church in Rome during the Vatican Council. The Dutch hierarchy was the only national episcopacy to command such an autonomous information center in Rome. The center, established in 1962, and entrusted to a team from the KRO broadcasting company, became the meeting point for Dutch journalists and broadcasters covering the Council. In 1962, DOC sponsored fourteen press conferences, eight theological conferences, and the publication of forty theological working papers dealing with the key issues of the Council. In 1963, DOC presented twenty press conferences (four in The Netherlands, sixteen in Rome) and published ten serious theological papers and working papers. Forty-five of DOC's papers, translated into five languages, enjoyed widespread circulation among the Council members. The DOC offices became the common meeting ground for progressive theologians from all over the world. Non-Dutch journalists came to receive a kind of news briefing denied them in the carefully controlled official Vatican press conferences. In attending or giving the press conferences or listening to theological sessions at their documentary center, the Dutch bishops were exposed to lectures from Hans Kung, Karl Rahner, M. D. Chenu, and John Courtney Murray. The mutual exposure of bishops and progressive theologians was made possible because in the Netherlands the Catholic Radio Broadcasting Company enjoys a substantial budget, derived from state funds, to maintain the kind of staff and office exemplified by DOC. No other national Catholic press service could begin to rival its coverage of the Council.

Not enough is usually made in reports of the Vatican Council of this unique communication center.[22] Its existence helps to explain Dutch preeminence at the Council and in theology in the years since the Council. The Dutch DOC became in 1965 the IDOC, International Documentary Center for the Council. The influential post-conciliar international theological journal, *Concilium,* grew out of

22. Franck, *The Exploding Church*, pp. 7–8, is one of the few authors who does justice to the role of DOC.

Dutch initiaties at DOC. A final point relates to what this center meant to Dutch Catholic journalism. If the Dutch press is heavily reformist and progressive in its staff, this is not a result of a conspiracy. The journalists went to school at DOC during the Council.

By the end of the Council in 1965, the Dutch bishops already constituted a collegial structure, exercising joint responsibility for their church province. They were, by that time, the only national episcopacy which spoke with one voice or with a clear pastoral policy. They had at their disposal an array of commissions, institutes, and secretaries to help in conceiving and implementing strategies for church influence. There was no question of episcopal commitment to pastoral coordination and planning.

COLLEGIAL STRUCTURES: BISHOP-PRIEST-LAY ROLES IN THE CHURCH

How did the Dutch bishops respond when lower clergy and lay elites began mobilizing for changes within the church? The most compelling evidence for weighing the episcopal response may be found by matching the bishops' persistent public pronouncements with their actual decisions on critical issues of change. What patterns of consistent meaning can be uncovered? Did the bishops allow for the free play of new ideas? Especially, how were the bishops handling the unresolved problem of finding new role definitions for bishop, priest, and laity?

In 1960, two newly appointed ordinaries explored, in letters to their dioceses, new images for the bishop. William Bekkers of Den Bosch stated that the church found itself in a changed milieu and called for a new experimental openness on the part of the church. In recalling that the laity also constituted the church, Bekkers warned that this truth must not remain mere theory any longer. He ended his letter with a remark unexpected from a bishop: "you do not have to worry about sparing me any criticism."[23] The other new bishop, Mgr. van Dodewaard of Haarlem, in a play upon the Latin term for bishop, pontifex, urged the concept of the bishop as a bridge builder: the bishop must be above parties in the church, bringing the various tendencies within Catholicism together, encouraging dialogue and listening to the desires of his people.[24] These themes became in time the persistent public pronouncement of the collective bishops.

23. See *KA,* XV, 3- (July 22, 1960), columns 721–724.
24. See *KA,* XV, 11 (March 11, 1960), columns 282–291.

The Dutch bishops commemorated Pope John's announcement of the Second Vatican Council by publishing a brochure-length letter for Christmas 1960. This remarkable letter, anticipating all of the major thematic shifts of the Second Vatican Council, had grown out of consultation between the bishops and a team of theologians, notably Jan Groot and Edward Schillebeeckx. It received wide press coverage in the Netherlands and was translated into several languages. In making a distinction between the church and the "reign of God through Jesus" announced by the gospels, the bishops saw the church called to dialogue with voices outside its boundaries. If the Holy Spirit was at work in other churches and in the "world," the church needed to reformulate its positions on ecumenism and secularization. Otherwise it would not be faithful to its task of seeking God's will. Further, the church, although an instrument of the "reign of God through Jesus," was situated in time, a pilgrim church on the march, bounded by space-time-culture limitations yet called to development.[25]

This Christmas letter represents the first essay, in any official Catholic document, on the concept of a collegial church. It is not the same as democracy.[26] A collegial church is not democratic in structure, because the papacy and the office of bishop and priest derive, according to Catholic theory, from the will of Christ and not from the desire of the body of believers. Nevertheless, collegiality reverses traditional Catholic priorities.

It can help us to understand some of the issues involved in Dutch Catholicism's efforts at achieving a collegial church if we transpose the theological concepts of collegiality into sociological language. I will draw upon some work of Guy E. Swanson to clarify the issues involved in collegiality.[27]

Swanson distinguishes two analytically distinct aspects of any group. From one point of view, every group is a *social system,* an organic collective unity which can be said to have purposes. As a social system, the group appears to be a collective actor. Individual members or sub-units of the system enact the group's purposes. They are agents—or in Swanson's terminology, *parts*—of the whole. Their

---

25. This and all following citations from the 1960 Christmas letter are from *KA*, XVI, *16* (April 21, 1961).
26. The Dutch bishops have always insisted in their public pronouncements that they were seeking "democratization" but not "democracy"; that is, they wanted the greatest degree of member participation in decision-making processes consonant with a hierarchical church.
27. See Guy E. Swanson, "To Live in Concord with Society," in *Cooley and Sociological Analysis,* Albert J. Reiss, ed. (Ann Arbor: University of Michigan Press, 1968).

rights and duties are subordinate to the purposes of the social system. One can say that the system "uses" them as its agents. When a social analyst wants to stress the unity, coherence, and interrelatedness of individuals and sub-units within a group, he considers the group as a *social system*.

From another point of view, every group is a collective bundling of the desires and purposes of autonomous individuals and sub-units which interact in the collectivity in pursuit of their own divergent interests, using the group as a market environment for exchange and barter to further certain interests and special purposes which are not collective. Individuals and sub-units claim rights and duties which are not derived from any given group, and they "use" their groups as agents of their independent purposes. They are, in Swanson's terms, *elements,* not reducible to parts, with which the collectivity must come to terms. When a social analyst stresses the problems of consensus, internal conflict, and asymmetrical purposes of individuals and sub-units within a group, he considers the group as an *association*.

The distinctions are analytic. Every group is a mixture of both. No pure cases of social systems or associations actually occur. There are no individuals or sub-units which are wholly parts or wholly elements. Nevertheless, the constitutional arrangements of groups, their founding myths and structures, differ in such a way that in some groups, arriving at consensus and unity and becoming a social system is especially problematic, while in other groups, attaining individual or sub-unit autonomy, and becoming an association, are problematic. The constitutional arrangements of some groups approximate the pure types of social system or association. Expressed simply, the main problem in groups which tend to overemphasize social system aspects in their myths and structures is that the group swallows up individual and sub-unit autonomy in its own purposes. The main problems in groups which tend to overemphasize association aspects in their constitutions is that the group has difficulty defining any collective purpose which transcends individual autonomous interests.

Swanson sees traditional Catholic corporatist church and society models as approximating a pure type of the social system.[28] The rights and duties of every agent in the church—from pope through bishop to priest and laymen—are subordinate and dependent upon the purposes of the whole. Incumbents of roles within the church are all seen, in different positions within the hierarchy, as agents of the church. Lower agents in the hierarchy are dependent upon cues from

28. See Guy E. Swanson, *Religion and Regime* (Ann Arbor: University of Michigan Press, 1968).

higher agents, who more perfectly embody the system's purposes. Of course, since no real group is a pure type of a social system, individuals and sub-units have always maneuvered for space within the church for their own interests and purposes. From the Council of Trent to the Second Vatican Council, there had been, however, no actual revisions of the founding myths and constitutional structures of the church, no redefinition of roles by including the aspect of rights and duties as elements.

If Dutch Catholicism and the Roman center came to embody two different visions of the church in the 1960s, the difference in these visions derive from varying recipes for the proper balance between the social-system and association aspects of the church. By choosing to open up the discussion to new ideas, Dutch Catholicism was fated by its structure and needs to place greater emphasis on the church as an association and on the rights and duties of individuals and units as elements. To do so, it turned to theories of collegiality and pluriformity within the church.

In their episcopal Christmas letter, the bishops saw the lay church as first in priority. In discussing the Catholic notion of infallibility (inerrancy in the witness and proclamation of true belief), the Dutch bishops affirmed that the pope was infallible because he was the special spokesman within an infallible college of the universal episcopate. His special irreducible charisma of infallibility derived from his particular role within *their* episcopal college. Neither pope nor bishop was simply an agent of the other's purposes. Both the pope and bishops are irreducible elements. The bishops, in their turn, constituted an infallible college, because they formulated the inerrant faith of the ordinary body of believers. "In fact, the personal infallibility of the pope rests upon his imbeddedness in the universal episcopacy which is itself collectively infallible, and the episcopacy, in its turn, is a carrier of the infallible belief of the entire community of the faithful." Collegiality replaces a hierarchical, pyramid view of authority with a consultative, feedback process. The emphasis shifts from command-obedience toward dialogue. No one in the church is purely an agent of anyone else. No one fully embodies in his own role the purposes of the whole system.

The Dutch bishops did not hesitate to embrace the corollary of the moral necessity to consult the faithful in matters of dogma. If the holy spirit is equally at work in the entire community and each position has its own gift and task as an element in the body, hierarchical leadership is unthinkable without the proper autonomous contribution of the laity. Indeed, in the forthcoming Council, the bishops would represent their people. "It is precisely as the bishop of a definite local church that the bishops are going to the ecumenical Council. Each of the bishops will become the voice of the entire community of faith entrusted to him. *That voice, of course, will have been previously led, guided, purified, corrected, and brought to life by each bishop in joint communion with the universal body of bishops.'*[29]

The Dutch bishops promised to embody a consultative and dialogic style even when the Council was completed: "Every individual believer is expected to be deeply involved in this Council not only before and during but after the Council as well. For if the Council finds no resonance in the community . . . it remains suspended, as it were, in mid-air. This Council will only be fully efficacious as an event in religious history if it is embraced by the people and worked out, in its implications, by the people in the daily life of the church."

The bishops ended their 1960 Christmas letter with an appeal for help and cooperation. They sought to tap the theological and practical expertise of priests and laity. They asked, in particular, for suggestions on liturgical renewal, catechesis, preaching, new forms of cooperation with Protestants and non-believers, and most especially, ways to determine the proper pastoral competencies of priest and laity within the church.

In this 1960 Christmas letter we meet a new kind of invitation to engage in discussion and brainstorming. This was not just an isolated episcopal enthusiasm on the eve of the Council. Throughout the Council the bishops repeated the same invitation in their letters. Thus, at the start of the Council sessions in 1962, they promised their people: "Your bishops will represent this community at the Council. They will see to it that your voice gets a hearing and they will be witnesses to your faith, your desires, and your needs."[30] Writing before the second session in 1963, they reiterated their invitation for new ideas to handle the sources of dissatisfaction within Catholicism by calling upon Catholics to join special kinds of discussion groups, "so that an open discussion is created between priests, religious, and laity about the broad questions which presently occupy the church."[31]

29. In its best-formulated versions as high theology, collegiality tries to maintain the balanced judgment that the church is both a social system and an association, and that incumbents of roles within the church are both parts and elements. The underlined phrase shows that the Dutch bishops had no intention of abdicating their special teaching role in the church. They merely would exercise it differently.
30. *KA*, XVII, *40* (October 5, 1972), column 950.
31. *KA*, XVIII, *40* (October 3, 1963), column 1001.

Again, in 1964, in a Lenten letter on the question of liturgical renewal, the bishops pointed out that there was more at issue than merely a new set of rites. What was needed was a new mentality, a new way of experiencing the church as consultative, collegial, and in dialogue. They asked that the faithful read their letter carefully and discuss it in groups, raising questions and proposing amendments. "We agree from our heart with those who claim *it is a task for all of us,* thus, for the bishops with their priests and the laity and the religious, to determine whether a truly new religious form of the liturgy can be created."[32]

In their letter on the occasion of the fourth session of the Council, the bishops returned to this theme. "Every believing member of the community is called upon to join us in this renewal. No one is excluded from this responsibility. . . . In this renewal the church— *thus, each of us*—is asked to show mutual listening, trust, and respect for one another."[33] There can be no question that the theme of collegiality and a call for creative thinking represented a persistent public pronouncement of the Dutch bishops between 1958 and 1965.

Three of the bishops stand out, in this period, for giving special encouragement to new ideas on the role definition of bishop-priest-laity within the church. By reason of his position as cardinal, the voice of Utrecht's Bernard Alfrink carried an extra weight in Dutch episcopal deliberations. The bishop of Breda, Mgr. De Vet, wrote a series of letters whose genial and intellectual formulation made them focal points in the discussion of role changes. The popular William Bekkers of Den Bosch embodied in his "style" an entirely new way of being a bishop.

Alfrink

In his many speeches in and out of the Netherlands during the Council years, Alfrink was urging the themes of collegiality, consultation within the church, the importance of the laity, and pluralism within the world church. In a speech to his priests on the eve of the Council, Alfrink deplored the narrow use of lay expertise in the preparation for the Council. He summed up what seemed to him the significant changes to expect of the bishops' gathering in Rome. "The possibilities of exchanging ideas that will take place *if the whole church gets involved in this Council* is very important. Also, the confrontation of the universal church with *its* central governing apparatus as that is

32. *KA*, XIX, *14* (April 3, 1964), column 398.
33. *KA*, XX, *38* (September 17, 1965), column 972.

exercised from out of the Roman center will be of importance. It will be important that we think through and implement the ideas which have been opened for discussion by this Council. It is significant that in the last years the church has finally catalyzed into movement.''[34] Alfrink reminded his priests that he and they would be spending a great deal of time after the Council putting its decisions into effect.

On his return from Rome after the first session of the Council, Alfrink told an audience at the dedication of a Catholic military canteen that at the Council, ''every cardinal or bishop is the witness to the faith and desires of his brother priests and the community of the faithful.''[35] In the spring of 1962, Alfrink took part in a special study week on the Council held at the Catholic Univesity in Nijmegen. Once again, he registered disappointment that the laity had not been consulted in the preparation of the Council. ''I consider it regrettable, especially in our age and in our Dutch situation (in other parts of the church the situation is entirely different than ours) that the consultation of the laity did not occur.'' He promised that in future councils the laity would be amply consulted.

Alfrink went on to criticize the one-sidedness of the Roman curia. He made clear that he did not intend to belittle the papacy in calling for a program of decentralization, pluriformity of national churches within the one Catholic church, and the internationalization of the central government of the church. In addressing possible objections to such a program, Alfrink stated, ''many will fear that this may lead to national churches or schism. I have already said that Vatican I has taught us all that to break with the pope is to break with the Roman Catholic church.''[36]

During a mass held in Utrecht to celebrate the Council, the Cardinal expressed his hopes for the Council in glowing, almost utopian, terms:

> The Second Vatican Council can usher in a genuine new period for the church—a phase in church history, moreover, which *all of us together* must go about giving a definite shape once the Council is over. Many in the church foster hopes that this new phase in the history of the church will be marked by a new and greater openness; by a truly joyful experiencing of what it means to have faith; by the falling away of many small-minded fears in the cherishing of love toward God and our fellowman; by an authentic piety which finds its roots in scriptures

34. *KA*, XVII, *24* (June 15, 1962), column 563. Italics mine.
35. *KA*, XVII, *1* (January 5, 1962), column 7.
36. *KA*, XVII, *18* (May 4, 1962), columns 409–414.

and the liturgy; by a proper understanding of *what belongs to the essence of the Catholic faith and what is best considered as mere peripheral historical accretion;* . . . by a straightforward search for unity with other believers in Christ, . . . by being open to everything that is good in humanity wherever it is to be found.[37]

At a press conference in Rome in the spring of 1963, Alfrink repeated his hopes that the Council would bring an internationalization of the Roman curia, along with consultation and pluriformity within the church: "An Italian newspaper . . . has written that I am anti-Roman. Anyone who really knows me, knows that I am Roman in heart and soul. But they also know that this attachment to Rome . . . is not the same as a blind infatuation. However 'Roman' I may be, I am always more Catholic than Roman. It is just for that very reason that it seems to me extremely important that *we involve the whole church* so far as possible in the implementation of this Council."[38]

In the winter of 1963 at a concelebrated eucharist attended by all of the Dutch bishops, Alfrink proposed joint prayer and discussion sessions between bishops, priests, and laity as the best means "to seek out ever more possibilities for bringing the insights into the faith which the church needs at the present time to fruition."[39]

De Vet

While Alfrink was articulating an invitation to brainstorming and consultation at every level of the church, Bishops De Vet and Bekkers addressed themselves to concrete redefinitions of the roles of bishop, priest, and laity. Bishop De Vet, consecrated as the new bishop of Breda in 1962, introduced his policies to his diocese by writing three letters. In his first communication to his priests, De Vet asked them to embody a spirit of service to the laity, while he promised to be at their disposal. In taking up the theme of collegiality, he averred, "I see you priests as my co-workers with your own responsibilities and your own pastoral experience." All ministry in the church is by its very nature consultative and collegial. "The pope is only pope because of his position *within* the college of bishops. *The bishop is not merely an agent of the pope.* He is also united in bonds of solidarity with the other bishops. He can only be a bishop in communion with the other bishops in the church."

37. *KA*, XVII, *41* (October 12, 1968), columns 953ff. Italics mine.
38. *KA*, XVIII, *18* (May 3, 1963), column 452. Italics mine, to indicate collegiality and consultation themes.
39. *KA*, XIX, *9* (February 28, 1964), column 117.

In De Vet's job description, it is the bishop, not the pope, who has the first responsibility for the governance of his diocese. The local bishop is also co-responsible for the church in other dioceses, especially the constituent dioceses of his church province. The bishop, moreover, must see himself as a leader of a team of his priests, the spokesman among equals. The priests, in their turn, must work in teams with one another within and across parish boundaries and with the laity. De Vet concluded his first letter with the exhortation, "We must come to find some way to arrive at a collective management of the diocese and a collective joint policy on a number of key issues."[40]

In 1963 and 1964 De Vet returned to many of these same themes. Thus, in a speech on the pastorate, he encouraged his priests to seek new approaches and methods, perhaps modeling their profession on that of counselors and social case workers. In their search for new pastoral forms, the priests should begin with three givens: (1) The pastorate is a common responsibility of the bishop, priests, and lay people. (2) The pastorate of the future must allow for new pluriformity beyond parish territorial boundaries. (3) The pastorate of the future will demand new client-centered techniques. The priest could not use spiritual coercion in his dealings with the laity. Priests have no directly profane tasks. Their role is that of spiritual advisor, liturgical leader, and counselor to the laity. The laity is autonomous, in its role as Christian citizen, in determining the forms of apostolate in the non-church milieu.[41] Note how De Vet's description parallels the hypothesis for priest-lay roles in the pastoral-cultural strategy outlined in Table 3. The use of motifs of service and client-centered methods presumes a certain autonomy in the laity as an *element* in their own right.

De Vet's position on the relation between priest and laity became the official position of the collective bishops in 1964, in a letter describing the priestly role in the confessional organizations; in this letter the bishops made clear that the spiritual advisor was not meant to have veto power over the autonomous actions of the laity.[42]

Bekkers

Since his appointment as bishop in 1960, William Bekkers had been stressing these same themes. In a speech delivered in 1962 to Pro Mundi Vita, an organization of lay Catholic pastoral workers, he

40. *KA*, XVII, *29* (July 20, 1962), columns 699–706 for De Vet's letter. Italics mine.
41. *KA*, XVIII, *31* (August 2, 1963), columns 777–796.
42. *KA*, XVIII, *24* (June 12, 1964), columns 655–660.

stated that laymen, as well as priests, should train the laity for Catholic apostolic units. "I do not believe in a training which is a one-way traffic between the priest and the layman. The word and witness which the laity has to give is of utmost importance for every participant in the church, not the least for the priest."[43]

In 1964, in an address to seminarians in Haaren, the bishop painted a "Vision of the Priest of Tomorrow." The fundamental problem in the traditional formation of priests lay in their being segregated from the laity during their formation and later, as priests, within a clerical caste. The priest of the future must remain "an ordinary human with other ordinary humans, especially a fellow man of the faith within the community of the faithful."[44] Clerical separation was the worse because priests spoke a special clerical jargon. "How powerless the church in the priest will be if he is not capable of engaging in dialogue because he talks the language of the church, which is so different from the ordinary language of our world."[45]

Bekkers urged that priests could not simply conceive of themselves as agents of the purposes of the organization. "The priest who thinks that he can rely upon the automatic operation of grace in his work and shows too little interest in his personal contributions to his ministry is a mere automaton or, to put it in blunt terms, a kind of magician."[46]

Although Bekkers' "Vision of the Priest of Tomorrow" involves an upgrading of the status of the layman vis à vis the priest, he saw the necessary reduction of functions within the priesthood as an opportunity for religious specialization rather than sheer loss of functions:

> You will remember how at a given moment in the past, the lay apostolate was discovered. Its very first characteristic was something like: to do those things for which the priest had no time. Catholic Action was, thus, the long arm of the hierarchy.
>
> The lay apostolate has pretty much lost this characteristic. The clergy, in growing numbers, has come to *the realization of the need to lose functions in order to arrive at the authentic fulfillment of its ministerial role.* The altar, the pulpit, the confessional, the baptismal font remain central in his understandings of his own proper task.[47]

43. *KA*, XVII, 29 (July 20, 1962), columns 705–710.
44. William Bekkers, "Het Priesterbeeld van Straks," in *Gods Volk Onderweg*, Michel van der Plas, ed. (Utrecht: Ambo Books, 1964), p. 107.
45. *Ibid.*, p. 109. To avoid clerical separation, the diocese of Groningen disbanded its minor seminary in 1962. In the following years, all minor seminaries in the Netherlands were closed.
46. *Ibid.*, p. 9.
47. *Ibid.*, p. 107.

Bishop Bekkers, who was known affectionately to his people as Willy, brought a new, more humane style to the exercise of the role of the bishop. Rarely wearing a uniform which set him off from his fellow priests, he adopted the stance of the bishop as common man. The teenage members of the Pax Christi group spontaneously bore him upon their shoulders when he joined their pilgrimage on foot through the cities of his diocese. He was seen on television at the press conferences in Rome as the bishop who sat at the feet of the Council theologians. He was the bishop who reminded his people that it was "God's people on the march."

Much more than de Vet or even Alfrink, Willy Bekkers was the man who typified, perhaps even created, the mutual trust and strong emotional attachment between bishop and population which is such a striking feature of Dutch Catholicism. He pioneered in breaking down centuries-old stereotypes in Catholic relations with non-Catholics in the Netherlands. He developed warm friendships with Protestant church leaders and theologians. A year before his death, Bekkers paid a personal visit to the non-churched chairman of the Dutch Society for Sexual Reform, Mrs. Mary Zeldenrust-Nordanus, thus initiating a detente with what had been one of Dutch Catholicism's strongest enemies. The remark of two Protestant theologians after an exchange with Bekkers captures some of the myth of the man: "He is the very first church leader we have ever met in our lives who made the deep and most disarming impression upon us of being, what few men are, a truly free man."[48]

The bishop's untimely death in 1966 provoked expressions of sincere grief and loss from every segment of the Dutch population. His funeral, carried live on national television, was an event of genuine national sorrow. Few viewers missed the poignancy of the fact that one of the two wreaths which adorned his coffin bore the inscription, "From the Dutch Society for Sexual Reform."

We saw earlier that Bekkers had a much more conservative past in his days as social charities director for the diocese of Den Bosch. The myth of Bekkers, still so strong in Dutch Catholicism that other bishops walk in his shadow, has repressed that past.

In the first winter of his office as bishop, 1960-1961, Bekkers decided to hold a series of twenty-two question-and-answer sessions with his priests as a way of getting acquainted. Several groups of the laity also asked for a chance to meet with him. He arranged for five meetings geographically spread throughout the diocese at which four

48. Personal communication from Jan van Kilsdonk, S.J.

representatives from each parish in the diocese would be in attendance. In response to these meetings, the bishop remarked that he thought the greatest problem was finding ways to bring the laity into decision making. As a concrete token of his desire to effect this sort of change, Bekkers directed that every parish in the diocese set up a lay advisory board. He also ordered that finances of the diocese and parishes be entrusted to competent groups of laymen. The first gesture toward structural change had been made. Bekkers' example of entrusting finances to the laity was followed in all the other dioceses. Further, in 1963 the diocese of Haarlem set up the first diocesan lay board of consultors to the bishop.

This first round of discussions in Den Bosch was so successful that Bekkers urged the formation of pastoral discussion groups throughout the diocese in which priests and laity could come together to discuss pastoral problems. From September through December 1963, 1,000 such groups met to debate the topic of confession. On January 24 and 25, 1964, delegates from the discussion groups met in congresses held in Nijmegen, Den Bosch, and Eindhoven to present their suggestions and conclusions. On the basis of these reports, Bekkers announced three policy conclusions: (1) Sermons at the eucharist should grow out of preparatory discussion sessions between the preacher and representatives of the congregation. (2) Confessors in the diocese were reminded that their role in the confessional was that of a forgiving father and not an examining judge. Bekkers instructed them to be discreet in questioning the penitent. (3) The bishop announced that the experiment with discussion groups would continue in the fall of 1964-1965 around the topic of the meaning of the eucharist.[49] Within a year of Bekkers' announcement, the collective bishops issued a letter on confession in which they made his position on confession their own.[50]

Bekkers' gesture in holding question-and-answer sessions with his priests and laity in 1960-1961, while undeniably effective as a sign of encouragement for a phase of brainstorming in the collective redefinition of group structures, could not serve as a permanent model for the structural embodiment of collegiality. It was too inefficient and time-consuming. Nevertheless, such a return to face-to-face dialogue dramatized the bishop's willingness to find better structures for exercising authority within the church, structures which would embody the fact that the lower clergy and laity were "elements." The switch

49. *KA*, XIX, *11* (March 13, 1964), columns 298–319.
50. *KA*, XX, *16* (April 16, 1965), columns 472–476.

to a new form in 1963-1965 had the advantages of mobilizing more participants within the diocese (10,000 instead of 1,750) and allowing the bishop to base his information on resumes abstracted for him by his staff.

The effectiveness of Bekkers' gesture rested upon his proclaiming an episcopal policy based on the suggestions of the groups at the end of the discussion group session. Within a short period, the collective body of bishops adopted Bekkers' policy. The myth which came to predominate within Dutch Catholic life was born out of this experience. According to the myth, energy, wisdom, and insight into needed structural changes exists at the grassroots; the wishes of people at the grassroots find a voice in their bishop; and when their bishop represents their desires in a council of fellow bishops, change is possible at the national level. The myth further suggests that shifts at the grassroots level can swiftly achieve a resonating response from the authorities. A further question was unavoidable. If the myth held true for the Dutch church, why not also at an international level, within the world church?

Bekkers enunciated this central myth during one of his fireside chats conducted for KRO television between 1960 and 1965: "What is alive within a people, always pushes itself to the surface. What is alive within the ordinary people of the church gives to the church its shape. Therefore, a church can never be static but must always be dynamic. Hence, a council of the church can never be a concluding point in history but the starting point."[51] The Den Bosch experiment with discussion groups spread to the other dioceses of the Netherlands from 1965 through 1969. As individuals and as a collective body, the bishops encouraged participation in the discussion groups as the best way to support their work at the Vatican Council.

While estimates vary and exact statistics are irrevocable, the best estimates are that about 20 percent of the adult Catholic population, or 500,000 adult Dutch Catholics, took part in discussion groups. Although it seems unlikely that this groundswell of popular participation actually determined episcopal policies, the significance of the movement should not be underestimated.

The popular discussion group movement of the mid-1960s, known as the *ecclesia* movement, is hard to capture in precise statistics. There were, to begin with, discussion groups serviced by the magazine *Ecclesia*. Secondly, there were diocesan-sponsored discussion group

51. Brandpunt television interview, November 25, 1964.

sessions for each diocese. Finally, there were independent discussion groups within parishes or with connections to some member of the lower clergy. For one given year, 1967-1968, using an index of ten per discussion group, PINK estimated that there were 180,000 participants in those groups. In a field interview, L. Koevoets of the staff of *Ecclesia* stated that his best estimates ran from 15-20 percent of the adult population. My own statistical information gathered from the pastoral centers of the seven Dutch dioceses shows an average of 13.8 percent of the adult Catholic population participating in the discussion group movement within "official" diocesan-sponsored discussion groups for the years 1966-1970. By any reckoning, 15 percent of the adult Catholic population is a massive and unparalleled kind of participation within a voluntary association. Compare, for example, the statistics for involvement in political parties in the Netherlands: in the 1972 election, 2 percent of the voters took an active role in any political gathering.[52]

In the mid-1960s the discussion group became, for a time, the primary model for the new experience of the reality of the church. At one point, indeed, some were suggesting that the priestly role was best defined as a discussion group leader. By proposing the discussion group as a model for a collegial church, the bishops raised expectations that dogmatic, pastoral, and structural positions within the church were reformable.

Since the majority of the discussion groups included a theologically trained resource person, the groups served as an unparalleled mobilization resource to socialize a broad base of the Dutch Catholic population in the new theology stemming from the Council. Resumes from these discussions show that the participants raised questions about almost every sort of topic touching the life and structures of the church. The discussion groups served, further, as training grounds for the cooperative exercise of new clerical and lay roles, co-equal if different elements within the body of the church. As one participant in the popular movement stated it, the solution to the problem of finding new structures in the church lay in "conducting collective consultation at the grassroots level and making our collective decisions known to the authorities . . . in some form of national assembly."[53]

52. *De Nederlandse Kieser* '72 (Alphen Aan den Rijn: Samson, 1973), p. 10. For a fuller treatment of the discussion-group movement, see L. Koevoets, *De Betekenis van de Kleine Kerkelijke Groep als Subject van Kerkelijk Handelen*, unpublished doctoral dissertation, Department of Theology, Nijmegen University, 1970, p. 109.
53. *Pastorale Gesprekken in Het Bisdom Roermond*, 1966. Stenciled.

THE TEST OF LAY AUTONOMY:
THE DOCTRINE OF CONTRACEPTION

The history of recent Catholic efforts at revising the traditional Catholic position on contraception is much too complex to reduce to one issue, or to discuss in full here. Throughout the world church, pressures to change the traditional doctrine which held that the use of all forms of birth regulations, except periodic continence, constituted an objectively grave sin, had built up in the period before and during the Council. The discovery of the contraceptive pill raised hopes for a resolution of the moral dilemmas of conscience of Catholic married couples, and their confessors.

Developments concerning contraception within the Netherlands can help us to exemplify some of the points we have been making. I will be especially interested in showing first the interplay of mobilization resources and the response of the authorities, and second the way in which the issue became a test case for lay autonomy.

The Netherlands had been more faithful in its period of traditional Catholicism to the official Catholic teaching than other European countries.[54] With Dutch Catholic economic emancipation, the pressures to change on this issue increased, and became especially acute because the Netherlands is the most heavily populated nation in the industrial world. Even by the mid-1950s Catholic elites showed a sensitivity to the need to rethink the church's position on contraception. Dutch mobilization resources lay at their disposal.

In 1947, the Catholics established a so-called Vormingscentrum—a center for retreat, reflection, and education for national service personnel at Ubbergen, just outside Nijmegen. Government subsidy financed the building and paid the salary of the staff. The armed services arranged for the release of Catholic recruits to attend the two-day courses conducted for about two hundred Catholic servicemen per week. The chaplains in charge of the center, especially P. C. Groenendijk, embodied an approach to religious topics decidedly less traditional than that to be found in an ordinary parish setting. Discussion played a large role in these formation weekends in which the participants were encouraged to arrive at a personal conviction on religious questions, even if their position did not agree with official church doctrine. Sexual morality formed a major topic. The staff avoided giving the impression that the church authorities had spoken

54. For the evidence to support this assertion, see F. van Heek, *Het Geboorte-Niveau der Nederlandse Rooms-Katholieken* (Leiden: H. Stenfert Kroese, 1954).

the last word on the subject, especially the use of contraceptives within marriage. The results of these discussions were published in a magazine for Catholic servicemen, *G-3*. It has been estimated that by the early 1960s these new ideas on sexuality had been exposed to 150,000 Dutch Catholic conscripts and that the magazine *G-3* reached one-sixth of the Dutch Catholic population.[55]

The Dutch bishops were situated at the nodal points of a unique communication and information network. It is not surprising, therefore, that Bernard Alfrink as early as 1959 showed an awareness of the pressures, such as those deriving from the *G-3* group, toward revising the Catholic position on contraception. In a 1959 speech addressed to the topic of "Family Problems in Our Time," Alfrink tried to assure his audience that he was aware of how pressing the problems of marital sexuality were. Nevertheless, he did not see how the church could change its position on contraception, and advised that expectations to the contrary were ill-founded. Still, he stated that he would encourage ways to make the traditional practice more palatable.[56] Mobilization resources lay at his disposal.

In the early 1960s, a Catholic psychiatrist, Dr. C. Trimbos, conducted a popular series of KRO broadcasts devoted to new views of human sexuality. These broadcasts reached a wide audience and provoked a critical rethinking of contraception within marriage. A Catholic magazine on family problems, *Wij in Huwelijk en Gezin*, followed the themes suggested by Trimbos. Catholic marriage counseling bureaus also followed suit. The annual congresses for Catholic university students pursued these same topics. By 1962 the Laennec Congress for Catholic doctors and medical students held sessions on the topics of sexuality within marriage, birth regulation, and the pill. The bishops were allowing the exploration of new ideas.

One of the points at issue in these discussions concerned lay autonomy, the competence of laymen to judge what constituted proper moral behavior within marriage. If the laity did not have prime responsibility here, then they remained mere agents of clerical purposes and not elements with their own unique contribution to the theological discussion.

As the discussion matured, Bishop Bekkers devoted three fireside chats on KRO television to the topic. His first broadcast on March 21,

55. See Peter McCaffery, "Some Groups at Present Seeking to Influence the Development of Roman Catholicism," unpublished thesis, Oxford University, 1971, pp. 31–36; L. M. Thomas "Vormingswerk: Kan dat in het leger?," in *G-3*, XXIII, *11* (November 1970), 295–296. Dutch Catholic servicemen had their own "Catholic" military canteens.
56. *KA*, XIV, *43* (November 20, 1959), columns 1029–1034.

1963, was the earliest public episcopal response anywhere within the Catholic world to the pressures being voiced by married couples:

> From within their human experience of the reality of marriage . . . the married couple—*and they alone*—can answer the question what God's vocation and task for them concretely means in their marriage, how large their families should be and what the spacing between children should be. Their human love and responsibility can move them to choose either a larger or a smaller family. . . . This is a *matter of conscience in which no one has the right to intrude.* The pastor, the doctor, or whoever is asked for advice, must as much as possible *grant to that personal conscience its rightful autonomy.* . . .

Bekkers refused to say that the use of contraceptives was always a subjectively grave sin. In raising the question whether the pill is morally allowable or not, he remarked that the answer to this question depended largely upon medical judgments of its effects: "Understand me well. I neither desire nor could I be a spokesman on these technical questions. I merely want to affirm one point. *There is definitely uncertainty in this question. We do not know.* No one should expect an over-hasty position from the bishop or priests."

The issue of contraception was not the only issue on which the Dutch bishops, in the early 1960s, stated that there was uncertainty. Bekkers ended his first broadcast by responding to objections that the bishops were being too vague in their recent policy statements: "Is it a question of vagueness or *room to explore?* There is such a thing as Christian incompleteness. To point that out is an important contribution to the effort at achieving Christian completeness."[57]

Bekkers' television broadcast provoked a discussion among leading moral theologians in the pages of the two national Catholic dailies about the Catholic teaching on contraception. The lack of consensus among the moral theologians only further underscored Bekkers' point that there was uncertainty on the issue of contraception. What was not uncertain in this whole discussion, however, was that the autonomous lay conscience of the Catholic married couple—not the hierarchy or the clergy—would have the last word on the question. Four and a half months after Bekkers' broadcast, the bishops issued a joint letter to their priests instructing them to honor this point in the confessional. After he had made certain that the penitent understood the traditional position of the church, the priest should not refuse

57. *Gods Volk Onderweg*, pp. 200–201, 205, 210, for the three Bekkers' citations.

absolution to penitents who, nevertheless, in good conscience chose to use contraceptives. "In the last instance, the personal conscience of the penitent shall be the deciding factor on this matter."[58]

The bishops' letter to their priests did not suggest that the priests had no role to play. The priests were to *inform* the conscience of the laity as counselors, not *impose* a conscience as higher agents of the church's purposes. This illustrates an attempt to balance the part-element character in both priestly and lay roles.

58. *KA,* XVIII, *32* (August 10, 1963), columns 672-678.

Chapter 5

Collective Redefinition: Free Institutions and New Roles, 1958-1965

PUBLIC OPINION WITHIN THE CHURCH

Traditional Dutch Catholicism supported a superb media apparatus. In 1960, for example, the following news sources were available to the 5,000,000 strong Catholic population. (1) A Roman Catholic Press Service for the Netherlands. (2) Twenty daily newspapers and two national dailies, providing general news and commentaries. (3) Twenty-two weekly newspapers serving small towns or communities with a large Catholic population. Although neither the dailies nor the weeklies were official religious organs of a diocese, they provided thorough coverage of Catholic church news. (4) One hundred and eighty-three weekly, biweekly, or monthly magazines and journals of opinion treating general religious topics. (5) Sixty-five magazines dealing with issues related to family life, education, and youth work. (6) Forty-two learned journals. (7) Twenty-two magazines treating issues related to social or church charity. (8) Seventy newspapers or magazines sponsored by official Catholic organizations. (9) Ten specialized periodicals devoted to music, theatre, sports, and so on.[1]

The journalists and broadcasters for the Catholic media had received secular training. They shared a newsman's eye for the curious and controversial. The newspapers and broadcasting company were under lay control. Traditional Dutch Catholicism provided a rich soil for the cultivation of public opinion within the church.

1. Source: *Pius Almanak*, Volume LXXXV (Amsterdam: De Tijd Press, 1960).

The Second Vatican Council placed international Catholic developments before the public eye in a new way. The news media punctured the myth of a Catholic monolith as they reported the work of the Council through the journalist's style of dramatic presentation around personalities, controversy, and the conflict of parties and visions. It is often forgotten that if the Council made pluriformity within Catholicism visible to an outsider, it did no less for the ordinary Catholic believer. Under the glare of publicity, long-submerged divisions and parties within Catholicism surfaced. Pluriformity of theologies and parties was a fact—but a fact without any legitimating theory within the Catholic corporatist model. Catholic tradition provided neither a theory nor an apparatus for the formation of genuinely free public opinion.

Before the Council, the ecclesiastical establishment could control information by hiding church decision-making behind bureaucratic secrecy and appeals to a united front for the beleagured Catholic minority. The "horror stories" which circulated widely among the clergy and the theologians had made clear, however, that bureaucratic oaths of secrecy covered a multitude of sins. Some of the fundamental issues raised by the Catholic pluriformity surfaced at the Council. Did Catholics have a right to information within the church? Was there such a thing as legitimate criticism? What were the limits of freedom of theological inquiry, speech, publication, and assembly? These issues are related to the question of the extent to which church members are elements as well as parts within the community.

How would the authorities react to this new development of pluriformity? The authorities in each country faced a dilemma. If they allowed free discussion and the open formulation of public opinion in the church as a way of coming to community consensus, would they not forfeit the controls necessary to maintain a dogmatic church? It is not possible to perpetuate a belief system based on unchanging dogmatic formulation in an atmosphere of free, open discussion in the search for truth. One cannot claim to be the repository of truths which are above and beyond history—hence, irreformable dogma—and simultaneously plunge into the dramatic give-and-take of historical dialogue. To allow institutions of free public opinion within the church and to give up the traditional controls over what can be published, who can teach theology, and whose sins can be forgiven, is to change the historic system of Roman Catholicism.

It may be helpful to list here some of the central controls and the sanction system which prevailed within traditional Catholicism until 1962: (1) Every priest or member of a religious order had to receive his bishop's or provincial's permission before publishing an article or making a public speech. (2) The Latin notes used for all courses within the seminary had to be sent to Rome for approval. (3) All teachers in seminaries were subject, in their appointment and dismissal, to the local bishop. Roman authorities could intervene to remove any teacher in any seminary. (4) Catholic publishing houses and lay Catholic authors were dependent upon the bishop for an Imprimatur. (5) The local bishop and higher Roman authorities could excommunicate priests or laymen or suspend priests from their function without granting a hearing to the person involved. (6) Priests could refuse absolution to penitents. A bishop could "reserve" certain sins which only he could forgive. (7) Priests, theologians, and even laymen were commonly required to take an oath of secrecy, promising not to reveal the content of discussions with higher superiors. The use of such totalitarian measures was mitigated somewhat, of course, by their humanitarian application by most officers in the church, or by restrictions of their abuse under the canon law.

Could these old controls be maintained in the climate of the Council and its aftermath? Again, was the church credible in its claim that the act of faith is a free choice of responsible men and compatible with secular knowledge and development if it must use totalitarian controls to limit the search for truth? At least in the free industrial world, the church authorities could not wish away the reforming voice or the fact of pluriformity.

When the Council opened the church to reexamination, the Dutch Catholic community sought the political freedoms of modern Western society within the church community itself. Throughout the 1960s the atmosphere within the church became like that of a modern political community. In a sense, free formation of public opinion within the church entailed open political processes: the formation of parties and pressure groups, each trying to enact its programs and defend its visions.

Because of the array of autonomous Catholic media, the Dutch bishops had very few direct tools to arrest the open development of public opinion within their church. There could be no question, once the Council was announced, of successful episcopal control or manipulation of information. With the announcement of the reforming Council, differences that already existed within Dutch Catholicism began to surface in the letters-to-the-editor columns of the Catholic dailies. We have seen that the Dutch bishops were obviously choosing to encourage ideas which would help to ease the dissatisfactions within the Catholic community. The bishops' stance seemed to say that it was wiser to contribute to a process which they could not, in any event, control.

In its Christmas letter of 1960, the Dutch episcopacy voiced a first cautious approval of criticism within the church and presented some rules for its conduct:

> Catholic criticism does not just come out of thin air. This criticism is thought through, not an emotional response but the result of serious reflection. Catholic criticism bears the burden not only of the love for truth but also the awareness of responsibility and the knowledge that the attainment of truth is always the product of tedious work. . . . Catholic criticism which is a right and duty for every believer is an expression of love which . . . does not undermine one's own commitment in faith or that of another.[2]

In the fall of 1962, Father Jan van Kilsdonk, S.J., gave an electrifying speech at the annual St. Adelbert congress entitled "The Need for a Loyal Opposition Within the Church." His speech, featured on national television, pointed to three recent actions of the Roman curia: the suppression of a book by the Italian Jesuit, Father Lombardi, *Concilio per Una Reforma Nella Carita;* the monitum of the Holy Office warning bishops not to allow their seminarians to read the works of Teilhard de Chardin; and the promulgation of the papal bull *Veterum Sapientiae,* reaffirming the central place of Latin as the teaching language within seminaries. Van Kilsdonk, in very emotional tones, pleaded for the Dutch episcopacy to fight against the autocratic controls of the papal curia. Soon thereafter Cardinal Alfrink responded to van Kilsdonk's fiery speech in an address to Catholic students. Alfrink ceded the right to criticism in the church. Nevertheless, he warned against sweeping condemnations of the Roman curia. Without mentioning his name, Alfrink branded van Kilsdonk's speech as irresponsible criticism.[3]

In the following years, Alfrink returned repeatedly to the theme of responsible public opinion within the church. On the occasion of the sixtieth birthday of the Catholic resistance hero in World War II and poet-professor at Nijmegen, Anton van Duinkerken, Alfrink defended freedom of speech within the church, even going so far as to suggest that bishops must sometimes stand up to the papal center,

2. *KA,* XVI, *16* (April 21, 1961), column 374.
3. For the texts of van Kilsdonk's and Alfrink's speech, see *Adelbert,* no volume indicated, No. 10 (November 1962), pp. 143–152.

just as St. Paul opposed St. Peter in Antioch.[4] In 1964 in a speech to the Thijm fellowship, Alfrink remarked that freedom of speech belonged to the very essense of the church. As he pointedly stated it, "Only God speaks in a monologue." The Cardinal suggested three rules for the exercise of free speech within the church: (1) Freedom of speech should contribute to the building up and not the tearing down of the Catholic faith. (2) Free speech should show respect for the faith of others in the church, the faith of church officers in Rome, and the unsophisticated faith of ordinary believers. (3) Free speech does not mean pushing your opinion on those unwilling to hear it.[5] Finally, in an address to the Dutch Catholic Journalists' Association in 1965, Alfrink frankly criticized the official conciliar press relations. He roundly affirmed the Catholic's right to open information, firmly rejecting censorship. Once again, Alfrink returned to the theme of responsibility. He asked the journalists to consider drawing up a code of ethics which included the right to information and norms of responsibility, especially in the delicate question of invasion of privacy. He requested that journalists maintain a distinction in their reports between free doctrinal disputes and matters of defined faith.

I have already outlined the traditional Catholic sanction or control system, which has largely disappeared in the post-Vatican church. Alfrink's appeal to the journalists to develop a code of ethics yields a clue to what was happening: a shift from *external* controls imposed by bishops or Rome to *internal* controls based on codes of professional ethics for sub-groups within the church, such as theologians, lower clergy, and journalists.

The Dutch Catholic media seized their new-found freedom to open their pages and channel time to the serious discussions taking place within the church. The Catholic dailies exposed pluriformity as they carried articles and letters to the editor presenting opposing views on such issues as the morality of contraception, liturgical renewal, the theology of the eucharist, and proposals for abolishing the office of the papal nuncio. The KRO, trying to serve the whole Catholic population and maintain its subscription level, balanced discussion panels treating controversial issues, and presented, in turns, traditionalist or modern liturgies in its biweekly televised eucharist.

In the process, the Dutch bishops and episcopal staffs were being schooled in giving press conferences and radio, press, and television

4. *KA*, XVIII, *1* and *2* (January 4 and 11, 1963), columns 50–52.
5. *KA*, XIX, *23* (June 5, 1964), columns 624–627.

interviews. Each diocese appointed a press relations officer. The bishops became accustomed to seeing cartoons of themselves in the daily press or reading criticism of their decisions. The Dutch episcopacy, firmly supporting the right to open information and discussion, was finding a new episcopal role, exemplified by Alfrink, as religious-ethical leaders, suggesting rules for the conduct of public opinion formation and providing exhortations to responsibility, openness, mutual trust, and unity. Through the bishops the diverse groups within the Catholic community could find a common meeting ground. The bishops, in their turn, stood above the parties within the church.

The free formation of public opinion requires, besides a free press, freedom of intellectual inquiry and the freedom of movement of persons. The latter was exercised as Dutch Catholics joined pressure groups or protest gatherings and circulated petitions and sent telegrams to Roman and Dutch authorities. Early in 1962, for example, thirty Catholics sent a protest telegram to the Roman curia objecting to the papal bull *Veterum Sapientiae,* which promulgated Latin as the unchanging language of the church. Their telegram reflects, in its first phrases, the climate within the Netherlands created by the persistent episcopal pronouncements: "The Undersigned feel themselves —partly on the grounds of the often repeated stimulus from authorities within the church encouraging active participation in the forthcoming council—to express their regret that. . . ."[6]

The right to freedom of inquiry found a test case in a theological debate in the early 1960s on the meaning of the eucharist. Several Dutch theologians were unhappy with the usual understandings and possible misinterpretations of the Tridentine formula of transubstantiation: the risen body of Jesus is truly present under the appearance of bread and wine in the eucharist. At the words of consecration pronounced by the priest at mass, the "substance" of the bread and wine are transformed into the "substance" of the risen body of Jesus, so that only the "accidents" or appearance of bread and wine remain.

These Dutch theologians felt that this Tridentine formula isolated too much the real presence of the risen Jesus during the eucharistic worship, localizing that presence too narrowly in space and time. The Tridentine formula did not do justice to the presence of the risen Jesus within the community of the faithful at the eucharist, or in the preached word of gospel and homily, His word. The theologians

6. Cited in *Le Croix,* March 12, 1962, p. 7.

wanted to emphasize that Jesus' presence in the bread and wine was a *directed* presence, whose only purpose was the personal and communal union between Jesus and believers. There were, moreover, problems inherent in expressing the real presence in culture-bound Aristotelian metaphysical categories of substance and accident. The theologians feared that the real presence was being conceived as the presence of an *object* occurring at a specific time and place, instead of the presence of a *person* who transcends, in his resurrected body, ordinary categories of space and time. They proposed a new description—labeled intentionality change or trans-finalization—which, they felt, would do greater justice to the whole of Catholic tradition on the eucharist presence.[7]

This eucharistic debate found resonance within the daily press and in church discussion groups. Some Catholics feared that the received Catholic sense of the real presence of Jesus in the eucharist was under attack. They requested that the bishops put an end to what they considered dangerous tinkering with essential truth.

In April 1965, the Dutch bishops responded in a collective letter on the meaning of the eucharist. I cite their joint response to show the way they tried to combine, within their new role as socio-ethical spokesmen in a situation of open public-opinion formation, elements of the traditional role of the bishop as the teacher of the true faith. The bishops began their letter by setting it within the context of the public discussion. There were divisions within the Dutch Catholic community on the formulation of the real presence. Some felt ancient values had been lost, mistrusting the good intentions of those who proposed new formulations. Others felt a need for revision of the received formulas in order to present ancient truths in a better, more understandable, indeed more Catholic, light. The bishops set as the first condition for the discussion that both sides agree upon the central importance of the eucharist.

The episcopacy, next, set forth the traditional theology of the eucharist. They added that they accepted the new insight of the theologians that Jesus' presence in the bread and wine is a *directed* presence, aimed at union with the community of the faithful. They affirmed, further, that Jesus was present within the eucharist in several forms, not just in the bread and wine. They refused to demand adherence to received formulas in setting terms for the discussion. "As long as the change of the bread and wine into the

7. The articles in question are by Dr. J. Moller in *Nederlands Katholiek Stemmen*, January 1960; and by Piet Schoonenberg in *Verbum*, December 19, 1964.

body and blood of the Lord and the actuality of his presence in the eucharistic species is accepted,'' free discussion can go on within the church. The bishops ended their letter by exhorting the faithful not to be too anxious or to give in to narrowness and small-mindedness. If each side tried to see the best intentions of the other, free discussion would not lead to unbridgeable divisions.[8]

It is evident that a free Catholic media and the freedom of Catholic assembly were institutionalized within Dutch Catholicism by 1965. The principle of free theological inquiry had been defended, although the institutional embodiment of the principle in autonomous centers of learning was not yet achieved.

ECUMENISM AND NEW COALITION PARTNERS

One of the most important shifts in the role of the Catholic episcopacy in the post-Vatican period is the way in which the bishop has become, in several countries, an ecumenical religious leader as well as a general socio-ethical leader. This development is especially pronounced within the Netherlands, where the bishops—Cardinal Alfrink and Bishop Bekkers in particular—are general Christian and national figures. The Dutch bishops achieved their new role by looking and speaking beyond their borders, employing the particularist Catholic symbol system to defend more general values shared by other groups within Dutch society. They found themselves, as a result, being addressed by individuals and groups from outside their borders.

Catholic ecumenism began in the Netherlands, as in most other Western nations, with conversation between theological elites in the late 1950s. The Catholic return to biblical sources during that period stimulated the development. Thus, for example, in 1958 the faculties of the Catholic seminary in Warmond and the Protestant theological department at Leiden began holding periodic exchanges for theological discussion. In 1959 in a speech on the topic of ecumenism, Alfrink proposed that Catholics abandon all nonessentials which might be stumbling blocks to Christian unity.[9] In the late 1950s Catholic priests and laity were taking part in bible retreats. In 1960 the Annual St. Thomas Aquinas Dispute for Catholic University students in Amsterdam invited the participation of members of the Netherlands Christian Student Association and the Free Thinking

8. *KA*, XX, *21* (May 21, 1965), columns 597–600.
9. *KA*, XIV, *43* (November 20, 1959), column 1029.

Christian Student Federation. In 1961, the bishops approved the statutes of a new Catholic bible society, commissioning the society to produce a new translation of the bible.

There was nothing, however, in those first gestures of Catholic ecumenism to suggest the explosion in ecumenism which characterized the late 1960s within Dutch Catholicism. Participation in the ecumenical movement was an elite movement limited largely to the theologians and university circles. The bishops' first reactions to any popular movement toward ecumenism, as evidenced by the inclusion of non-Catholic partners in the church discussion-group movement, were decidedly cool, with the bishops recommending severe caution in undertaking Catholic-Protestant popular discussions. Here again, we see the pattern whereby the authorities' first response is a holding action.[10]

The Dutch bishops first began to show signs of looking beyond their borders in 1961. In a collective letter announcing the meeting of the World Council of Churches in New Delhi, the bishops remarked: "What is happening in New Delhi is not a matter of indifference to us Catholics. The scandal of division among Christians must be felt by us too as a genuine scandal." They directed that a mass be offered in every Catholic parish during the week of November 19-26 for the success of Protestant unity in New Delhi.[11] The bishops addressed their letter of September 5, 1961, which announced their hopes for the second session of the Vatican Council, to all Protestants and non-believers, following the lead of John XXIII.[12] They continued this practice in 1964, addressing a collective letter to "Everyman" within Dutch society.

The bishops' approach to Christians beyond their own Catholic borders provoked an echo from Protestant Netherlands. In 1961, Cardinal Alfrink received an open letter from the Protestant Netherlands requesting that he voice its concerns at the Council for specific changes which would lower the barriers separating Catholics and Protestants, such as Catholic teaching on Mary and the authoritative role of the bible in the church. The following year, the Cardinal received a second open letter from Protestants asking him to favor changes in the Council document "On Revelation," which would

10. See the bishops' letter in *KA*, XVII, *3* (January 19, 1962), columns 59–66, where the bishops reminded such discussion groups that they must have no pretension of being "official" and, if meeting regularly, must include a theological expert.
11. *KA*, XVI, *48* (December 1, 1961), columns 1139–1140.
12. *KA*, XVIII, *40* (October 4, 1963), columns 999–1002.

emphasize the irreducible primacy of scripture in the life of the Roman Church.[13]

The interventions and votes of the Dutch episcopacy at the Council gave a response to the questions and requests posed in these open letters from the Protestant Netherlands. During the discussion of the schema "On the Church," for example, Cardinal Alfrink led the successful Council fight against attempts to include new titles for Mary within the Council document, titles such as "Mary, Mediatrix of all Graces" and "Mary, the Mother of the Church." Mgr. van Dodewaard of Haarlem, in a Council intervention, claimed that the ecumenical movement was the work of the Holy Spirit. He also intervened in the Council discussion on the document "On Revelation" to appeal for a statement which declared that all of divine revelation could be found in scripture. Bishop Bekkers once put his position on ecumenism this way: "We must go together to the very edge of the gap which divides us until we are moved to go even further."[14]

The Catholic Conversion of Princess Irene

The announcement of the conversion of Princess Irene to Roman Catholicism in January 1964 was a very important precipitant for official Catholic-Protestant discussions. A Dutch newspaper reporter accidently discovered Irene in Madrid communicating at a Catholic mass. Irene declared to the reporter that she had already been secretly received into the church by Cardinal Alfrink. Asked about the reason for her conversion, she offered the jaunty comment, "I did it to increase religious tolerance and ecumenism."

Irene's secret conversion raised several serious questions in the mind of the Moderamen of the General Synod of the Dutch Reformed Church, which addressed a public letter to Cardinal Alfrink asking whether the Princess had been rebaptized upon her reception into the Catholic church. They also wanted to know why her conversion had been kept secret. Finally, they inquired whether the Cardinal agreed with the seeming import of the Princess' statement that individual conversion was the best way to achieve ecumenism.

The Cardinal, embarrassed by this challenge of his rebaptism of Irene, at first refused to answer the letter, claiming that his answer

13. For these Protestant requests, see *KA*, XVI, *46* (November 15, 1961), columns 945ff; and *KA*, XVII, *18* (May 4, 1962), columns 409ff.
14. For Alfrink's action at the Council, see Ton Oostveen, *Bernard Alfrink, Katholiek*, p. 76; Dodewaard at the Council in *KA*, XX, *6* (February 5, 1965), columns 195–196; *KA*, XX, *51* and *52* (December 17–24, 1965), columns 1381–1408; Bekkers' quote from *KA*, XX, *18* (April 30, 1965), columns 531–532.

would betray a personal pastoral relationship. The Moderamen, however, pressed its claim for information with the reminder that a rebaptism ignored the doctrine that even non-Catholic baptisms are valid. At last, the Cardinal gave way and apologized for his ecumenical faux pas, claiming that he had acceded to an expressed wish of Irene's, in part because he lacked precise information about the circumstances of her initial baptism in London during the war. This ecumenical blunder would, in ensuing years, lead to a far-reaching joint agreement between Dutch Catholics and Protestants on baptism. Alfrink also answered another question posed by the Moderamen, speaking this time in the name of all Dutch bishops: ''According to Catholic convictions the way to Christian unity does not consist in attempts to win individual converts.''

The headstrong Irene insisted on active participation in Carlist political rallies, thereby causing embarrassment to the Dutch government's relations with Spain and violating the constitutional principle that the monarchy remain above politics. The government, under a Catholic prime minister, finally determined that the Princess should marry the Carlist pretender to the throne without parliamentary consent, thus forfeiting her right of succession.

Irene's conversion and abdication raised the theoretical question in Dutch political life of whether a Catholic monarch would be acceptable to the nation. This question had much the same symbolic import in Dutch society as John F. Kennedy's presidential candidacy in the United States. Neither country had an established religion. Neither country's constitution contained any religious test for the head of state. The question was of symbolic importance to the Catholic populations of both countries. In both countries the symbolic question registers an important shift in the civil religion, outside the body of any church.

Irene's mother, Queen Juliana, shies away from formal relations with any of the main Dutch churches. She attends, by choice, the services of a small, unimportant Dutch congregation. Official publicity for Queen Juliana stresses the point that her religious education was personally provided by her mother, Queen Wilhelmina. The four crown princesses attended non-religious schools. The Dutch monarchy, in the classical period of columnization, was one of the few important public symbols of national unity. In a strange way, the monarchical house mirrors almost every strand of Dutch society. While the Queen and her husband are Protestants, the Queen's mother-in-law and one of her daughters are Catholics. Two of her sons-in-law are Catholic, two are Protestant. One of her daughters is non-church. The monarchy in Dutch society is not only a political instrument above party politics; it is also the most concrete embodiment of Dutch civil religion.

The theoretical question about a Catholic monarch raised to public consciousness the issue of Dutch civil religion. Was the civil religion Protestant? Was the Netherlands still a Protestant nation? Dutch Protestants, especially the supporters of the Christian Historical Party in the parliament, clung to the House of Orange as a particularist Protestant symbol.

When the leader of the Catholic Party in parliament, Dr. Norbert Schmelzer, posed the theoretical question of a Catholic monarch in parliament, the parliamentary caucuses of the Catholic KVP, the Socialist PVDA, and the Liberal VVD reported that it went without saying that a Catholic could be monarch, although the VVD contained some opposition to this view. The Protestant parties refused at first to answer Schmelzer's question, and finally delivered a hedged response which reflected genuine opposition within their parties to the idea.

In a public-opinion poll conducted among a representative sample of the population, Dutchmen were asked at the time, "Must a monarch who converts to Catholicism abdicate the right to the throne?" Seventy-three percent saw no contradiction between being a Catholic and occupying the throne. Twenty-three percent thought a Catholic monarch would have to abdicate, and 4 percent gave no answer. The percentages by political party were:

	Can remain	Must abdicate	No opinion
Catholic KVP	97%		3%
Socialist PVDA	66%	29%	5%
Liberal VVD	70%	30%	
Protestant Parties	50%	46%	4%

By the mid-1960s, the symbolic issue of majority acceptance of the rightful inclusion of Catholics within Dutch culture had been resolved.[15]

15. The documents for following the Irene Affair in Dutch political life are available in *KA*, XIX, *13* (March 27, 1964), columns 372ff; the handling by Alfrink of the rebaptism is found in

CONGREGATIONAL FORM FOR SPECIALIZED PARISHES

The traditional chain of command in Catholic decision-making led from pope and Roman curia through the papal nuncio to the local bishop and from the bishop to the pastor of territorially based parishes. Within his parish, the pastor had final authority over the disposition of funds, the allocation of work assignments of his priest assistants, and the determination of services for lay clients. Assistant priests and laity were ''parts'' of his parish as he, in turn, was a ''part'' of the diocese.

We have already seen that in the post-Vatican church, intermediare structures, in the form of episcopal conferences, increasingly intervene between Rome and the local bishop. Full coordination of pastoral strategy would seem to require intermediate units between the bishop and the territorial parish. There are three lingering problems in international Catholicism in planning at the diocesan level: (1) finding effective sub-units within the diocese; (2) coordinating efforts of diocesan and religious-order priests; and (3) finding a functional congregational micro-unit to replace or supplement the parish.

In the late 1960s Dutch Catholicism witnessed far-reaching experiments directed toward solving these problems. Dutch dioceses, even in the period of traditional Catholicism, made much more of the concept of deaneries—territorial sub-units within the diocese—and the office of the dean, a senior priest with responsibilities over several parish units, than is customary, for example, in the American church. In the 1960s the deaneries and the office of dean gained even more importance. By the beginning of the 1970s the longstanding rivalries between religious-order priests and diocesan priests had also vanished.

Were new models emerging, between 1958 and 1965, for pluriform parishes with specialized liturgies and services catering to different religious needs within the Catholic population? If so, what was the reaction of the social authorities? Did they encourage or stifle the new endeavors?

In the larger Dutch cities at least, long before Vatican II, individual Catholics voted with their feet, by attending the diocesan or religious-order church of their choice. One of Alfrink's first difficulties when

---

KA, XIX, *21* (May 22, 1964), columns 567–569. The constitutional issue of a Catholic monarch (no problem) is handled in J. P. van Banning, *Het Huwelijk van Hare Koninklijk Hoogheid Prinses Irene* (Zaltbommel: Europese Bibliotheek, 1964), pp. 11–18. For the general concept of civil religion, see Russell E. Richey and Donald Jones, eds., *American Civil Religion* (New York: Harper and Row, 1974).

he was still co-adjutor Archbishop of Utrecht in 1952 came from his attempts to stop Catholics in the village of Huissen from attending a Dominican church instead of their local parish church.[16]

The aim of the congregational micro-unit in my hypothesis of a post-Vatican "cultural-pastoral" strategy (Table 3) is the socialization of a layman able to live in a pluralistic secular society as a Christian and a citizen simultaneously; he is to be the key agent of Catholic influence. The clergyman's main role is one of teacher-counselor or pastor, who aids the members of his congregation without infringing upon their individual autonomy.

Some questions about new models for pluriform parishes are answered by observing the developments within a student parish, the Student Ecclesia, in Amsterdam in its first years.[17] In September 1960, the two Jesuit moderators of Catholic University students in Amsterdam inaugurated a special student Sunday liturgy in Amsterdam. They used, in their services, Dutch translations of the Psalms put to music by the French liturgist, J. Gelineau. They employed hymns based on biblical themes and composed in contemporary Dutch by Theo Naastepad and Huub Oosterhuis, to replace the introit, gradual, and communion texts as prescribed for the mass according to the Roman rite. Similar experiments were taking place in other parishes, such as the Bos chapel in Nijmegen and the student parish in Leiden.

Within the first year, with the able assistance of a liturgical composer, Bernard Huybers, the Amsterdam student church featured hymns which emphasized "rhythm, improvisation, genuine give and take between instruments, choir, and community song." This was a startling innovation in a Catholic world mainly accustomed to Gregorian chant or traditional hymnal music. There was an effort to divide chores between priest, choir, congregation, and lay readers, so that no one need feel that he was a passive "part" and not an element in the liturgical happening.[18] In the fall of 1961, the campus minister Jan van Kilsdonk announced a sermon series around bible themes, liturgical songs, texts, and scripture readings to replace texts and readings approved by the Roman rite for the mass.

These campus ministers saw the Catholic university milieu as one of great importance, because it embraced a crucial target group for the

16. Oostveen, *Bernard Alfrink, Katholiek*, pp. 30–31.
17. Unless otherwise specified the following account follows C. Stuldreher, "De Amsterdamse Studenten Ecclesia—Over de Oorsprong van Een Conflict," in *Alternatieve Groepen in de Kerk*, pp. 24–58.
18. Bernard Huybers makes the point that everyone at the eucharist must feel that he is a vital element in his *Door Podium en Zaal Tegelijk* (Hilversum: Gooi and Sticht, 1969).

church's pastoral activities (given the dangers of lapsing) and because it could produce Catholics capable of approaching their faith "critically" as autonomous adults. The sermons, inaugurated in 1961, avoided moralizing exhortations or dogmatic conclusions, and concentrated instead upon creating an atmosphere which would lead to personal reflection and responsibility. Statistical analysis of these early sermons and other liturgical texts indicates a shift, in comparison with the Roman rite texts, from themes of transcendence to themes of immanence, from non-biblical to biblical and from normative to suggestive language. The shift in language illustrates the emerging autonomy of the laity: the new liturgy was leaving the concrete application of Catholic principles to the lay congregation.[19]

The Amsterdam liturgical experiment was such a success that by the second year, a third Sunday service had to be added to accommodate the crowds, which included many non-university students. Consultation with the local territorial pastor led to the expansion of liturgical services to include baptisms and weddings, alongside the eucharist, confession, and counseling service. The student church became a parish without boundaries.

In 1962 the staff of campus ministers was expanded to include several new members, among them Huub Oosterhuis, an internationally known poet and liturgist. Oosterhuis self-consciously experimented with the creation of new liturgical forms, using music and texts adapted to modern Dutch language and thought patterns. In November 1962 Oosterhuis wrote an article entitled "Responsibility for a Liturgical Experiment," for the leading Dutch periodical on the liturgy, *Tijdschift Voor Liturgie,* in which he described and defended his efforts. A sample of the new liturgy for Advent used at the student church was published that same year by the bishops' publishing house, Gooi and Sticht.

As the experiments at the student church began to gain some national prominence, Oosterhuis was invited to address the Liturgical Center in the diocese of Den Bosch on March 24-25, 1963. Bishop Bekkers' response to the Amsterdam liturgical experiment was enthusiastic. Bekkers closed the two-day session by remarking: "Experiment fits in very well with the structure of the church. We must try to adapt to the spirit of our own times in our reflections upon new liturgical experiments. I must add this: if this is the kind of 'experiment'

19. See Andre Agterof, Pim LeCor, and Joop van Velzen, "De Aksieradius van Kontemplasie-Een Onderzoek Naar Preken en Liturgiese Teksten in de Rooms-Katholiek Studenten Ekklesia te Amsterdam," unpublished paper, Catholic Institute of Theology, Amsterdam, 1973.

we can expect, then experiment will fit in very well indeed with the structure of the church and shall be absolutely indispensable."

On December 22, 1963, two episcopal visitors were commissioned by Mgr. van Dodewaard of Haarlem to report upon the experimental service in the student church. They wrote a long and carefully written report to the bishop giving their judgment: "Father van Kilsdonk gave a fine homily. . . . He justly enjoyed the rapt attention of his audience. . . . The service was both simple and tasteful. Everything went without flaw and as a genuine *community* celebration. . . . The combination of community song and a choir singing in parts lent to the service a tone of the highest quality. It was a feast!" Nevertheless, they added: "This service is completely contrary to the Ignatian principle: nothing without the bishops' permission. Leaving aside for the moment the older church decrees, the concluding speech of Pope Paul at the end of the Second Session of the present Council and The Constitution on the Liturgy, Section 22, Paragraph 3, expressly forbids what was done here. We can only regret it."

Despite the fact that the liturgy at the student church was against the juridical norms of the church, the official visitors recommended that the experiment be sustained. "It seems to us that a demand that this service, despite everything, be made to conform with the presently governing regulations would be a mistake. The service itself was extremely worthwhile. *It relates our future intellectuals to the Church,* and, hence, to Christ."

The episcopal visitors suggested that the bishop petition the Holy See for permission to grant the student parish a three-year experimental status. "In this way we can avoid a great deal of unnecessary conflict. The service can only be labeled 'out of place' because current church law allows no room for it."

On April 19, 1964, the campus ministers announced at the Sunday eucharist that the bishops had given temporary approval to their liturgical center as a pilot project for a new Dutch liturgy. Long-term approval awaited visitation by a delegation of the national commission on the liturgy. In the meantime, however, the student church had introduced two new variations within the liturgy. The priests began to distribute the bread into the outstretched hands of the congregation at communion instead of on their tongues, giving as justification for the novelty both the words of Jesus, *"Take and eat"* and the practice of the early church. In explaining this change, the church bulletin claimed that the gesture indicated a *more adult* response than allowing oneself to be fed. The second innovation was more startling: the use of a Dutch canon of the mass composed by Huub Oosterhuis to replace the prescribed Latin canon.

The visitation by the delegates from the Dutch episcopal commission took place on January 31, 1965. Upon receiving their recommendation for approval, the Dutch bishops petitioned Rome for approval of the experiment. After months of waiting, the bishops received a letter in November 1965 from the secretary of the Vatican commission on the liturgy, Father A. Bugnini, forbidding the use of Oosterhuis' Dutch canon, effective December 1, 1965, and directing that the student church return to universal church practice.

The Dutch bishops and their advisors felt relatively certain that the use of the vernacular in the canon of the mass would shortly be a universal Catholic practice. The bishops took the Roman directive under consideration. At their episcopal conference meeting, Bishop Bluyssen urged a compromise formula for repetitioning Rome which had been suggested to him by the Amsterdam group. In their new request the Dutch bishops sought experimental status for five parishes.

In the beginning of 1966 the request was granted. Dutch Catholicism had five pilot churches—non-territorial communities with specialized liturgies and services. Each of these parishes included a collegial team of priests, each member with a pastoral specialization. The visibility and success of the student parish and its contacts with priests and seminarians throughout the country promoted wide acceptance, especially among the younger clergy, of this new role definition of the priest. Liturgical texts from the five experimental centers became nationally available for use through the bishops' publishing house. All of the Catholic Netherlands saw the results of the new liturgy on the biweekly Sunday morning KRO television broadcasts.

The initial success of the student parish points to two themes which would become extremely prominent in the following years: First, the Dutch authorities were mindful of the need for church order. They feared that wildcat experimentation would lead to pastoral chaos and confusion. If the *juridical* order of the Roman church did not offer solutions for genuinely felt pastoral needs, the bishops were willing to experiment with a *pastoral* order for their church province. They preferred open experiments which could be monitored to driving experimentation underground. Second, the experience with the student church in the early 1960s gave credence to a widely held belief that what was being done today in the Netherlands by way of experimentation would be approved tomorrow for the universal church. And in fact, the view of liturgical renewal proposed by the student church in 1965 was mirrored, almost literally, in the Vatican document for the whole church issued by A. Bugnini in June 1968.[20] Within a few years, distributing communion in the hand and the recitation of a vernacular canon became the common practice of the European church. By the mid-1960s the Dutch were an avant-garde, and they were aware of it.

CONTESTATION GROUPS

Not all Dutch Catholics, as we would expect, were equally enthusiastic about the structural change. Already in their Lenten letter of 1958, the bishops saw two streams within Dutch Catholicism. The first wanted speedier change because it saw the alternatives as reform versus defection from the church. The second thought the changes were touching the very essence of the church. The bishops tried to assure both sides that they felt their problems as their own. The episcopal remedy was dialogue: "You must continue to talk to one another."[21]

The letters to the editor in the national dailies *De Tijd* and *De Volkskrant* registered the unrest among more traditional Catholics. There were those who saw the switch to the vernacular in the liturgy, inaugurated in 1964, as the work of a small pressure group within the church. One of the letter writers complained about the liturgical changes, "Every attempt of the individual to concentrate upon his private prayer is impossible because of the racket. The holy mass has become a show!"[22]

In 1965 the bishops reflected once again on these divisions in a Lenten letter on catechesis. They announced the forthcoming new Dutch catechism. They knew that many were pleased with changes and others were wary that received truths were being undermined. The bishops tried to explain the new methods in catechesis. The best contemporary insights into pedagogy suggested that the traditional method of question and answer or memorizing of formulas was not successful in educating and involving youth in the faith. Besides, faith did not consist of formulas. "Belief is not a question of learning something but primarily of living something." They ended the letter by calling all parties in the church to work together to form a church

---

20. See Stuldreher, "De Amsterdamse Studenten Ecclesia—Over de Oorsprong van Een Conflict," p. 56.
21. *KA*, XIII, 9 (February 28, 1958), columns 215–220.
22. *De Volkskrant*, January 16, 1965, p. 10.

where "each individual has his own active role to fulfill within the community of God's people. . . . *Giving a new content to the proper role of each individual believer in the church,* from pope to bishops, priests, religious, laity—is one of the most important tasks which the Council has set for itself."[23]

In the spring of 1965 a group of sixteen Catholics, disturbed by the developments, sent a public letter to Cardinal Alfrink. The group had started its own stenciled magazine, *Confrontatie,* in 1964. They complained about unlawful experiments in catechesis, dogma, and the liturgy. They sought normative and not experimental leadership from bishops and priests. They attacked the "illusion" that young people or even adult Catholics could be trusted to form their own conscience properly on questions of faith and morals, citing a passage from Paul VI's encyclical *Ecclesiam Suam* to justify their point. The letter charged that theologians were presenting their own views instead of church dogma, thus opening all questions to discussion. They listed, as examples, new opinions about the divinity of Jesus, miracles, the resurrection, the real presence in the eucharist, the possibility of remarriage after divorce, the existence of a separately created spiritual soul, and obedience to the pope. They cited the words of Pope Paul VI on June 18, 1965, condemning "exaggerated ecumenism." The group sought at least one Latin mass in every Dutch parish every Sunday. They ended by telling the bishops the kind of leadership they looked for: "We shall be very happy if we hear from you more open, clear warnings against dangerous errors in our church province and the denial or minimizing of papal authority."[24]

The bishops were inclined in 1965 to dismiss this rather small *Confrontie* group as a tiny reactionary segment of integralist Catholics reflecting a position of cultural deprivation in the face of change. I have mentioned them here because they are the only example of a separate contestation group within Dutch Catholicism in the period before 1965. Also, they bear witness to my point that the Dutch bishops were permitting new ideas to gain ground.

CENTER-PERIPHERY CONFLICTS: HOLLAND VS. ROME

It would be very difficult to speak of real conflicts between Dutch Catholicism and the Roman authorities prior to 1962. There were

23. *KA,* XX, *16* (April 16, 1965), columns 466–469. Italics mine.
24. *KA,* XX, *24* (June 11, 1965), columns 676–680.

irritations, of course. In the 1950s progressives were irked by a negative review of Professor Rogier's monumental history of Dutch Catholicism in *L'Osservatore Romano,* in which the reviewer found Rogier too jaundiced in his judgments of the Roman handling of the restoration of the Dutch hierarchy in 1853 and of the modernist crisis. Progressives chafed at the visitation of Sebastian Tromp, S.J., to the bishops' seminaries in 1954 and the Catholic University in Nijmegen in 1955 to report on their orthodoxy. They exchanged "horror stories" when the popular Professor Steur was relieved of his teaching post at the seminary in Waarmond as a result of the Tromp visitation. Clerical wags, with a play upon his last name, his new pastorate, and his safe removal by Rome from the Waarmond seminary, spoke of his being "pasteurized." Still, traditional Dutch Catholicism probably had fewer of these "horror stories" than other national churches.

The Dutch bishops' 1960 Christmas letter was translated into several foreign languages. In June 1962, however, the Salesian fathers in Rome were instructed to remove the Italian translation of the Christmas letter from their bookstore. The story circulated in the Netherlands that several Roman curial theologians at the Lateran University in Rome were planning articles in their theological journal, *Divinitas,* which would protest against the Christmas letter's novel concept of collegiality, with the argument that it undermined papal infallibility and contained dangerous overtones of the heresies of laicism and conciliarism.

The chairman of the St. Willibrord Association, Jan Groot, himself a co-author of the letter, especially the sections on collegiality, dismissed the censorship action in a KRO national television interview with the remark that it revealed "the textbook mentality of the Roman theologians." Cardinal Alfrink was more diplomatic in his public assessment of the Curia's reasons for this gross act of censorship: "Let us put it this way. Although the letter was considered in every way acceptable and worthwhile, some found that in a few passages the formulation could have been more carefully worded or the presentation fuller. They feared that these passages might be misunderstood by the readers. At no point did they entertain the slightest doubt about the orthodoxy of what the authors actually intended to say."[25] The controversy died down. The case involved, at any event, censorship in another part of the church.

Reactions were much less cool, however, when the Curia tried to impose censorship on Dutch soil. Van Kilsdonk's speech asking the

25. *KA*, XVII, *26* (June 29, 1962), columns 625–628.

Dutch bishops to form a loyal opposition against the Roman Curia did not go unnoticed in Rome. Evidently, Alfrink's rebuke of van Kilsdonk was not enough. Even after protracted consultations during the first session of the Second Vatican Council between the Dutch bishops and the officials of the Holy Office, especially Mgr. Parente, then assessor for the Holy Office, the Curia demanded sterner episcopal measures than Alfrink's guidelines of responsibility within public discussion. On December 3, 1962, the Holy Office informed van Kilsdonk's bishop, Mgr. van Dodewaard, that "a man who is capable of such utterance is not suitable to function as a moderator for Catholic students." The Holy Office directed that van Dodewaard remove van Kilsdonk from his function and suppress the publication of his speech in the annual St. Adelbert issue. When van Dodewaard hesitated to comply, the Holy Office leaked its letter to him to *L'Osservatore Romano.*

Rumors about the incident and later publicity rallied support for the beleagured van Kilsdonk. The editors of the magazine threatened to publish blank pages where the speech should have been, and to inform its readers that it had been suppressed on instructions from the Holy Office. The Council of Catholic Campus Ministers, a group of Dutch Reformed theologians, and nine teachers at the Gereformeerden Free University sent telegrams to van Dodewaard and Alfrink protesting the curial attempt at suppressing free speech in the church. In January 1963, van Dodewaard announced to the press that he had no intention of removing van Kilsdonk.

Foiled in its efforts to gain episcopal cooperation, the Holy Office put pressure upon the Jesuit Vicar General in Rome. The Vicar General, Fr. Swain, informed van Kilsdonk that he was imposing a three-year sentence of silence upon him. Van Kilsdonk was told to refrain from any publication or public remarks until 1965. His Dutch superiors, however, were very supple in interpreting the command. Thus, Bishop Bekkers immediately invited him to give the official retreats for the priests of Den Bosch for the following two summers. Van Kilsdonk's Jesuit superiors looked the other way as he continued to write the weekly bulletins for the student parish. These bulletins, amounting to theological tracts for the times, enjoyed a wide circulation among the clergy and laity beyond the Amsterdam parish. There was little support among the authorities for Roman efforts to impose the old controls.[26]

26. The public evidence and all citations used here can be found in *KA*, XVIII, *1* and *2* (January 4–11, 1963).

The Nieuwe Linie Affair

Religious orders and congregations have long been a Roman foil against excessive local or national autonomy. On more than one occasion, religious-order priests in a national setting have been the primary agents of Roman purposes, acting as watchdogs of orthodoxy or sending reports and recommendations, without the knowledge of the local authorities, to Rome. The fathers-general of the religious orders reside in Rome. Their "subjects" in various countries are directly answerable to their religious-order provincial and to the father-general, and not to the local bishop. The older orders enjoy privileges of "exemption," that is, they can conduct specific religious activities exempt from the rules binding upon the local diocesan clergy.

Many of the received concepts about religious-order priests no longer apply in the post-Vatican church. In particular, the Roman authorities can no longer assume automatic compliance with their directives. Indeed, in several countries, the religious-order priests have provided the leadership in protest movements. These developments are too large to relate here. Put in simple terms, however, the religious orders have also been experiencing shifts in role definitions in response to demands for greater personal or local autonomy, for recognition that participant members of the order are elements whose talents and wishes must be respected and not merely parts of the social system.

The shift among the religious orders in the Netherlands became very pronounced in the 1960s. Dutch Jesuits, Dominicans, and Augustinians experienced a series of conflicts with their religious superiors in Rome over the meaning of obedience.[27] Dutch religious-order priests often found that their ties with the local bishop and diocesan priests within the national setting were closer than those with fellow-members in other countries.

The Jesuits in Holland published a widely read weekly called *De Linie*. In the early 1960s the structure and editorial policy of *De Linie* were changed. It was renamed *De Nieuwe Linie*, and combined Jesuit and lay control of the editorial board.[28] The editor-in-chief was a layman. The structural change was hailed as a symbol of a new era of clerical-lay cooperation in the church. Joint control also gave the

27. On conflicts between Dutch Augustinians and their Roman superiors, see "Renewal of Religious Life: The Dutch Augustinians," in *IDOC*, no volume indicated, 3 (May 9, 1970), 38–62.
28. Full accounts and documents for the *Nieuwe Linie* affair are available in *KA*, XIX, 22 (May 29, 1964), columns 609–614, and Nos. 34–35 (August 21–28, 1964), column 913.

magazine more freedom in its dealings with church authorities, who have more difficulty in controlling the laity than the clergy, the clergy being bound by a vow of obedience. *De Nieuwe Linie* was also new in that it pursued a more critical, "leftist" policy in its treatment of church and national politics.

The Roman authorities were unhappy with the newspaper's new direction. The Jesuit father-general tried to persuade the editors to pursue a softer policy; when the editors refused to conform, he was pressured to take more drastic steps. On April 27, 1964, the Dutch provincial of the Jesuits reluctantly informed the Jesuit staff of *De Nieuwe Linie* that he had received instructions from Rome that they must resign their positions on the paper.

The story was carried the following day in *De Tijd*. The Annual General Disputation for Catholic Students, meeting in Amsterdam, immediately sent a telegram to the father-general protesting the lack of dialogue and the scandal to clergy-lay relations involved in his decision. On May 2, 1964, the editor-in-chief of *De Nieuwe Linie*, Gerard van den Boomen, printed a personal editorial stating his deep regret. Van den Boomen praised the Dutch Jesuit provincial for his handling of the crisis. The provincial and his staff had been open and encouraging in the new cooperative effort between lay and Jesuit staff, and the provincial had tried to dissuade the general from his decision. Van den Boomen protested that the magazine staff had never been consulted. A telephone call by the editorial board to the Roman authorities requesting a meeting had been unanswered.

The *Nieuwe Linie* affair provoked a chain reaction within the Dutch Catholic public. The annual meeting of the Dutch Catholic Journalists' Association, gathering in Maastricht, sent telegrams to the Jesuit father-general and the press services, protesting both the lack of consultation and the Roman authorities' injustice in breaking three contracts without prior consultation. The Union of Catholic Student Associations sent their protests to Cardinal Alfrink and the Jesuit father-general. The protest reiterated the theme of a right of consultation, adding that the *De Nieuwe Linie* experiment of cooperative lay-clerical control provided "an excellent illustration . . . *of the modern idea of the church* which invites everyone, priest and lay alike, *on an equal footing* and according to each one's abilities, to realize the values of Christianity." In the issue of *De Tijd* for March 5, 1964, Professor J. J. van de Ven, professor of law at the University of Utrecht, commented: "Our problem is no longer so much the emancipation of the laity from clerical control as the attempts to stifle the integrity of the priest."

The *Nieuwe Linie* affair illustrates how intensely the issues of free public opinion, dialogue, and experiments in priest-lay relations were being experienced in the mid-1960s. In other countries the loss of church subsidy for a journal would have meant its death.[29] The fact that the *Nieuwe Linie* has continued to publish without church subsidy is a sign that Dutch Catholicism has resources to support a free press. The Dutch authorities found ways to continue the *Nieuwe Linie* experiment of lay-clergy cooperation. In August 1964, two of the Jesuit editors, Jos Arts and Nico van Hees, after full consultation with their local Jesuit provincial and Bishop Bekkers, requested permission to leave the Jesuits. They were received as priests in Bekkers' diocese with permission to continue their work as editors on the *Nieuwe Linie*.

The Terruwe Affair

Historical revisionism plays an important role in freeing a collectivity to reexamine its past in ways which open up new possibilities for collective experimentation. There were two important symptoms of this sort of revisionism during the period 1958-1965. Their impact, although difficult to measure, was still being referred to a decade later by Dutch Catholics as major turning points in the rethinking of traditional Catholicism.

In 1963, the Catholic journalist, Michel van der Plas, compiled a documentary history of Roman Catholicism for the years 1925-1935, entitled *From the Period of the Rich Roman Life*. His book, an immediate bestseller, was a compilation of excerpts from sermons, newspaper articles, advertisements, parish bulletins, photos, and cartoons from that period of triumphalist separatism. An outsider reading the book today gasps at the Catholic self-satisfaction and intolerance, the inflated clericalism and sticky piety that passed for "the rich Roman life." Dutch Catholics who lived through the period described by the book testify that they had the same reaction upon first reading the book—a shock of recognition. *From the Period of the Rich Roman Life* is often one-sided, negative, and debunking in its selection of documentary material. It leaves out much of the more whimsical side, and also the deeply spiritual side, of "the rich Roman life." The principles governing the choice of items for the book seemed to be van der Plas' opposition to columnization, clericalism, and lay passivity within the church, and his dislike of exaggerated obeisance to

---

29. Compare the failure of progressive journals to survive without subsidy from church officers in the case of *Herder Correspondence* in England and *Publik* in Germany.

Rome and sentimental otherworldly piety.[30] However, the phrase "the rich Roman life" became overnight a catch-phrase among Catholics to refer to how bad things were before.

A second indicator of a debunking spirit is in the phonograph records and theatre and television appearance of the popular Dutch Catholic comedian, Frons Jansen, who packed theatres in the early 1960s with his jokes. "In our church formerly everything was forbidden, except what was allowed—and you had to do that!"[31]

In the midst of this period of historical revisionism, Dutch Catholicism was confronted with a painful memory from its recent past which led many in the community to take a new hard look at the adjective "Roman" modifying "Catholic." In 1950 a commission of moral theologians was deputed to investigate the moral teachings of Professor W. J. Duijnstee, C.S.S.R., of the Catholic University of Nijmegen and the psychiatrist Dr. Anna Terruwe. The commission, headed by Professor F. Feron, requested that Dr. Terruwe render an account of her thought and practice in the areas of sexual morality. When Terruwe wrote her account and forwarded it to the commission, the commission met and gave its report to Cardinal De Jong. He and the other bishops accepted the commission's finding and sent a jointly signed report to the Holy Office.

In their report, the Dutch bishops affirmed that Dr. Terruwe followed Catholic principles. They found that her book contained no theological errors. The bishops stated that Terruwe denied Roman charges that she counseled masturbation. The bishops' report ended by saying that the investigating commission was convinced of Terruwe's sincerity and that she was "orthodox in belief and prudent in her practice."

The matter rested there until the visitation of Sebastian Tromp to Nijmegen University in 1955. Tromp, a Dutch theologian who served at that time as consultor for the Holy Office, had been commissioned by the Holy Office to reinvestigate Terruwe and three priests on the theology faculty, especially Professor Duinstee. Tromp's visitation resulted in a letter to the Dutch bishops from the Holy Office in 1956. The bishops were commanded to publish the letter in the

---

30. Michel van der Plas, ed., *Uit Het Rijke Roomsche Leven* (Utrecht: Ambo Books, 1962). This Catholic revisionism triggered parallel attempts to debunk its own past from the Protestant and Socialist columns two years later. See A. C. de Gooyer, ed., *Het Beeld der Vad'ren* (Utrecht: Ambo Books, 1964) (Protestant) and D. van der Stoep, ed., *De Rode Rakkers* (Utrecht: Ambo Books, 1964) (Socialist).

31. Jansen's joke is cited in J. M. Thurlings, *De Wankele Zuil* (Amersfoort: De Hoorstink, 1971), p. 153.

analecta for each diocese. The Holy Office's letter began, "The Holy See . . . is acquainted with false teaching and practice in the area of sexuality and asceticism." The letter listed eight errors to be found within Dutch Catholicism: (1) Some Catholic psychiatrists too easily see self-denial and self-control as instances of psychological repression. (2) Those psychiatrists approach sexual difficulties as psychoneurotic problems. (3) Supported by certain moral theologians, the psychiatrists claim that psychoneurotic patients lack the necessary freedom to be morally responsible for their actions. (4) The psychiatrists claim that in order to achieve freedom for the patient, the analyst must dispel the patient's fears, even the fear of God. (5) These analysts deny the doctrine of freedom of the will. (6) The analysts claim that everything is possible sexually, without anxiety and fear. (7) The psychiatrists hold that "completely healthy persons can put themselves at the disposal of the psychoneurotic from a motive of Christian charity. They can engage in objectively impermissible sexual behavior without being implicated in any moral evil." (8) On many occasions the psychiatrists conducted patients to a house of prostitution. Even priests and members of religious orders were advised to "gaze upon a completely naked person of the opposite sex and to have sexual relations with her with the goal of relieving sexual frustrations or dispelling morbid curiosity." While this letter named no names, it took little skill in the art of curial nuance to know that it was directed at Dr. Terruwe and her friend, Professor Duijnstee. The Dutch bishops informed Dr. Terruwe of the contents of the letter of the Holy Office.

Within a few months, the Dutch bishops received a letter from the Vatican instructing the bishops to abide by the following directives: No seminarian may consult a female psychiatrist; if it seems necessary for his cure that he consult a female psychiatrist, he should be sent away from the seminary; his need for a woman psychiatrist is a sign from God that he lacks a vocation; no priest should be allowed to consult a female psychiatrist.

The letter from the Congregation of the Seminaries was an obvious reference to Dr. Terruwe, one of the few female psychiatrists in the Netherlands with a practice including priests and seminarians. The papal nuncio sent a copy of the letter on July 8, 1957, to all of the religious superiors of priest orders and congregations.

Like so many Catholics before and since, the Dutch sought the device of nuance to maneuver for space. The Vatican missive, they claimed, was directed against abstract, dangerous propositions; it did not apply to Dr. Terruwe and Professor Duijnstee since they did not hold these propositions. The basis of the nuance was that Alfrink received a letter from Cardinal Ottaviani asking Terruwe to write a defense of her practice in the light of the eight points enumerated in the letter of 1956. Terruwe did so, claiming that her practice was worlds apart from the bizarre picture painted by the Holy Office. Her letter was sent to Rome with a covering letter signed by the Dutch bishops attesting to her good practice.

A letter of the Holy Office to the chairman of the Conference of Religious Superiors of Men, dated February 17, 1958, refuted the nuance: "It appears from responses which the nuncio has received that there are rumors being spread about that the Holy Office has approved the teaching and practice of the Reverend Father Duijnstee, C.S.S.R., and Miss Terruwe. This most Holy Congregation deems it opportune—indeed, absolutely necessary—to inform you as chairman of the Conference of Provincials of Religious Congregations in Holland that such rumors are absolutely false."

Finally, in 1964, Dr. Terruwe, having received no answer to her communications with the Holy Office, published a brochure setting out the history and documents of the Terruwe affair. She did so, she claimed, because her good name, practice, and theoretical work suffered serious harm from the innuendos based on the Holy Office documents. The Terruwe affair catalyzed Dutch public opinion.

Bishop Bekkers, interviewed on the KRO "Brandpunt" program on October 24, 1964, was asked to comment on the Terruwe affair and to say whether he thought such injustices could happen again. Bekkers answered: "It was unbelievable. She received no opportunity to defend herself personally against the charges, no answer to her letters to the Holy Office." In 1965 Cardinal Ottaviani publicly, if reluctantly and half-heartedly, rehabilitated the reputation of Dr. Terruwe in a declaration that pronouncements of the Holy Office always concern abstract propositions and not the actual teaching of any person.[32]

It is not surprising, therefore, that the bishops, with the memory of these wounds fresh in their minds, spoke consistently at the Vatican Council of the need to decentralize the church government, internationalize the curia, and reduce the curia's central position. At the Council, they pleaded for a permanent synod for the world episcopacy to continue the work of reform in the church.

32. All of the evidence about the Terruwe affair, the Roman documents and my citations, can be found in *KA*, XIX, *48* (November 27, 1964), columns 1307–1335, and *KA*, XX, *24* (June 11, 1965), column 691.

That there was a division of opinion between Alfrink and prominent members of the Roman Curia was freely acknowledged by both sides. Alfrink has publicly attributed his appointment as one of the four permanent chairmen of the Council presidium to a gesture of Pope John XXIII to rehabilitate him against curial counselors. This personal concern of the Pope for Cardinal Alfrink meant that higher Roman authorities were hamstrung in their attempts to intervene within the Dutch church in the crucial period of reexamination which coincided with the years of the Council. Moreover, the Curia was too preoccupied with defending its own interests against the threat to its position by the Council. It is clear that Pope John did not support those in the Curia who wanted to force a different, more conservative and authoritarian reaction on the authorities within the Netherlands. On his deathbed, Pope John told his private secretary, Mgr. Capovilla, to give a reliquary of the great reforming Pope, Gregory VII, to Cardinal Alfrink. At the base of the reliquary stands the inscription: "May the church remain free, untainted, and Catholic."[33]

The relationship between Alfrink and Pope Paul was hardly that of natural enemies. When Paul was Archbishop of Milan, he frequently had Alfrink as a house guest. Alfrink seems to have championed his candidacy in the conclave which led to Paul's election. It does not seem likely that Pope Paul's encyclical on the eucharist, *Mysterium Fidei,* issued in 1965, was intended as a gesture of distrust of the Dutch bishops' handling of the same issues in their earlier letter, although *Mysterium Fidei* is less open to free discussion. Someone else in Rome besides the Pope was planting stories in the Italian newspapers—notably *La Stampa, Il Tempo,* and Milan's *De Corriere della Siera*—about a "Dutch schism," "the worst crisis in the Netherlands since the Reformation," "a serious crisis in orthodoxy." On the day the encyclical appeared, Alfrink's personal theologian at the Council, Edward Schillebeeckx, declared to the press in the name of Alfrink that the Dutch had no problems accepting the papal encyclical. The encyclical did not condemn any propositions which the Dutch theologians proposed, and the Dutch theologians did not propose any propositions which the encyclical condemned.[34]

In a spirited discourse delivered at the DOC center in Rome, Alfrink gave a speech which captures the three major themes, the chief collective representations or myths, which were emerging within Dutch Catholicism between 1958 and 1965:

33. Oostveen, *Bernard Alfrink, Katholiek,* p. 71.
34. See *KA,* XX, 40 (October 1, 1965), column 1031.

1. The mutual identification of bishop and national church:

> When I was personally attacked in the last year of this Council by
> certain elements of the Italian press, I always kept silent. That seemed
> to me—considering the source from which the attacks came—the most
> reasonable stance. But now that the Catholic community over which I
> have been placed has been attacked in its entirety, I feel that my
> people have a right to a word of defense to set the record straight, even
> though one can only fear that the campaign against the Catholic
> Netherlands will continue unabated.

2. The bishop as both teacher and spokesman for what is alive in
his community:

> A bishop at the Council is the witness to the faith of his church. That
> is to say, he brings witness to what is alive within his church, to the
> faith as that is experienced there, to the desires and hopes that exist in
> his church.

To serve as a witness in this way, the bishop must consult the faithful,
and respect their autonomy and independent contribution. It is true
that the bishop is also an agent of the purposes of the whole church in
his capacity as judge of the faith. Here, however, according to
Alfrink, the bishop must be careful to find out what the past
formulas of the faith really intended to say, rather than simply
repeating the formulas as such. He needs the advice of theological
experts to help him to be critical in determining what belongs to the
faith and what does not.

3. Open public opinion as the means to arrive at church consensus:

> What in other lands is thought about or spoken about in secret is in
> our case openly published. But it would be a great mistake if someone
> concluded from the fact that certain opinions or thoughts do not
> surface that the problem does not exist. . . . Some people object, for
> example, that in the Dutch Catholic community there are discussions
> about the value of priestly celibacy wherein negative remarks are heard
> alongside the positive ones. Don't let anyone be so mistaken as to
> think that because of an absence of such open discussion, the prob-
> lems do not exist. . . . No one should suppose that problems do not
> exist because no one in their land has or is allowed to have the courage
> to speak out publicly.

Alfrink also responded to charges that the Dutch church was anti-
Roman.

If you mean by this anti-papal, I can categorically deny this with a peaceful conscience. But if you mean by this that certain persons within the Dutch Catholic community have objections—and perhaps strongly worded ones—against certain methods of the Roman Curia and against the way in which certain persons employ these methods, I neither could nor would deny that. . . . Yet, it would be a supreme mistake if someone thought that this anti-Roman spirit shows itself only in the Netherlands. One finds it, *un peu partout*—one finds it even in Rome.[35]

CONCLUSION: CHAPTERS FOUR AND FIVE

I have turned in these two chapters to anecdote, persistent episcopal pronouncements, and the action of the church authorities in order to seek answers to questions about structural change. We have seen the beginnings of new coalitions and conflicts within Dutch Catholicism, and new relations between it and Rome. It will be helpful, by way of summary and conclusion, to return to the structural concerns which have informed my reading of this history. These chapters sustain several main propositions:

1. The period 1958-1965 represents, within Dutch Catholicism, the fourth stage in the hypothesized sequence of structural differentiation (Table 2, Chapter One), the stage wherein the authorities encourage new ideas to handle dissatisfactions.

2. The Catholic structural differentiation is a redefinition of roles within the church community which is caused in part by the differentiation of the civil religion from the body of the churches and the differentiated autonomy of secular realms of experience.[36]

3. Within the church itself, the church as a community of faith differentiates from the church as an organizational apparatus for separate confessional purposes within secular society. In the case of the Netherlands, the ideology and sanctions perpetuating Catholic columnization had lapsed by 1965.

4. Within the church as a community of faith, the structural changes—new role definitions, sanctions, norms, and organizational

35. For Alfrink's speech, see *KA*, XX, *40* (October 1, 1965), columns 1020–1025.
36. For a broader analysis of the differentiation of the civil religion from the body of the churches which informs my implicit use of civil religion, see Talcott Parsons, "Belief, Unbelief and Disbelief" in *The Culture of Unbelief*, Rocco Caporale and Antonio Grumelli, eds. (Berkeley: University of California Press, 1971), pp. 207–245.

arrangements—are postulated to follow the hypotheses of a post-Vatican pastoral-cultural strategy (see Table 3, Chapter One).

5. In the Dutch case, the following ideas for new role definitions in accord with these hypotheses emerged in the period 1958-1965.

(a) For the Catholic Bishop: A shift from the role of religious king to that of socio-ethical leader within his own Catholic community and in the wider secular community. Within the church his teaching role as part of the Magisterium is seen to presuppose consultation and open opinion formation.

(b) For the Catholic Priest: A shift from the role of missionary leader and militant organizer of Catholic confessional organizations to that of teacher-counselor-pastor, who provides services to the laity within an agent-client relationship.

(c) For the Catholic Layman: A shift from hierarchical auxiliary to autonomous Christian citizen.

6. Traditional sanctions used to maintain a dogmatic church—censorship, control over course content and teachers in Catholic institutions, suppression of information, and so on—fall into disuse and are replaced by new controls: specifically, by codes of ethics for subgroups within the church and by the bishops' use of their socio-ethical role to call for responsibility and fidelity to tradition. In the Dutch case, the social authorities allowed the traditional sanctions to lapse between 1958 and 1965.

7. The organizational mode shifts from one of emphasis on controlled contact with the secular milieu to one of integrated autonomy. Within the church, organization develops in the direction of national coordinating units, with the local congregation as a pastoral micro-unit. Church planning focuses on groups in critical danger of lapsing: the young and the intellectuals. We see evidence for each of these shifts in the period 1958-1965.

8. The speed of structural change within Dutch Catholicism was made possible by a unique combination of an infrastructure capable of mobilizing for change and the presence of social authorities sympathetic to change. Attempts by higher social authorities in Rome to stop the changes were either checked by the Pope (John XXIII), foiled by local authorities (uncooperative Dutch bishops and superiors of religious orders), or discredited when exposed to the light of a free press.

By 1965, Dutch Catholicism was ready to progress beyond its "brainstorming" phase into further experiments with and implementation of new structures for the church. When Paul VI received the Dutch episcopacy in a private audience in 1965, he stated: "The Catholics of the Netherlands stand out in a definite degree when compared to any group of Catholics in the world. They bear, therefore, a greater responsibility. . . . You can be sure that I will be following everything that goes on in your land with very special care."[37] The pope seemed to sense that Dutch Catholicism was a "pilot church," a pioneer in making the structural changes that were occurring everywhere in the church.

37. *KA*, XX, 3 (January 15, 1965), column 75.

Chapter 6

Collective Redefinition: New Institutional Forms, 1966–1974

There is a set of evidence which needs to be confronted by anyone who is tempted to interpret Dutch Catholicism too narrowly through the lens of a model of rational interest-maximization. We need to find a hypothesis which helps us to understand and interpret the following five points.

1. Both opponents and supporters of the changes recognize that the rapidity of change was nothing less than startling, and had few analogues in recent Dutch history. We have seen that Italian sources were referring to Dutch developments as "the worst crisis since the Reformation." Dr. Walter Goddijn, one of the architects of the Dutch reform, has used similar language: "There can be no doubt that the church finds itself in a crisis that can be likened to the crisis of the time of the Reformation in the sixteenth century."[1] Within five or six years, received and ancient practices and traditional role structures, sanctions, and norms were completely overturned. Every commentator on Dutch Catholicism has seemed puzzled about this. How is it possible that the church which in 1958 was the most dutiful daughter of Rome became, a decade later, the enfant terrible of international Catholicism? How did it happen that a church with relatively poor ecumenical relations in the mid-1950s could hardly be contained from ecumenical experiments ten years later? Most of the rational models of explanation do not seem to do justice to this explosion of change. The Dutch themselves look back in wonder at it. As a Protestant minister expressed it in the last session of the Dutch Pastoral Council in 1970: "If you were to ask me now what made the

---

1. See the article reporting Goddijn's lecture to a group of Dutch business managers in *De Tijd*, December 7, 1971, p. 10.

deepest impression on me in these last ten years, I would have to say: how the Catholic world which was so used to being governed from the top down and, then, here at the Council began a vigorous experiment in democracy, *has learned in four years' time* to provide a platform for the voice of the ordinary churchman, and that *in a most unusual way.*"[2]

2. Dutch Catholicism between 1966 and 1970 exhibited an élan, enthusiasm, intensity, and self-confidence which clearly set those years apart both from what went before and what came after. It was not just through manipulated publicity that Dutch Catholicism pre-empted disproportionate space devoted to church news in the world press, and prompted French travel agents to advertise tours to the Netherlands not to see the tulips but "to see Dutch Catholicism for oneself."[3] When I came to the Netherlands in the spring of 1971 to conduct research, I found that both supporters and opponents of the new developments agreed about the remarkable élan in the period 1966-1970, and they confirmed my suspicions that the intense collective enthusiasm of those years, so special and elusive, had faded away. Most commentators remained puzzled as to the best explanation for what had occurred in those years.

·3. What was further curious about the Dutch Catholic explosion was what seemed to be the decidedly un-Dutch character of this élan, with its overt emotional enthusiasm and conflicts. Although generalizations about national character are always potentially misleading, convergences of opinion, over the years, by foreign visitors and residents of the society in question can tell us something about underlying realities. Since the seventeenth century, foreigners and Dutchmen alike have tended to point to the rather unromantic, pragmatic, anti-speculative mentality of most Dutch people; they have called the Netherlands a nation with the soul of a shopkeeper—thrifty, cautious, honest, trustworthy, eminently practical, undogmatic, and inclined to avoid unnecessary conflicts.[4] Compared to other industrial nations, the Netherlands has witnessed very few riots, social movements, strikes, or conflicts. It has known no revolutions or civil wars

2. Remarks of Professor L. van Holk in *Pastoraal Concilie van de Nederlandse Kerk Provincie,* Volume 7 (Amersfoort: Katholiek Archief, 1970), p. 257. Italics mine. Hereafter cited as *Pastoraal Concilie.*

3. See *En bref. tourisme aux Pays-Bas* (on vient "voir" le Catholicisme Hollandais) in *Informations Catholiques Internationales,* No. 340 (August 8, 1969), 20.

4. For a Dutch attempt to portray national character which reviews the comments of famous foreign visitors, see A. Chorus, *De Nederlander Uiterlijk en Innerlijk* (Leiden: A. W. Sijhoff, 1965). For a foreigner's view, see William Z. Shetter, *The Pillars of Society* (The Hague: Martinus Nijhoff, 1971).

and few collective social explosions. Hence the Catholic outburst between 1966 and 1970 has taken most experts on Dutch society a little off guard. Dutch Catholics in the late 1960s exhibited an almost unbridled enthusiasm about their renewal which is difficult to reconcile with the supposedly cautious Dutch character.

The beginning of one of the discussion reports of the Netherlands Pastoral Council illustrates the point:

> Just as the world in which we live, so also the people of God are filled with an immense anticipation and inflicted with fear. In a new world we look for a renewed church. In our estimation *we stand at the edge of something brand new, something never before thought of* but at the same time we are held back by anxiety. The new is not only a yet unknown horizon but also the abyss of the unknown in which many of our beloved old traditions shall perish, in which we must find our way without any trusted compass points. Is what is coming, perhaps, not a labyrinth in which we will be lost? . . . Is the Lord truly present *in the storm of our passionate longing?* Must we also walk over the water? From time to time *we experience that it is once again Pentecost.*[5]

We could, perhaps, dismiss this passage as an atypical excess of apocalyptic rhetoric, were it not that such rhetoric actually dominates the speeches, sermons, and events within Dutch Catholicism between 1966 and 1970. Consider, for example, the following passages from the letter of Bishop Peter Nierman of Groningen issued on October 16, 1966, announcing the Dutch Pastoral Council: "I feel in writing you like Moses before the burning bush as I stand before a moment of history, an event that history before us has never before seen and of which we do not know how it will turn out." He said he did not feel like a bishop who gave instructions. "I feel as one of you." Nierman had attended plenty of gatherings of church dignitaries making church decisions, "but never before in history has an entire people gone in council to discuss those matters which most deeply touch their lives."

Nierman reminded his people that no one could predict what the Pastoral Council would mean, what sweeping changes it might make, but "there is one thing we know for sure: there is no turning back. God has set us in movement."

> When we come together, then, you will not, as previously, only just sit down to listen to leaders and the learned. We are coming together now as equals. Every voice is indispensable. Every one of you belong

---

5. Discussion paper, "The Unity which the Lord Brings About," in *Pastoraal Concilie*, Vol. VII, pp. 47–48. Italics mine to underscore the apocalyptic rhetoric.

in the consultation. Each individually and all together, we must feel responsible and let our voice be heard. There will be no leaders and no presiding officers. Everyone is invited to speak his piece, led by God's spirit and employing all his energy. Hence, everyone can make his views known and share his experiences. Thus, too, everyone will bear his share of the responsibility for the church: *a people of God, speaking as on the first Pentecost, each one in his own language.*[6]

The speeches, books, and comments of Dutch Catholics between 1966 and 1970 were filled with emotional terms such as "adventure,", "the church of tomorrow," and "risk"; they bristled with comparisons between the Dutch Catholic situation and that of the Jewish people in the Exodus, leaving their trusted and traditional home in search of a new land, or that of the early church bursting with enthusiasm at Pentecost.[7] As the episcopal advisor for ecumenical questions, Professor H. Fiolet, said in a speech during the Dutch Pastoral Council: "The Roman Catholic Church in the Netherlands has been catalyzed into movement, together with all the other churches, because we are in search of *a new way of being the church.*"[8]

It seems to me that the rhetoric by which Dutch Catholics in the period were describing themselves has to be taken seriously as evidence. It is also apparent that the euphoric rhetoric came into full bloom around 1966 and began to fade away around 1970. It was a far cry from the adjective most chosen by the Dutch to describe themselves and by their foreign observers: *nuchter*—sober, hard-headed, down-to-earth.

4. There exists, as a residue of the collective élan in the 1970s, a set of predictable slogans which continually, almost monotonously, crop up in discussions, during crisis points when the new church appears to be under threat, in commentaries on the Dutch-Roman conflicts, in conversations and in sermons: "experiment, democratization, dialogue, new church, a church in movement, in search, finding out what is alive within the church, groping and searching faith, pluriformity, the grassroots, collegiality."[9] These words or slogans have the quality of being more than concepts.

6. For Bishop Nierman's letter, see *KA*, XXI, 50 (December 16, 1966), columns 1348–1353. Italics mine.
7. See the books in the series "The Church of Tomorrow" published by the Pastoral Institute of the Dutch Church Province between 1966–1970, also "Risking Church," *Riskante Kerk: Vijf Jaar PINK* (Amersfoort: Katholiek Archief, 1968).
8. *Pastoraal Concilie*, Vol. VII, p. 202.
9. In Dutch: "ruimte, experiment, democratisering, overleg, nieuwe kerk, een kerk in beweging, op zoek, vinden wat in de kerk leeft, tastende, zoekende geloof, pluriformiteit, grondvlak, collegialiteit."

5. The last piece of evidence is more subjective. I present it because it is related to the previous points. In innumerable contacts, conversations, and participant observations over two and a half years, I was struck by the fact that even intellectual elites or theologians, who were purportedly using slogans such as pluriformity, collegiality, democratization, or experiment as intellectual concepts, did so with a kind of persistence, tenacity, and enthusiasm which led me to surmise that nonrational, mythic factors were in play. I suspected that these collective slogans or symbols were "over-determined" in the Freudian sense, that they were symbols which contain more than is available to conscious rational inspection because they are related to residues of events in the unconscious. The more I heard the intellectual elites present rational justifications for the inevitability and wisdom of the Dutch Catholic developments, the more convinced I became that some non-rational factor underlay their arguments.

What are the factors involved in items 1 to 5 which call for interpretation? We can sum them up as follows: revolutionary tempo of change; reported feelings of psycho-social collective élan; the frequent use of euphoric rhetoric with few parallels in Dutch national life; a residue, after the élan, of slogans which repeatedly crop up in public discussions; and my own subjective intuition of a certain over-determination, in the Freudian sense, in the use of these slogans by reformers.

While it is possible to understand the tempo of change by means of ordinary sociological models, as we did in the preceding chapters, these models miss this evidence of the non-rational. Again, it does not do justice to the range of this evidence merely to state obvious truths that most reforming groups tend to glorify the future and villify the past, or that those who react to traditional distortions often tend to overstate their case for the new. Other commentators have used metaphors such as "steam kettle effect," to suggest that long-brewing pressures finally exploded, or "safety-valve" effect, to suggest that widespread dissaffection produced by social changes such as industrialization did not explode from the church in France, Belgium, or Germany because critical voices had long since left the church in those countries. In the Netherlands, where the Catholics exhibited unusual communal strength, the criticism turned inward.[10]

10. For the metaphor of the "steam kettle," see the remarks of Edward Schillebeeckx in "Are There Crisis Elements in Catholic Netherlands?" KA, XXI, 11 (March 18, 1966), column 351; for the "safety valve" image, see Leo Laeyendecker, "Theologische Veranderingen Sociologisch Beschouwd," Sociologische Gids, XV, 4 (June–July 1968), 247–259.

We must permit ourselves, then, the luxury of trying out what may seem a speculative interpretation, because our own general model does not leave much room for the evidence in items 1 to 5. We turn therefore to the concepts of Emile Durkheim.

COLLECTIVE EFFERVESCENCE

Emile Durkheim argued that the fundamental nature of any society consists of a set of "collective representations," commonly held myths, ideas, or symbols which exist in the minds of the members of the group. For Durkheim, every cohering collectivity is founded upon and sustained by commonly accepted myths. Even what at first glance appear to be concepts rather than symbols—such as the ideas of democracy, individualism, reason, and freedom—are often essentially myths which direct consensus. Because the collectively held myths transcend any given individual, the group, for Durkheim, is a reality sui generis instead of merely an additive statistical property of individuals, although he was careful to avoid the dubious concept of a group mind. Society does not exist except in the minds of its individual members. As a set of collective representations, however, society transcends the mind of any given member.

In trying to explain the origin, reinforcement, or major reinterpretation of the collective myths, Durkheim asked, "Where do the collective representations come from and how do they get into people's heads?" He turned to the concept of collective effervescence for his explanation. In his book *The Elementary Forms of Religious Life,* Durkheim employed the concept of collective effervescence to refer to the sort of group frenzy that seemed to accompany the ritual gatherings of Australian aborigenes.[11] He also claimed to see collective effervescence in outbursts such as the French Revolution. Robert Bellah has suggested that Durkheim's notion of collective effervescence is "a concept much like that of the unconscious—it could almost be called a social unconscious."[12]

Why have these concepts, so central to Emile Durkheim, been largely overlooked in the sociological literature? Many sociologists, to be sure, are intensely aware of collective representations, the group myths and symbols which form the cultural base of any community. The problem lies in the elusive, almost mystical quality of the concept

11. Emile Durkheim, *The Elementary Forms of the Religious Life* (London: Allen and Unwin, 1954), Book 2, Chapter VII.
12. Robert N. Bellah, *Beyond Belief* (New York: Harper and Row), p. 239.

of collective effervescence. Is it possible to find quantifiable indicators for the concept which might make it a more useful tool for the social sciences, a tool related to the central myths of a group's cultural matrix?

There have been two kinds of attempts within sociology to employ these central notions of Durkheim. The first can be seen in the work of Robert Bales, Philip Slater, and their associates in their studies of the emergence of structure and culture within originally leaderless and unstructured ad hoc discussion groups. By defining a group as a communication network and counting and labeling various kinds of communication within discussion groups, Bales and Slater discovered a pattern of sequences in achieving group structures and culture as well as a relation between increases in the volume both of the units of communication and the number of channels used to conduct the flow of communication and the emergence of common group symbols.[13] Thus, in his book *Microcosm,* Slater shows that in "successful" discussion groups—groups in which a structure and common symbolic culture emerge which enables the group to achieve effective solutions to problems—the dominant myths emerge in a relatively early sequence in the development of the group when the volume of units of information and channels used to direct information flow is at its highest point.[14] For the study of discussion groups, then, we can take the increase of volume in units and channels of information as a quantifiable measure to operationalize Durkheim's concept of effervescence. When we do so, as Slater did, Durkheim's contention about the relationship between collective effervescence and collective representation is confirmed.

A second set of sociological studies which use analogues of Durkheim's concepts of effervescence and representations is available in the sub-discipline of "collective behavior"—the study of relatively uninstitutionalized action such as spontaneous crowds, panics, riots, bandwagon effects, and social protest movements. If we count the number of riots, protest movements, and crowds over time for a specified society, we notice that they often bunch up for a given year or number of years; for example, the bread riots in France increase in volume immediately before the French Revolution, and the number of riots, protest movements, and crowds in American society increases

13. For one statement, see Robert Bales and Philip E. Slater, "Role Differentiation in Small Decision Making Groups," in *Family, Socialization and Interaction Process,* Talcott Parsons and Robert F. Bales, eds. (London: Routledge and Kegan Paul, 1956), pp. 259–306.
14. Philip E. Slater, *Microcosm* (New York: John Wiley, 1966).

dramatically in the 1960s in comparison with the 1950s. Further, if we relate this increase in the volume of episodes of collective behavior to central cultural myths—"Liberty, Equality, and Fraternity" or "Manifest Destiny"—we uncover a relationship between increased volume of episodes of collective behavior such as riots and protest movements, used as a quantifiable index of "collective effervescence," and the origin or major reinterpretations of the group's central myths, the collective representations.[15] Once again, Durkheim's contention seems confirmed.

Let us assume, then, from these two examples, that the psychological feelings of excitement and élan within discussion groups or societies in periods when episodes of collective behavior bunch up are vague psychological registers of an increase in the volume of units and channels of information within a group—an increase which, though never perfectly mapped, is in principle mathematically mapable. Since the feelings of élan relate to quantifiable shifts that are never perfectly mapped, we can call these shifts "a social unconscious."

The Dutch Pastoral Council as an Expression of Collective Effervescence

Can we find something analogous to collective effervescence within Dutch Catholicism between 1966 and 1970, and does it relate to the origin of new collective representations? Further, can we point to any quantifiable indicators of effervescence, to an increase in volume in units and channels of information flow? Finally, is there anything similar to a kind of social unconscious operating in the relation between the new collective representations and the episode of collective effervescence?

The central event within Dutch Roman Catholicism between 1966 and 1970 was the National Pastoral Council, first announced at a press conference on March 16, 1966, by Bishop De Vet, who stated that the bishops sought from the Council "the achievement of acceptable decisions which since they will come out of the body of the church can also be lived with by the body of the church . . . there must be special care that the whole of the church truly feels itself involved in this council."[16]

15. For a survey of the literature on collective behavior which relates these episodes to the collective representations, see Neil J. Smelser, *Theory of Collective Behavior* (New York: The Free Press, 1962). Smelser refers to the representations as "the growth of generalized belief."
16. Press conference of Mgr. G. de Vet in *Pastoraal Concilie*, Vol. I, citations from pp. 12–13.

On November 27, 1966, the Dutch Pastoral Council officially opened. The first plenary session met on January 3-5, 1968. There were six plenary sessions between 1968 and the last session, April 5-8, 1970.

The Dutch bishops announced the Pastoral Council in the most solemn possible terms. At a press conference held on November 14, 1966, Cardinal Alfrink averred:

> In the church today, the course of our Pastoral Council can only be a progressive one. . . . *We are a Church in movement* and in that movement we desire to follow the Lord . . . to follow him means that we must go forward. . . . It is very important that we take the community of faith of the Dutch Church very seriously as a community of all the faithful and guarantee the right to participation and voice to all. That is communication, and *for that all of the new channels for communication flow have been set up* during this period of preparation. . . . Our Council is going to begin. It seems a *risky adventure* but one can also see it as the fruit of the Spirit.[17]

In a collective letter issued November 17, 1966, the Dutch bishops told their people: "We want to ask you to speak your opinion about a whole number of issues, surely also in the discussion groups that are everywhere being formed. We promise you that we will take what comes to us from these discussion groups into account to the fullest extent possible. . . . May your *discussion and search* be full of mutual understanding because this discussion *must help to form the church.* . . . May God give us, may we give to one another, *a new élan.*"[18] In a public telegram sent to Alfrink from St. Peter's on November 23, 1966, Pope Paul VI stressed that the Dutch Pastoral Council "is a delicate and most demanding undertaking, something that is entirely new and unique."[19]

The Council as a Social Movement

The Dutch Pastoral Council was, in a sense, a social movement as well as a kind of church parliament. In its plenary sessions as a parliament, the bulk of the body was constituted by elected representatives, with laymen in the majority. The laity joined priests, members of religious orders, theologians, sociologists, diocesan curia specialists, and bishops in open discussions and voting on issues of pastoral policy such as

---

17. *Pastoraal Concilie*, Vol. I, citation from pp. 31 and 35. Italics mine.
18. *Pastoraal Concilie*, Vol. I, citation from pp. 45 and 46. Italics mine, to indicate the equation between church, "discussion and search," and élan.
19. *Pastoraal Concilie*, Vol. I, p. 38.

preaching, ecumenism, peace and justice, the exercise of authority in the church, catechetics, the seminary formation of priests, birth-control, and celibacy. Never before or since has a national church within Catholicism involved such a large and representative body of its ordinary faithful in key decision areas. We will return to discuss the structure and some of the issues connected with the plenary sessions of the Pastoral Council later. First we will look at the Council as a social movement.

The Dutch bishops had proposed the experiment of the Pastoral Council as a new way of experiencing the church. They recommended that participation in the popular discussion movement was the best means for ordinary believers to take part in the business of the Council. It is by looking at what went on parallel to and in preparation for the six plenary sessions that we can get some idea of what might serve as indicators of the increase in volume by units and channels of information-flow as a way to operationalize Durkheim's concept.

We can begin by considering the popular discussion-group movement which was under the partial direction of *Ecclesia* magazine. A pastoral commission in each diocese prepared résumés of the discussions to send to the discussion-group commission of the Council. *Ecclesia,* providing printed resource material for the discussion groups, pre-dated the Dutch Pastoral Council by a decade. Its subscription averaged 8,000 in the period 1958-1965, spurted in 1966, climbed to its highest point of about 18,000 in 1969, and began to decline in the early 1970s to an average of 7,500 copies. We can use these subscription figures, then, as one index for the dramatic increase in volume of intra-church communication between 1966 and 1970.[20]

There are other indicators to show that the volume of units and channels of communication flow reached dramatic heights in this period. For example, the Pastoral Council secretariat maintained a central post office box to which ordinary Catholics could write with suggestions or reactions concerning topics under discussion. The secretariat enlisted student seminarians and members of religious orders to respond to the thousands of letter writers. Further, from 1966 to 1970 the number of committee meetings, study commissions, and open hearings concerned with the work of the Council were unusually high. We can sample the volume and frequency of these

20. Statistics from an interview with Mr. L. Koevoets of *Ecclesia* magazine.

gatherings by looking at the chronicle of the preparation period for the Pastoral Council, which lists fifty-eight different extraordinary official meetings for the period December 1966 to September 1967.[21]

The Pastoral Council commissioned fifteen study groups with a total of 131 theological and lay experts to write the working papers for the discussion and votes at the plenary sessions. Separate commissions were set up consisting of professional theologians, canonists, Catholic sociologists and psychologists. There were separate gatherings of the deans of all dioceses and representatives from thirty-three Catholic organizations, two large congresses open to all priests in the country, a mock student council called Stucon, and so forth. It would be a serious mistake, then, to look only at what went on in the plenary sessions of the Council, for we would miss the extent to which the council was also a broad-based social movement.

During these same years the emergence of consultative councils serving the bishop of each diocese and consisting of elected lay and clerical representatives gave rise to innumerable meetings at the parish level and within each diocese. Further, the number of ad hoc meetings to send protest telegrams or to lobby for or against proposals of the Council show record numbers for the period 1966-1970. There can be no question that there are sufficient indicators that the volume of units of internal communication within Dutch Catholicism was higher in this period than in previous periods; it was also higher than in the 1970s, when the new structural changes began to be implemented, causing a certain streamlining and new structuring of channels of communication between bishops, diocesan and national service bureaucracies, theologians, sociologists, and Protestant ecumenical elites. The vague reported feelings of a Catholic élan during these years is related to real shifts in the volume of intra-church communication.

Again, the elated feeling of change is related to the new direction and multiplying channels of information. The Council invited representatives from eleven Dutch non-Catholic churches or organizations not only to observe, as at the Second Vatican Council, but to speak and serve on preparatory commissions and to comment on positions or resolutions passed by the Council which might be injurious to good ecumenical relations. Hence, Catholic and Protestant ecumenical experts were in more constant communication than previously. Theologians were talking to sociologists, and diocesan bureaucracy staffs

21. *Pastoraal Concilie*, Vol. I, pp. 48–144.

were in conversation with students or housewives. It would not be very difficult, therefore, to demystify Durkheim's concept of collective effervescence in operationalizing it for Dutch Catholicism between 1966 and 1970.

We also know that the collective slogans so prominent in Dutch Catholic rhetoric—experiment, a new church, collegiality, and the rest—were becoming communal mythic symbols precisely in this period. They are to be seen on almost every page of the minutes of the plenary sessions of the Council.

As a further point, almost all of the national and diocesan service bureaucracies, theologians, canonists, lay representatives, or priests who took an active part in the preparation for and the sessions of the Dutch Pastoral Council remain enthusiastic about the experience of a church in council, and they have recurrently used the collective slogans in public pronouncements or protests against threats to the "new church" which have come after the Council. There is, therefore, a specifiable relation between the collective effervescence which resulted from the bishops' decision to hold a new kind of pastoral council, the emergence within Dutch Catholicism of new collective myths of communal identity, and active participation in the Council.

Is there anything akin to a social unconscious which might help us to understand the over-determined reactions of these supporters of the new collective myths? By a social unconscious we will mean a real experience, difficult to bring under conceptual analysis or precise words; we therefore examine the collective slogans not entirely as intellectual concepts but as symbolic pointers to a shared experience. The social authorities had invited Dutch Catholics to experience the church in a new way, as a church in council or in discussion groups. A large portion of the Dutch Catholic population and the overwhelming majority of church elites had answered their summons to this new experience. At the time, the experience defied exact characterization.

For example, one of the documents of the Pastoral Council suggests that confidence in the new pastoral policy rests on an experience which is beyond words or conceptual argument because it derives from active participation in the collective effervescence. "A person can only have this confidence if he has participated in the growth process and dared to plunge into the midst of something like this Pastoral Council."[22] Again, in preparing a résumé of reports from the

---

22. See the report, "Contemporary Experience of the Faith and Renewal of the Practice of the Faith in the Church," *Pastoraal Concilie*, Vol. V, p. 141.

popular discussion-group movement, the conciliar reporter remarked that these discussion groups "experience their togetherness no longer only—indeed, no longer primarily—as a means to bring information [to the Council top] but as a togetherness which is *an experience of being-the-church.* . . . Much more occurs in the groups than is registered in the reports. The emotional atmosphere, the experience of being the church together, the possible charismatic happening and preaching are not captured by the reports. *This second aspect can only be experienced and is almost impossible to capture in words.*"[23]

Those who participated in the Council tend to speak of the experience in the way people involved in sensitivity-training groups talk enthusiastically about a group dynamics experience which is difficult to express in words.

A great number, but not all, of the Dutch Catholics underwent, in discussion groups and through the Pastoral Council, an intense emotional experience of a new way of "being the church." Out of that experience emerged a new set of collective symbols for the church. The number of Dutch professional theologians, diocesan and national service bureaucrats, and so on is relatively small. Almost all of them were involved in this intense group experience. There are, for example, only sixty members of the Catholic Theological Work Association, which includes all active professional Catholic theologians in the Netherlands, excluding biblical exegetes and canonists. Almost all continue to champion the slogans for a new church.

In the controversies and conflicts between progressives and conservatives in the 1970s, or in conflicts with Rome about the wisdom and appropriateness of the new structural arrangements, there is a non-rational underside barely hidden behind conceptual terminology.

Dutch conservatives often refer to a cabal or conspiracy by the intellectual elites to take over, imposing their new concepts. Such charges seem to miss the real dynamics of what happened. It is difficult to avoid the conclusion that the post-Pastoral Council fight in the 1970s and the apparent polarization between conservatives and progressives is much less about rational concepts, strategies, and programs than about the collective symbols which mediate divergent experiences of what it means to be a member of the Roman Catholic church and tradition. What seems to be at stake are fundamental personal and collective identities.

In the remainder of this chapter and in Chapter Seven we will return to the same seven rubrics we used in the preceding two

23. *Pastoraal Concilie,* Vol. II, pp. 29–30.

chapters to chronicle structural changes. It was necessary, however, to address at the beginning of this chapter evidence which does not immediately fit these models.

NATIONAL COORDINATING UNITS

We have already seen how Dutch Catholicism began to develop new ideas for service bureaucracies and institutes for the coordination of pastoral planning for liturgy, catechetics, and preaching at the national level. In this chapter we will be interested in watching the attempts at specifying and establishing the new institutional forms for national coordination. It will be my contention here and in the following chapter that the period 1966–1974 represents the completion of stages five and six of the sequence of structural differentiation —attempts at specifying and establishing the new institutional forms (1966–1970)—and a stormy beginning to stage seven, in which the collectivity consolidates the new structures even against the threat of counter-revolution (1971–1974).

The Pastoral Institute of the Netherlands Church
In 1963, the Dutch bishops inaugurated the Pastoral Institute of the Netherlands Church (PINK) under the leadership of a professional priest-sociologist, Dr. Walter Goddijn, O.F.M., and a staff of canonical and social-science specialists. In 1966, PINK was entrusted with planning, coordinating, and carrying out the recommendations of the Dutch Pastoral Council. Thus, between 1966 and 1970, and indeed until its dissolution in 1972, PINK served as an executive secretariat both for the Dutch bishops and for the Netherlands Conference of Superiors of Religious Men.[24]

During the years of the Pastoral Council, Dr. Goddijn and his associates at PINK enjoyed relative autonomy to commission reports, set up study groups, and finance social surveys dealing with a wide range of issues affecting the church. The relative autonomy of this bishops' executive secretariat entailed several consequences in the years under study. First, the PINK staff, while at the service of the bishops, used their freedom from the bishops to establish contacts with groups and movements at the periphery of Dutch Catholicism. They served as a channel to transmit the voice of more radical

24. The phrase "religious men" is a technical term to refer to men within the Catholic religious orders and congregations.

Catholic groups to the bishops and vice versa.[25] Hence, PINK ensured that channels of communication remained open in the period of specifying and establishing new institutional forms, thereby preventing movements of underground leftist protest of the sort that emerged in other national settings. Secondly, the director of PINK used his authority to commission a wide range of sociological surveys and polls. PINK guaranteed, therefore, that elites were being confronted with a great deal of empirical data when making policy decisions. PINK's use of sociological surveys on several controversial issues, notably the issue of celibacy for priests, set a climate which encouraged the formation of pressure groups. PINK's activities helped to open up free expression of public opinion.

Dr. Goddijn had responsibilities and tasks of national importance as director of PINK which made him a leader on the same level as the bishops, although his role lacked any jurisdiction within hierarchical structures. Through the years, his extraordinary visibility and increasingly clear position as a champion of reform made him less palatable to conservatives within the church, who chafed especially at his critical stance vis à vis Rome. His replacement in 1972 by a relatively unknown church bureaucrat was widely interpreted as a move to appease conservative elements who blamed him, rather than Alfrink or the new structure, for the rapidity and direction of the changes. In serving as a scapegoat for conservative frustrations, his removal diverted attention from the fact that the functions of PINK have been structurally consolidated.

After almost ten years of experimentation with the national structure of PINK, on September 1, 1972, the Dutch bishops and the Conference of Religious Superiors of Men set up a new executive secretariat, the secretariat of the Roman Catholic Church Province in the Netherlands, under the leadership of a new secretary-general, Dr. P. Vriens, with a staff of eleven service bureaucrats. This secretariat combines the functions of PINK as a sort of information-gathering center with those of the secretariat for the episcopal conference. As a joint secretariat for the bishops and the superiors of religious men, it coordinates activities between the diocesan and religious priests. At the same time, the bishops established a national management and policy committee consisting of one vicar-general from each of the

25. See the letter of Dr. Goddijn to the Amsterdam Student Parish about the "long way" (a married clergy through collegiality discussions at the Synod of World Bishops) and the "short way" (a married clergy through one-sided action by the Dutch Catholics), *KA*, XXIV, 5 (January 31, 1969), columns 123-126.

seven Dutch dioceses, the chairman of the Conference of Religious Superiors of Men, and three lay members. This management and policy committee, which serves as the agenda committee for the bishops' conference, also controls the preparations for the ongoing national pastoral dialogue.[26]

While this secretariat and national policy committee appear to be merely efficient service bureaucracies, they have introduced, in their statutes, several novelties within the international Roman Catholic structure. First, laymen occupy key policy-making posts within the national service bureaucracy. Thus, prominent lay Catholic politicians and university professors—such as Minister Marga Klompe, Senator Piet Steenkamp, and Professor R. de Moor—have had corresponding posts of responsibility within the church. Second, the bishop's conference has yielded its former absolute control over its own agenda. This means, among other things, that the bishops cannot insulate themselves from problems within the church which they would rather not deal with. Further, since the agenda of the bishops' meeting is made public two weeks before their monthly conference, interested parties have a chance to make their voice heard.

The clear superiority in staff and central administration at the national level institutionally guarantees the continuance of national policy on pastoral matters. Ivan Vallier has argued that the diocese is the key unit for comparative studies of Roman Catholicism because the individual bishop is a sort of religious king in his territory.[27] In the Netherlands, however, it is almost impossible, structurally, for a bishop to pursue pastoral policies completely uncoordinated with those of the other bishops. He is as much, if not more, a member of a national governing college for the church province as he is the territorial officer for the church in his own diocese. Indeed, the structural realities of Dutch Catholicism are such that the national unit takes priority over the local territorial diocese.

Experimental to Permanent Forms of Council

We have considered some of the aspects of the Dutch Pastoral Council as a social movement. During the Second Vatican Council, the Dutch bishops decided to hold a pastoral council for their own

26. For the statutes of the executive secretariat and the national management and policy committee, see "De Struktuur en de Funktie van Het Centraal Bureau van de R. K. Provincie in Nederland," available from the Episcopal Conference of the Roman Catholic Church in the Netherlands.
27. Ivan Vallier, "Comparative Studies of Roman Catholicism: Dioceses as Strategic Units," *Social Compass,* XVI (Spring 1969), 147–184.

church province in order to apply and extend the decisions of the Vatican Council to their situation. While the traditional canon law provided for provincial councils as territorial follow-ups to general church councils, it saw these councils as deliberative meetings consisting of the bishops, regional superiors of religious orders, and diocesan curial elites—in short, as exclusively hierarchical decision-making bodies at the local or regional level.[28]

As we have seen, the Dutch bishops were championing a model of authority around the concept of collegiality and consultation. Hence, they determined to experiment with a new conciliar structure, one that embodied the reality that every member is both an element and a part of the church, each with his own proper contribution to authoritative decisions and proclamations of faith. The bishops and Catholic elites showed sensitivity to the fact that the crises in credibility concerning officeholders in the church, and the assertion that authority could only be responsible if it showed itself truly responsive by allowing participatory access to decision-makers, were related to similar crises in the credibility of officeholders in most institutions within Western industrial societies. How would it be possible to combine participatory collegial forms of authority with the traditional teaching role of the episcopacy?[29]

The Structure of the Council. The statutes of the Dutch Pastoral Council tried to embody three fundamental principles which protected the hierarchical role while allowing democratization:

1. The plenary session must be as much as possible a body wherein the whole of the church membership is represented. Therefore, it consists in the bishops and, for the most part, in elected representatives [three priests and seven laity from each diocese, ten elected representatives of religious congregations]; the bishops have the right, if it appears that certain groups are insufficiently represented by the electoral process, to appoint a maximum of fifteen members.

2. The open handling of reports must be as insightful as possible, so that those in the nation interested in the issues being discussed can follow the progress of the discussions. In this way, the discussions in the plenary sessions can contribute to the development and maturation of the concept being handled within the whole church membership. Consequently, the working documents must be published promptly.

28. For the status of the Pastoral Council in the canon law, see Ruud Huysmans, "Het Pastoraal Concilie in Canoniek Perspectief," *Bijdragen*, XXXI, 4 (November 1970), 373–289.
29. For comparisons of the authority crisis within the church to a general authority crisis in the Western world, see "The Conceptualization and Exercise of Authority," *Pastoraal Concilie*, II,

In accordance with this desire for open deliberations at the Pastoral Council, it was decided to allow journalists and radio and television broadcasting access for all plenary sessions. Approximately one hundred Dutch or foreign journalists were in attendance at each of the six sessions. Further, not only the working papers but the study commission reactions to these papers, as well as the minutes of the plenary session, were officially published and distributed. The Catholic and secular daily press gave wide coverage to the issues and conflicts connected with resolutions at the Council.

> 3. The structure and procedure of the plenary session must be such that the organic relation between the bishops, as the teachers and shepherds of the church in the Netherlands, and the other members of the plenary session, as representatives of the whole church membership in all of the church's parts, is expressed and functions as well as possible.
>
> (a) The fact that the whole church membership has a genuine responsibility in all areas must be embodied: *they are all, indeed, active and, therefore, co-responsible members of the church*. . . . Only when the whole of the church membership in its representatives knows that it is really responsible, shall they speak in a responsible way. Therefore, it has been most consciously decided that the plenary session does not only issue advice . . . but that the plenary session itself, together with, presided over by and under the leadership of the bishops, approves and passes all final resolutions.
>
> (b) The proper and irreducible authority of the bishops must be given a clear and positive form and forum within the structure of the plenary session.[30]

Dutch Catholics were looking for an institutional form which would embody the collegial ideas, something that was neither a parliament set apart from the bishops as executive officers nor a mere consultative open hearing. They were also seeking an electoral procedure which would guarantee to every group within the church a chance to have an active voice in the deliberations. Within the Pastoral Council structures, the bishops constituted the Council Presidium. They had the right to call the plenary gatherings into session and the responsibility for presiding over the deliberations. On issues put to a vote at the Council, they voted first. Only after their vote was publicly recorded would a vote be taken by the remainder of the delegates. Further, the bishops could refrain from voting on issues

---

pp. 6–10; and the speech of Bishop Bluyssen of Den Bosch on the contemporary crisis of authority, in *KA*, XXIV, *34* (August 25, 1967), columns 849–858.
30. *Pastoraal Concilie*, 1, pp. 134–135.

to which they did not wish to commit themselves, thus making such a vote a recommendation of the rest of the body to the bishops rather than a resolution of the whole council. Moreover, they had the right to appoint the central steering commission of the council, which consisted of two bishops, two representatives of the national church service bureaucracy, and three laymen. Finally, the bishops could send a working paper back to committee or hold their own separate consultation on it before the plenary session. During the plenary session, the college of bishops could put an end to the discussions, bring a motion to a vote, or suspend the session. In effect, then, the bishops had absolute veto power. At the Council, however, they rarely chose to exercise that power.[31]

The Presidium and Steering Commission controlled the agenda of the council and appointed the eleven members of the Council Commission. The Council Commission, in turn, appointed members to working committees to prepare and refine the working papers for each session.

The statutes of the Pastoral Council determined that the voting body should consist of no more than 150 members. In practice, each session consisted of 110 representatives with the right to vote. These voting members included:

1. The seven Dutch bishops.

2. Eighty elected representatives: 21 priests, 10 members of religious congregations, and 49 laymen. The priests and the laymen were elected by an electoral college consisting of the pastoral council of each diocese, which in turn had been elected by direct elections at the parish or deanery level. The ten representatives for the religious congregations were chosen by the members of all Dutch religious orders through direct elections.

3. The bishops could nominate 15 members of the plenary session to guarantee electoral balance.[32]

Besides these voting members, the Pastoral Council was attended by an average of one hundred representatives or observers—who came from other national episcopal conferences or from Protestant churches, or who were resource persons especially invited by the bishops to attend a given session. Some of these observers had the right to speak out but not the right to vote. In particular, the eleven representatives of non-Catholic churches and the Dutch Humanist Association had the right to take active part in the deliberations. The

31. *Ibid.*, pp. 136–137.
32. *Ibid.*, pp. 126–127.

Protestant churches were expected to speak to the question of how the resolutions might affect the dialogue between the Christian churches, while the Humanist Association was invited to discuss implications for dialogue with nonbelievers. Many of the Protestant or Humanist observers were full members of the preparatory study commissions.

The structures and procedures of the Pastoral Council sought to achieve a balance between the concept of the church as both a social system and an association and the concept of roles in the church as combining aspects of a part and an element. The bishops were not merely executive agents independent of an elected deliberative body. Nor was the deliberative body simply dependent upon the good wishes and purposes of the bishops.

During the fourth plenary session of the Council, on April 9, 1969, Alfrink tried to explain the episcopal self-understanding of the relationship of the Council to the bishops:

> I will raise, then, two questions. Is this Pastoral Council a hearing wherein the faithful get a chance to speak out their insights and desires together with experts, and where afterwards the bishops then make the actual decisions? Or is this a democratic parliament wherein the representative assembly makes the decisions and then passes them on to the bishops as an executive power? The first does not do justice to the responsibility of the faithful, the second does not do justice to the responsibility of the bishops. . . .
>
> Every adult Christian has true responsibility for all of the facets of what it means to be Christian or the church; for renewal and conservation; for the vitality of the local community and for the solidarity between the local church and the world church. The faithful have, therefore, *the right and the duty* not only to speak out their desires and to present petitions to the bishops *but also to bear the balance,* I could almost have said "Catholicity," of their desires. . . . The bishops, on their part, have an irreducibly proper responsibility. They cannot content themselves with being the spokesmen for the voice of their people but they must also hold up the word of the Lord before their people's eyes. . . . Within the council of all believers itself, the bishops must let their own voice be heard. Not just as the voice of one other believer among many, but as the voice of one who is "sent," as the one who presides. The bishops must do this not as a means of restricting the freedom of opinion or cutting off dialogue but as a way to make their own proper episcopal contribution to the formation of judgment. Bishops and faithful must learn to understand one another in this. It is something brand new. Neither the bishops nor the faithful are used to this type of episcopal pronouncement. We are not used to it because formerly bishops usually only spoke to settle a

matter once and for all. You are not used to it, for you have a tendency to ask: is the bishop speaking as the final decision-maker? The intermediate form wherein the bishop speaks in the role of one who is sent to the community as the presiding officer in the faith—that is, both as an ordinary believer and at the same time as someone who has the task to provide leadership in preaching and executive decisions within the community of faith—this intermediate form is something we hardly know.[33]

The Pastoral Council as Representative. Was the Pastoral Council representative of Dutch Catholics or was it, as some Roman sources and Dutch conservatives suggested, a rigged platform for a small party of radicals and progressives? Did the Pastoral Council do justice to or did it undermine episcopal authority? The Pastoral Council was certainly representative of the Dutch episcopacy, professional theologians, and the national and diocesan church service bureaucracy, because almost the entire population sample of these three categories was involved in the Council either as voting members or in the preparatory commissions. The ten representatives of religious orders were directly elected by all members of the congregations of priests, nuns, and brothers. The eighty representatives of priests and laity from the seven dioceses were chosen, however, by an indirect method of election by stages. The National Pastoral Council representatives were elected by the seven diocesan pastoral councils, although not necessarily from their own body. Separate elections were held for each of the six sessions of the Council. Each session usually contained anywhere from 26 to 50 new delegates. The members of the diocesan pastoral councils, in their turn, were for the most part chosen by the deanery councils of priests and the directly elected parish councils at specially announced election meetings.

Indirect election favored those priests and laymen most actively engaged at the parish or deanery level. At each step in the election procedure—parish, deanery, diocese—those who were most extreme to the right or the left had less chance to be elected. Many of the Dutch conservatives, disapproving of the introduction of democratization within the church, did not take an active part. Thus, the conservative voice was slightly under-represented at the council.

The Dutch bishops used their power of appointment to redress some of the imbalances caused by the electoral procedure. Thus they appointed Adrien Simonis, later bishop of Rotterdam, to most of the sessions to represent the conservative voice. In a session devoted to the

33. *Pastoraal Concilie,* V, citation from pp. 201 and 202.

question of the church's relation to youth, the bishops appointed mainly student leaders, and at another session, they appointed chiefly young members of religious orders and congregations. They also appointed several prominent members of the reactionary Confrontatie group to serve on planning commissions and as delegates to the plenary sessions. The feed-in channels to the Council permitted those who felt that their voice was not being heard in the electoral process either to write letters or to join the discussion groups which relayed their recommendations to the Council.

It was, in particular, on the issue of clerical celibacy that the question of the representativeness of the Dutch Pastoral Council was first seriously raised. The fifth session of the Council voted on four different resolutions urging revision of the celibacy rule for priests. The bishops did not vote on any of these resolutions. The four resolutions passed the assembly by votes, respectively, of 90 for, 6 against, 2 blank; 86 for, 3 against, 8 blank, and 1 abstaining; 94 for, 1 against, 2 blank, and 1 abstaining; 93 for, 2 against, and 3 blank.[34] How representative was this vote for the feelings and opinions of Dutch priests and laity?

Luckily, the propensity of PINK and other organizations to conduct social surveys on church issues can help answer the question. In a national sample survey of all Dutch Catholics conducted by Intomart and commissioned by the KRO Broadcasting Company, 59 percent of Dutch Catholics claimed that they thought the Pastoral Council was genuinely representative of the Catholic community.[35] On the issue of celibacy, a series of surveys show that the overwhelming majority favored a change. In a survey conducted in 1966 by the market research firm of Attwood Statistics, it was found that, in a sample of 554 Catholics, only 29 percent chose the first alternative when asked the question, "As you know, Catholic priests may not marry. Is that in your opinion a good thing or a bad thing?"

In another survey conducted by the Psychological Laboratory at Nijmegen University, with a sample of 292 respondents evenly divided by sex, only 17 percent of the men and 33 percent of the women answered "Yes" when asked, "Do you consider that the rule obliging all priests to stay celibate must remain in force?" Another 1966 survey conducted by the Nijmegen Institute of Applied Sociology asked a sample of 820 parents of Catholic primary-school children to choose between four categories of answers to the question:

34. For the discussion and votes on the resolutions for changing the celibacy rule for priests, see *Pastoraal Concilie*, VI, pp. 297–323.
35. Reported on KRO Radio transcript, "Riskante Kerk" for February 13, 1970.

"Do you see the unmarried state of the priest as: (1) truly meaningful? (2) desirable in practice? (3) unnecessary? (4) disadvantageous?" Eighteen percent of the sample chose the first answer and 28 percent the second.

A survey of all Dutch priests in 1967 shows that 68 percent of the 381 respondents were in favor of allowing priests who married, under certain circumstances, to continue in the ministry. Finally, a random sample of 1,200 lay Catholics surveyed in 1969 by the Netherlands Institute for Public Opinion (NIPO) found that 24 percent desired that compulsory priestly celibacy be maintained while 72 percent thought the decision between celibacy and marriage should be left to the discretion of the individual priest.[36] Seventy percent of the Catholics in the NIPO poll said that they would be willing to accept married priests in their own parish. Even 48 percent of those who self-chose the label "conservative Catholic" had no objections to a married clergy. If there is some question about how representative the first three samples are, there can be no question about the sampling technique in the priest study or the NIPO poll.

These surveys attest that between 1966 and 1969, a minority of about 25 and 30 percent of lay and clerical Catholics opposed a change in the celibacy rule for priests. An overwhelming majority of priests and laity supported the change. Presumably, therefore, even if the Pastoral Council had been an absolutely perfect mirror of Dutch lay and clerical opinions, the resolutions supporting a change in the celibacy rule would have mustered the two-thirds vote necessary in accord with the statutes of the Pastoral Council for passage. Neither the method of election of representatives of the Pastoral Council, nor an inspection of its membership rolls, nor any of its votes lend support to contentions that the Council was a rigged forum of radical Catholics whose opinions dramatically differed from the ordinary Catholic population.

The Pastoral Council and Episcopal Authority. A second question concerns the relation between the Pastoral Council and the authority of the bishops. Did the Pastoral Council undermine episcopal authority? In the explanatory note accompanying the statutes for the

36. For the Attwood Survey, see G. H. Zeegers, ed., *God in Nederland* (Amsterdam: Van Ditmar, 1966), Table 26, pp. 144–147; the Psychological Laboratory Study is reported in *Hoe Denken de Gelovigen Over de Celibaatswet?*, J. M. van de Lans, ed. (Amersfoort: Katholiek Archief, 1968), pp. 8–11 and 14–21. The study of the Nijmegen Institute of Sociology is found in J. G. M. Sterk and J. J. Poeisz, *De Leek Over Het Ambt* (Nijmegen: Instituut voor Toegepaste Sociologie, 1965), p. 58; the priests' survey in *Ambtscelibaat in eeen Veranderende Kerk* (Amersfoort: Katholiek Archief, 1969), p. 47; the NIPO poll is reported in *KA*, XXIV, 22 (May 13, 1969), columns 536ff.

Pastoral Council, the expectations of the drafters of the statutes on this point were clearly stated:

> The bishops are asked as individuals and as a college to speak out openly and to give their reasons in the course of the discussion. In that way, they give true and effective leadership in the process of forming opinion and judgment. It is expected that in this way the solidarity of the church membership with the bishops will grow and the episcopal authority will be strengthened.[37]

Although the seven bishops, in particular Cardinal Alfrink, took an active and leading part in the discussion and deliberations of the Council, they did not demonstrably intimidate the other participants from speaking out. On many issues the bishops disagreed among themselves and did not vote as a bloc. They consistently allowed themselves to be interrogated on their positions and policies. Throughout the Council, when the bishops thought that the discussion was overemphasizing one pole of a paired concept in theology or church structure, they came forward to call for balance, although almost always some other member of the Council—sometimes a Protestant observer—could be counted on to add balance to the discussions.

Even though the statutes of the Pastoral Council foresaw the possibility that the bishops and the other representatives might be at loggerheads on an issue—hence, the demand for a two-thirds majority to carry any resolution and the provision for effective episcopal veto even against a two-thirds majority—no such occasion occurred during the six sessions. In the midst of an emotion-packed discussion in the first session, for example, several delegates wanted to send representatives to Rome to clear up what they felt was unresponsiveness and poor communication. "Many of the decisions of the central authority in Rome are clearly not consonant with the feelings of the church. The value of the central authority of the church is, thereby, undermined." Cardinal Alfrink intervened to point out that, while he too desired improvement in communication between Rome and the local churches, he did not think that sending a delegation to Rome would be helpful. He also warned the Council to be careful about overgeneralizing about the Roman Curia. Bishops Bluyssen of Den Bosch and Nierman of Groningen supported Alfrink's position. When the issue of sending a delegation to Rome was put to a vote, the bishops, voting first, split 1–6 against, Mgr. Jansen of Rotterdam

37. *Pastoraal Concilie*, XXXIX, *1*, p. 137.

voting for. The Council followed the bishops' lead, voting 37 for, 61 against, and 4 blank.[38]

The bishops spoke repeatedly, as officers of a world church, to implications for the relationship between Dutch Catholics and Rome or with other national Catholic churches. At several points, the bishops decisively determined what lay within the province of decision-making of a national church and what could be decided only in dialogue with the pope and the other world bishops.

Before, during, and after the Council, all of the Dutch bishops who participated expressed enthusiasm and support for the new role of being a bishop in council. Hence, after six sessions and four years of experience, the Dutch bishops determined, in 1970, to institutionalize the experimental structure in a permanent body. In his closing speech to the Council at the final session, Alfrink tried to reflect on his own experience of this new episcopal role, that of a bishop serving as the leading spokesman within a representative national body of Catholics:

> The Pastoral Council has shown that in dialogue with all the parts of the church, the bishops do not need to be isolated as a college from the rest of the church which sets itself against the bishops. Some have remarked that we bishops in the last few years have given too little leadership. I will not, for myself, try to deny the charge out of hand. But I am happy to have the opportunity to make clear that we have consciously chosen to learn to understand our leadership function as the exercise of authority in dialogue, and that we have tried to avoid the appearance of wanting to hold on to an authoritarian manner of acting, as was formerly done and which is, perhaps, the most obvious role for a bishop.[39]

The Dutch episcopacy also learned that the more authoritarian manner of exercising the episcopacy in several other countries led to noisy conflicts between the bishops and members of their lower clergy. At the gatherings of the European episcopacy in Chur, Switzerland, and again at the meetings of the Synod of World Bishops in Rome in 1969 and 1971, many of the world episcopacy seemed unable to cope or communicate with the extra parliamentary opposition of the members of their own lower clergy noisily protesting outside. Upon their return from the meeting in Chur, the Dutch bishops wrote:

38. *Pastoraal Concilie*, II, pp. 111–113.
39. *Pastoraal Concilie*, VII, p. 266.

In the publicity about the symposium in Chur, the isolation of bishops was repeatedly mentioned. We want, to the extent that it lies in our power, to avoid such isolation. We consider it essential to have open communication with the community, especially with the priests. We feel ourselves bound in conscience to maintain a close tie with the college of priests and with the conscientious views of all the faithful.[40]

It is not surprising, therefore, that, in a representative random sample of Dutch Catholics surveyed in 1969, 88 percent claimed strong confidence in the leadership of their bishops.[41] The Dutch bishops' mandate compares very favorably with that of secular officials in the Netherlands: in 1972 54 percent of voters claimed that they had trust in the leadership of Dutch governmental officials against 27 percent who had no trust.[42]

Perhaps an anecdote, chosen from among many within the events of the Council, will convey both the new way in which the Dutch bishops were exercising their role and the sort of experience of the church in council which has generated an enthusiasm among Dutch Catholics which they find difficult to capture in words. In the Catholic student parish in Utrecht, the three campus' ministers had permitted a Protestant minister to celebrate the eucharist for the Sunday liturgy. In the early months of 1969, Alfrink and these pastors came to an impasse on the question. The cardinal felt compelled to suspend the pastors from the exercise of their function as priests until they agreed to discontinue this ecumenical experiment. Support for the position of the Utrecht pastors was mobilized by pastors in other student parishes throughout the Netherlands. During the fourth session of the Council, April 9–11, 1969, one of the suspended pastors, Dr. J. H. Kamphuis, was in attendance as a representative for the study commission entitled "Renewal of the Practice of Faith in the Church." During the discussions at the Council on April 10, 1969, the unresolved conflict between Cardinal Alfrink and the Utrecht student parish was brought up. The cardinal, reacting very cautiously, stated that he found it rather uncomfortable to talk about the issue in public, since it involved a relation with persons. Because many of the delegates were disturbed by the unresolved tensions between Alfrink and Kamphuis, the vicar-general of the diocese of Breda, Mgr. H. Ruygers, took it upon himself to approach the Council leadership, Cardinal Alfrink, and Dr. Kamphuis to suggest a

40. *KA*, XXIV, *38* and *39* (September 19–26, 1969), column 923.
41. Reported in *KA*, XXIV, *22* (May 13, 1969), column 536.
42. *De Nederlandse Kiezer '72* (Alphen aan den Rijn: Samson, 1973), p. 76.

mediation commission to facilitate resolution of the conflict. All sides agreed to the suggestion. The following morning, April 11, 1969, the daily newspapers, which had earlier carried stories of the conflict and ultimate suspension of the three Utrecht priests, announced the formation of the mediation commission which had been chosen by the dean of Utrecht. Within a short time, the conflict was resolved—without noice or rancor—to the mutual satisfaction of the cardinal and the campus ministers, who agreed to suspend their unauthorized liturgical experiment. Experience of this kind helps to explain the mutual confidence between the Dutch bishops and their lower clergy, theologians, and lay elites. It is to the emotional newness and satisfaction with such experiences that the Dutch elites seem to be pointing when they energetically use the symbolic slogans and collective representations for the new church.

When Mgr. Ruygers announced the successful resolution of the impasse between Alfrink and Kamphuis, he could hardly contain his enthusiasm about this new experience of being-the-church-together: "For me personally and also for many others here it has been a most unusual and deeply moving religious and church experience that a bishop who suspends and the priest he suspended were, nevertheless, together in the same Council chambers."[43]

Toward Permanent Structures?

In 1970, after four years of experimentation with a national council, the bishops commissioned a study group under the chairmanship of a leading Catholic politician, Professor P. Steenkamp, to draw up the definitive charter for a permanent national structure of a church in continuous council. The documents for this permanent National Pastoral Council clearly set out the goal and jurisdiction of the new body. "The goal of the Pastoral Council is to give form to the involvement of all Catholics in the Netherlands in a mutually determined national pastoral policy." Article I, Section 1a, of the statutes defines its jurisdiction. "Such a Council is a policy-forming organ and thus more than an ad hoc organ for dialogue. It is, together with the bishops' conference, responsible for pastoral policy."

Article II, Section 3b, states, "This formula, which recognizes the increase in scale from a diocesan to a national church, does not exclude activity at the diocesan level. Rather, it presupposes and

43. *Pastoraal Concilie*, V, p. 253.

builds upon it." Article I, Section 1, No. 1b, specifies that the co-responsibility of the pastoral council for pastoral policy does not preempt the separate position and responsibility of the episcopal conference. The college of bishops has the exclusive right to approve or change the statutes of the Pastoral Council or dissolve the institution. Further, the bishops constitute the continuous policy-making body for the church. Finally, they are always present at the council sessions as active, participating leaders, constituting a presidium.

The steering committee and executive secretariat of the permanent Council consists of 17 persons: the seven Dutch bishops, one representative of the Conference of Religious Superiors of Men, and nine members chosen by the body of the Pastoral Council. The main task of this committee is the maintenance of contact between the National Pastoral Council and the diocesan councils and the holding of hearings or surveys on pastoral issues which will be discussed at the general session.

The members of the National Pastoral Council are elected for three-year periods with an opportunity for reelection. One-third of the members would be elected each year. The election procedure foresaw that 56 members would be chosen by diocesan pastoral councils. An explanatory note to Article II, Section 4, No. 1, states the presumption that the diocesan pastoral councils would not normally choose these 56 members from their own membership. An additional 25 members would be chosen by an electoral college consisting of three members from the steering committee and three members chosen by the general session of the pastoral council. Groups which felt that they were being discriminated against by the electoral procedure of the diocesan councils were invited to submit names of nominees to the special electoral college. A bishop was to act as presiding officer both of the steering committee and of the electoral college.[44]

On August 13, 1972, the Dutch bishops issued a press communiqué announcing the suspension of the planned first session of the permanent Dutch council because of Roman objections which claimed that the Dutch council was inopportune because the Curia was still studying the question of statutes for diocesan councils. The Vatican Congregation for the Clergy had sent a letter, dated November 25, 1970, to all the bishops' conferences in which it presented its

44 See "Statuten van de Landelijke Pastorale Raad van de Nederlandse Kerk Provincie," available from the Episcopal Conference of the Roman Catholic Church in the Netherlands.

own guidelines for diocesan councils. The Dutch council differed from the proposed Roman model on several important points. The Roman document presumed that members of diocesan councils would be appointees of the bishop, not elected. Secondly, such councils would have no juridically permanent character; each bishop was to be free to erect a pastoral council for his diocese or not. Further, every diocesan council was to avoid the appearance of being a representative body of the faithful; individual members of such councils were to be considered acting strictly as individuals. Again, the Roman document proposed that it was somehow confusing to combine, as the Dutch models did, priests and laity in a single episcopal advisory council.[45]

In what seemed an obvious reference to the Dutch Pastoral Council, the Roman document stated, "All believers, indeed, have the right and duty to take an active part in the mission which Christ has given to his church . . . *but they do not have either the right or duty to give advice to the hierarchy in their exercise of their pastoral task.*"[46]

The Congregation of the Clergy proposed that a pastoral council can have only a consultative voice, for two reasons: (1) there are no questions which the bishop has to place before the council; and (2) the bishop has no duty to act according to the advice which the council gives him. The Roman document is firm in rejecting the idea that councils are co-responsible for pastoral policies. Finally, the Congregation suggested that councils at a regional or national level have no juridical status and seemed inopportune. Rome had some difficulty pressing this last point with any credibility against the Netherlands, because it had allowed national synods in East and West Germany and in Denmark, and had permitted regional synods in Flanders and Switzerland.

In their communiqué of August 13, 1972, the Dutch bishops stated: "The curial organs are preparing a document about pastoral councils that in a short while will be sent to the world episcopacy. They considered that the authority of the bishops and their proper

45. I am grateful to Dr. Paul Dresen of the Diocesan pastoral council of Haarlem for informing me of the reason why the diocese combined the priest and lay councils in one body. The laity had elected several priest members to their council and asked the priests' council to merge with them because they felt separation to be somewhat artificial for Dutch Catholicism.
46. See *Archief van de Kerken,* XXVII, 40 and 41 (October 3–10, 1972), columns 913–923. The *Katholiek Archief* changed its title in 1969 to include non-Catholic church news. Hereafter cited as *AK.*

place in the church was not sufficiently safeguarded by the statutes of our national pastoral council. They considered, further, that the time was not ripe to set up a pastoral council at the national level.''[47] The Dutch bishops disagreed with the Roman judgment and promised to find a way to continue dialogue at the national level.

In a prime-time television interview on the *Brandpunt* program of August 14, 1972, Cardinal Alfrink referred to two visions in the church on how authority should be expressed. When the interviewer asked him, ''You mean that Rome holds on to the more authoritarian way of exercising authority?'' Alfrink replied, rather nonchalantly, ''You could put it that way.'' In the same interview the cardinal tried to give assurance that the bishops would find some way to facilitate dialogue, even if the resultant structure was only an ''advisory organ,'' not ''co-responsible for pastoral policy.'' ''In practice I should think that the term advisory organ will not make that much difference because it depends primarily on the way in which such a council functions. And when people work together in mutual trust and respect I should think that even such a structure that has only an advisory capacity would, nonetheless, have real influence on the policy which the bishops will follow.''[48]

Alfrink traveled to Rome during the week of October 15-22, 1972, to discuss the Dutch-Roman differences. Upon his return he announced that the bishops would take active part on January 26-28, 1973, in a national pastoral dialogue based on the model used in the Dutch-speaking dioceses of Belgium. In this new form, the bishops were present as individuals and not as a presidium. They were present, further, as auditors and not as leaders within a co-responsible deliberative body. Significantly, however, the topic for discussion and the members at this meeting were the original topics and members proposed for the first meeting of the permanent National Pastoral Council whose statutes were opposed by Rome. Whatever the statutes the meeting showed much of the dynamics and openness of the Dutch Pastoral Council, including a frank discussion of the differences between the policy vision of the lower clergy and the controversial new bishop of Roermond, Msg. Jan Gijsen. While the other six Dutch bishops took an open and active part in these discussions similar to the role they played at the original pastoral council, Gijsen,

47. *AK*, XXVII, *15* (August 29, 1972), column 764.
48. The text of the television interview in columns 765-770 of the same issue (August 29, 1972).

pointedly, remained silent. Upon completion of the 1973 pastoral dialogue, the Dutch bishops announced a second one which was to be held in 1975. The structure would seem to be a permanent part of Dutch Catholic life.

Coordination between Diocesan Priests and Religious Orders

In the mid-1960s Dutch Catholicism began to lay to rest long-standing and, often, intense rivalries and jealousies between diocesan and religious-order priests. Traditionally, the priests of religious orders have been directly responsible to their own superiors and only indirectly responsible to the bishops. The history of post-Tridentine Catholicism is filled with conflicts, jealousies, and uncoordinated pastoral efforts between the two groups. As we saw in the preceding chapter, the religious orders have historically afforded Rome leverage for exerting its influence locally. Since 1963, the Dutch episcopal conference and the Conference of Religious Superiors of Men share a national executive secretariat. Hence their activities support rather than undercut each other. Before announcing their position on the question of a change in the celibacy rule for priests, for example, the Dutch bishops met with the superiors of religious orders so that the bishop's final position represented a joint policy. Moreover, a representative from the National Conference of Religious Superiors of Men is present on almost every commission entrusted with coordinating national pastoral policies.[49]

The good relationship between the diocesan and religious-order priests is important, especially since the religious-order priests outnumber the diocesan priests, 4,309 to 3,680. As in so many areas, the development of new coordination between diocesan and religious-order priests in the Netherlands has undergone a rapid evolution. Since 1967, the students for the priesthood for religious orders and those for the diocesan priesthood pursue their studies in shared theological centers rather than in separate seminaries. This new joint theologate would seem to ensure continued cooperation between the two kinds of Catholic clergy. In the Netherlands religious priests hold several diocesan-wide curial posts, such as vicar-general, dean, or

---

49. For the lack of such coordination between the episcopal conference and the Conference of Religious Superiors in the American church, see John P. Marschall, "Diocesan and Religious Clergy: the History of a Relationship, 1789–1969," in John Tracy Ellis, ed., *The Catholic Priest in the United States* (Collegeville, Minnesota: St. John's University Press, 1971), pp. 385–423.

member of the cathedral chapter, which in other national churches tend to be rather jealously preserved for the diocesan clergy. For example, seven of the twenty-one diocesan vicars are members of religious orders. The percentage of religious-order deans varies from six of the eleven deans in the diocese of Groningen to four of the thirty-one deans in the diocese of Den Bosch. The prestigious post of dean of the Hague is held by a Jesuit. The secretary-general of the church province is a Capuchin. All of these developments have occurred since the mid-1960s.

In 1971 the priests of the cathedral chapter in Rotterdam proposed a religious-order priest as their first choice from a list of nominees for bishop, something that would be unthinkable in almost any other church in Western Europe or North America.[50] Again, in the past several years, pastoral teams of priests in parishes have included diocesan priests in the team of religious-order churches and vice versa. This new spirit of cooperative planning between the religious orders and the diocesan clergy is a little noted fact in the stormy story of structural differentiation in the Dutch church.

Like any institutional solution to a problem, however, the growing cooperation and integration between religious-order and diocesan priests has created its own problems. Thus many religious-order groups have complained about a sort of "identity" crisis in the meaning of the religious order when it begins to think of itself too much in terms of the local or national church.[51] Many of the religious orders in the Netherlands have had problems similar to those of the diocesan priests in finding acceptance for the new collective symbols, such as that of collegiality, in their headquarters in Rome. Some of the religious orders in the Netherlands have faced the same conflict between Rome and Holland that has checkered Dutch attempts to specify, institutionalize, and consolidate new institutional forms. In the post-Vatican era, Dutch religious orders have placed great emphasis on the order's service within the local and national church setting. Indeed, many of them have chosen the local setting in situations where there was a conflict of loyalties. In 1967, when the Dominican master-general in Rome brought objections against the progressive policy of the Dutch Dominican magazine *De Bazuin*, Dutch Dominicans found ways to place the magazine outside of Dominican jurisdiction to ensure its continued freedom. This conflict of loyalty between Rome

50. The nominee was Dr. C. G. F. Braun, M.S.C., the vicar-general of the diocese.
51. See the remarks in *Pastoraal Concilie*, VI, p. 23.

and the national church is again reflected, for example, in a letter sent on March 11, 1972, to Cardinal Alfrink by six Dutch fathers-general and twelve top functionaries of international religious congregations with headquarters in Rome, expressing their solidarity with the Dutch bishops. These Dutch elites in international orders especially noted "the good internal communication which has been brought about in the Netherlands."[52]

Behind the stormy conflict, symbolic skirmishes, and personal and institutional clashes within Dutch Catholicism between 1966 and 1974, then, there is a discernible pattern by which new institutional structures for national planning and coordination of pastoral policies have been specified, erected, and consolidated. It is clear that, in this period, Dutch Catholics were mainly engaged in the tasks implied by stages five and six in structural differentiation: the collectivity specifies the new forms and embodies them in new institutional arrangements. As we will see later, the Dutch church is already in the seventh stage specified by our model: the collectivity attempts to consolidate the new institutional forms. The continuing conflicts within the college of bishops in the Netherlands apparent since 1972, which are between groups within Dutch Catholicism and between Rome and Holland, however, show that some groups do not agree with what the majority of Dutch Catholics decided was the best institutional form for easing dissatisfactions. These conflicts seem to center mainly on role definitions regarding bishop, priest, and laity within the Roman Catholic Church. A change in the role definition of any one affects each of the other roles, and that of the papacy and the Roman Curia as well.

COLLEGIALITY: BISHOP-PRIEST-LAY ROLES IN THE CHURCH

Bishops

We are fortunate in having, to chart the massive structural changes within the Dutch church, a great deal of public evidence for understanding how the Dutch bishops were defining the role of a bishop within his diocese, the national church, and the world church. The Dutch bishops' responses to television and newspaper interviewers as well as the public record of their discussion during the Pastoral

52. Reported in *De Tijd*, March 11, 1972, p. 3.

Council about the role of a Roman Catholic bishop, when coupled
with the pattern of their collective decisions, leave little doubt that
the Dutch episcopacy was defining the role of a bishop in dramatically new ways in accord with its understanding of collegial
authority.

We will want to see how the Dutch bishops were defining the role
of the individual bishop to: (1) the college of other Dutch bishops
within the episcopal conference; (2) other bishops in the world
episcopacy; (3) the pope and Roman Curial bureaucracy; (4) their
lower clergy and theologians; (5) the Catholic laity; and (6) wider
Dutch society. Only after reviewing the evidence which provides some
answers to these six questions can we begin to understand and evaluate the revolutionary developments in role definition for a bishop.

The Individual Bishop and the Episcopal Conference. In traditional Catholic structures, the line of command went from pope and
Roman Curia through their representative, the papal nuncio, to the
individual bishop in the diocese. Since Vatican II, however, the
national episcopal conferences of bishops have gained jurisdiction
over several pastoral questions (liturgy, ecumenism, social issues, and
forms of ministry, such as the married diaconate), which has introduced genuine restrictions upon the former absolute legislative power
of an individual bishop in his own diocese. Throughout the international church, this new institution of an episcopal conference has
led to the revision of traditional rights and duties. Nevertheless, few
of the episcopal conferences refer to themselves, as the Dutch
bishops do, as a college of bishops co-responsible for pastoral coordination at the national level. Most national episcopacies tend to be
cautiously slow in revising the absolute jurisdiction of a bishop.

The Dutch bishops seem to be attempting to reverse the direction
of flow within the world church into a line which runs just as much
from individual bishop to episcopal conference, episcopal conference
to the collegial body of world bishops, and through that body to its
head, the pope, as vice versa. In the Netherlands, at any rate, an
individual bishop is as much, if not more, a member of the college of
Dutch bishops as he is a sovereign territorial church officer in his own
diocese. This development toward a national church reflects Dutch
institutional realities. The Netherlands is one small, compact, unitary
state with a well-developed communication network and increasing
mobility, so that older territorial localisms have lost their meaning.
Political, economic, or cultural events in any one of the provinces

soon become national issues. Roman Catholicism shares the same sense of national unity which transcends the arbitrary territorial boundaries of one diocese.

It may help to cite examples to illustrate this point. If the bishop of Utrecht allows the non-Catholic party in a mixed marriage to receive communion at the Catholic eucharist while his neighboring bishop of Den Bosch does not, the Catholics in each diocese will be confused, frustrated, or jealous of one another. Again, if the bishop of Haarlem approves the use of a catechism series for his school system in Amsterdam which the bishop of Utrecht (twenty minutes away by train) declares unorthodox, Catholics in the two dioceses—who will know the next day about the dispute from the Catholic daily press or on television—will be needlessly confused. In the process, episcopal authority will be undermined. Such situations are avoidable if the bishops jointly plan important pastoral activities across dioceses.

In their response to this real problem, found everywhere within the international church as one result of structurally defining a bishop as a kind of religious king, but especially prominent in the Netherlands, the Dutch bishops have increasingly decided most pastoral questions in joint conference through decisions binding upon all dioceses. In recent years, the statutes of most Catholic organizations place them under the responsibility of the collective body of bishops. These seemingly unavoidable institutional arrangements militate against the traditional absolute sovereignty of the local bishop.

A concrete example of how this institution of the episcopal conference works will illustrate the point. In 1971, the bishop of Haarlem, Mgr. Zwartkruis, was asked to approve the statutes for a non-parochial "critical community of Catholics" which would operate outside of parochial or deanery territorial boundaries but would be directly responsible to the bishop. Zwartkruis knew that his approval of this far-reaching experiment would be prominently reported in the Catholic press, thus confronting the bishops in other dioceses with the possibility of demands for similar experiments. Although Zwartkruis had theoretical rights, according to Catholic canon law, to act any way he pleased, he took the question to the bishops' conference for joint decision before his final approval of the far-reaching experiment.[53]

53. See Jan Ruyter and Richard Auwerda, *Welkom en Ongewenst* (Hilversum: Gooi and Sticht, 1971), pp. 145–147.

The constant—sometimes weekly— 'nsultation between the Dutch bishops has made their episcopal conference a unique episcopal body. Naturally, a small body meeting several times monthly on key pastoral issues takes on, over the years, a collective face and joint outlook. In that sense, the college of Dutch bishops constitutes a kind of club.

The Dutch episcopal conference has also emerged as a concrete institutional embodiment of the collegial concept of bishops. The Second Vatican Council developed a theology of the college of world bishops as infallible, with the pope as head of the church *within* rather than *above* the college. The institutional embodiments of this collegial idea include ecumenical councils of the world bishops, the synod of bishops which meets every two years in Rome, and the new body that constitutes the consistory to elect the pope. The Dutch bishops have in recent years developed rituals and symbols of their episcopal conference as an ongoing collegial sub-unit of the world college of bishops. Since 1966 the naming of new bishops has provided ritual reinforcement to the Dutch episcopacy's embodiment of the myths for a collegial church.

There were six new bishops appointed to the Dutch hierarchy between 1966 and 1974: Mgr. Zwartkruis of Haarlem (1966); Mgr. Bluyssen of Den Bosch (1966); Mgr. Ernst of Breda (1967); Mgr. Moller of Groningen (1969); Mgr. Simonis of Rotterdam (1971); and Mgr. Gijsen of Roermond (1972). We will analyze the structural issues involved in the controversial appointments of the last two men in a later chapter. The first four were nominated following the procedure by which all Dutch bishops have been named in accordance with a privilege granted to the Dutch church in 1853 and reaffirmed by Rome in 1956 when two new dioceses were erected. The cathedral chapter in each diocese sends a list of three candidates to the episcopal conference and to the papal nuncio for their independent comments, which are then sent on separately to Rome. The pope has the right to name a new bishop according to his own wishes, but between 1853 and 1971 Rome has always picked the new bishop from the list suggested by the cathedral chapter.

Between the announcement of the pope's choice of a new bishop and the actual consecration of the nominee, several months usually elapsed in which the nominee, in a sort of on-the-job apprenticeship, got the chance to talk to his consultors in the cathedral chapter and the diocesan service bureaucracy, as well as to sit in as an auditor on the episcopal conference. Consecrated upon the Roman proclamation of his nomination, the new bishop's first official act was to compose a letter to his diocese.

We get some idea of the way the Dutch church was embodying the new collegial models by looking at this important ritual of episcopal consecration and installment. Emile Durkheim contended that the group myths which originated during periods of collective effervescence were solemnly reaffirmed during crises or turning points, such as the inauguration of new leaders. For him, solemn group rituals were fundamental indicators of communal solidarity. Moreover, the use of the rhetoric of the collective representations during crises further reinforces the "social unconscious" which binds the members of a collectivity together. Hence, those who follow Durkheim's lead in sociology are not likely to dismiss public rhetoric as "mere" rhetoric.

The Dutch bishops have used each of the six episcopal nominations since 1966 to reaffirm the myths of collegiality, dialogue, democratizing, a church in movement, and so on. On each occasion, they have affirmed the solidarity of the new bishop to their episcopal college and *through* that college to the college of the world bishops with the pope as its head. Finally, on each occasion the national episcopal college has claimed its right to be considered an element in the church and not merely an agent of papal or Roman purposes.

At the consecration of Mgrs. Zwartkruis, Bluyssen, Ernst, and Moller, all of the Catholic Netherlands could watch on television as the college of Dutch bishops assembled around their new colleague. Further, the new bishop was surrounded by bishops from other parts of Europe and the missionary territories, as if to underwrite the Dutch bishops' independent solidarity with the world episcopacy. Finally, the presence of the papal nuncio symbolized the Dutch church's desires to maintain communion with Rome. In recent years, representatives from non-Catholic churches have also been present at the consecration.

In his sermons at these solemn consecrations, Cardinal Alfrink reiterated the themes of collegial solidarity of the new bishop with his fellow Dutch bishops, with all the world bishops, and with the pope. He used these occasions to reinforce the myth of a collegial church at all levels. Thus, for example, in his sermon at the consecration of Mgr. Ernst of Breda, Alfrink remarked, "the possibilities which *the local churches can find for their own life* within the essential structure of the church have not always been the same in the course of the centuries. But the collegial character of the bishops' college will always continue to ask that these possibilities be brought into actuality *within the structure of that college* and not outside of it.''[54]

The four new bishops (1966–1969) underscored the bishop's collegial relationship with his priests and people: in dialogue, together with the bishop as leader of a team of priests, they are God's people on the march. Thus, Mgr. Zwartkruis' first letter to the deans of the diocese of Haarlem stressed dialogue and cooperation. In his first letter to the whole diocese, Zwartkruis showed his solidarity with his fellow Dutch bishops by publicly praising the New Dutch Catechism, which had come under attack from conservative groups. In this letter, Zwartkruis also spoke of the need for experiment: ''No one can live without risks.'' He ended his letter by promising that he would try to promote unity within pluriformity.[55]

The first letter of Bishop Bluyssen to his faithful in Den Bosch was emphatic on his acceptance of collegiality: ''The task which we are together facing must from the very beginning be thought through together and mutually brought to realization. I am saying it with conscious deliberation: the task which we are together facing. Because my episcopal task is also your task. My responsibility is also your responsibility.'' Bluyssen pleaded that his Catholics show openness to change and room for experiment. He ended his letter by reminding his people, as his predecessor William Bekkers had done, that a bishop was an ordinary mortal who would make mistakes, asking the faithful for patience and encouraging them to criticize him when he erred.[56]

The Dutch Episcopal Conference and the World College of Bishops.

The Dutch episcopacy has exhibited an unusual sensitivity to their connections with the world college of bishops and their corresponsibility, as bishops, for the unity, credibility, and needs of the entire world church. Since 1966 the Dutch bishops, as individuals and as a body, have sent numerous letters to fellow bishops about situations of human injustice, especially in the developing world.[57] In return,

54. *KA*, XXIII, *1* (January 5, 1968), column 11. Italics mine to stress the balance between assertion of an ''element'' as well as a ''part'' role in the office of a bishop. For another inaugural sermon by Alfrink, see *KA*, XXIV, *31* (August 1, 1969), columns 740–743—a sermon at the consecration of Mgr. Moller of Groningen.
55. *KA*, XXI, *45* (November 11, 1966), columns 1216–1220.
56. Bluyssen's first letter is in *KA*, XXI, *48* (December 21, 1966), columns 1290–1293. See also Ernst's first letter, *KA*, XXII, *46* (November 17, 1967), column 1153; and Moller's first letter, in XXIV, *31* (August 1, 1969), columns 743–745.
57. For examples, see the letter signed by Bishops Ernst, Bluyssen, Jansen, Moller, and Zwartkruis to a Spanish bishop protesting the infringement of human rights in the condemnation of sixteen members of the Basque resistance movement, cited in Jan Ruyter, editor, *Informatie Septuagint* (Hilversum: Gooi and Sticht, 1971), p. 22; the telegram of Cardinal Alfrink to the minister of justice in Brazil protesting the illegal procedures applied to Brazilian

bishops from other national churches, especially international elite bishops such as Cardinal Silva of Santiago, Chile, and Archbishop Helder Camara of Recife in Brazil, have sent special messages or made "state visits" to the Catholics of the Netherlands.[58] Camara, for example, has made three state visits to the Dutch Catholics since 1967. This style of independent episcopal exchange recalls practices of the church in the first five centuries. Since the Second Vatican Council, Cardinal Alfrink has traveled widely as an international figure in the church.

It was only fitting, perhaps, that the first international conference of European bishops was held in Noordwijkerhout in the Netherlands. At the Dutch Pastoral Council, observer bishops or delegates from episcopal conferences in Belgium, Scandinavia, Germany, France, Switzerland, and Indonesia were in attendance. The Dutch Pastoral Council, especially PINK, maintained contacts with representatives of Cardinal Konig of Vienna, the German bishops' conference, the bishop of Denmark, and the Swiss bishops' conference—all of whom have since held pastoral councils of their own.[59] The bishops and Dutch Catholic media have given prominent play to international bishops' conferences and the sessions of the world synod of bishops. Informal exchanges or acts of independent collegiality have taken place between Dutch and German bishops and between a Dutch bishop and the French episcopal conference.[60] The Dutch vigorously opposed a Roman suggestion that the mission societies in each country channel their funds through Rome, instead of dispersing them directly from the national church to mission projects of their own choice. Dutch objections centered on the argument that Roman financial centralization would undermine direct and independent collegial contacts between national churches.

The Celibacy Dispute. The most dramatic instance of Dutch insistence on a right to collegial contact occurred in connection with the Dutch bishops' decision, following upon the vote of their Pastoral Council, to reopen discussion in the world church on the question of the celibacy rule for priests, even after the pope had decided to

---

prisoners, wherein Alfrink shows his solidarity with Brazilian Bishop Arns, in *AK,* XXVII, *42* (October 17, 1972), column 945.

58. Silva's "Letter to Dutch Catholics" in *AK,* XXVII, *18* (May 2, 1972), columns 403–407.

59. For evidence that the German national synod contained themes reminiscent of the Dutch Pastoral Council, see Karl Rahner, *The Shape of the Church to Come* (New York: Seabury, 1974).

60. See report of an informal exchange of pastoral experiences between six German and four Dutch bishops in *AK,* XXVI, *13* (March 26, 1971), column 301. Bishop Moller was the Dutch representative to the Synod of the German Church in 1972.

reserve the decision to himself. There had been no public discussion of the celibacy rule by the bishops at the Second Vatican Council when they voted on a document on priests; the pope had removed the question from the Council agenda because he considered its decision a papal prerogative.

It will be helpful for the following discussion to distinguish three different forms of the celibacy rule: (1) the Roman Catholic rule for the Latin rite: only celibates can be ordained, and they must remain celibate after ordination or give up the priesthood by being "reduced to the lay state"; (2) the Orthodox rule followed by the Orthodox churches as well as the Greek, Syrian, Russian, and Chaldean rites in union with Rome: marriage is allowable before ordination but not afterward; (3) the Anglican rule: marriage is allowable both before and after ordination. The Dutch appealed for both the Orthodox and the Anglican rule.

During the preparatory period of the Dutch Pastoral Council (1966-1968), the Dutch bishops at first tried to veto discussion of the celibacy rule. They were opposed by the Council advisory commission, which viewed the inclusion of the celibacy question on the agenda as a test case.[61] When, in 1967, Pope Paul VI issued a papal encyclical, *Sacerdotalis Celibatus,* reiterating the classic Catholic case for the celibacy rule, a large number of bishops, theologians, and members of the lower clergy in the world church did not feel that the discussion was closed.

As we have seen, the Dutch bishops had at their disposal a series of sociological surveys of Dutch priests and people which showed that approximately 65–75 percent of the Dutch church (1966–1970) favored some change in the rule. The survey of all Dutch priests showed, further, that 83 percent of those priests already ordained judged that they would probably remain celibate under a more liberal rule.[62] Discussion did not threaten the stability of the ministry. Some groups within Dutch Catholicism at this time were arguing that the bishops should change the celibacy rule on their own and confront Rome with a fait accompli. The survey of Dutch priests revealed that a surprising total of 46 percent agreed with the statement, "Do you think that the Dutch Church Province should pursue its own policy in connection with the requirement of celibacy for the ministry?" Only 40 percent disagreed.[63]

61. *Pastoraal Concilie,* I, p. 71.
62. *Ambtscelibaat in een Veranderende Kerk,* p. 51.
63. *Ibid.,* p. 46. The proportion of those favoring a go-it-alone policy is considerably higher if we remove retired priests and Dutch missionaries home on leave from the sample.

By the time the discussion on celibacy began at the fifth session of the Dutch Pastoral Council, January 4–7, 1970, the issue had been the subject of almost seven years of public discussions, surveys, and lobbying for and against within Dutch Catholicism. Shortly before this council session, Pope Paul wrote a letter to the Dutch bishops in which he expressed his reservations about the discussion report listing five specific objections. The pope ended his letter with a plea that the bishops support his position in *Sacerdotalis Celibatus:* "Whether it is a question of doctrine or discipline, we are certain . . . that the best service which you, your priests, and your believers can give at the moment—in particular, during the forthcoming gathering of the Pastoral Council—will be if you calmly witness to your full and unconditional agreement with the universal church on the disputed points."[64]

Despite Paul's plea, the Dutch bishops decided that the Pastoral Council had the right to discuss the original working document and that it was their duty as bishops to champion this right. In a long opening speech to the Pastoral Council, Cardinal Alfrink asserted the bishops' own rights by setting the terms on which discussion could take place. (1) The original "working paper" was merely a draft proposal for discussion, not a final document expressing the opinion of the Council and the bishops. (2) The bishops exercised their right, as officers of the world church and the presidium of the Council, to rule out of the discussion any suggestions of a "short way" by which the Dutch Church would change the celibacy rule on its own. The Dutch bishops declared in advance of the discussion that they would abide by the collegial decision of the world episcopacy under the pope. (3) According to Alfrink's ground rules, the only question at issue was whether the Council had a right to vote on resolutions informing the bishops of their collective opinion on the celibacy rule. Since the bishops did not intend to vote on the issue, the Council vote would be only consultative not deliberative. (4) The Dutch bishops intended to meet separately with the Conference of Religious Superiors of Men before announcing whether they would inform the pope and the world episcopacy of their own opinion on the celibacy rule. Emotions ran high before the fifth session. The papal nuncio boycotted the fifth session of the Pastoral Council. Despite the bishops' clear position that they were merely going *to discuss* the celibacy rule, conservative Dutch Catholics hired an airplane trailing

64. *AK,* XXV, 4 (January 23, 1970), column 79.

the message "Unity with Rome" to fly over Cardinal Alfrink's home on the Maliebaan in Utrecht. The cardinal referred to the incident at the Council session: "If you did not have a sense of humor you could, perhaps, find it very tragic that some people, even after so many years, have so little knowledge of their Archbishop."[65]

During the discussion of the report on the ministry, Bishop Moller of Groningen, in an intervention in the name of the whole episcopacy, urged, as objections of the Dutch episcopacy, the five specific objections to the report listed in the pope's letter, without, however, mentioning it specifically because it was not yet public.[66]

Before any vote on resolutions about the celibacy rule was taken at the Council, the Dutch bishops exercised their right to invite non-elected members to speak to issues under discussion. Dean J. Joosten of Echt from the diocese of Roermond, leader of the conservative Catholic group Katholiek Leven, was permitted to address the assembly in the name of a group of Dutch Catholics disturbed by the possibility of a positive resolution of the Council for change. Immediately before the vote on the resolutions on the celibacy rule was taken, Alfrink reiterated the episcopal understanding and decisive definition of the state of the question: "Despite every genuine dependence that a person has upon the Holy Father—whether purely on objective grounds or even because of personal ties—it can, nonetheless, be a definite task and duty of the bishops to inform him about what is to be found at work and alive in their church province and what is desired by their church province. I do not believe that someone can see this as a sort of disobedience or opposition—or whatever word one might use."[67]

Between the overwhelming vote supporting the four resolutions to change the celibacy rule for priests on January 7, 1970, and the final announcement of the Dutch bishops making their own position public on January 19, Vatican sources leaked the pope's letter to *L'Osservatore Romano*. Despite this pressure tactic, the Dutch bishops announced to the press on January 19:

> The bishops bear the responsibility for their own portion of the church but also, at the same time, they bear a responsibility for the whole church. That is the genuine content of collegiality as it was announced by the Second Vatican Council. In the light of this responsibility the bishops feel that it is their task, in the first place, to let the Holy Father

65. *Pastoraal Concilie*, VI, pp. 221–227.
66. *Ibid.*, pp. 270–271.
67. *Ibid.*, p. 311.

know the exact situation in their own local church and the insights and desires that are found here, in the conviction that these are to be found not only in the Netherlands.

The bishops are of the opinion that their community of faith would profit if, besides the priesthood of those who have chosen celibacy in clear freedom, the Latin church would be able to allow a married priesthood, so that married men would be ordained priests, and, in special cases, priests who have entered into marriage, under certain conditions, would be reinstated into the ministry. But no one church province can bring this about on its own, without dialogue with the Holy Father and the world church. A consultation of the whole church about such a weighty and urgent problem, which affects the whole church, can only be a service to the church.[68]

On February 1, 1970, Paul VI gave a speech on the Catholic devotional practice of the "Angelus" in which he asked his audience for prayers for "the holy celibacy" of priests. "It is a principal law of our Latin Church. We cannot give it up or bring it into discussion. To do that will mean that we are taking a step backwards." The same day, the Dutch bishops issued a press communiqué that they were still in contact with the Vatican. "We do not have the impression that the speech of Pope Paul was intended as an answer to the concerns which we have laid before him."[69] On February 2, Paul wrote a long public letter to Cardinal J. Villot, Secretary of State of the Vatican, expressing his deep sorrow over the Dutch position and asking Villot, "In the first place, we ask ourselves in a humble and absolutely sincere heart, if there is not some responsibility on our part in respect to such unfelicitous decisions that diverge so much from our position and from that, so we thought, of the whole church."[70]

In his letter to Villot, Paul VI stated that he was not only against the idea but also against allowing any discussion of the question of allowing priests who marry subsequent to ordination to continue in the ministry. On the other hand, he did not rule out discussions about ordaining already married men for missionary situations.

On February 3, 1970, the Dutch bishops made public that the pope had agreed to speak with them about the question of priests in the Netherlands. The public character of the difference of opinion between the Dutch church and Rome led to discussions of the celibacy rule by other bishops and episcopal conferences. On February

68. *Ibid.*, pp. 338–339.
69. For the pope's Angelus speech, see *AK,* XXV, 7 and *8* (February 13–20, 1970). Dutch bishops' press communiqué in column 140.
70. *AK,* XXV, 7 and *8* (February 13–20, 1970), column 141.

25, 1970, *L'Osservatore Romano* published a series of telegrams and resolutions of unanimous support for the pope's position from bishops' conferences throughout the world.[71] But not all of the world's bishops distanced themselves from the Dutch bishops. Some—the Brazilian bishops, for example—asked for the Orthodox celibacy rule for the Latin rite. Cardinals Koning of Vienna and Suenens of Brussels as well as the Archbishop of Ottawa praised Dutch Catholicism in public interviews. The Dutch bishops also received many telegrams of support from priests' groups in Spain, France, Argentina, Germany, and the influential Federation of Priests Senates in the United States.

Meanwhile, throughout the winter and spring of 1970, the conflict between Rome and the Dutch episcopacy over the possibility of discussing the celibacy rule remained unresolved. On May 12, 1970, Cardinal Leon Suenens of Brussels granted an interview to *Le Monde* in which he suggested that the impasse between Rome and Holland over possible discussion of change could be best broken through if the bishops in each national church undertook a survey and dialogue about a number of questions, including that of celibacy. He proposed, further, that the entire question of priestly ministry be placed before the 1971 meeting of the World Synod of Bishops. Suenens praised the Dutch bishops in this interview, dismissing the almost solid support from bishops' conferences for the pope's position:

> The Center expects from the bishops only complete support for a decision that may not come under study. As a result, the bishops join their voices to the papal decision almost à priori, out of loyalty, out of solidarity and, undoubtedly, in great part, also because they share the same viewpoint and the same fears. . . . The telegrams sent to Rome by the bishops are a source of disquiet because they were sent over the heads and without consulting the priests.[72]

It seems that both the Dutch bishops and Cardinal Suenens were trying to force Rome's hand in order to get the celibacy rule on the agenda of the Synod of Bishops.

On June 28, 1970, the Dutch bishops issued a pastoral letter, to be read in all Dutch parishes, on the indispensable place of the pope within the Roman Catholic church. They con-celebrated that same day, in the Hague, a mass, with the papal nuncio as principal celebrant and Cardinal Alfrink as the preacher, to commemorate the

71. For these resolutions from bishop's conferences, see *AK*, XXV, *11* and *12* (March 13-20, 1970), columns 235-263.
72. *Le Monde*, May 12, 1970, p. 8.

pope's fiftieth anniversary as a priest. The ceremony was carried live on Dutch national television. On July 8, 1970, Alfrink was finally granted permission to have an audience with the pope and Cardinal Villot to discuss the celibacy rule. In the press communiqué dated July 30, 1970, which reported the results of this meeting, the Dutch bishops announced that the pope and Alfrink agreed that the bishops' synod of 1971 would be a good occasion for further discussion of the question, although they did not agree on several substantive issues. In a special television interview on the same day, Alfrink warned that priests who married and continued the ministry on their own would betray a commitment to the church which they accepted at their ordination, and risk bringing about a schism.[73]

At the second general session of the synod of world bishops in Rome, September 30 to November 6, 1971, Cardinal Alfrink did not plead, in his interventions, for revising the rule of celibacy for previously ordained priests, giving as his reason that such a change did not have much collegial support among the world bishops and that it lacked foundation within the tradition of the Latin and Orthodox churches. A resolution at this synod supporting the celibacy rule for previously ordained priests was opposed by only 22 bishops, with 7 abstaining; 169 voted in favor. On the question of ordaining already married men to the priesthood, the bishops at the world synod supported the papal position, although over 40 percent voted in favor of the ordination of married men.[74]

Since the world synod vote, the Dutch bishops no longer encourage the discussion of allowing married priests to be reinstated in the ministry, although they still champion the ordination of married men. They have consistently resisted, under penalty of a declaration that such priests and communities lie "outside the responsibility of the bishop," any attempts of married priests to continue their functions. Between 1970 and 1976, the Dutch bishops had to issue such declarations of "non-responsibility" in only three instances, which involved the student parishes in Amsterdam and Leiden and the "critical community" in Beverwijk (the Kritische Gemeente, a non-parochial community of Catholics dedicated to political activism and inter-church justice). The public declaration occurred only after prior attempts to dissuade the priests or groups involved had failed, and after consultation with them. Even in its use of the negative sanction

73. For the press communiqué and interview, see AK, XXV, 33 (August 14, 1970), columns 719–721.
74. AK, XXVI, 51 (December 17, 1971), column 1146.

system, the Dutch bishops have adopted a collegial, consultative style.

I have stated earlier that internal conflicts found everywhere within the post-Vatican Roman Catholic church are largely due to efforts at redressing overemphases on the church as a social system and roles within the church as "parts" of the system. The collegial models which have emerged since the Vatican Council permit greater room for conceiving of the church as an association as well as a social system, and for seeing roles within the church as "elements" as well as "parts." Let us translate this terminology into the language of "rights and duties" for incumbents of roles in the church. Not to recognize that a role has certain specified rights is to reduce it to a part, while granting it those rights is to view it as an element as well as a part. A shift in any specification of the rights of one role in a social structure will entail shifts in the set of rights and duties for other roles.

Prior to Vatican Council II, the canon law of the church recognized almost no rights of the laity within the church, except the right not to be refused the sacraments when they made reasonable requests for them. A priest in respect to his bishop had very few rights in canon law. A priest had the right to appeal to Rome for redress under certain conditions, although the frequent Roman practice was to return the case to the disputed bishop for decision.

This top-heaviness can be seen in the fact that prior to Vatican II, the rights of the papacy in respect to the episcopacy were better defined than the corresponding rights of the episcopacy to the papacy. The rights of the bishop in respect to his priests were better defined than the corresponding rights of the priest to the bishop. The rights of a pastor over his priest assistants and laity were better defined than the corresponding rights of an assistant priest or the laity. The laity, however, could always take a passive attitude toward church authority, which was more difficult for priests. The top-heaviness of the pre-Vatican II church is also apparent in the pre-Vatican use of "duty-language," appeals to obedience, humility, the cross of Jesus, self-sacrifice. While this would seem to be a feature of any Christian rhetoric system, it is not clear that the single or primary meaning of these terms is that lower agents in the church must always give up self-will and freedom at the bidding of higher agents. Although the practice and exercise of rights and duties within the pre-Vatican church was much less authoritarian than this formally authoritarian structure for the church would indicate, because most of the officers in the church did not always press their rights or lower agents' duties, and because the informal system in the church was able to counteract the one-sidedness of the formal structure's stress on duty, there was very little protection in the pre-Vatican authoritarian structures against the frequent ''authoritarian personality'' in the post of bishop, pastor, or assistant priest.

At the Second Vatican Council, the body of world bishops claimed new rights for the episcopacy vis-à-vis Rome and for the laity. They created a new rhetoric system which stressed the reciprocal duties of higher officers to respect the rights of lower agents: service, dialogue, pluriformity, collegiality, and consultation were called for. Because the adjustment of rights and duties between papacy, bishops, priests and laity has not been completed, the post-Vatican church has witnessed new kinds of internal conflicts between higher and lower officers (papacy versus Dutch bishops; other bishops versus members of their lower clergy as well as some laity); frequently, however, these conflicts are masked by the use of two competing rhetoric systems— what, for simplicity's sake, we can call the system of preponderant duty-language to preserve the social system's unity (obedience, humility, and so on) and the rhetoric system of right-and-duty language to encourage a new balance (dialogue, service, collegiality, and so on).

In the celibacy dispute, while the papacy consistently championed a one-sided view of the church as a social system, the Dutch bishops urged a balanced view. They fully acknowledged papal rights and their own duties as part of the world church, but only on the condition that the papacy recognize their independent rights as elements and its own duties as part of the world episcopacy.

The Dutch bishops had been developing new institutional arrangements which simultaneously guaranteed their own rightful authority to make final decisions on almost any issue and also recognized their duty to respect the right of the lower clergy and laity to discuss that issue before a final decision. The Dutch collegial model includes rights and duties for all officers and agents. On innumerable occasions in the past, the Dutch episcopacy has risked serious conflict with Rome to champion rights of their own lower clergy and laity. Thus, for example, the Dutch bishops have resisted suggestions that priests who leave the ministry with permission to marry are traitors. Indeed, the episcopal conference has generously financed a personnel bureau for ''laicized'' priests and members of religious orders to help them find new employment and support their psychological adjustment to a new status within the church. The bishops have, moreover, championed the rights of the ex-priests to serve as pastoral workers on parish teams or to teach theology in Catholic schools, even against Roman efforts to deny these rights. The Dutch position has been that a "laicized" ex-priest has all of the rights of a Catholic layman.

When, therefore, the Dutch bishops claim their own rights as officers of the world church to make final decisions after everyone has had the right to be heard, it is difficult for groups in the Dutch church to make a case that the bishops are authoritarian or failing in their duty to other roles. Hence, the absence of any effective underground church or leftist contestation groups opposing episcopal authority in the Netherlands is not very surprising. A collegial style seems to enhance rather than undermine episcopal authority.

The Dutch Bishops and the Pope and Roman Curia. The Dutch episcopacy is also trying to find new ways of expressing the relationship of the episcopal conference to the institution of the papacy. Perhaps because of a continuous cold war between the Netherlands and Rome after 1966, but also because the Dutch bishops had been championing a new view of the collegial church, there has been greater two-way communication between Holland and Rome than between Rome and any other episcopal conference. Since the late 1960s, the Dutch bishops travel to Rome, often three or four times a year, to discuss their differences directly with the heads of curial congregations and the pope instead of handling problems exclusively by letter or through the papal nuncio. The ordinary practice in the Catholic church is, of course, that local bishops journey to Rome only once every five years. A large number of Roman documents directed to the entire world church derive from a certain preoccupation of the Roman authorities with Dutch Catholicism, and are hardly understandable except as responses to Dutch initiatives. As examples, we might cite the 1965 papal encyclical, *Mysterium Fidei;* the 1970 letter of the Congregation of the Clergy on pastoral councils; the 1972 letter of Cardinal Villot on a new way to appoint bishops in consultation with the national hierarchies (two months after the controversial appointment of Mgr. Jan Gijsen in Roermond); and a 1972 letter of the Sacred Congregation of Doctrine and Faith on the Trinity.

The Dutch episcopal conference has also, in recent years, championed two distinctions which were not prevalent in the pre-Vatican church, although they seem to have emerged among many Catholic elites: a distinction between the pope and the Vatican career bureaucracy in the curia; and a distinction between the person and office of the papacy. In this sense, the post-Vatican church has a loyal opposition within the international church which is different from anything found before the Vatican Council.

Relation of the Dutch Bishops to Wider Dutch Society. Within the Dutch Catholic community itself, the bishops have been defining their role primarily as that of the first pastor and preacher of the diocese. They have largely delegated direct administrative authority over management of financial affairs to lower officers, sometimes laymen, within the diocesan curial staffs. Indeed, in most of the dioceses a rather careful job description for various responsibilities is available, so that vicars of the diocese are similar to cabinet ministers with a definite portfolio. In this sense, the Dutch bishops have conceived of their role less as managers than as pastors. The greatest portion of the bishop's time within the diocese is mainly devoted to conversation with groups of Catholic laity and clergy; with working visits to the deaneries and parishes, where the bishop is visibly present as the sign of unity within a pluriform church; with the administration of the sacraments of ordination and confirmation; and with coordination of pastoral planning within the diocese. The role as a national officer within the bishops' college consumes probably half of his time and energy. The Dutch bishops have also tested out a new role vis-à-vis the wider Dutch non-Catholic society.

I have previously suggested that the civil religion has been differentiated, in modern industrial societies, from an exclusive locus within the body of the churches. Because of its structures of columnization, Dutch civil religion was never very well articulated, and certainly less so than the civil religion of the United States, France, or Israel. Nevertheless, one can pinpoint some of the items of belief, rituals, and institutions which embody classic Dutch moral consensus and conscience: democracy; personal liberty; internationalism; tolerance; compromise and proportionality in politics; honesty and probity in comportment; acceptance of various life styles; and national unity in the face of foreigners who attempt to impose their structures on Dutch society. In one sense, this civil religion is the moral consensus which provides the arch across Dutch columns. The monarchical house, as well as international organizations such as the World Court of Justice of the Hague, institutionally, embody this set of beliefs which represents Dutch moral conscience and consensus—its civil religion. The shrines and national heroes of the society, or the rituals which bind Dutch Catholics, Protestants, Socialists, and Liberals into a unity which transcends the differences, tend to commemorate this moral conscience and consensus. Thus the memory of heroes such as Michael de Ruyter, who fought for liberty and democracy in the Dutch revolt against Spain, or the ritual wreath-laying to recall the dead who fell under Nazi occupation, help to embody Dutch civil religion and keep its memory alive.

Institutional change within Dutch society since the Second World War has taken place within this framework. Several examples will illustrate the point. The left and right within Dutch politics disagree on the question of the Netherlands' place within NATO and the heavy defense budgeting required to maintain a Dutch NATO force. Both, however, appeal in support of their opposing cases to what will best serve the cause of democracy, personal liberty, acceptance of pluriformity, internationalism, and so on. A second example from the political arena will make the same point. The Socialists, Liberals, and other non-confessional parties oppose "confessional columnization." Yet, as if to make the point that this stance is not inimical to tolerance, compromise, and proportionality in politics, and the respect for differing life-visions, the Socialist cabinet *formateur,* when putting together the socialist-confessional party coalition government in 1973, nominated two Catholics from non-Catholic political parties for ministerial posts most sensitive to the church blocs' interest in state subsidy: the ministry of education and the ministry of culture, welfare, and social work. This was more than a clever maneuver, for it expressed the respect for differing life-visions which is a firm part of the national conscience.

There is a peculiar elective affinity between Dutch civil religion and the collegial models of the new church championed by the Dutch bishops since Vatican II around the concepts of consultation, democratization, international responsibilities for the national church, acceptance of pluriform visions within the church, tolerance, compromise and proportionality in determining church decisions, and honesty and probity in church comportment. It is not surprising, therefore, that their policy receives unusual attention in non-Catholic circles. The bishops—especially Cardinal Alfrink—have become national heroes. The Socialist and Protestant press almost always presents the cardinal and the bishops' collective decisions in a favorable light.

The greatest problems in traditional Dutch society—pressures due to columnization and the existence of separate "nations" in the one land—have been greatly eased by the new collegial models. There are few voices at the top calling for a return to the period of separatism, although nostalgic groups at the periphery sometimes express pain at the loss or reinterpretation of the symbols which united the columns internally in the period of classic columnization. In the process of

what Dutch commentators call "de-confessionalization," the episcopacy has emerged as the personal collective embodiment of a new
structural solution for Catholics which also relieves larger communal
pressures in cooperation with the monarchy and the Protestant
churches.

The Roman Catholic church is a full member of the Dutch
National Council of Churches. The Catholic bishops appear frequently on public occasions with Protestant ministers, such as the
chief officer of the Dutch Reformed Church. The bishops, in recent
years, have brilliantly used their own particularist Catholic tradition
and symbol system and joined it to more general, ecumenically
Christian symbols to articulate values and moral goals which can
claim wider Dutch support and consensus. Recent episcopal letters
and Christian television marathons calling for Dutch action to aid the
developing nations or to help the victims of famine and war in Biafra,
Bengladesh, North Ireland, and Vietnam provide examples of this
new episcopal stance, the bishops as spokesmen for the national
moral conscience. It seems indisputable that the striking success with
which the Dutch bishops have embodied this new role for a bishop is
linked to their own definition of a similar role for the bishop within
the Catholic community as the bridge-builder who embodies the
values of tolerance, unity, and consensus.

We get a striking illustration of this new episcopal voice as an
institution of moral authority for the whole society if we compare the
non-Catholic reactions to the episcopal Mandatory Letter of 1954 with
those of the episcopal Lenten pastoral, "Welfare, Responsibility, and
Frugality," in 1973. In their 1954 letter, the Dutch bishops, using
traditional Catholic sanctions of excommunication, imposed a definite political program upon the consciences of their Catholics and
indirectly upon the whole society. The non-Catholic responses to this
episcopal meddling in concrete political questions were hostile.

The bishops' 1973 letter, "Welfare, Responsibility, and Frugality," is a moral document with serious political implications. The
document, which has already been translated into five languages,
respects the legitimate separation of church and state. Although it has
genuine political import, it skirts commitments to a partisan political
position. It also avoids the restriction of church pronouncements on
political issues to sentimental statements of patriotism. It is moral
without being moralistic, political without being partisan, specific
without being unduly concrete. The bishops carefully avoided supporting any one political program: "Because we are convinced that

the believer himself can best decide in his own situation what his responsibilities are to find the desired form of welfare, responsibility, and frugality, we restrain ourselves here from closer specifications. The concrete applications are left to each person's imaginative capacities."[75]

On the other hand, the bishops forthrightly faced specific moral problems which they considered pressing within Dutch society: the injustices suffered by foreign migratory workers, the "guest workers" who represent almost 10 percent of the Common Market's labor force; a growing disparity between the rich nations and the poor nations, which invites despair about the possibilities of international justice; false values for a welfare state, such as rugged individualism, unthinking consumerism, unqualified acceptance of status-seeking, and false competition inculcated through the school system; and, most specifically, disparity in incomes within Dutch society.

The bishops began and ended their pastoral letter with a humble recognition that Christians have no monopoly on moral conscience or on answers to common Dutch problems:

> The word "frugality" has begun cautiously to come again into prominence within a viewpoint which is different from the biblical viewpoint. The Christian community is neither the sole nor the principal community which . . . begins anew to surmise a positive value in "frugality" for the sake of a more just order. . . .
>
> The optimism by which Christians, despite everything, can set themselves to the task of realizing a more just and humane society finds its roots in a deeper trust, not in some better insight. It is the person of Jesus, understood in the light of our faith in the Resurrection, who can make us free to face our responsibilities.[76]

After a review of the biblical evidence on the question of wealth versus poverty and a society of welfare, the bishops remarked: "In opposition to people who want to place the emphasis of religion on ritual and holiness, the bible repeatedly and emphatically shows that liturgy and piety are insincere and objectionable unless they go hand in hand with an active concern for social justice."[77]

They strongly criticized the individualism and status competition built into a consumer society of unlimited productivity, which is institutionalized in the school system. They became specific by proposing a review of Dutch income policy, including especially the uniform

75. *Welvaart, Verantwoordelijkheid, Versobering*, p. 18.
76. *Ibid.*, pp. 2 and 20.
77. *Ibid.*, p. 9.

percentage wage freeze proposed by the government to combat inflation. "We need to reflect on the question whether it might not be a
Christian duty to accept the moderating or freezing of the highest
incomes and, thereby, accept that the distance between one's own
level of welfare and that of others [ought] be somewhat less
dramatic."[78]

The 1973 pastoral letter became, within weeks, a bestseller of more
than 100,000 copies in several editions. It evoked sympathetic comment from the national Protestant and socialist press and from
members of the Socialist party. Socialist and Protestant labor unions
used the letter as a basis for discussion at union meetings. What
would have been unthinkable twenty years ago in the Netherlands
has occurred. Catholic bishops have become socio-ethical leaders
within the whole society and spokesmen for that moral consensus and
conscience which we refer to as the civil religion.[79]

The Role of Priest

The collegial model for the church which the Dutch bishops have
been applying to the redefinition of their own role has also been
extended to cover the relation between bishop and priests, the relations of priests between themselves, and the role-relation of priest to
laity. How is the role of priest being reinterpreted? We can begin by
looking to a thematic description of the priest's role and, next, to the
institutional arrangements adopted to embody this new role.

Among the many statements of the collegial theme as applicable to
the bishop-priest relation, as well as the bishop-laity relation, we can
cite a remark by Bishop Bluyssen of Den Bosch:

> The consideration that we are the people of God contains the duty to
> work toward true democratization. If my authority as bishop comes
> from God, yours, as a member of the priestly people of God, comes no
> less from God. If my competence as bishop is indispensable, yours is
> no less so. If you must account for your opinions, I must do the same
> thing if I want to be a genuine authority for you. If you are expected
> to listen to me as your bishop, I have also to listen to you, to what you
> have to say to me as believers, and, yes, even as doubting members or
> non-believers.[80]

78. *Ibid.*, p. 17. For another example of the bishop as spokesman for national consensus and
conscience, see the April 10, 1973, reactions in the Protestant newspaper *Trouw* and the Liberal
NC Handelsblad to Cardinal Alfrink's April 7 speech in London on the obligation to work for
disarmament.
79. For non-Catholic reactions to the Dutch bishops' Lenten letter, see *De Tijd*, March 10,
1973, p. 4.
80. *KA*, XXII, *34* (August 25, 1967), column 849.

The controversial report of the fifth session of the Dutch Pastoral Council, "Toward a Fruitful and Renewed Functioning of the Ministry," is perhaps the best guide for understanding the redefinition of role requirements for the Catholic priest:

> The minister shall try in word and gesture to express *what there is to be found alive and at work* in the values among the faithful in the midst of whom he works. He shall try to formulate what we understand by the terms "holiness," "redemption," "being made free." He shall try to put into words how the faithful understand the gospel in the midst of contemporary reality. The minister's task is to give a name to this experience. . . . More than anyone else, the minister has the duty to bring a corrective voice to the occasions when the community does violence to the best sense of the gospel.[81]

This report on renewed ministry sums up the role designation of the clergyman under three general rubrics: spokesman for the congregation; prophetic critic; and symbol of unity in the parish and with the other parishes of the diocese under the bishop. The main tasks of the priests are described in a core package: preaching and catechetics; the liturgy and celebration of the sacraments; individual pastoral work and the creation of local religious communities. The report pleads for a purification of functions for the priest. As a suggestion for institutionalizing religious specialization, the report recommends that no one be ordained before he undertakes a year's pastoral apprenticeship under professional supervision. It also suggests that already ordained priests be given a chance to gain in-service retraining through pastoral courses, study groups, and work groups.

The report goes on to make a plea for differentiation and pastoral specialization. It foresaw that instead of being a jack-of-all-trades (catechist, preacher, liturgist, administrator, counselor, leader of youth clubs, social worker) a priest would take his place on a pastoral team, each member of which had a specialty which met the religious needs of the parish or community.

In its call for a collegial understanding of the priestly role, the report commented:

> Collegial cooperation appears, over and over again, to be a difficult task. People use the word in season and out of season. People speak about it often in idealistic and glib terms. It has to do, actually, with three hard facts: (1) Each person has his own responsibility for his own job; (2) further, each person is co-responsible for the whole work; no one can escape this responsibility or pull back into "his own turf"; (3)

81. *Pastoraal Concilie*, VI, p. 91. The whole report covers pp. 68–150.

finally, each person bears responsibilities for the other person, so that he can function and prove himself. This has much meaning. So clerical individualism has to make room for new forms of cooperation. . . .[82]

The suggestions of the pastoral council that no one be ordained without a year's pastoral apprenticeship in a specialized ministry and that in-service retraining for priests be provided have both been implemented since 1970. Even religious order priests must undergo the pastoral apprenticeship.

There are three new institutional arrangements which embody this new sense of collegiality between the bishop and his priests.

1. Every Dutch diocese has inaugurated a diocesan pastoral council which consists of elected members of the lower clergy and the laity. The council, serving as a consulting board for the bishop on diocesan policy, is considered co-responsible for diocesan-wide policy. Besides these mixed bodies of clergy-lay representatives, most of the dioceses have specially elected councils of the clergy to address specifically ministerial questions such as appointments, professional training, salary, and retirement.

2. Dutch dioceses have introduced personnel management committees or officers as an intermediate body between the bishop and the priests to mediate the sensitive question of the assignment of the priests. The assumption which underlies the introduction of personnel management committees is that it is both legitimate and necessary to consider the desires and capabilities of the individual priest and the needs and desires of the individual parishes and extra-parochial pastoral teams in making appointments. Although there is some variety in the form of this new structural arrangement, the various forms are functional alternatives to achieve similar goals. Thus in some of the dioceses (Rotterdam, Haarlem, Utrecht) appointments are handled by a personnel management officer. In some (Groningen, Breda), an appointment committee of the lower clergy meets ad hoc to determine appointments. In others (Den Bosch, Roermond), appointments are handled by the diocesan vicars-general in unison with a personnel manager who serves in the diocesan service bureaucracy.

In each case, the responsible persons or agencies are expected to fit vacancies with job applications. In a further development, in several dioceses, parishes and pastoral works have developed a kind of solicitation system, placing "Help Wanted" and "Position Sought" ads

82. Ibid., p. 116.

in the local or national Catholic press.[83] The new arrangement for appointments differs dramatically from the pre-Vatican pattern, by which the local bishop exercised full sovereignty in assigning priests to a parish irrespective of the priest's or the parish's desires. It was assumed that the priest and the parish would accept the assignment in obedience.

The reasons for the popularity of the new arrangement among members of the lower clergy should be apparent. The priest now has a voice in determining, to some extent, the place and conditions for his exercise of the professional ministry. The traditional method of priestly appointment was not always free from charges of episcopal favoritism or the punishing of non-conformist priests. It was also subject to the whims of the bishop. Thus, in a moment of bizarre humor, a former bishop of the diocese of Haarlem decreed that only priests who had allusions to fish in their surnames (for example, Visser, Haring) would be assigned to the Catholic fishing villages which dot the area north of Amsterdam.

3. The traditional Catholic position of the dean of a diocese as a sort of senior priest responsible for pastoral coordination for the territorial sub-units of the diocese has been upgraded and given new responsibilities. Whereas previous to the Vatican Council, all deans were appointees of the bishop, since 1966 a mixed pattern has emerged within Dutch dioceses in which some deans are elected by their fellow priests within the territorial unit. Further, the collective body of all deans of a diocese hold periodic meetings to discuss important issues or conflicts at the diocesan level, serving as a second, exclusively clerical, advisory board for the bishop, alongside the diocesan pastoral council.[84] Indeed, the council of the deans is the most important counterbalance within the diocese to the absolute power of the bishop.

If the above examples point to a collegiality between the bishop and the lower clergy, there is also evidence of new institutional arrangements to embody collegiality at the local parish or community level—collegiality among priests themselves and between priests and laity. The priest-lay collegiality can be seen in the fact that by 1971, 59 percent of the 1,847 Dutch parishes contained elected lay parish councils. Discussion groups to evaluate pastoral problems or to aid the parish priest in preparing his sermons and the parish liturgy were

83. For evidence of similar developments in the American church, see the solicitation ads in the weekly issues of *The National Catholic Reporter*.
84. This new arrangement has American parallels, notably the restructuring into deaneries in Cardinal Deardon's diocese of Detroit.

available on an average of three to four discussion groups per parish, with a total of 71,400 participating lay members throughout the country.[85]

The adoption of a new appointment policy for priests has altered the position of the local pastor in a parish. In order to solicit new team members for the parish staff, the pastor tries to make the position attractive by guaranteeing the other priests on the staff some areas of personal autonomy and task specialization. Indeed, since the late 1960s, several dioceses, notably the diocese of Haarlem, have abolished the canonical title of pastor. In its place these dioceses have created the title of *deservitor*—temporary administrator of the parish, or team leader. The abolition of the canonical title of pastor has been introduced with suppleness. None of the priests presently holding the canonical rights of the pastor have been deprived of their position. When vacancies occur, however, the new appointment does not include the title and canonical rights of a pastor. In another development, all of the Dutch dioceses have suppressed an earlier rule for pastoral appointment—one still operative in the American church— by which a priest is appointed pastor or to the position of senior administrator of the parish purely on the basis of seniority rule, without regard to personal aptitude for administration.

A symbolic development with implication for breaking down a clerical caste mentality and supporting priest-lay collegiality is the shedding by the Dutch clergy, between 1968 and 1973, of the previously customary special clerical uniform of black suit and clerical collar. In another move to remove the clerical caste mentality, the Dutch church has ceased granting the honorary title of Monsignor to senior priests or members of the curial service bureaucracy.

The training of future priests has likewise undergone dramatic institutional change since 1967, when all minor and major seminaries as separate academic and living communities for students for the diocesan and religious-order priesthood were closed. Since that time the candidates for priestly ministry for dioceses and religious congregations pursue their studies in the following five theological centers:

1. The Catholic Institute of Theology in Utrecht, which has been integrated with the Protestant theological faculty of the University of Utrecht. In 1974 this Catholic institute had a student body of 177, including 19 female theology students.

2. The Catholic Institute of Theology in Amsterdam, which has

---

85. Statistics from a KASKI memorandum for March 1971, reported in *Internationale Katholieke Informatie*, V, 8 (April 15–30, 1971), 3.

informal cooperative arrangements with the Protestant theological faculties of the University of Amsterdam and the Free University of Amsterdam for the exchange of courses and the granting of degrees. In 1974 this institute included 165 students.

3. The theological faculty of the Catholic Institute of Economics in Tilburg, with 192 students in 1974. This faculty is a constitutive member of the state-supported University of Tilburg.

4. The theological faculty of the Catholic University of Nijmegen, with 360 students in 1974. This faculty is also state-supported.

5. The Catholic Institute of Theology in Heerlen, with 152 students in 1974.

These five theological centers receive either full or major state subsidy. The future priests of the Netherlands pursue their theological training in ecumenical contexts, with other students who do not plan to be ordained. Indeed, non-priest candidates represent a majority of the student body in all of the centers. While the number of ordinations of Catholic men to the celibate priesthood has dropped dramatically in the Netherlands—as it has, indeed, in most industrial nations in the past two decades—from a total of 393 for the year 1948 to 49 in 1971 and 26 in 1972—the Dutch church has developed new forms of lay ministry to help supplement the diminishing ranks of the celibate priesthood: pastoral workers who are appointed by the episcopal appointments bureau for pastoral counseling, catechetics, or lay preaching in parishes. These new lay ministers in the church are known by the title past*or* to distinguish them from the ordained priests, who are called past*oor*. The similarity of titles, however, suggests that lay and ordained ministry do not widely diverge. The Dutch bishops have, moreover, requested for their own church a new form of non-priestly ministry which has emerged in the post-Vatican church, the celibate or married deacon who officiates at baptisms, weddings, and church burials. The Dutch church has also permitted former priests who marry to continue to perform non-specific priestly pastoral work, or to work as teachers of theology or catechists in Catholic institutions, provided that they desire to continue to use their pastoral specializations for the service of the church and are acceptable to the communities in which they serve. Increasingly, therefore, the celibate priesthood will be exercised in pastoral teams which include lay, unmarried, and married pastoral workers, both male and female.[86]

86. See American parallels in the institution of a married diaconate and the "lay theologian" in parishes. The move away from isolated seminaries to university centers can be similarly documented for the post-Vatican church in the United States.

The Role of Layman

The period 1966–1974 also saw the emergence of a new content for the role of the laity. The layman is no longer in a residual category, an appendage to the "real" church which is clerical. He has an autonomous role as a Christian citizen in a pluralistic society. He has become the key agent in the strategy of church influence. It is evident that he has become more than the extension of the hierarchy in the secular sphere. Thus, for example, both the Dutch episcopacy and the lower clergy have avoided, in recent years, making partisan political statements which would be binding upon the conscience of the laity. They have moved away from direct involvement in or support for the KVP party.

The laity is also finding a new voice within the church. They are represented on parish councils, the diocesan and national pastoral councils, and even within the service bureaucracy at the diocesan and national levels. The laity have assumed pastoral tasks within the parish which were formerly reserved for the clergy, such as parish visitation of the sick. A new lay ministry is being developed.

The administrative officers and employees of the Catholic organizations are almost exclusively lay. The Dutch church can financially afford a lay church because of generous state subsidies. In a sense, it cannot afford not to be a lay church. To retain the good will and energetic commitment of its lay members, the church must grant them a voice in the deliberations which affect them. One reason why the Dutch episcopacy and lower clergy strongly support the concept of lay collegial co-responsibility within the church, even against Roman objections, is that the new role definitions for the laity are part of a structural fit which includes new role definitions for priest and bishop. To attack the concept of collegiality at any level is to attack it, implicitly, at all levels. To attack the new collegial roles is to undermine the new cultural-pastoral strategy for the church. Since this new strategy fits underlying structural needs within Dutch society, one should not be surprised that the Dutch church has been vigorous, even wily, in its efforts at warding off attacks upon its collegial changes.

Chapter 7

Collective Redefinition: Contestation and Conflict, 1966–1974

A free Catholic press, radio, and television was already fully institutionalized prior to 1966. Those who oppose pluriformity in Catholic theology have had to try, so far unsuccessfully, to form their own "authentically" Catholic press and broadcasting company.

PUBLIC OPINION WITHIN THE CHURCH

The major institutional changes in the area of public opinion between 1966 and 1974 focused on finding an institutional guarantee for some pluriformity and freedom of academic theology. Thus, for example, the five centers in which academic theology and the training of priests or pastoral workers take place have achieved freedom from absolute control by a bishop or the Roman center. The acceptance of state subsidy for the maintenance of these theological centers places some restrictions on interference. The state presumes that academic institutions have definite rules for appointments, tenure, and promotion. Moreover, since these centers are responsible to the collective body of bishops and superiors of the congregations of religious men, no one bishop or superior can immediately veto or dismiss a member of the faculty.[1] These five centers employ the overwhelming majority of professional theologians, scripture exegetes, and canon lawyers active

---

1. This assertion needs qualification since the events of 1974, when Bishop Gijsen opened an old-style seminary in Rolduc, disassociating himself from the theological center in Heerlen, see *KA*, 29, 20, October 1, 1974, column 899. The dismissal of a tenured professor at the *Katholieke Hoogeschool Amsterdam* under pressure from Bishop Simonis also raised questions about the academic freedom of theology in the Netherlands; see *KA*, XXIX, 23 (November 12, 1974), columns 1045–1054. Dutch institutional arrangements for theology are, nevertheless, still freer than in most other national churches.

within Dutch Catholicism. The new arrangements have won the support of the theologians. Hence, it is highly unlikely that a return to the old-style seminary directly responsible to one bishop has much chance of recruiting a respected faculty. While conservatives have called for such a return, it could only be achieved by pitting a conservative bishop against the majority of theologians. Under the new arrangement of five theological centers, no one bishop or even the body of all bishops has full control over the important symbol system of theology. The basis for pluralism of theological thought is institutionally guaranteed.

The bishops and theologians have sought indirect means, such as codes of ethics of Catholic responsibility for theological societies, which would allow a continued two-way consultation and control. For example, the Catholic Theological Institute in Amsterdam has devised a formula in its statutes whereby the collective body of bishops has the right to stay temporarily an appointment made by the theological faculty. In cases of unresolved differences an intermediate body, the curatorium of the school, nominated by the bishops but in continuous contact with the faculty as the school's functioning board of trustees, serves as middleman to resolve conflicts and find compromises.

This new institutional arrangement is very similar to the informal arrangements between American bishops and the centers of theology in the American Catholic universities. The American bishops, also, do not have direct control over the symbol system of theology, because appointments to university theology faculties in America are governed by faculty vote and approval of the board of trustees. Of course, such institutional arrangements have long been in effect in Switzerland, Austria, and Germany, which partially explains the preeminence of German Catholic theology in the pre-Vatican church. It had some measure of academic freedom.

The attitude of the Dutch episcopacy toward academic freedom is probably best formulated in a long response which it wrote to a letter by Cardinal Ottaviani, dated July 24, 1966, in which Ottaviani asked the world episcopal conferences to respond to ten questions about "errors" whose condemnation the Holy Office had taken under consideration. The Dutch bishops remarked in their letter that they did not see much point in trotting out again old warnings and condemnations because the condemnations tend to miss the truth that lies hidden behind every error: "these condemnations are more likely to get in the way of living and authentic faith than to further it—as all of history has taught us.''[2]

> Furthermore, it is to be feared that precisely the core of truth that lies at the base of every overemphasis or one-sided position will be so much nipped in the bud that it will have no further chance of survival in the first years which follow the condemnation. This would be disadvantageous for the faithful who find help, strength, and inspiration for their faith not in the overemphasized aspect itself but in the core of truth which lies behind it. . . . The narrow preoccupation in pointing out the dangers connected with new formulas is seen by many believers as a mistrust in their sincere desire to be Catholic believers.

The Dutch bishops defended the theologians who favored pluriformity.

> It is, indeed, the conviction of our Catholic theologians that, on the one hand, the words whereby the truth is expressed and conceptual formulas whereby the faith is summarized are dependent, to a certain degree, upon the culture and nature of a given community . . . and, therefore, are receptive to change or closer precision, but that on the other hand, the dogmatic meaning (that which was truly meant in an old, yes even obsoletely old, formulation) remains an unchangeable norm of faith and must also be expressed in the new formula.

In defending this position against charges of relativism, the bishops stated that they were merely following St. Thomas Aquinas in his *Summa Theologiae* (II-II, q. 1, a. 2, ad 2): the act of faith finds its object not in words and formulas but in reality. Against an attempt to impose a new literalism or the demand that the Catholic faith must be expressed only in ancient formulas derived from other places, times, cultures, and language systems, the Dutch bishops urged a pastoral reason for allowing new theological formulas: ''The faithful who do not understand what the ancient formulas mean find precisely in the new formulas the ancient, unchangeable faith. If we shall try to hold the line against this development, that will entail a disaster for the faithful and could lead to many, once again, leaving the church.''

The Dutch bishops thought that the best way to preserve fidelity to tradition consists in allowing mutual disagreements among

---

2. For this and the following citations from the letter of Ottaviani, see *KA*, XXII, 5 (February 2, 1968), columns 126–140. Professor Edward Schillebeeckx wrote the draft of the Dutch bishops' response to Ottaviani.

theologians to act as a built-in corrective of self-censorship. They suggested that the reason this freedom of discussion had not always worked was because many theologians were afraid that ecclesiastical sanctions would be invoked against them.

The Dutch bishops staunchly defended the right of the theologians to express the Catholic faith in new formulas in a long battle with the Roman authorities on the question of the bestseller, *The New Dutch Catechism for Adult Believers,* and against an investigation by the Roman Congregation of Doctrine and Faith of the works of Edward Schillebeeckx. In respect to Schillebeeckx, the bishops issued a press communiqué on October 8, 1968, as soon as rumors of the investigation became public in the international Catholic press. "The bishops . . . are amazed that any doubts exist among the Congregation of Doctrine and Faith about this theologian, in whom the bishops have placed such great trust." In a telegram sent to Rome, the Dutch bishops remarked:

> The Dutch Bishops' Conference in its monthly gathering has taken note, with great perturbation, of reports in the international press concerning an investigation into the orthodoxy of Professor Schillebeeckx. They feel it necessary to express their full trust in this theologian who has always shown the greatest concern for the orthodoxy of modern theology. They regret most deeply this event, which brings great damage to the church and causes much pain to someone who has devoted himself entirely to the church.[3]

Schillebeeckx's orthodoxy was finally dismissed as a topic of interest at the Congregation of Doctrine and Faith, when the internationally prominent Karl Rahner offered to defend Schillebeeckx. The investigation surprised most of the Catholic world, because his orthodoxy seemed beyond question. Schillebeeckx's own estimation of the investigation was that "it did not really concern me. It was an act against Dutch Catholicism."[4] Vatican watchers look for nuances in papal speeches as signals to which party has gained the upper hand within a curia dispute. After several months of conflict between Dutch Catholicism and the Congregation of Doctrine and Faith over the Schillebeeckx investigation, the pope signaled that the battle was over by innocuously citing a passage from one of Schillebeeckx's writings, without mentioning his name, in a papal audience. Roman preoccupation with *bella figura* does not, of course, allow papal sources to admit forthrightly that they have made a mistake.

3. See *KA,* XXIII, 5 (October 18, 1968), columns 1048–1051.
4. Richard Auwerda, *Dossier Schillebeeckx* (Bilthoven: H. Nelissen, 1969), p. 88.

The creativity of the Dutch episcopacy can be seen in its efforts to find a new control system based on internal codes of ethics for the theologians within an atmosphere of free inquiry. The bishops' stance seems to be that "catholicity" is best expressed by keeping all theological positions in contact with each other and thus corrective of each other's one-sidedness.

ECUMENISM AND NEW COALITION PARTNERS

In the late 1960s and early 1970s Catholics and Protestants embarked on a new set of relations which have made them much more coalition partners than competitors. After listing some of these institutional arrangements, we can ask how the new coalitions shed light upon some of the conflicts within Dutch Catholicism and between Holland and Rome.

1. Beginning in 1967, following the example set by a local council of churches in Zeist, 140 local and regional councils of churches have been formed throughout the Netherlands with representatives from both the Catholic and Protestant churches. These councils engage in ecumenical discussions, propose ecumenical experiments (such as a common baptismal roll, visiting one another's services, exchanging pulpits, inter-communion) and make joint ecumenical declarations. As might also be expected, their participation in these councils leads many Protestants and Catholics to think of a Christian unity in faith which transcends denominational differences and particularist symbol systems.

2. On June 11, 1968, the Roman Catholic Church, the Gereformeerden, the Dutch Reformed, and other Christian churches joined together in a national council of churches. Dutch Catholicism is the only national Catholic church to maintain full membership in a national council of churches.

In 1968, the member churches of the national council agreed upon a joint recognition of the full validity of one another's baptisms. They proposed a joint policy on the question of mixed marriage which involves new directions for the traditional Catholic teaching on marriage. Since the Council of Trent, Catholics had held that a baptized Catholic is not legitimately married unless his wedding takes place before a priest and two witnesses.

Mixed marriages between Catholics and non-Catholics were traditionally discouraged. They were permitted only if a dispensation from the rule forbidding them was granted by the local bishop. Such dispensations were conditional upon the non-Catholic party signing a written promise that he or she would not interfere with the Catholic partner's practice of the faith and would raise any children from the marriage as Catholics.

During the period of traditional Catholicism, the Dutch bishops had followed a particularly stringent course in interpreting the rules for mixed marriage. As a result, Dutch Catholics had the lowest rate of out-group marriage of any of the churches in the Netherlands, and a considerably lower rate of out-group marriage than Catholics in Germany, Switzerland, or the United States. On the other hand, 78 percent of all Dutch Catholic marriages with non-Catholics were performed outside the church.[5] One result of these strict church rules on mixed marriage, as Table 13 illustrates, is that the proportion of purely civil wedding ceremonies was considerably higher than in several comparable countries.[6]

A careful statistical study of all mixed marriages in the Netherlands between 1938 and 1971 shows that of the mixed marriages 20 percent of the marriages were homogeneous (both partners Catholic, both Protestant, or both non-churched) within five years of the marriage; that 40 percent were homogeneous within 15 years; and that 50 percent were homogeneous within 20 years.[7]

It became clear from these statistics that the price the churches were paying to maintain their identity by discouraging mixed marriage was an increasing loss of members to the ranks of the non-churched. This loss is further borne out by 1968 statistics which show that of the 20,686 children from mixed marriages (Catholic and non-Catholic spouses), only 22.5 percent were registered under state law as Catholics and only 16.9 percent were baptized as Catholics.[8]

In order to counteract the losses, then, the churches were willing to compromise their separate identities somewhat by agreeing to a far-reaching new mutual policy on mixed marriages:

(a) All of the Dutch churches agreed to a statement which, without using the traditional Catholic language of marriage as a "sacrament," comes to much the same thing by maintaining that a marriage in the church means "God himself instituted marriage as a sign of the covenant of trust between him and his people. . . . Thus, a marriage is a marriage in the Lord, *a concrete sign* of the relation between Christ and his community."

5. For this statistic, see C. P. van Andel *et al.*, *Het Gemegde Huwelijk* (The Hague: Boeken Centrum N.W., 1971), p. 69.
6. See *ibid.*, p. 88.
7. *Ibid.*, p. 99.
8. *Ibid.*, p. 104.

TABLE 13.
Percent of Those Married in Religious vs.
Non-Religious Ceremonies

Country	Year	Kind of Ceremony			
		Catholic	Protestant	Jewish	No Church
Netherlands	1968	44.3	35.0	0.1	20.6
West Germany	1967	44.6	52.9	0.04	2.5
Switzerland	1968	49.3	38.9	0.2	1.6
Austria	1967	89.5	7.9	0.1	2.5
Canada	1966	48.3	50.6	1.1	0.05

(b) The right of a church member to choose his own marriage partner, even someone from outside his religious group, was recognized as a legitimate right.

(c) The church blessing of the marriage takes place in only one of the two churches involved in the mixed marriage, with the choice of the church once again being left to the couple. It is assumed that the priest and Protestant minister will work closely together in arranging premarital instructions to the couple and determining the rite of marriage to be used.

(d) "It goes without saying that no other questions will be asked of the couple to be married than those which are openly asked: Will they live their marriage in mutual respect for each other's belief and raise their children in the spirit of the gospel of Jesus Christ?" This remark rescinds the earlier Catholic marriage rule that the non-Catholic party must explicitly promise to raise the children as Catholics and that both parties promise to refrain from the use of contraceptives within marriage.

(e) The choice of the church into which the children are baptized lies with the couple, although "as a sign of recognition of this baptism the Protestant congregation or Catholic parish where the service did not take place can register the baptism in its own baptismal roll." The ecumenical practice of registering children in two church rolls is growing in the Netherlands.

(f) The Dutch churches remarked that they assumed "that it is desirable that the family orient itself toward one church."[9]

We are dealing here with something more than a vague ecumenical movement. Mutual recognition of baptisms, official cooperation between the highest officers of the churches to set a unified policy for

9. "Common Declaration on Mixed Marriage within the Churches," in *ibid.*, pp. 11–17.

mixed marriages and approve a common rite for the marriage service, as well as the involvement of Catholic and Protestant clergy and couples in executing that policy and service, indicate that the churches in the Netherlands have gone beyond the stage of ecumenical dialogue to some kind of federative coalition.

This important institutional shift is mirrored in dramatic changes in attitudes and practices. Table 14 illustrates the change in attitudes toward mixed marriages between 1959 and 1970.[10]

The adoption, since 1968, of a new policy for mixed marriages has led to an increase in the number of mixed marriages involving a Catholic which have been blessed in the church from only 26.6 percent in 1960 (2,133 of the 8,000 mixed marriages involving a Catholic party) to 44.9 percent in 1969 (7,379 out of the 16,547 mixed marriages involving a Catholic).[11] The earlier stringent practice on mixed marriages had led to the overwhelming majority of Catholics in mixed marriages leaving the church and not raising their children as Catholics. A recent study indicates that the number of mixed marriages blessed by the church since the new policy was adopted in 1968 has almost doubled. The study concludes that ''a comparison of marriages between two Catholics and mixed marriages involving a Catholic, when both are blessed in a church, leads to the cautious conclusion that there are no measurably great differences in subsequent church practice.''[12]

3. In 1969, to provide a token of the new spirit of ecumenical cooperation, there was a merger between the service bureaucracies of the *Church and World* staff of the Dutch Reformed Church and of the Saint Willibrord Association, which functions as the official advisory commission for the Catholic bishops, priests, and parishes. They were joined in the merger by the Roman Catholic de Horstink Foundation, which serves as a Catholic publishing house and a documentary and orientation center. The three institutes then constituted one Ecumenical Action Center with headquarters in Driebergen.

This unique ecumenical institution, a common Protestant-Catholic national service bureaucracy, with financial and federative ties both to the Roman Catholic Church and the Dutch Reformed Church, publishes a series of influential joint magazines: *Kosmos en Oecumene,*

10. *Ibid.*, p. 72.
11. *Ibid.*, p. 76.
12. *Ibid.*, p. 106. The two best single sources for comparative statistics on mixed marriage in the Netherlands are P. A. van Leeuwen, *Het Gemengde Huwelijk* (Assen: Van Gorcum, 1959), and van Leeuwen, ''Kerkelijk Gemengde Huwelijk in Cijfers,'' in *Het Gemengde Huwelijk*, C. P. van Andel *et al.*, pp. 68–106.

TABLE 14.
Dutch Attitudes on Mixed Marriage as Response to the Question:
Do You Think it a Desirable or Undesirable Thing
that Catholics and Protestants Marry Each Other?

Response by Year	1959	1970		
Desirable	21%	66%		
Undesirable	60%	15%		
No Opinion	19%	19%		

1970 Response by Church	Catholic	Dutch Reformed	Gerefor-meerden	None
Desirable	66%	63%	47%	76%
Undesirable	14%	23%	32%	4%
No Opinion	20%	14%	21%	20%

1970 Response by Age	23–34	35–54	55 +	
Desirable	74%	66%	57%	
Undesirable	7%	15%	24%	
No Opinion	19%	19%	19%	

Ecclesia, and *Archief van de Kerken.* The Ecumenical Action Center served, moreover, as an advice bureau for local parishes and councils of churches in stimulating ecumenical experiments. A survey of the written advice given by the Center between 1969 and 1972 uncovers a pattern of great flexibility in its interpretation of official church documents. Thus the center advised Catholic parishes that Protestant ministers can legitimately distribute communion at the Catholic eucharist. Moreover, in listing what he considered "official" (not experimental) ecumenical cooperation, the Catholic secretary of the Action Center enumerated: (a) visiting in each other's service (such visits to a Protestant service fulfill, for the Catholics, the Sunday mass obligation); (b) exchange of pulpits; (c) a common baptismal service; (d) cooperative catechesis; (e) a unified pastorate for mixed marriage; (f) united missionary projects; and (g) limited communion at one another's eucharist.[13]

13. *Oekumene: Advies en Begeleiding van de Oekumene op Het Grondvlak* (Driebergen: Ecumenical Action Center, 1971), see Appendix IV. Mimeographed manuscript.

4. The Roman Catholic and Protestant churches sponsor yearly a joint fund-raising program for overseas missions. Dutch Protestants and Catholics sponsor and fund one another's missionary work. In 1972, for example, this fund-raising action, called "Come Over the Bridge," mobilized 250,000 church volunteers in a door-to-door collection. Within twenty-four hours, the volunteers had raised 60 million guilders (about 25 million dollars).

5. Rather far-reaching cooperation and federative ties exist between the Catholic and Protestant churches in what is called the "categorical pastorate," composed of non-parochial pastoral apostolates directed to special groups, such as servicemen, students, homosexuals, migratory workers, the mentally or physically handicapped, and industrial workers. Almost all of the student parishes in the Netherlands have ecumenical services in which the Catholic priest preaches at the Protestant service or the Protestant minister distributes communion at the Catholic eucharist. The emergence of ecumenical teams in the categorical pastorate is dictated largely by the necessity of joint cooperation in order to obtain state subsidy.

Thus an ecumenical team servicing the Bijlermeer, a new city on the outskirts of Amsterdam, receives state subsidy. So do the Protestant or Catholic centers for continuing education, the Vormingswerk. The Protestant churches help pay the salary for a Catholic full-time chaplain in Het Dorp, a model city near Arnhem exclusively for the physically handicapped.

6. The new ecumenism affects the way Catholic theology in the Netherlands is done. Most of the separate Catholic-Protestant theological societies for the study of scripture, church history, or systematic theology have either merged or meet in joint congresses. The Catholic Thijm fellowship, for example, is now ecumenical. We have already seen that two of the five theological centers for the study of Catholic theology have federative ties with the Protestant faculties in Utrecht and Amsterdam.[14]

7. In several parts of the Netherlands—notably in the dioceses of Rotterdam, Groningen, and Haarlem—new liturgical communities have emerged whose congregation is mixed Catholic-Protestant; examples are the city church in Groningen, the "critical communities" in Beverwijk and Het Gooi, and St. Thomas Church in Amsterdam. In some instances, Catholics and Protestants share one building for services. Informal expectations may dictate that the appointment

14. Compare the ecumenical federative ties of Catholic theological centers in Boston, New York, Chicago, St. Louis, and Berkeley.

of a Protestant pastor (for the Reformed Congregation in Beverwijk, for example) or a Roman Catholic dean (such as the Dean of Breda) be based on his proven openness to ecumenical cooperation and experiment. The popular discussion-group movement within Dutch Catholicism in the 1960s has emerged in the 1970s as a new movement of ecumenically constituted groups. Where this pattern has been most pronounced, in the predominantly Protestant province of Drenthe, an ecumenical pastoral council for the Netherlands, held on the campus of the University of Enschede in 1971, drew 2,000 Catholic-Protestant participants to discuss a common ecumenical pastorate for the Netherlands.

This somewhat sketchy checklist of ecumenical experiments indicates that new semi-federative ties between the Catholic and Protestant churches, however much they may remain incipient, are both real and far-reaching. They form a necessary background if we are to understand pressures and conflicts within Dutch Catholicism and between it and Rome. The Dutch bishops and national service bureaucracy are situated at the confluence of two streams, one calling for further room to experiment (the key issues being open communion at the eucharist and mutual recognition of one another's ministry), and the other calling upon the bishops to crack down on what some Catholic groups consider over-hasty ecumenical experimentation, if not outright betrayal. The episcopacy has to chart waters between the Scylla of the activist reformers, who claim that the ecumenical movement has had enough time to talk and must act now, and the Charybdis of conservative Catholic groups, who feel that the faith of their fathers is under siege.

As if this set of intra-Dutch cross pressures were not enough, the bishops and national service bureaucracy are also caught in a dilemma of choosing between their loyalties to the new federative ties in the Dutch Catholic-Protestant coalition and their commitment to maintain the bond of unity to world Catholicism. If the episcopal bureaucracy, for example, refuses permission for open communion for the Protestant observers at the National Pastoral Council, it will come under fire from many of its own Catholic elites who see this act as timid conservatism; on the other hand, if it allows open communion, it will inevitably be featured on Dutch television or in the press, so that some Catholic is likely to report the deviation to Rome, once again bringing pressure from Rome. The general policy of the bishops and national service bureaucracy is to permit, even encourage, every ecumenical experiment which is clearly allowable by the Roman authorities, to stretch the meaning of Roman documents to give them the most liberal interpretation, and to wink at some experiments which are not yet legitimate. They try, at the same time, to avoid conflict situations.

The new federative coalition is not unlike the grand coalitions of Dutch political life, which have effectively insulated or co-opted the extreme right and extreme left by providing a succession of moderately progressive governments. In the church case, the extreme left in the church, impatient with the prerequisite compromises inherent in any institution, is likely to drop out of the church altogether or sit on the edge, half in and half out. On the margins, it continues to be Catholic in sympathy but free to pursue cooperation with liberal Protestants.

The extreme right wings of Protestantism or Catholicism are also insulated. Although both are unhappy with the progressive ecumenical coalition and charge that it is undermining what they consider Protestant or Catholic orthodoxy, they are not likely to find one another as coalition partners; they live with very divergent identity symbols which have sprung from years of Catholic-Protestant polemics, so that the norms they use to determine orthodoxy (the literal inerrancy of scripture *vs.* the literal inerrancy of papal pronouncement) and underwrite their securities in the midst of a changing society, do not offer much room for coalition compromise. These right-wing groups, then, are faced with difficult choices. For the Protestants the choices lie in sectarian withdrawal into like-minded groups, which only accentuates their insulation or compromise within the larger liberal church. For the Catholics, there is besides sectarian withdrawal, a further option: counter-revolution in alliance with Rome.

CONGREGATIONAL FORM FOR SPECIALIZED PARISHES

Between 1966 and 1974, Dutch dioceses and parishes experimented with new congregational forms organized around specialized liturgies and services catering to different religious needs of the Catholic population. The Amsterdam City Church has served as a kind of model for the new congregational form. The inner city of Amsterdam has been made into one deanery of the diocese. The various parishes which traditionally serviced what is now a rapidly changing inner-city population have been grouped together under one coordinated plan.

Some parishes have been consolidated, with a subsequent closing of one or more of the churches. The parishes which remain specialize in varying kinds of liturgies and devotional practices. Within walking distance in downtown Amsterdam, for example, one finds Catholic churches which continue to provide Latin Gregorian or polyphonic Palestrina masses (the Papagaai and Duif parishes); other churches which provide new, thematic liturgies as a sort of adult catechumenate (the student church and the Dominican church); and a church used mainly for non-Dutch-speaking Catholics, which serves during the week as a center for new forms of meditation and prayer. Another church in this inner-city pastorate specializes in children's masses and dialogue homilies on Sundays, while during the week it functions as a social action center. One church which works with the theatrical community periodically enacts dramatic liturgies or modern equivalents of the medieval miracle plays. During the summer, the Franciscan church, The Moses and Aaron Church, is available for the "hippie" students who use the baroque church as a teahouse and a place to rest and congregate. On Sundays during summers, there are international youth masses for this special transient population. Besides the ordinary staff of the participant churches, a core team of priests and pastoral workers engages in a program of house visitation to the resident population within the inner city.[15]

While the Amsterdam City Church plan was designed to meet a special problem peculiar to the inner city in Amsterdam, there have been efforts to consolidate churches in other cities. The closing of inner-city Catholic churches, for example, has rallied opposition among traditionalist Catholics in Maastricht, Utrecht, and Den Bosch. At least in the cities, the formation of specialist parishes devoted to new thematic liturgies in a modern Dutch idiom, or to youth masses, ecumenical services, or traditional Latin or polyphonic masses has become the organizational ideal. Even within one parish team, different types of liturgical and pastoral services have been designed to cater to young, progressive, moderate, or traditionalist groups. What seems remarkable for Dutch Catholicism, as compared, for example, to the American church, is the continued availability in every large city of centers for Latin, Gregorian, or traditional polyphonic masses. It would be very difficult in any large American city to find Catholic parishes which schedule traditionalist Latin masses for the public. In America, such masses have been driven underground.

15. See Dr. B. A. M. Peters, ed., *Pastoral Plan Binnenstad Amsterdam* (Nijmegen: Dekker and Van de Vegt, 1969).

The Dutch practice accords with the Dutch bishops' desire to provide genuine diversity.

The majority of Dutch parishes still seem to aim at presenting one liturgical service which will cover the divergent religious tastes and needs of the whole parish population. It is noteworthy that the growing number of parishes which have developed a specialized liturgical style have been more successful in avoiding large declines in their Sunday mass attendance than parishes which have not tried to specialize. It seems likely, as this evidence of success through specialization becomes more obvious, that the pattern of specialized liturgies and services catering to different religious needs of the Catholic population will continue, especially since it is a trend which can be noted in more than one national setting.[16]

CONTESTATION GROUPS

What kind of support have the bishops found for the policy of collegiality, pluriformity, dialogue, and priestly specialization in pastoral tasks? As the Dutch church was specifying and institutionalizing new structures to embody the "cultural-pastoral strategy," what forces provided the coalition of support for or opposition to these sweeping structural changes?

We can look, first, at the evidence of the distribution of attitudes among the Catholic laity, and, next, among the clergy. We shall then look at six contestation or pressure groups within Dutch Catholicism during the period 1966–1974.

Lay Catholic Attitudes

A national sample survey of parents of secondary-school children in Catholic schools conducted in 1967 by J. G. M. Sterk and J. J. Poeisz, dividing the 764 respondents by social class, urbanization, and percentage of Catholics in the surrounding environment, sorted out Catholics as "traditional" or "liberal" on the basis of their acceptance or rejection of three propositions:

"As a good Catholic you must accept all that the church prescribes."

16. For some statistical evidence that parishes which specialize in either traditionalist or new liturgies have maintained or increased levels of Sunday attendance, see the KASKI report, "Liturgie en Kerkgang te Amsterdam," in *Notanda*, bulletin of the Amsterdam deanery, February 1970. This statistical evidence accords with my experience as a participant observer at diverse liturgies throughout the Netherlands between 1971 and 1973.

"Someone who neglects his Sunday mass obligation cannot be a good Catholic."

"It is desirable not only to have separate Catholic schools but separate Catholic recreational facilities of all kinds as well."

The authors defined a respondent as a traditional Catholic if he agreed with all three statements. This description applied to 47 percent of the sample. The remaining 52 percent were defined as liberal.[17] Table 15 reproduces the distribution of traditionals and liberals by social class.[18] Note that traditionalism increases as one goes down the social class scale, reaching a very high level among the farming community.

Table 16 shows, further, that liberalism outweighs traditionalism among all groups of Dutch Catholics except those in strictly rural areas.[19] It increases in proportion to the degree of urbanization, except for the three largest cities, where Catholics represent only 17 percent of the population. Presumably, minority position explains the greater percentage of traditionalism in the three largest cities. Table 17 demonstrates that the density of Catholics in the surrounding environment has a small but statistically significant effect.[20]

It should be noted that the social-class distribution of Catholics in the Netherlands approximates that of the total population (working-class members are as likely to belong to the church as the rest of the population). In general, the Dutch Catholics and Gereformeerden approximate the social class distribution of the total population, while the Dutch Reformed are predominantly middle class. The non-churched Liberal group contains proportionately higher percentages of upper and middle class, while the Socialists contain higher proportions of the lower and working classes than the total population. In the Netherlands, because of the peculiar structure of columnization, class distribution is less an indicator of religious position than in other countries.

The Sterk-Poeisz survey uncovered not only a majority of liberals among their Catholic sample but also strong majorities precisely in those groups most likely to participate actively in the church and,

17. See J. G. Sterk and J. J. Poeisz, *De Leek Over Het Ambt* (Nijmegen: Instituut voor Toegepaste Sociologie, 1967), pp. 6–15.
18. *Ibid.,* Appendix III, p. 23.
19. *Ibid.,* Appendix IV, p. 26.
20. *Ibid.,* Appendix IV, p. 30. This relation between rural location and traditionalism is replicated in P. van Hooijdonk and J. P. Groot, *Platteland en Kerkvernieuwing* (Hilversum: Gooi and Sticht, 1968), pp. 106–107 and 111–112.

TABLE 15.
Percentages of Traditional and Liberal
by Social Class

	Percentage		
	Traditionalist	Liberal	N
1. Managerial and Professional	28	72	110
2. Self-employed Middle Class	43	57	
3. Lower Non-Manual	46	54	115
4. Skilled Manual	42	58	122
5. Unskilled Manual	55	45	175
6. Farming	86	14	68[a]

[a] N of sample too small to be statistically significant but included to indicate general probabilities.

generally, in voluntary associations: the managerial, professional, self-employed, and lower non-manual classes. Again, the percentage of liberals was highest precisely in those areas where the greatest bulk of the Dutch Catholic population is concentrated: middle-sized cities, towns, and built-up rural areas.

A much more sophisticated survey, conducted by J. A. van Kemenade, *Catholics and Their Education System,* interviewed 75 headmasters, 75 teachers of religion, 490 general curriculum teachers, and 762 parents of pupils in the Catholic secondary school system. Van Kemenade's study employed 33 different scale items measuring both religious participation and conformity to the traditionalist, pre-Vatican Catholic normative system.[21] Using factor analysis on these 33 items, van Kemenade defined six different types of Dutch Catholics:

1. Orthodox: strong religious participation and very strong normative orientation.

2. Traditionalist: Moderate religious participation and "strong to modest" normative orientation.

21. See J. A. van Kemenade, *De Katholieken en Hun Onderwijs* (Meppel: J. A. Boom and Sons, 1968).

TABLE 16.
Percentage of Urbanization and Liberalism

	Percent		
	Traditional	Liberal	N
1. Amsterdam, Rotterdam, The Hague	46	54	97
2. Other Cities	31	69	111
3. Towns	38	62	201
4. Built-up Rural Areas	49	51	210
5. Rural Areas (Farming)	79	21	34[a]

[a]N of sample too small to be statistically significant but included to indicate general probabilities.

3. Progressive: Very strong or strong religious participation and weak normative orientation.

4. Participating Modernists: Moderate religious participation and weak normative orientation.

5. Non-Participating Modernist: Weak religious participation and weak normative orientation.

If we label the first three groups "traditionalists" and the remaining three "progressive" we get respective proportions of 48 percent traditional and 52 percent progressive.[22] A national sample of all Dutch Catholics conducted in 1969 by NIPO asked respondents to label themselves as conservative, progressive, and so on. This NIPO poll yielded the results shown on Table 19.[23]

If we label groups 1 and 2 in Table 19 "conservative" and groups 3 and 4 "progressive," we get the respective proportions of 41 percent conservative and 59 percent progressive. These surveys would seem to discount positions which maintain that the radical structural changes in the church in the Netherlands were engineered by a cabal of the clergy against the wishes of some silent majority of traditionalists.

22. See *ibid.*, p. 352.
23. Reported in *KA*, XXIV, *22* (May 13, 1969), column 536.

TABLE 17.
Percentages of Traditional and Liberal by Catholic
Density in the Surrounding Environment

	Percent Traditional	Liberal	N =
0– 80% Catholics in the Neighbor-hood	42	58	383
81–100% Catholics in the Neighbor-hood	51	49	379

Dutch Catholic Clergy Attitudes

The distribution of attitudes about structural changes found among the clergy is, of course, even more important than those to be found among the laity, because the causal thrust of a church, like that of a political party or labor union, is better seen by looking at full-time workers in the organization rather than part-time volunteers or passive consumers of the organization's product. We can distill evidence about clergy attitudes from three different sociological studies of Dutch priests. In a sample of Dutch priests, using the instrument designed by Marie Augusta Neal for the study of traditional-progressive attitudes among Boston Catholic clergymen, J. Driesen found that almost all of his respondents fell under Neal's first type: value-change oriented.[24] A second survey, a full population study of all Dutch priests, deacons, and sub-deacons undertaken for the bishops by the Department of Sociology, Nijmegen University, did not ask explicitly about a progressive versus traditionalist orientation of the priests. Nevertheless, a clear pattern of change orientation among the Dutch clergy appeared in the answers to the survey's questions. Thus, 68 percent of all respondents stated that they supported the position

24. For Marie Augusta Neal's instrument, see *Values and Interests in Social Change* (Englewood Cliffs, New Jersey: Prentice-Hall, Inc., 1965). The Dutch retest is in J. Driesen, "Veranderingsgezinheid bij Priesters. Een Herhaling van Een Onderzoek van M. A. Neal," report filed in the Department of Sociology, Nijmegen, 1969.

TABLE 18.
Percentage of Catholic Types as
Measured by Religious Participation
and Normative Orientation

Type	Percent
1. Orthodox	13
2. Traditionalist	26
3. Moderate Traditionalist	9
4. Progressive	19
5. Participating Modernists	18
6. Non-Participating Modernists	15

that priests should be allowed to marry, while 81 percent supported the ordination of married men. In the same survey, as many as 29 percent of the Dutch priests declared that they were opposed to a strong teaching authority in the church. Fifty-six percent accepted the statement, ''the church must encourage continuous and free dialogue about the truths of faith.'' Fifty-three percent agreed that the church must take the ordinary reality of the world as the starting point for its theological reflection.[25]

A third survey of 150 priests, conducted in the fall of 1966, corroborates the impression given by these first two surveys that the Dutch church contains a strong proportion of change-oriented priests. The study, *Zielzorger in Nederland,* provides us with evidence that there is rather substantial support among the Dutch lower clergy for what I have described as the bishops' policy of building a new church around the slogans of collegiality, democratization, a searching faith, free public-opinion formation, and so on.[26] In general, both this study and the previously cited population survey of the Dutch Catholic clergy *(Ambtscelibaat in een Veranderende Kerk)* show a high degree of job satisfaction among Dutch priests, surprisingly small differences between pastors and assistant priests, and very strong acceptance of lay autonomy and priestly specialization around the task of specifically pastoral or religious jobs. *Ambtscelibaat* also demonstrates that both religious-order and diocesan priests show generally similar profiles on change orientation.

25. *Ambtscelibaat in een Veranderende Kerk* (Nijmegen, 1969), *passim.*
26. J. B. Faber, Y. de Jonge, *et al., Zielzorger in Nederland* (Meppel: J. A. Boom and Sons, 1968).

TABLE 19.
Self-Ratings by Dutch Catholics

	Percent
1. Conservative	10
2. Moderate Conservative	31
3. Moderate Progressive	41
4. Progressive	18

Six Contestation Groups

The range of attitudes found in surveys and public-opinion polls, however valuable a piece of knowledge it might be, is almost always time-bound and does not tell us very much about whether the opinion expressed will lead to action, or what active forces actually shape decisions in an organization, or which attitudes gain a hearing by decision makers. We can learn much more about the strength of the progressive coalition supporting the Dutch bishops' policy, or the coalition opposing it, if we take note of three factors: the emergence, the active and passive clientele, and the object of protest for six different national contestation groups within Dutch Catholicism between 1966 and 1974. Each group's position on two issues within Dutch Catholicism—participant democracy within the church and the need for clarity on dogmatic formulas of the faith—will be of special interest. It will not be possible here, of course, to give more than a telescopic view of the range of positions and nuances encompassed within each of the six groups.

While the existence of a spectrum of such pressure groups within Dutch Catholicism is a post-Vatican II development, the Dutch church is not alone in the period after the Council in spawning polarized left-right Catholic lobbies within the church.[27] My main focus will be on the way these Dutch groups line up within shifting coalition forces. The six groups, listed from right to left in the Catholic spectrum are:

Sint Michael's Legion	(1968–)
Confrontatie	(1964–)
Katholiek Leven	(1968–)

27. I was greatly helped by Peter McCaffery, "Some Groups at Present Seeking to Influence the Development of Roman Catholicism in the Netherlands," unpublished thesis, Oxford University, 1970.

Action Group World Church   (1969–1971)
Action Group Open Church   (1972–)
Septuagint   (1968–1973)

Sint Michael's Legion. The Sint Michael's Legion grew out of informal meetings, which began in 1964, of between ten to eighty-five persons in Amsterdam. The group's founder, L. Knuvelder, had earlier been active in the Dutch church as a promoter of devotions concerned with special visions of the Blessed Virgin and her messages to the church. In the mid-1960s, the group wrote an open letter to the bishops protesting episcopal tolerance toward innovative members of the clergy. This letter, featured in the Catholic daily press, drew 2,500 letters of support for its viewpoint.

Formally constituted in 1968, the group chose its name from the angel Michael who casts out demons, implying, thereby, that its opponents' activities are due to the influence of evil spirits. The Sint Michael's Legion regularly attacks the Dutch bishops' leniency toward what they consider unorthodoxy. They have also attacked the pope for not removing the Dutch bishops from office. While the group claims a membership of 3,000, the Catholic press generally credits it with less than a quarter of this total on the basis of the attendance statistics at annual national meetings. The bulk of the Sint Michael's membership is urban, deriving mainly from Dutch cities such as Amsterdam and Utrecht, where Catholics represent a minority of the population. The Sint Michael's Legion publishes its own Catholic catechism, hires churches for traditional devotional celebrations, such as processions in honor of the Virgin Mary, and circulates a bulletin in which it informs its members about which churches are served by traditionalist priests. The bulletin also comments on the orthodoxy of catechists in the Catholic school system. The group's most ambitious project, thus far unrealized, is to raise 15,000 subscriptions to form a radio and television broadcasting company. Fifteen thousand members would entitle it to a 30-minute television program four times a year and a 15-minute radio broadcast every two weeks on the national Dutch networks.

The leaders of Sint Michael's Legion were received in audience by Mgr. Zwartkruis of Haarlem in 1968, as part of the bishops' policy of maintaining contact with all groups in the church. This meeting only seemed to confirm the Sint Michael's group in its suspicions that the bishops are disloyal to the pope. Cardinal Alfrink once wrote a letter to a priest in contact with the group stating his appreciation for the group's concern for the church but expressing his own fears that it would become a sect, owing allegiance to no bishop.

Significantly, another traditionalist group, Confrontatie, has refused to accept announcements of the Sint Michael Legion's activities in its magazine and avoids any coopertaion in its affairs. This split within the right wing of Dutch Catholicism only further diminishes what little influence it has. Sint Michael's Legion shows no sympathy for either democratization or the Dutch bishops' encouragement for those seeking new formulations of the traditional faith. The group has little visible influence on decision-makers either within the Dutch church or in Rome.

Confrontatie.   Confrontatie was founded in 1964 by two Catholic laymen, J. Asberg and P. den Ottolander. Its first major public action was a protest letter to the Dutch bishops against what it considered departures from orthodoxy in the New Dutch Catechism for Adults. Unsatisfied with the bishops' response, Confrontatie sent a petition to the pope asking him to order revisions in the catechism. Within months of this petition, the Roman Congregation for the Faith and Doctrine set up a commission of theologians to investigate the New Cathechism and listed the very same objections to the New Catechism as those proposed by the Confrontatie group.

Confrontatie, which calls itself "a movement for orthodoxy" and not a pressure group, publishes a monthly magazine with a circulation of about 9,000 to 10,000 subscriptions. The group also sponsors some twenty-eight discussion groups which organize "orthodox" masses, usually in Latin, orthodox catechetics to supplement the catechesis in the Catholic school system, and special gatherings for prayer and traditional devotions, such as the Benediction of the Blessed Sacrament. In several cities, such as The Hague, Amsterdam, Utrecht, and Tilburg, Confrontatie groups sponsor "Credo" meetings around lectures on theological topics.

Confrontatie defines itself as an intellectualist and legitimist movement which engages in polemical controversy with the new theology current since Vatican Council II. Among the fifty regular contributors since the magazine's inception, one finds mainly senior citizens and retired professors from Dutch or missionary theology centers. One-tenth of its contributors are conservative Dutch priests-in-exile who have sought a more congenial climate under more traditionalist German bishops, such as the bishop of Essen and the bishop of Regensberg, whose letters are frequently quoted with approval in the magazine in opposition to the letters of the Dutch episcopacy.

Several efforts by the Dutch bishops to win the group over to the new structural reforms have not proved very effective. Cardinal Alfrink arranged a dialogue between members of the Confrontatie group and leading progressive theologians in 1968 and appointed three Confrontatie contributors to the Dutch Pastoral Council.[28] The group refused, however, to accept any seats at the last sessions of the Council, which it branded a "freethinking synod." The editors of the magazine justify their opposition to dialogue and pluriformity under the motto "No Dogmatic Coexistence." The group seems, however, to distinguish between dialogue within the church and dialogue between the churches, although there is no evidence that the Confrontatie group engages in the latter. "Within the Church, no dogmatic coexistence on essential questions is possible. With other churches and groups it is allowable—inter-confessional, then— indeed, certainly to be encouraged." The only ground rule for dialogue within the church which the group accepts is based on papal literalism. "The unbroken and unclouded trust in the essentials of our faith—as these are formulated and presented by the highest teaching authority, the pope."[29]

In the course of its ten years' existence, the magazine has attacked six of the seven Dutch bishops, along with almost all of the episcopal vicars and vicars-general and heads of Catholic institutions. It accuses some bishops by name (Mgrs. Bluyssen, Ernst, and Zwartkruis) of being themselves unorthodox; others (Cardinal Alfrink, Bishops Bekkers and Simonis) it sees as soft, weak-willed "Pilates" who have washed their hands of responsibility for the growing unorthodoxy. The co-editor of the magazine summed up the group's position on the Dutch bishops: "The bishops in the Netherlands are certainly legal because they have been named by the pope. About certain of them you could put it this way: they are certainly legal because they have not yet been deposed."[30]

The Confrontatie group has a network of part-time workers who assemble "horror" stories and samples from parish sermons, public talks, and parish bulletins which contain what they consider aberrations or unorthodox departures from their papal fundamentalism. Confrontatie also attacks the orthodoxy of the Catholic People's Party, the Catholic Radio Broadcasting Company, the national

28. The minutes for the Confrontatie-Progressive dialogue are found in *KA*, XXIII, 45 (August 11, 1968), columns 1102–1114.
29. *Confrontatie*, Nos. 18–19 (January–February, 1967), p. 3.
30. *Ibid.*, No. 77 (October–November, 1971), p. 735.

Catholic press, and the Catholic theological centers and school system, urging the founding of new authentically Catholic parties, newspapers, and broadcasting companies. One of the magazine's regular contributors, an eighty-year old priest-hero from the period of the "Rich Roman Life," Father Henri de Greeve, was one of the co-founders of a new orthodox Roman Catholic Party in the Netherlands which stood candidates for the national elections in 1972. This new party won 3 percent of the vote of all Catholics who voted in 1972.[31]

Content analysis of the group's publication, *Confrontatie*, over a ten-year period yields several reasonable assumptions about its membership.

1. The group is comprised mainly of an older, senior-citizen age category. Thus, the magazine's contributors are priests and laymen whose average age is sixty-eight. Further, the articles in the magazine frequently use analogies comparing the position of the Dutch church today to that of the Dutch nation before the German invasion in 1940. Again, the articles contain frequent exhortations to its membership not to give up courage in the fight against the "occupation of the Church" by the progressives.[32]

2. The group is largely well-educated. *Confrontatie* articles are mainly written in the technical, abstract language of post-Reformation Catholic scholastic theology. Some of the articles quote or appear untranslated in German, French, and English.

3. The group is mainly concentrated in the southeast corner of the Netherlands, where Catholics represent 90 percent of the population. Active members throughout the country represent approximately 800 Dutch Catholics, although as the electoral success of their orthodox Catholic party shows, they can rely upon almost 3 percent of the Catholic population for passive support.[33]

4. Confrontatie includes a high proportion of well-to-do people who contribute money to keep the magazine's subscription prices very low or raise the funds (approximately $1,500) to place full-page advertisements in the national Catholic press.

Confrontatie recognizes that it is a tiny minority among Dutch

31. *De Nederlandse Kiezer '72*, p. 34.

32. *Confrontatie*, No. 64 (October 1970), p. 99. An appeal to emeritus pastors to subscribe is found in *Confrontatie*, Nos. 51–52 (August-September 1969), p. 77.

33. I base the figure 800 on a multiple of 30 (average attendance at five different meetings in five different locales where I engaged in participant observation) by the twenty-eight groups advertised in *Confrontatie*. Participant observation at meetings confirmed the senior-citizen character of the movement. The assumption that the group is mainly concentrated in the southeast corner of the Netherlands is based on the fact that 50 percent of the magazine's contributors come from that area, whereas less than a third of the nation's Catholics live there. The area is predominantly Catholic (90 percent).

Catholics, comparing itself to a biblical "remnant" called upon to preserve the true faith. The magazine complains of the difficulty of finding priests to conduct its orthodox retreats, and assumes that 80 percent of the catechism being taught in the Catholic school system is false since it is under the control of heretical progressives. Its advice to the remnant true Catholic parent runs: "If your catechist is not generally known to be orthodox (people currently point the finger at the orthodox), then he is not orthodox."[34] Confrontatie considers itself a fighter for true orthodoxy in occupied territory. "We know that the restoration of all things in Christ is not a question of weeks or months but of many, many years—of decades. There is so much destroyed and shoveled under the ground, so much adapted to the prevailing culture, that a restoration seems hardly possible."[35]

Confrontatie, then, shows all of the classic traits of a sociological sect: purity of fundamentalist belief with no compromises with the world; the creation of a special intentional community to justify the sect's correctness against the aberrations of the world; and a sense of divine vocation to bring the true faith to the world. Its membership, similarly, exhibits most of the sociological characteristics of members of sectarian societies: persons who are marginal in age and social location within the culture and institutional life of the society.

Since Confrontatie has refused any cooperation with either the Sint Michael's Legion or the more moderate Action Group World Church, it would not seem a very powerful candidate for building a coalition force within Dutch society to counteract the new church of pluriformity, democratization, and collegiality. What makes Confrontatie a force to be reckoned with within Dutch Catholicism, however, is the coalition it seems to have forged with crucial decision-makers within the international church in Rome.

From the Dutch-Roman conflict about the New Catechism for Adults (1966–1968) to the naming of two conservative bishops to vacant Dutch sees (1971, 1972), bishops who had held lectures for the Confrontatie group, *Confrontatie* magazine is the best single advance indicator of Dutch-Roman disputes. Thus, as early as May 1970 *Confrontatie* gave indications that the new bishop of Rotterdam would be a man more to their liking, instead of a member of "the Dutch episcopacy which rebels against the church."[36] In October

---

34. *Confrontatie*, Nos. 74–75 (July-August 1971), p. 558. On page 586 one finds the estimate that 80 percent of the catechism is in alien, unorthodox, hands.
35. *Ibid.*, Nos. 71–72 (April-May 1972), p. 317.
36. Indication of a different kind of bishop in Rotterdam in *Confrontatie*, No. 59 (May 1970), p. 25 (Mgr. Simonis was appointed on December 30, 1970).

1970 *Confrontatie* advertised a forthcoming sermon of Dr. A. Simonis for a prayer-action, sponsored by one of their groups. When Simonis was named bishop in December 1971, *Confrontatie* rejoiced at getting, at last, an orthodox bishop.[37] Nine months before the dispute between Rome and the Dutch Catholics about a mimeographed experimental catechism used in the Catholic school system for the dioceses of Breda and Den Bosch became public, *Confrontatie* published articles criticizing the catechism's orthodoxy and calling upon Rome to take action.[38]

In the summer of 1971 *Confrontatie* suggested that Dr. Jan Gijsen, whose brochure attacking the Dutch bishops was featured in their October 1970 issue, would be the new bishop of Roermond, although it was clear that his name would never be submitted by the Cathedral chapter. In the fall of 1971 *Confrontatie* told its readers that the new bishop of Roermond would be appointed outside this nomination list of the Cathedral chapter.[39]

When its candidate, Dr. Gijsen, was finally appointed by Rome as bishop of Roermond, *Confrontatie* claimed him as its man, stating "we won't have to go directly to Rome any more." They set forth what they expected from their new bishop: "From this bishop is asked: orthodoxy, tact, courage, and tenacity of purpose in reorganizing. He can use the dove in his bishop's coat of arms instead of a broom, so long as it is a dove with claws!"[40] There is a remarkable similarity in the points and language used in Roman documents disputing Dutch developments and those used by *Confrontatie*. Whether this is because Roman sources take their information from this one-sided sectarian picture of Dutch Catholicism, or because Roman sources leak their objections to *Confrontatie*, is not clear. What seems very clear is that the connections between some members of the Roman curia and *Confrontatie* are not the product of chance. The Dutch Catholic press plays up the many contacts between the

---

37. Simonis' talk to a Confrontatie Prayer Group is advertised in *Confrontatie*, No. 64 (October 1970), p. 3; Confrontatie's welcome to "their" new bishop is found in *Confrontatie*, No. 68 (January 1971), pp. 3–4.

38. *Confrontatie*, No. 69 (February 1971), p. 154. The differences between Rome and the dioceses of Breda and Den Bosch were made public on November 6, 1971; see *AK*, XXVI, *48* (November 26, 1971), column 1087.

39. Rumor that Gijsen would be appointed, in *Confrontatie*, No. 74–75 (July-August 1971), p. 552. *Confrontatie* ad for Gijsen's brochure attacking the bishops, in *Confrontatie*, No. 64 (October 1970), p. 3; announcement that the new bishop did not appear on the nomination list of the Cathedral Chapter, in *Confrontatie*, No. 77 (October-November 1971), p. 726. Gijsen was appointed bishop on January 18, 1972.

40. For Confrontatie reactions to the Gijsen appointment, see *Confrontatie*, No. 81 (February 1972), p. 79ff, and the citation from p. 153.

papal nuncio in the Hague, Mgr. A. Felici, and prominent members of the Confrontatie group. It also seems clear that the moral authority of Rome is seriously compromised in the Netherlands to the extent that Rome is seen as supportive of this stridently sectarian right-wing group.

Confrontatie tends to view the church as a purified orthodox sect maintaining its membership by creating an intentional community of like-minded true believers. A frequent plea in *Confrontatie* articles is that Dutch moderates, progressives, and radicals should act logically and leave the church. Since Confrontatie does not accept the principles of pluriformity, democratization, or dialogue in the church, it cuts itself off from any direct influence on the strategy adopted by the decision-makers at the national or diocesan level. Nevertheless, the decision-makers seem very concerned about this group, fearing that it will actually become a splinter sect. Mainstream Dutch Catholicism has created room for these reactionary, sect-like Catholics within a pluriform church even though the group uses that room to undermine the very principle of pluriformity. Much of the vitriolic polemic of *Confrontatie* is best seen as a cry for comfort by a culturally deprived group at the margins of Dutch institutional society, a group which has become equally marginal within Dutch Catholicism in the 1970s.

Katholiek Leven. While Sint Michael's Legion and Confrontatie were founded by laymen, Katholiek Leven grew out of informal meetings of between thirty to one hundred of the seven hundred clergymen active in the area of Vaals and Sittard in the diocese of Roermond. In 1968 the group formally announced its purposes: "The restoration of unity in authentic faith in obedience to the supreme authority of the pope." On December 4, 1968, the group published announcements of their purposes in *De Volkskrant* and *De Tijd,* which elicited approximately 14,000 letters of support. In January 1969, Katholiek Leven began publication of a monthly magazine, *Waarheid en Leven,* with a circulation of about 10,000.

Waarheid en Leven tends to devote a larger portion of its pages to defending orthodoxy than, as in *Confrontatie,* to directly attacking persons or serving as a clearing house for all the aberrations in Dutch Catholicism. While the Dutch bishops are criticized by the *Waarheid en Leven* articles, the criticism is generally on tactical rather than doctrinal grounds: for summoning the National Pastoral Council too soon after the Second Vatican Council, for example, or for not preserving perfect representativeness at the Pastoral Council, or for tolerating criticism of the pope. From time to time, the group places advertisements in the Catholic daily press which set out traditional Catholic teaching on topics such as the nature of the church, the meaning of the priesthood, and the resurrection of Jesus, again usually without directly attacking other persons by name. One of its full-page advertisements calling for signatures to a petition declaring Dutch Catholics' loyalty to the pope drew 70,000 responses, or about 2 percent of all Catholics over the age of fourteen.

Although *Waarheid en Leven* gives publicity to meetings held by the Confrontatie group, the Katholiek Leven group seems much more open to the idea of democratization in the church than does Confrontatie. Again, the group does not see itself as engaged in polemic or polarization within the church. The editor of *Waarheid en Leven*, Dean J. Joosten of Echt, is a member of the diocesan Pastoral Council in Roermond and has formed a pastoral council of elected laymen in his own parish. Joosten accepted an invitation to address the National Pastoral Council before the vote on the celibacy rule was taken. Katholiek Leven, like Confrontatie, is a traditionalist, legitimist group. Unlike Confrontatie, the group does not organize its own sect-like sub-groups for liturgy and catechesis. It extends its legitimist stand, moreover, to acknowledge its duty to accept not only Rome but the Dutch bishops as well.

Action Group World Church.   Action Group World Church was founded in 1969 as a center party under the joint initiative of Professor H. Hoefnagels, a professor of sociology at the University of Nijmegen and recognized proponent of democratization, and Dr. W. Kusters, the lay sociologist chairman of KASKI.[41] The group began with the premise that a right and left wing in the church was an existential fact and that there was room for the concept of a "loyal opposition" within the church, so long as this opposition took place in open and continuous dialogue. World Church opposed the position of the left-wing Septuagint group, which suggested that the Dutch church undertake unilateral action in respect to the celibacy rule. The World Church group took a middle position on the question of doctrinal reformulations, on the one hand considering literal formulas less important than the underlying unity in belief which the formulas were intended to express and, on the other hand, calling for continuity with past generations as a safeguard against current intellectual fads. Although the group once received 25,000 letters of

---

41. Dr. Hoefnagels is a Jesuit priest, the author of a plea for democratizing in the church, *Demokratisierung der Kirchlichen Autoritat* (Freiburg, 1969). All of the six contestation groups include about equal numbers of priest and lay members.

support for its position, the thirty-member national council which released press communiqués commenting on controversial issues within Dutch Catholicism met only sporadically and disbanded by late 1971. Action Group World Church had a difficult time maintaining a clear profile and seemed to be contesting more the existence of the Septuagint group, or undemocratic methods in the church from the side of Rome, than the Dutch bishops whom they consistently supported. Perhaps the contestation purposes of the group could be summed up best by saying that Action Group World Church contested groups whom they considered to be opponents of the Dutch bishops.

Action Group Open Church. Action Group Open Church was founded in the spring of 1972 in response to the nomination of Dr. Jan Gijsen as bishop of Roermond. The group had held several national congresses with some five to six hundred members in attendance, and it holds regular regional meetings in several Dutch cities. The group's purpose is to support the new structures and policy of the Dutch bishops against threats of counter-revolution by Rome, Mgr. Gijsen, or Dutch conservative groups. It has elicited support from a wide range of national elites who helped to form the first National Pastoral Council, such as Dr. Walter Goddijn, Dr. J. Tans (one of the chairmen of the National Pastoral Council sessions), Professor F. Haarsma, and Professor Leo Laeyendecker. One would surmise from the heavy representation of middle-level church officials in its membership that Action Group Open Church is the most influential of the six groups under review. Open Church releases press commentaries on controversial issues. It threatened to form its own national pastoral council without the bishops if the bishops did not find a way to get around the Roman objections in 1972 to a continuation of the National Pastoral Council. Like Action Group World Church, Action Group Open Church supports democratization, seeks new ways to formulate the traditional faith, and contests groups whom they consider opponents of the Dutch bishops.[42]

Septuagint. In order to compare the Septuagint group against the cultural-pastoral strategy hypothesis (see Table 3, Chapter One) and assess the influence of this group within Dutch Catholicism, we will need to bear two factors in mind. First, Septuagint is a relatively amorphous pressure group. Not all of its members or passive sympathizers would agree with the profile which emerges from its published

---

42. My sources on Action Group Open Church include participant observation at both national congresses in the spring and fall of 1972 and a reading of the bulletins published by the group between March 1972 and December 1974.

work or its program as articulated by its leading spokesmen. Secondly, internal changes within the group since 1970 have altered its potential influence in comparison with the late 1960s.[43]

Septuagint was most active between 1968 and 1971. Founded in an initial meeting of seventy priests of the Haarlem diocese in December 1968, as a pressure group to support the claims of a priest in the Amsterdam Student Church who wished to marry and retain the ministry, the group had grown to 150 members, representing several dioceses, by a second meeting in February 1969. Although by no means the only factor involved in the successful resolution of the impasse between Bishop Zwartkruis and Joe Vrijburg of the Student Church, Septuagint's moral support for Vrijburg undoubtedly played a role in bringing Zwartkruis to take a novel step in breaking the impasse over a married priest by approving a formula by which he could remain on the pastoral team of the Student Church and preach so long as he agreed not to celebrate the eucharist or other sacraments.[44]

In March 1969, the group's steering committee sent a letter to all Dutch priests announcing Septuagint's relatively vague program: a married clergy; freedom from clericalism in the church; collegiality; dialogue; experiment; the church as champion of the oppressed within society; democratization; the erection of local, "critical" congregations which would act as watchdogs against totalitarian abuses in church or society; pluriformity; the abolition of titles of honor in the church—in short, a program with many points in common with mainstream Dutch Catholicism. The central theme of the group's letter ran, "Free the church in order to free the world!" This initial letter elicited passive support in responses in the form of letters or telegrams from approximately one in six of the Dutch clergy, although very few of these passive supporters turned into active dues-paying and meeting-attending members.

By the summer of 1969, Septuagint had a core of fifty members serving as its steering committee, including such leading liturgists as

43. My information on Septuagint comes from Jan Ruyter, ed., *Septuagint van Chur Naar Rome* (Amersfort: Katholiek Archief, 1969); *Van Rome Naar Utrecht* (Amersfort: Katholiek Archief, 1969); *Van Utrecht Naar Huis?* (Amersfort: Katholiek Archief van de Kerken, 1970); *Informatie Septuagint* (Hilversum: N. V. Gooi and Sticht, 1971). I also worked through the archives of Septuagint for 1968–1972, and conducted field interviews with five of its steering committee members.

44. For a chronicle and documents of this first conflict between bishop and the student church over the question of a married priest, see Lucien Roy and Forrest L. Ingram, eds., *Step Beyond Impasse* (New York: Newman Press, 1969). Not long after the impasse, however, Vriburg retired from the ministry.

Huub Oosterhuis, Ben Huybers, Herman Verbeek, and Pastor J. Keet. Indeed, it is notable that almost all of the recognizable liturgical renewers in the Dutch church have shown active or passive support of Septuagint. Regional sub-groups met in Amst, Alkmaar, Haarlem, Nijmegen, Arnhem, Breda, Eindhoven, and Limburg. Furthermore, Septuagint took the initiative, early in 1969, in establishing contact with similar groups in other lands, writing to fifty foreign contestation groups of priests to invite them to join Septuagint in a kind of extra-parliamentary opposition to the meeting of European bishops in Chur in Switzerland. While none of these groups from other lands had direct contact with their own episcopacy, Septuagint spokesmen were received by Cardinal Alfrink and Bishop Bluyssen. That Septuagint, in its beginning phase, was not hostile to the Dutch episcopacy is evident from a letter which the group sent to the Dutch bishops before the meeting in Chur: "As a group, we in Septuagint desire from our hearts to be able to depend upon you . . . we wish you much courage and promise you our full support for your work for the church to make it a hopeful and freeing sign of Christ in the world."[45]

The extra-parliamentary opposition failed to gain any access to the collective bishops in Chur. The bishops argued that the priest delegates at Chur were unrepresentative radicals and, moreover, unofficial, since none of them were sent to Chur as delegates from priest senates. Responding to this charge, the priests' council for the diocese of Haarlem commissioned two Septuagint members to represent them at a second extra-parliamentary action at the World Synod of Bishops held in Rome in the fall of 1969. At this synod, Septuagint leaders gained a hearing for their position in separate audiences with members of the papal theological commission and with several bishops. An interview with a Septuagint member was carried on Vatican radio. During this second extra-parliamentary session, Joos Reuten of Septuagint was elected by the delegates as the first president of the European Assembly of United Priests. Although a request for an audience with Paul VI was not granted, Cardinal Alfrink met with fifteen Septuagint members during this synod session at the Netherlands College in Rome. When urged by one of the leaders of the group to risk conflict with Rome, Alfrink replied, "I must continue as long as possible to try to maintain the relation with the whole of the church. That is the responsibility of a bishop and no one

45. *Septuagint van Chur Naar Rome*, p. 86.

can take that responsibility away from him. I hope that it will never come to the sort of conflict that you are proposing."[46] Although he disagreed with many of the aims and tactics of Septuagint, he thought it useful that the group keep in contact with the bishops.

Before the preparatory sessions for the fifth session of the Pastoral Council, which discussed the celibacy rule for priests, Septuagint members actively lobbied for a married clergy and a "short way" by which Dutch Catholicism could institute a married clergy on its own, even against the wishes of Rome and the world college of bishops. Septuagint sent delegates to a national meeting of priests and bishops held in Doorn, November 24–25, 1969, to try to influence the clergy's vote on celibacy. There were, however, only two members of Septuagint among the 110 voting delegates at the Pastoral Council.[47]

When the Dutch bishops ruled out any discussion of a "short way" in January 1970, Septuagint became more radical in its program and tactics. In 1970 it switched from an earlier emphasis on institutional reform of the church to the establishment of separate "critical" communities, relatively free from episcopal supervision or formal Catholic ties and identities, declaring that it found "the structures, rules, and organizational forms of all existing churches lacking in credibility."[48] In part, this was a tactic for preparing communities which would accept a married priest, if necessary against the wishes of the bishop.

Instead of an institutional church, Septuagint sought a free movement of Catholics, Protestants, and even non-believers who joined together to perform a critical, prophetic, even revolutionary role in society. Increasingly, Septuagint chose to see itself—perhaps as a result of the fact that several of its founders were pastors to students— according to political models of the New Left student movements in France and Germany in the late 1960s. Christian charity must be translated into direct, concrete political action. For the church, "the social and political action of groups is the most important instrument for contact with reality and forms the means for realizing 'love' for fellowmen."[49]

In the spring of 1970, Septuagint members traveled to France, England, Switzerland, and Germany to establish contacts with similar

46. *Van Rome Naar Utrecht*, p. 52.
47. That Septuagint actively lobbied for support for a radical position on a married clergy is clear from the minutes of the steering committee meetings during 1969. On the other hand, the minutes of December 20, 1969, show that a request by the group to receive a special place at the Dutch Pastoral Council was denied by the bishops.
48. *Van Utrecht Naar Huis?*, p. 8.
49. *Van Rome Naar Utrecht*, p. 81.

groups. Indeed, Septuagint proved the cement which forged these groups into a loose, international movement. At the congress of the European Assembly of United Priests, held in Amsterdam under Septuagint's auspices, September 28 to October 3, 1970, with delegates from contestation groups of priests from all over Europe in attendance, the rhetoric and ideology approximated the neo-Marxist ideology of the student movement. "The temple must be destroyed. Once again as so often before in our three-thousand-year-old history, the time for the exodus has arrived."[50] The group at the congress asked itself whether "this congress might not signal the beginning of an international movement of revolutionary Christians."[51]

The Septuagint group became increasingly concrete in its political program, which it saw as the necessary ethical consequence of the gospels. The church must "in her concrete, historical situation choose for the poor, the persecuted, and the oppressed."[52] In practice, this meant a break with the political regimes in Spain, South Vietnam, the Philippines, Portugal, Greece, and Turkey and direct church support for the political aspirations of Hanoi and the rebels in Angola, Mozambique, and Brazil.

The first major conflict between Septuagint and the Dutch bishops occurred in the fall of 1970 when one of the Septuagint founders, Huub Oosterhuis, defied the bishops' "long way" of collegiality by celebrating the eucharist as a married priest for the Amsterdam Student Church. His bishop, Mgr. Zwartkruis of Haarlem, declared the Student Church "outside the responsibility of the bishop." On October 23, 1970, Septuagint published a public letter announcing its intention to ask which married priests in the Netherlands were willing to continue as active priests and which communities, even Protestant communities, were willing to accept such priests on their staff. Cardinal Alfrink called the Septuagint leadership to task, reprimanding them for this act against episcopal authority. The group soon gave up the project. When, in 1972, the president of Septuagint, Jan Ruyter, married, his community in Beverwijk which approved his continued celebration of the eucharist was also declared by Zwartkruis as "outside the responsibility of the bishop." Zwartkruis' first impulse was to excommunicate Oosterhuis. He was dissuaded from doing so on grounds that most of what the Student Church was doing was praiseworthy and in accord with fundamental gospel values. Furthermore, the question was one of discipline, not dogma.

50. *Informatie Septuagint,* p. 8.
51. *Ibid.,* p. 6.
52. *Van Rome Naar Utrecht,* p. 83.

Could the bishop refuse the same kind of openness toward a group with clear Catholic origins and inspirations as that being accorded to Protestants in the new ecumenical climate? Dutch conservatives are very unhappy with the ambiguity in the formula "outside the responsibility of the bishop." They demand clear and unequivocal condemnation. In so doing, they have developed a rather labored distinction between centripetal and centrifugal groups to justify ecumenical dialogue with Protestants while closing off dialogue with groups such as that of Jan Ruyter and the Student Church. The distinction betrays, of course, in its use of the centripetal imagery, the older Catholic view that ecumenism means that other churches must "come home" to Rome.

The bishops feel that they cannot condemn a whole movement outright for one act which they disapprove. The following, from a field interview, illustrated the attitude of church officers:

> We do not want to be responsible for a group turning into a schismatic sect. If they become a sect let it be clear that it came from their side. A bishop is called to bring Catholics to unity. He tells this group that he does not approve of some of their innovations and does not go out of his way to advertise that they are his brand of what it means to be a Catholic. Yet, they do so many good things that you cannot condemn the good with the bad. Ordinary Catholics in the diocese get the bishop's message. But the right wing? They want the bishop to excommunicate 95 percent of the church!

Oddly enough, the pastors of the Student Church do not see the formula as being very ambiguous; they have taken it as outright condemnation, and since its issuance, the Student Church has assumed a rather strident attitude. The status of both the Student Church and Beverwijk remain, however, ambiguous. Jan van Kilsdonk of the Student Church continues as a Jesuit priest in good standing; his salary as a student pastor is paid by the diocese of Haarlem. Jan Ruyter has adopted a stance for his community in Beverwijk of finding "deeper and more real bonds with the bishop" than juridical ones, in order to preserve his community from the danger of sectarian isolation. The two communities, together, represent about 800 Catholics. Both draw almost half of their congregations from non-Catholic milieus.

In the fall of 1971, Septuagint again organized an extra-parliamentary opposition in Rome during the World Synod of Bishops. Since that time, however, the group has been relatively dormant, increasingly retreating from inner-church affairs to concentrate on reflection and the formation of small cells or political action.

Where does Septuagint's strategy agree and where does it disagree with the cultural-pastoral strategy? The general points of agreement would seem to be acceptance for democratization, pluriformity, dialogue, the stress on greater engagement in the wider society, new roles for the laity in the church, and the importance of the local congregation as the primary though not exclusive locus for religious action and commitment. Septuagint has, then, points of contact with mainstream Dutch Catholicism. Through these contacts, the group tries to urge the decision-makers to place greater emphasis on issues of justice, world peace, and concern for the poor. In this, it acts as a critical gadfly for the church establishment.

On the other hand, Septuagint's strategy would seem to differ from the cultural-pastoral strategy on several crucial points. It criticizes the Dutch church for too great an integration within the national society. Both in theory and in practice, the group discounts or minimizes the role or importance of bishops. While it stresses the local congregation as the "real" church, it shows little enthusiasm for the need to coordinate these local units at the macro-level. It tends to define the priest as a political man acting on behalf of the poor, oppressed, or forgotten.

In general, Septuagint dismisses the idea of structures for the church, appealing to models of the church as a non-institutionalized social movement. Priests are to be charismatic prophets who arise out of local charismatic, critical communities.[53]

In choosing to align themselves rather closely with Dutch leftist parties and political programs, or to identify the gospel with one political program in highly complex political issues (so that financial aid to Saigon is reprehensible while aid to Hanoi is a Christian responsibility), the radicals tend to resurrect a very old and dangerous strategy for the church which seems to suggest that Catholics have ready-made political answers. The Dutch church, which can still recall formal or informal pressures from the pulpit to vote KVP, will probably not be well served by similar tactics supporting the Socialist PVDA or the radical PPR. In that sense, I do not see the strategy of the Catholic radicals as particularly new or fruitful.

Just how much influence does Septuagint exercise in the Dutch church? Because of its support for a married clergy, the short-way

53. See *Informatie Septuagint*, p. 18, for this non-institutional model of the church as a charismatic social movement.

strategy of Dutch-Roman conflict, and extra-parliamentary actions critical of some bishops and Rome, Septuagint is anathema to many conservative groups within Dutch Catholicism and in Rome. These groups generally exaggerate the actual influence of Septuagint or its very articulate leaders—notably Huub Oosterhuis, Jan Ruyter, and Jan van Kilsdonk—as if all of Dutch Catholicism is best understood painted in the colors of Septuagint's militant, critical rhetoric. Because Septuagint includes prominent Dutch liturgists and journalists, the group has gained wide exposure for its programs or actions in the Catholic media. Members of the group have contact with important middle-level decision-makers and elites in Dutch Catholicism and have, on occasion, drawn prominent theologians such as Edward Schillebeeckx or F. Haarsma to participate in its programs.

On the other hand, the power of the group to influence church opinion has considerably waned since 1970, because many of its prominent members "lie outside the responsibility of the bishop" or have retired from the ministry. The goals of Septuagint became more diffuse when 150 Protestant ministers and theologians joined it in 1970. The steering committee spent over a year on the question of the theology of Septuagint in this new ecumenical form without coming up with any clear profile. Direct action by the group declined. Like many social movements, Septuagint seems to have dissipated its power as a lobbying group within the church by shifting from relatively concrete goals to an amorphous platform similar to Dutch leftist political parties. It has lost its unique organizational purpose for being. This loss of influence may be reflected in Septuagint's increasing movement away from church politics and into secular politics.

Moreover, the firm resistance of the Dutch episcopacy to a married clergy, until it is approved for the world church, has robbed Septuagint of its prime plank for its inner-church program. Consisting largely of clergymen who are engaged only part-time in the work of the pressure group, Septuagint is not very likely to produce effective political action for non-church goals. While the decision-makers at the center of Dutch Catholicism seem open to the valuable liturgical work or certain specific social-action programs of Septuagint members, they do not share its view of the church as a loose social movement of charismatics drawn together around concrete leftist political programs. They also oppose a too-close equation of the religious and the political. Indeed, Septuagint seems to have been aware of what mainstream Dutch Catholicism will accept. In a meeting of the steering committee for January 10, 1970, in Utrecht, one of the members remarked: "Dutch Catholics want renewal in the church, but they want it without overt conflicts with Rome."[54]

The six contestation groups just reviewed represent the spectrum of differing attitudes and positions to be found within Dutch Catholicism during its period of specifying, institutionalizing, and consolidating the structures of the new church. Indeed, the right-to-left spectrum of these contestation groups corresponds almost perfectly with the range of self-chosen positions shown for all Dutch Catholics in sociological surveys of lay and clergy attitudes. The Dutch bishops' policy of a collegial church commands strong support, although it rests on shifting forces of coalition. The bishops' strategy represents a clear majority position within Dutch Catholicism. This sometimes shifting coalition of forces would seem to lie behind the 88 percent of Dutch Catholics in the NIPO poll who thought that their bishops exhibited strong and creative leadership.

DUTCH-ROMAN CONFLICTS—
ISSUES, RHETORIC, AND TACTICS

Between 1966 and 1974 Dutch Catholicism and the Roman social authorities engaged in continuous conflict on a series of issues. The issues are complicated enough to have divided individuals and groups both within the Dutch church and within the entire international church—and perhaps even in the Roman center. Rather than engage in the theological value judgments which would be necessary to resolve the issues, I will simply catalogue the major substantive and procedural issues which underlay the ecclesiastical cold war.

It will be my contention that the substantive issues are closely connected to procedural ones: who has the right to control information and symbols within both the national and international church, and what kind of control system is legitimate in the post-Vatican II era?

Substantive Issues
Dispute over The New Dutch Catechism for Adults. In their press conference announcing the publication of *The New Dutch*

---

54. Cited from Septuagint archives, 1970. I am grateful to Jan Ruyter for allowing me full access to these archives.

Catechism for Adults, on October 4, 1966, the Dutch bishops claimed that the book was a safe guide to help the faithful pursue the new Vatican II insights in continuity with tradition. It was hoped that the book would encourage trust in the renewal going on within the church. In his speech at the press conference, Cardinal Alfrink tried to make clear that the book was a new kind of catechism. Not "everything that is written in this book has the characteristic of infallible gospel. . . . No book or written document can or should replace the personal preaching of the gospel."

The New Dutch Catechism, which became an instant bestseller, is a new kind of catechism, one that avoids technical, theological language to express the faith in a modern, lively, almost poetic idiom. It combines the best in contemporary biblical and historical scholarship with a popular and moving religious style. The book was the result of a four-year collaboration between theologians (principally Edward Schillebeeckx, Piet Schoonenberg, and Gerard Mulders), catechists trained in modern pedagogical technique, and ordinary Catholics who had tested the book's materials in discussion-group sessions. The catechism ventures new formulations for a series of Catholic dogmas such as the meaning of miracles, original sin, the real presence of Jesus in the eucharist, the sacrifice character of the mass, the direct creation of the human soul, and the role of sexuality within Christian marriage. In general terms, the theology of the new catechism tries to overcome an absolute dichotomy between God and the world by restating the classic positions on nature and the supernatural. The book exudes an atmosphere of ecumenism, respect for human freedom, and a collegial church. On certain issues, such as the question of the biological virginity of Mary, the catechism purposely chose vague formulas which, though compatible with orthodox interpretation, leave openings for further doctrinal development.

From the beginning, the bishops' endorsement of the catechism was contested by the Confrontatie group, which saw the book as misleading, unorthodox, and heretical. Within months of its publication, the catechism came under investigation by the curial Congregation of the Vatican Council. Rome entrusted a select and secret committee of Vatican theologians with the task of reporting on the catechism's orthodoxy. This commission suggested that the Dutch bishops revise several sections. The bishops, however, followed the advice of their own theologians and catechists, who argued that the Roman objections represented only one among several legitimate theological positions within the church—and one, moreover, which is uninformed by modern catechetics.

Roman pressures for revision continued. On April 8-10, 1967, a dialogue took place in Gazzada, Italy, between three theologians appointed by Rome (Edward Dhanis, B. Lemeer, and J. Visser) and three theologians representing the Netherlands (Edward Schille-beeckx, Piet Schoonenberg, and Willem Bless). The Roman theologians claimed to find twelve major doctrinal errors in the catechism and scores of minor objectionable points. The dialogue in Gazzada did not lead to any resolution. One point of objection from the Dutch side was that the Roman team did not include a catechist to parallel their own Willem Bless. They felt, moreover, that the new catechism was being judged as a technical theological book, upon criteria which would not allow any genuinely new catechism. The Roman team objected, on its part, to the use of the term ''catechism'' for a book which included new theological insights which had not yet been fully developed or tested.

In the summer of 1967, a commission of six generally conservative cardinals (Cardinals Fringe, Lefebrve, Jaeger, Florit, Browne, and Journet) was appointed to judge the doctrinal purity of the catechism and determine what changes had to be made before the book appeared in new editions or in translation. For this task, they sought the advice of a secret committee of theologians. They did not, however, grant an audience to the authors of *The New Dutch Catechism* to defend their position, or to Cardinal Alfrink. The Dutch bishops found themselves during this period of tense negotiation in the position of having to claim that they had no knowledge of the secret procedures of the commission of cardinals, or of the process by which episcopal imprimaturs were first granted and then mysteriously rescinded for German and English translations of the catechism.

Although the cardinals largely sided with the initial objections of the three Roman theologians at Gazzada, there is some confusion about the commission's vote because of claims that its own report was changed by Edward Dhanis before final publication. The cardinals' commission left the work of precise revision of the catechism, in accord with their objections, to a new commission of four theologians: Edward Dhanis and Jan Visser (appointees of Rome), and G. Mulders and H. Fortmann (appointees of the Dutch bishops). In the midst of negotiations, Mulders resigned from the commission on the grounds that the changes suggested by the cardinals' commission were commands, not suggestions. As a catechist, Mulders found that the Roman suggestions would violate the intent and spirit of the new catechism. Rome was demanding long citations from church councils in the technical, scholastic language of post-Tridentine theology, which the authors of the catechism had assiduously avoided in their efforts at making the faith understandable to modern man.

Throughout 1967 and 1968 the Dutch bishops continued to champion the orthodox intentions of their theologians and catechists. They sought some compromise that would assuage the Roman objections and still do justice to the intentions of the authors of the new catechism. On October 15, 1968, the cardinals' commission published its final report, which demanded substantial changes in the book and the inclusion of a separate brochure in technical, scholastic language which set out the traditional doctrinal formulations on disputed points. Finally yielding to Roman pressure, the Dutch episcopacy published the Roman scholastic text—but as a separate, expensive brochure, rather than including it as an appendix to the original, inexpensive catechism. In a press communiqué on December 10, 1968, the Dutch bishops remarked: "When the changes and additions which the commission of cardinals has demanded are published, every competent judge will be able to see that people can continue to discuss the points of difference. Out of respect for the wishes of the pope, the bishops have decided to forego further discussion."

In an interview granted on December 2, 1968, Mgr. F. Vallainc, the press secretary for the Vatican, remarked that Rome had found no heresies in the catechism. Roman objections centered upon vague or sometimes infelicitous expressions. The index, presenting the Roman scholastic positions, was necessary if the book was to be called a "catechism." When the dispute had settled down, it seemed to Dutch theologians that the Roman methods of investigation had aimed at undermining the authority of the Dutch bishops by sowing doubts about the orthodoxy of a book they had commissioned. The theologians saw the Roman scholastic brochure, which purportly "corrects and completes" the original catechism, as an attempt at reducing pluriformity of theology within the church to a uniform acceptance of Roman (centrally controlled) theology. The issue in the dispute was primarily about who controlled theological symbols in the church and how that control was exercised. Do bishops as well as the Roman Curia possess teaching authority for the whole church? Should control over the symbols of faith take place in dialogue and trust, or through authoritarian and secret processes?

On the issue of secrecy versus open dialogue, it is significant that whereas the Dutch theologians have published a dossier with documents presenting the procedures and positions of the Dutch church in the dispute, the Roman case rests, ultimately, on appeals to the final authority of edicts. Despite the Roman objections, the Dutch publishers of *The New Dutch Catechism* introduced a second edition of the catechism in 1973 without including the Roman brochure as part of the text.[55]

The OMO-MAVO Catechism Dispute. The issues involved in the *New Dutch Catechism* dispute remain unresolved. Since 1971 Roman authorities have exerted pressure to suppress an experimental mimeographed catechism used in the secondary schools of the dioceses of Den Bosch and Breda, which are known as the OMO-MAVO schools. Once again, Dutch partners to the dispute contend that Rome lacks a sufficient sense of the demands of modern catechesis. The several volumes of the OMO-MAVO catechism claim to be orthodox in all that they present, since the catechism writers think it irresponsible catechesis to present everything at once. They also want to avoid the implication that Christianity is primarily a set of doctrines, rather than a lived experience of searching faith. The Dutch bishops, Mgrs. Bluyssen and Ernst, personally defended their catechists by intervening in the dispute. Both journeyed to Rome on several occasions to plead for a continuation of the experimental catechism, or at least for a reasonable time in which to make necessary revisions. When Cardinals Seper and Wright demanded that the entire approach of the catechism be abandoned as irredeemable, Bluyssen and Ernst argued for the possibility of revision. As in the earlier dispute on *The New Dutch Catechism,* the Dutch position sought procedures of collegial dialogue between bishops, theologians, and catechists which would allow new formulations of faith for a searching church, a legitimate pluriformity in theology, and open procedures for judgment in the church. Rome seemed to fear that an unresolvable pluralism was being introduced into the church which needed to be checked by stern, even authoritarian, measures.[56]

The Issue of Laicized Former Priests. The Dutch bishops have been in contention with the Roman authorities about the question of laicized former priests. In general, the Dutch authorities have argued for a fair and expeditious procedure by which priests who wish to marry may be laicized. Moreover, they have urged that former priests

---

55. For documentation on the *New Catechism* dispute, see W. Bless, ed., *Witboek Over de Nieuwe Katechismus* (Utrecht: Ambo Books, 1969). Citation from the Dutch bishops' press conference from page 288. The original text and the Roman additions can be found in the American edition of the catechism, *The New Dutch Catechism for Adults* (New York: Herder and Herder, 1970).

56. For the OMO-MAVO dispute, see *AK,* XXVII, *46* (November 14, 1972), columns 1021–1025.

who marry with the approval of the church have all the rights of laymen. The bishops have resisted efforts by Roman authorities to exclude laicized former priests from certain pastoral ministeries which are ordinarily open to Catholic laymen, such as teaching theology or pastoral service on parish teams. The most sensitive area concerns the presence of former priests on the theological faculties where future candidates for the priesthood study. Here again, Dutch problems are not unique. Thus married laymen and even Protestant ministers teach in seminaries in the United States. Why not former priests? Is the removal of a teacher from the faculty merely because of his marital status an unjust infringement of legitimate academic freedom? Like the church in the Netherlands, the United States church has been unwilling or unable to follow Roman directives that married former priests may not teach theology in Catholic schools. Most American Catholic university theology departments include former priests.[57]

The Issue of Marriage Legislation in the Church. Since the 1960s Dutch dioceses have been experimenting with new procedures for church annulments which differ from those allowed by the Roman Rota. The Dutch claim that they remain faithful to the Catholic tradition that a sacramental marriage does not allow the possibility of dissolution and remarriage within the church. In the new Dutch procedures, greater weight is placed on the testimony of the married couple as to the meaning and intent of their marriage than is usual in the Roman practice. Secondly, the defender of the bond—a canon lawyer charged with the task of upholding the validity of marriages— need not automatically appeal cases in which the tribunal judges that an initial marriage is null and void. Appeal remains an option, however, if the defender of the bond judges that the grounds for the declaration of nullity are debatable. This new procedure streamlines the annulment procedure, because in ordinary church practice a marriage must be declared null by two separate tribunals before a final verdict is granted.

The Dutch "officiales"—church officers of the diocese charged with regulating annulment procedures—have met regularly in recent years in order to adopt a common policy on church annulment across

---

57. The removal of Professor Henk van Luik from his position at the Catholic Institute for Theology, Amsterdam, in September 1974 would seem to be a Dutch compromise with the Roman position, although significantly other married former priests continue to teach there and in other Dutch theological centers. Indeed, Alfrink's successor, Cardinal Willebrands, successfully opposed their removal by Rome in 1976.

dioceses. They hope, thereby, to avoid pastoral confusion. Further-more, instead of an impersonal judgment removed from the couple involved, who normally have no direct contact either with their canon lawyer or the judges of the marriage tribunal, the Dutch dioceses look upon church annulment more as a pastoral than a purely juridical reality. They see marriage more as a sacrament of personal commit-ment than as a mere legal contract. They object that traditional annulment procedures are often pastorally irresponsible and unfaith-ful to the gospel injunction for forgiveness and mercy. They fault those who neglect to streamline procedures and open new possibilities for second marriages in the church in ways which would protect the classic Catholic doctrine of the indissolubility of sacramental mar-riage. Roman authorities are reluctant to give up their ultimate control over annulment procedures and cautious about introducing reform. They also question the introduction of new grounds for granting annulments, such as a plea of moral impotence to contract marriage based on psychological evidence about the moral maturity of the contracting partners. They have questioned whether Dutch procedures might not be tantamount to a genuine justification of the dissolubility of sacramental marriage.

Part of the difficulty between the Netherlands and Rome on mar-riage annulment lies in the realm of doctrine, the preservation of the Catholic doctrine of indissolubility of a sacramental marriage. Part lies in divergent views about the role of law in society. Part of the difficulty, finally, revolves around procedures. Should "law" in the church be applied more in a pastoral or in a juridical manner? Should the parties to a marriage have the right to personal contact with their canon lawyers and the judges in the marriage tribunal? Should proce-dures for annulment be streamlined, presuming the good faith and honest testimony of those seeking church annulments, or should they be multiplied to protect the theoretical ideal of marriage?[58]

The Issue of the Role of the Papal Nuncio. In the years immedi-ately following the council, Dutch Catholics urged a re-examination of the role of the papal nuncio in the national church. The nuncio is both a diplomatic representative of the Vatican to the national government and a Vatican liaison officer for the national church. It is

---

58. Dutch Catholicism was not alone in its difficulties with the Roman Rota. American dioceses also had difficulties with the Rota for following new procedures not allowed by Rome. The best statement of the Dutch position on church annulments, with the clear judgment that it deals with annulment and not divorce, is found in Dr. H. W. J. Kuipers, "Kerk Orde en Huwelijk in de Practijk," *Theologie en Pastoraat,* LXXXV 9, 291–299.

difficult to play both roles at once. It is not clear whether the papal nuncio is a sort of super-bishop within the national church who controls and channels the information flow between Rome and the national churches. The Dutch bishops have, on several occasions, sidestepped the nuncio to try to handle affairs directly with the pope and the Roman authorities. They argue that the primary line of communication between Rome and the national church should run through the episcopal conference and not the nuncio. But because the role of the nuncio is an integral part of the Vatican bureaucratic structure, Rome has resisted attempts at reducing the ecclesiastical importance of the nuncio. Dutch impatience with the nuncio system is perhaps highlighted if we recall that during the sensitive years 1966–1969, when the Dutch catechism dispute was being handled, the nuncio, Mgr. Felici, was passing judgments about the Dutch church on to his superiors in Rome without even being able to speak the Dutch language.[59]

Procedural Issues

Behind this list of substantive differences between the Netherlands and Rome lie two different visions for the church and models of procedures in the church. Perhaps the best way to uncover these two views is to rehearse some of the procedural issues involved in the above disputes, as well as other differences, such as the legitimacy of lay voice within national pastoral councils and open discussion of the celibacy rule. I list these procedural issues as alternate questions which reflect each side's difficulties with the other's vision.

1. Do the Dutch bishops achieve sufficient clarity in their formulations to guarantee fidelity to the Catholic tradition? Was Roman clarity, on the other hand, a narrow choice of one theology, scholastic fundamentalism, among the pluriform theologies allowable within the Catholic tradition?

2. Do bishops have any independent rights and autonomy over their local churches, and if so, did the Dutch bishops exceed their rights in exercising independent autonomy in their role as bishops by allowing new experiments in liturgy, catechesis, and pastoral practice? Does Rome have duties in respect to bishops, and if so, did

59. The redefinition of the position of the papal nuncio is a sore point in several national churches. For a non-Dutch objection to the traditional nuncio role, see José de Broucker, ed., *The Suenens' Dossier* (London: Gill and MacMillan, 1970), pp. 257–258.

Rome neglect its duties to respect the rights of bishops to collegial consultation? Were the Dutch endangering church unity by developing on their own a new church order based on pastoral needs? Was Roman caution in permitting changes a contributing factor in pastoral chaos and the breakdown in church order?

3. Did the Dutch bishops, even if they were merely exercising their rights, undermine the authority of the papacy in its difficult period of crisis in the post-Vatican church? Did the Roman authorities, even if they were only exercising their rights, undermine the authority of the Dutch episcopacy in its difficult period of crisis?

Even within the Dutch church itself, there arose the problem of the way in which each side controlled its supporters. Thus some members of the Roman Curia did not think that the Dutch bishops exercised sufficient control over certain progressive groups within the Dutch church who were loyal to the bishops yet displeasing to Rome—for example, Septuagint. On the other hand, Dutch Catholics asked whether the Roman authorities might not exert influence upon certain conservative groups who were loyal to Rome but displeasing to the Dutch bishops—for example, Confrontatie.

4. Would leakage from the church into the ranks of the non-churched best be prevented by renewing doctrinal formulations or by preserving older formulations? By a firm "law-and-order" use of the traditional sanction system of excommunications and interdicts, or by developing a new, more supple, sanction system? There is some question whether the church could reinstate the traditional sanction system of excommunications, prior censorship of theological writings, oaths of secrecy, and public declarations of books or persons as "unorthodox" even if it wanted to. There is also the question whether such sanctions are consonant with the fundamental gospel values of freedom and mutual, if sometimes corrective, love. Even if one finds the sanction system theoretically legitimate, is it pastorally wise or practically applicable in the post-Vatican church? Some would argue that the church cannot preserve its doctrinal unity and fidelity to tradition without such sanctions. A further issue is whether the loss of the traditional, pre-Vatican II sanctions necessarily means chaotic unorthodoxy. Can the authorities in the church find new ways of exercising control, such as the Dutch bishops were developing, by means of internal codes of ethics or a declaration of episcopal non-responsibility for groups or persons whom, after consultation, the bishops decide are not sufficiently attentive to their duties?

5. It is a moot question whether the church can suppress free information and public discussion within the church and still expect energetic commitment from an emancipated laity and lower clergy. On the other hand, will the church, if it allows free inquiry, alienate the simple faithful? Is it not better to maintain a united front and keep controversial issues or disagreements under wraps so that the dirty linen of the church is not visible to the outside world? The rejoinder is that there would not, perhaps, be so much conflict and dirty linen if the church did allow free discussion in its midst.

The substantive and procedural issues listed above can be best summed up in the question of who has the right to control—and how—information and symbols within both the national and international church. Cardinal Alfrink has repeatedly referred to two different visions of the way in which authority is to be exercised within the church, visions which lie at the bottom of the continuing conflict between Rome and the Netherlands. Because these two different visions are to be found among bishops, theologians, lower clergy, and laity throughout the international church since Vatican II, the Dutch church has become, whether it desires it or not, a symbolic center for those who support one of the two visions. While the Dutch bishops repeatedly claim that they do not seek to export their brand of Catholicism, what happens in the Netherlands gains attention in other lands. Thus, at the Catholic Study Day held in Essen in 1968, progressive German Catholics cheered the very mention of *The New Dutch Catechism*. A conservative French Catholic group, "The Silent Majority in the Church," held a congress in Versailles, November 7 and 8, 1970, on the topic, "Will the French church follow the example of the church in the Netherlands?" Three Dutch traditionalist guests were received with enthusiasm by the congress. One of them was chief celebrant at a high mass at which a Dutch choir sang Latin hymns.[60]

In the course of the ecclesiastical cold war between Rome and the Netherlands, each side has developed its own rhetoric to defend its vision of the church from attack by the other side. The Roman rhetoric relies heavily on "duty language," with appeals to obedience, humility, unity, self-sacrifice, and *legitimate* pluriformity (that which is permitted by Rome). The Dutch rhetoric system relies more on language stressing rights and duties within the collegial model of

60. *AK*, XXVI, 2 and 3 (January 8–15, 1971), columns 66–68.

the church, with pleas for dialogue, mutual respect, service, and legitimate *pluriformity* (that which arises out of the legitimate autonomy of national churches). Rome accuses the Dutch of preparing a schism. The Dutch accuse the Romans of a despotic and authoritarian exercise of power.

In its conflict with Dutch Catholicism, Rome has four chief tactics at its disposal.

1. Rome can try to isolate the Dutch episcopacy from the world episcopacy, as it did in *The New Dutch Catechism* dispute, by appointing an international commission of cardinals to judge Dutch documents. Rome saw to it that no national hierarchy granted an imprimatur in the translations of *The New Dutch Catechism* into English, German, Spanish, French, and Italian until the Roman corrections were included in the appendix, although the book was already a Catholic bestseller. The national hierarchies were unable to stop Catholic publishing houses from distributing the book without an imprimatur, or to effectively dissuade the Catholic clergy and laity from reading it. The imprimatur for the American edition of the catechism had already been granted when Rome put pressure on the Bishop of Burlington, Vermont, to rescind his authorization. Between 1966 and 1971 the catechism sold 1,230,026 copies in six languages, and became an international Catholic bestseller.

Again, in the celibacy rule dispute, Rome tried to isolate the Dutch hierarchy by publishing telegrams of episcopal support for the Roman position, although this proved to be less than solid support, once the issue was brought to the open forum of the World Synod of Bishops.

2. Rome can refuse to grant final approval to the Dutch bishops' experiments with a new pastoral order for the church, thus denying them the status of law within the church. In a period, however, when the pre-Vatican II code of canon law, codified in 1917, is largely superseded by legislation since Vatican Council II or in abeyance awaiting a new codification, this Roman weapon is not very potent. There is a great deal of confusion about what has the status of law within the church as the church awaits this new codification. Moreover, the fact that Rome has, on several occasions since 1966, approved for the whole church experiments which began in Dutch Catholicism makes it difficult to urge the ultimate seriousness of Roman objections.

3. Rome can declare Dutch documents "unorthodox" or suspect, thus robbing them of full legitimacy either within the national

church or in other lands. Here, too, there is growing confusion about what constitutes legitimacy in the post-Vatican church, so that this tactic is less powerful than it was before the Vatican Council.

4. As a final and most potent tactic, the Roman authorities could take the drastic—and unlikely—step of removing Dutch bishops from office or appointing bishops more to its liking to vacant episcopal sees. Since 1970, Rome has followed this latter course in two controversial episcopal appointments. We will examine the fruits of this course of action in the following chapter.

In the conflicts with Rome, the Dutch bishops have several tactics of their own:

1. The Dutch bishops have at their disposal the willing resources of theologians and canonists who try to legitimate Dutch positions in a theological dispute by appeals to precedents, tradition, or pastoral need. A great deal of Dutch theology has grown out of this need to justify pastoral experiment. Furthermore, elite international theologians in other countries have been producing justifications for the kind of pluriform collegial church embodied in the new Dutch structures. In this sense, the Netherlands rather than Rome usually has the majority of elite international theologians on its side.

2. The Dutch bishops can countenance or openly support innovative structures as an exercise of the sort of legitimate pluriformity within the church recognized at Vatican II. In time, these structures carry the weight of accepted custom behind them, which makes them more difficult to dismantle. Furthermore, the bishops can act as buffers between the Roman authorities and catechists or theologians who come under Roman investigation, thus forcing a long process of negotiation and compromise instead of unilateral decisions from above.

3. Dutch Catholicism's most powerful tactic is its reliance upon the free flow of information and public discussion in the church, the publishing of dossiers with full documentation of Roman and Dutch documents on a disputed issue, and a pro-Dutch slant in influential international journals or newspapers such as *Herder Correspondence, Informations Catholiques Internationales, Le Monde, La Figaro, Concilium, Orienterung, Pro Mundi Vita, Commonweal,* the *National Catholic Reporter,* and *America.* On occasion, especially when the conflict on an issue is peculiarly intense, Cardinal Alfrink grants interviews to Italian national newspapers, in which he gives full coverage to the Dutch position. Indeed, because of his exposure in

the Italian press, Alfrink has become something of a celebrity in Italy. Open communications in the church is an issue close to Alfrink's heart.

In a peculiar way, the most powerful tactics are those most dreaded by each side and most calculated to unite each against the other. The Roman service bureaucracy, like all bureaucracies, depends upon secrecy and the control of information for its power. Dutch Catholicism's tactic of free information and public discussion weakens this secrecy and control of information. On the other hand, some of Rome's strongest moves in the conflict only unite the Dutch church even more, and evoke support from non-Catholic groups, to the extent that the Roman position seems to be authoritarian, shock therapy instead of dialogue, and a foreign power's intervention against the Dutch civil consensus favoring democracy, personal liberty, tolerance, compromise and proportionality in politics, honesty and probity in comportment, and acceptance of pluralism. The continual opposition undoubtedly compromised the authority of the Dutch bishops within segments of their own church and the authority of Rome both in Dutch Catholicism and within the world church.

CONCLUSION: CHAPTERS SIX AND SEVEN

In these two chapters I have been using history and the study of documents to test whether the period 1966–1974 represented stages five and six in the hypothetical seven sequences of structural differentiation (Table 2, Chapter One). During the years of its National Pastoral Council, Dutch Catholicism specified and institutionalized new structures for the church: (a) national coordinating units, such as the Secretariat of the Roman Catholic Church Province and the ongoing National Pastoral Council; (b) new collegial structures, such as the episcopal conference, diocesan and parish pastoral councils, and personnel management committees to handle appointments and grievances of the lower clergy; (c) new arrangements for theological reflection in five autonomous centers. We have seen the way in which the role understandings of bishop, priest, and layman in the church underwent redefinition in accord with the hypotheses about a new cultural-pastoral strategy for exerting church influence (see Table 3, Chapter One). The major base of church influence shifts from the differentiated Catholic organizations to new styles of socio-ethical leadership in the wider society. The local congregation becomes a key unit of emphasis, with the priest's main role being that of pastor and spiritual leader and the layman's being that of Christian citizen. Besides these role shifts, we have also looked at the new norms of freedom of speech and inquiry which have emerged, as well as at a revised sanction system which presupposes consultation.

The magnitude of the changes I have been attempting to map has demanded a sometimes broad outline of the evidence for strategy, coalition, and conflict within the Dutch setting. The concept of coalition throws some light on unresolved conflicts. Democratization entails open political processes within the church and the subsequent emergence of pressure groups lobbying for change. Rather than viewing Dutch Catholicism as uniformly radical or progressive, we have seen that there exists a whole spectrum of attitudes. A moderate coalition of pressure groups has gained ascendency, leaving the extreme left and right wings isolated. The ecumenical coalitions confront the social authorities with conflicting loyalties vis-à-vis Protestant coalition partners and Rome. The Roman authorities, increasingly hostile toward Dutch developments, were unsuccessful in arresting the change. They could not suppress the new theology which provides cultural legitimation for the structural changes. This theology became popularized in catechisms for adult and student populations. The Dutch authorities, continuing their sympathy for renewal, protected their theologians and catechists from attack and found a functional alternative for the National Pastoral Council when it was forbidden by Rome.

It has been my contention that Dutch Catholics are less deviant in the directions in which they have been moving than in the speed and tempo with which they have institutionalized the new collegial structures and disseminated the theology of Vatican II. These collegial models and the theology which justifies them have since become international. Throughout, I have tried to use a conceptual model for studying change which invites comparative research and analysis across national boundaries. The speed of Dutch institutionalization is best explained by a combination of factors: (1) mobilization resources inherited from the period of columnization; (2) social authorities favorable to change; (3) an elective affinity between Vatican II collegial models and Dutch needs created by the pressure of columnization; and (4) an intense founding experience in a period of collective effervescence.

It is my judgment that Dutch Catholicism is currently in the final stage of structural differentiation in which the collectivity attempts to consolidate the new structure, even against the threat of counter-revolution. We can perhaps best see both the strength of the new structures and the extent to which they already represent institutional expectations if we review two "battles" in the cold war of two visions for the church: the controversial appointments of two new bishops for the Netherlands, Bishop Adrien Simonis of Rotterdam and Bishop Jan Gijsen of Roermond.

Chapter 8

New Bishops in the Netherlands: The Collectivity Consolidates the New Institutions

On December 30, 1970, Adrien J. Simonis, the episcopal nominee to represent the conservative voice at the Dutch Pastoral Council, was appointed by Rome as the new bishop of Rotterdam. Mgr. M. A. Jansen of Rotterdam had tendered his resignation on January 3, 1970, upon reaching his sixty-fifth birthday. The Cathedral Chapter of Rotterdam had agreed to wide consultation before deciding on its list of three nominees to send to Rome.[1] Wider consultation had earlier been experimented with, with happy results, for the nominations of Bishops Bluyssen and Ernst. It was decided, however, to extend the consultation beyond the more informal procedures used in those two cases. The chapter commissioned a survey, completed by 80,000 lay Catholics in the diocese, to suggest a profile of what the laity sought in a new bishop. The profile shows how the new institutions of collegiality had taken deep root within Dutch Catholicism:

> The bishop must be someone who can listen well to other people: to find out *what is alive and at work within them;* . . . He must be a man who is open to other opinions, who allows them their say . . . [a man] *who encourages the faithful to find out doctrine for themselves.* . . . It is expected that he seek, *together with his faithful,* as one who is inspiring and creative, *new ways* to give their faith shape in the world. He must stand in the middle of *a church in renewal,* with a feel for tradition, certainly, but especially with the courage to trust in the

---

1. The movement toward involving priests and laity in the choice of bishops can be seen also in the American church. In 1968, for example, groups of priests asked to have a voice in the appointment of new bishops for New York City, Green Bay, Wisconsin, Wilmington, Delaware, Saint Louis, Missouri, and Des Moines, Iowa; see *KA,* XXIII, 6 and 7 (February 9–16, 1968), column 195.

future. . . . If he is not to lose contact with the various age groups, then he must take into account that the religious sensitivities of his people are *in movement* throughout all age groups. . . . He should go to work according to good *democratic* rules. . . .[2]

The Cathedral Chapter asked 1,100 priests and laymen in the diocese to suggest to them names of priests whom they thought might fill this profile. All of the priests of the diocese, the members of the deanery councils, and the conference of religious orders were instructed that the list of the eight most mentioned names would be sent by the chapter to three separate meetings, which would consist, respectively, of the fourteen deans of the diocese, the chief officers of diocesan curial bureaus, and the faculty of the Catholic Theological Institute in Amsterdam for advice. Each of these groups was asked to list the eight names according to its order of preference. It was felt that this procedure would guarantee the choice of a bishop who could command the respect of the staffs with whom he would most closely work.

Finally, the list of eight names, ranked according to the order of preference of the three groups of deans, chief officers of curial bureaus, and faculty was sent to the diocesan pastoral council. The pastoral council chose five names from the list of eight to forward, in alphabetical order, to the Cathedral Chapter. It was stipulated from the beginning that the procedure was not an election but a multi-level consultation, with the Cathedral Chapter retaining its ancient privilege to decide on three nominees after the consultation. The chapter sent its list of three nominees to Rome, and to the episcopal conference and the papal nuncio, for their independent comments. Probably never before in history has a Catholic diocese undertaken such a thorough search for a bishop.

Of the eighty names suggested during the diocesan nominating process, Adrien Simonis' name was the one second most mentioned by 15 percent of those nominating. Eighty-five percent of the vote split over other, moderately progressive, candidates. In their list of preferences for the top eight nominees, however, the deans of the diocese, chief curial officers, and theological faculty placed Simonis' name last. His name did not appear on the list of five nominees chosen from the eight by the diocesan pastoral council, of which

---

2. *AK,* XXVI, 6 and 7 (February 5–12, 1971), column 129. All of the following citations in connection with the Simonis appointment are taken from the dossier on the appointment published in columns 117–158. Italics throughout are mine, to indicate the collective representations.

Simonis was a member, nor on the final nominee list of the chapter, of which he was also a member.

RESPONSE TO THE SIMONIS APPOINTMENT

When Simonis' appointment—breaking Rome's tradition of honoring the Cathedral Chapter's nominee list—was announced on December 30, 1970, a tense month of emergency meetings, press communiqués, and protest telegrams followed, itself a sort of collective effervescence. During a two-week period, thirty-two different meetings of priests, deans, and pastoral councils were held throughout the country to marshal support for or against Simonis.

Simonis' conservative positions during the Dutch Pastoral Council led many to fear that the new collegial church was in serious danger. In particular, many were uneasy because of an interview which Simonis held for the Catholic daily De Volkskrant, on December 31, 1970, in which he seemed to oppose the Dutch bishops' collegial policy.

Although Simonis stated that he was a supporter of diocesan and national pastoral councils, he agreed with Roman objections that such councils must be conceived of as purely advisory and not co-responsible with the bishops for the teaching authority of the church. While his nomination was cheered by Dutch conservatives, he distanced himself from both the Confrontatie group and the left-wing Septuagint group; but he did remark, "When it comes to the question of the truth of the faith, I think that Confrontatie and such groups take it more seriously and are closer to it than Septuagint."

The institutional arrangements of a collegial church seemed under threat. In the burst of public pronouncements, protest telegrams, and argument, the collective representations for the new church came to the fore. The president of the council of deans for the diocese, Dean L. van Noort, commented that Simonis did not seem to answer to the profile which saw the bishop as a bridge-builder between different groups in a pluriform church. Simonis belonged too much and too clearly to the conservative group. The executive secretariat of the diocesan pastoral council of Rotterdam issued a statement on December 30, 1970, to the effect that "a bishop must be a binding figure. It is to be feared that this bishop, despite his many fine qualities, will be a sign of contradiction in the diocese." The fourteen deans of the diocese unanimously agreed on December 31, 1970, in their objections to Dr. Simonis: (1) He was not ready to bridge over polarizations; his policy might, on the contrary, lead to a hardening of positions. (2) He could not work cooperatively with the pastoral administrative officers of the diocese. (3) His position and the manner in which he had expressed his views would most seriously endanger the common policy within the college of bishops.

Throughout the process of consultation for a new nominee, the members of the Cathedral Chapter and the pastoral council, and other officials involved in the consultative process, had honored a request by the nuncio that the names of the eight candidates being considered be kept secret. When the nuncio, publicly leaking the fact that Simonis had stood second on the list of names sent to the Cathedral Chapter, accused the Dutch officials, in what he knew to be an untruth, of "manipulation," the Rotterdam diocesan pastoral council issued a strong statement to the press on January 2, 1971:

> Although the nuncio sought with insistence that we maintain secrecy as to the names of the candidates, he has now himself broken the rules of discretion by making known that Chaplain Simonis stood second on the list of candidates, thereby suggesting the conclusion that the diocesan pastoral council manipulated the list of candidates. Taking account of the violation of professional secrecy on the part of the nuncio, we feel justified in this issue to give further disclosure of the facts. . . . We must now with great disappointment and indignation declare that the pope, without giving any reasons, has cast aside the advice which the council, after much deliberation, gave to him. All of the consultation seems to have been in vain! The appointment of Chaplain Simonis shows an intervention from above whose clear meaning leaves little doubt, namely to drive a wedge within the Dutch episcopate and the policy which the episcopacy has until now followed. Further, to stop the tendency toward *democratization* which, thanks to the leadership of the Netherlands bishops, has been allowed to develop within our church province.

The council stated its objections to its fellow-member, Simonis: "His lack of ability to intuit *what is alive* in the lives of people, his lack of *collegiality*—as recently shown by several remarks which Chaplain Simonis made in interviews for the press, radio, and television *without consultation* with the cardinal and the other bishops and without any consultation with the vicars of the diocese—and his one-sided views make him unqualified to be bishop of Rotterdam."

In a communiqué of solidarity with the curial service bureaucracy, which had advised Simonis to turn down the appointment, the gathering of the pastoral council for the Rotterdam deanery voted 75 to 3 for this resolution: "the executive college of the diocese, as it has functioned up to now, has shown a policy choice for *a searching church*. We declare ourselves in solidarity with that policy."

The fact that the Rotterdam pastoral council, all of the deans of the diocese, and the chief officers of the diocesan curial staffs unanimously opposed Simonis' nomination, and indeed suggested that he refuse it when appointed, gives some indication of how firmly the collegial concepts had penetrated the administrative elites in Rotterdam. How firmly were they entrenched among the Dutch clergy and laity? In a representative survey of all Dutch priests conducted by Intromart, 61 percent stated that they could not agree with the nomination, 17 percent supported it, and 22 percent gave no opinion. To a question, "the nomination deserves to be accepted because the pope has the right to name bishops according to his own lights and is not bound to follow advice," 55 percent disagreed, 25 percent agreed, and 20 percent gave no opinion. On the other hand, 55 percent stated that, although they would have preferred to see another bishop in Rotterdam, they believed that people should now accept the nomination as a fact. A representative sample survey testing reactions to the nomination conducted by the Netherlands Institute of Public Opinion (NIPO) showed that 53 percent of the Dutch laity accepted the nomination of Simonis while 30 percent expressed dissatisfaction. The same NIPO survey, probing non-Catholic reactions, found 36 percent of the Dutch non-Catholics in disagreement with the Simonis nomination and 32 percent in support, the rest giving no opinion.[3]

The Simonis nomination provoked, further, a national response among Dutch Catholics. Thus Katholiek Leven, Septuagint, and Action Group World Church all sent telegrams of support or protest. The Katholiek Leven reaction to the Simonis nomination indicates that the new symbols had penetrated even into the camp of those who were critical of the new church. Katholiek Leven suggested that the action of the Rotterdam deans, in opposing Simonis, was inconsistent with the principle of pluriformity. More conservative groups in the church had a right to their voice being heard in the bishops' conference. Moreover, Katholiek Leven protested that the deans were failing to be what they claimed a new bishop should be, a unifying figure who could bridge over the differing visions of the church. Action Group World Church argued that Simonis should be given a

3. That nearly 70 percent of the Dutch non-Catholic population had an opinion on Simonis supports my earlier point that a bishop in the Netherlands is a national figure.

chance to show whether "he will be able to leave *room* for positions that differ from his own but are accepted by the body of the Dutch bishops." Similar responses of protest or calls to moderation were issued by the diocesan pastoral councils in Breda, Den Bosch, and Groningen.

If there was some question about the bishop's commitment to a collegial view of the church, there was none about that of the other bishops. On December 31, Dr. Simonis met for the first time with the two vicars-general and the financial advisor of his Rotterdam diocese. On January 2, 1971, he held a three-hour interview with Cardinal Alfrink. Alfrink and the other Dutch bishops remained curiously silent about the Simonis nomination between December 30, 1970, and January 12, 1971, when most of the protest meetings took place, except to announce that they would deal with the Simonis appointment in their gathering on January 7 in Utrecht. On January 12, 1971, the Dutch bishops met for a second time to discuss the Simonis nomination, this time inviting Simonis to be present for a portion of their meeting. As if to underscore their commitment to a collegial church at all levels, they invited the vicars and financial advisors of the Rotterdam diocese to this consultation.

At the end of their January 12, 1971, consultation, the Dutch bishops issued a press communiqué which read in part:

> Concerned about the unrest and the divisions which have arisen as the result of the naming of the new bishop of Rotterdam, the bishops have established contact with the Holy See.
>
> These contacts have made clear that this appointment, in the mind of the pope, has a definitive character. Paul VI considers that this appointment, which took place after long and careful consultation by the Holy See and whereby the pope desires to serve the Dutch church, must be sustained. Therefore, *the bishops* accept Dr. A. Simonis as the new bishop of Rotterdam *into their college*. They have trust in an open and honest cooperation for the good of the community of faith.
>
> In conversation with the newly named bishop, the bishops have come to the conviction that he is ready to cooperate, while he regrets that several of his remarks after his appointment might have given the impression that he desires to set himself against the Netherlands bishop-college.

The bishops made very clear their disapproval of the insinuations of the nuncio and Roman authorities that the Dutch had manipulated the nomination: "The bishops feel that they must clearly disavow the assumption or contention that the diocese of Rotterdam, in the preparation for this appointment, conducted itself in a dishonest or untruthful way.'' They concluded their press statement with exhortations to all parties in the church to show united support for the new bishop.

Once the bishops had spoken in support of the new bishop, the protest against the Simonis nomination almost immediately died down. On January 17, Mgr. Zwartkruis of Haarlem left the country to conduct consultations in Rome. On the next day, Alfrink and Mgr. Moller of Groningen also went to Rome with the promise that they would bring up the difficult situation of the Simonis nomination in their consultation with the pope and the Roman Curia. While in Rome for this visit, Alfrink granted an interview in the Italian daily *La Stampa*, in which he gave all of the facts about the nomination. He categorically denied Roman charges of Dutch manipulation as ''absolutely false and without grounds, despite the tenacity of the voices which claim the contrary.'' Alfrink, in deploring the breakdown in communications between the Netherlands and Rome, which brought the unity of the church into danger, stated that, while he thought the Holy Father must be free in his choice of bishops, ''A procedure that lets the pope know the opinion of the episcopal conference and gives to the faithful of a diocese the chance to feel involved in one or another way in the choice of their bishop shall considerably help the mission to which a bishop is called: to bring unity and peace to the church.''

During the same interview, in answer to charges that the priests who opposed Simonis' nomination were rebellious and disobedient, Alfrink underscored the new Dutch Catholic concepts of legitimate right to ''loyal opposition'' within the church. ''It would be unfair to view the expressions of disagreement which occurred in the Netherlands after the appointment of Mgr. Simonis as rebellion or to have any doubt about the sincerity of the concern for the church which came to the fore therein.'' Alfrink ended the interview by describing what has become known in the Netherlands as ''the bishops' policy'':

> In the Netherlands, problems are very openly discussed and we bishops have always tried to further the freedom of speech, so that the real problems do not remain underground or get resolved in an underground church outside the authoritative instances. We do not pretend always to find the right solutions or solutions for export. Within the legitimate pluriformity of the universal church, that seems to us the task of the local church. The Dutch episcopacy gives preference to this pastoral method—which does not mean the superficial

or glib giving up of eternal truths—over a stance of resolute intransigency which can bring with it the danger of persecution or threaten to drive a large number of the faithful from the church because these faithful get the impression that the church does not understand their problems or merely pretends to understand them.[4]

Between his appointment and his actual consecration as bishop on March 20, 1971, Adrien Simonis underwent an apprenticeship in collegial dialogue. The curial chiefs of the diocese and the pastoral council presented him with their own versions of a pastoral policy on issues of ecumenism, preaching, catechetics, and collegial structures within the church, and asked him whether he found them acceptable. If he found them unacceptable, they would tender their resignations. In a letter to Simonis dated January 21, 1971, the executive college for the diocese of Rotterdam, of which he would be the presiding officer, remarked: "In the communiqué of the Dutch bishops for January 12, 1971, it once more appears clear that the Dutch bishops' college considers itself co-responsible for all the Dutch dioceses . . . the situation in the Netherlands church province shall indeed be chaotic if you shall distance yourself from the policy of the Dutch bishops' college of which you, yourself, without losing your identity as the bishop of Rotterdam, are going to be a part."

By March 20, 1971, the Dutch bishops, curial officials, and lay bodies had pledged their support to the new bishop. On his part, Simonis agreed to function as bishop within a new structural arrangement, operative in the diocese of Rotterdam since 1968, in which a college, consisting of the bishop and the vicars-general, is the final authority. A set of statutes defines the independent competencies of the bishops and vicars, by which the vicars enjoy a co-responsibility for pastoral policy unique in diocesan structures. Simonis also agreed to work with the existing episcopal staff.

On March 20, Simonis was formally consecrated bishop in the cathedral of Rotterdam, surrounded by all of the Dutch bishops, five bishops from mission dioceses in Tanzania, Brazil, China, and New Guinea, and the bishops from the Russian Orthodox and Old Catholic churches. Cardinal Alfrink's sermon at this consecration was a classic restatement of the collective representations for a collegial church:

> We are going to consecrate a new bishop for the church in Rotterdam. We are going to take him into the bishops' college of the universal

4. Alfrink's interview is in *AK,* XXVI, 6 and 7 (February 5–12, 1971), column 153.

church. . . . The bishops' college is not conceivable without the bishop of Rome, the pope, who is placed at the head of the college of bishops. No one can legitimately enter the college without the authorization of the pope. That is the meaning of the papal letter of appointment which was just read.

On the basis of this authorization, *the bishops of the Netherlands are going to take their new colleague into their college and thereby into the college of bishops of the whole church.* They do this with the readiness to work together openly and honestly—with the expectation and conviction that the same readiness also exists from the other side. . . .

The installment of a new bishop can be of historical impact. Therefore, it should be something that speaks for itself that by such an extremely important decision for a church province, ways would be sought that this comes about in *open and mutually trusting dialogue* between the center of the church and the local hierarchy.

In speaking to the divided reactions in response to the Simonis nomination, Alfrink painted a picture of a bishop as a moral symbol of unity for all factions:

I will gladly take this opportunity to state that in my estimation these reactions *from both sides* arose out of genuine concern for the church and in faithful solicitude for the best in the church. . . . The most regrettable thing is that this situation could have been avoided if people had chosen another procedure. . . . *Bishops of a church province cannot identify themselves with a definite group.* They have the commission under God to be shepherd *for the whole flock.* . . . This is not a question of compromise, but it is certainly a question of avoiding one-sidedness or intransigency and of an understanding of *pluriformity* where the unity of the faith allows that. . . .

Alfrink ended his sermon by turning to address Simonis personally:

I bid you welcome into our ranks. . . . In a collegial government, the contribution of each of the members has its own separate value. I can assure you that the bishops are ready to accept you with your contribution. Our mutual task will be to preserve the church of the Netherlands in the present situation in unity with the universal church, which is not conceivable without the successor to the Apostle Peter.[5]

If there had been some questions about Simonis' acceptance of a collegial church before his consecration as bishop, there can be few, judging by his public utterances and actions, since. Even his detractors, who feel that his heart is not in the new church, give him high

5. The text of Alfrink's sermon is found in *AK,* XXVI, *14* (April 2, 1971), columns 302–307.

marks for cooperation with collegiality. In his many television and journal interviews during his years as bishop, the young bishop sometimes supports theological positions which many Dutch elites consider of pre-Vatican II vintage or too negative in their evaluations of modern trends. Although he is always sympathetic to positions espoused by the pope and the Roman Curia, he has never openly criticized the joint policy of the Dutch bishops. Indeed, his only public remarks on the question of the episcopal conference have been to deny that he distances himself in any way from it. He appears frequently on public occasions flanked by his fellow Dutch bishops or with non-Catholic Christian leaders. Even though there was talk at the time of the appointment of a second conservative bishop of a 5–2 split within the ranks of the episcopal conference, Simonis' loyal acceptance of collegiality has dispelled it. Indeed, in time, church gossip spoke of a 6–1 division, on the assumption that Simonis was part of the majority policy for a new church.

Simonis' public statements show that he is especially sympathetic with those segments of the church who feel that the true and ancient doctrines are under attack. Thus he defends the traditional theological positions, although in an irenic style which avoids naming groups or persons within Dutch Catholicism or impugning the motives or dedication to the church of those who oppose his own views. Simonis seems to have taken seriously the model of the bishop as a bridge-builder who remains in contact with diverse groups. He confers with student groups and senior citizens. Again, while Simonis has made staff changes in his diocesan curia since his appointment, he has always done so in consultation with the curial staff. His appointments, moreover, have been men who support the collective bishops' policy.

The young bishop faithfully consults the diocesan pastoral council and works within the structure of the council of deans of the diocese. At no point has he invoked traditional sanctions of excommunication or suspension, although he has maintained the sanction imposed by his predecessor, Mgr. Jansen, which declared the celebration of the eucharist by a married priest in the student parish in Leiden as outside the bishop's responsibility. Even here, Simonis has exhibited surprising tolerance, having appeared at public congresses on the same platform with the suspended priests of the student parish.

Since the first week after his appointment, there have been few conflicts between the bishop and groups of priests or laity in Rotterdam. The diocese contains no groups which consider themselves an underground or alternative church. The Confrontatie group, which at first cheered his nomination, has since criticized his lack of spunk in stamping out heresy. Simonis has rejected proposals that he sponsor an old-style seminary. He supported his diocese's handling of marriage annulments even in the face of Roman objections, and pleaded for a new and more collegial method of nominating bishops when Rome appointed a second conservative, Dr. Jan Gijsen. In retrospect, the Simonis nomination does not seem to have been a genuine threat to the new structures of Dutch Catholicism. The bishop seems to have changed because of the new structures, which guarantee him maximum exposure to information, more than he has tried to change these structures in some kind of counter-revolution. On one occasion, Simonis even remarked, somewhat guilelessly, that he was, perhaps, "encapsulated by the new collegial structures."[6]

THE GIJSEN AFFAIR

A few weeks after the appointment of Bishop Simonis in Rotterdam, the Cathedral Chapter in the diocese of Roermond began its own process of drawing up a list of names for its nomination of a successor to Mgr. P. J. Moors, who had tendered his resignation to the pope upon reaching his sixty-fifth birthday. The chapter wanted at all costs to avoid another Simonis affair, which might divide the diocese into warring ecclesiastical camps. From the beginning, the chapter informed both the papal nuncio and the Roman authorities about its nominating procedure. The chapter commissioned a survey, conducted by the Sociological Institute of the University of Nijmegen, which questioned a representative sample of the Catholic population of the diocese. The aim was merely to gain a profile of what the Catholics sought in a new bishop. The summary stated that: "The new bishop of Roermond should be someone between forty and forty-nine years old, a man of faith who thoroughly understands social developments, not a sacred figure who cuts himself off from the various groups within the Catholic population, capable of working in a team, a man who knows how to show leadership."[7]

6. For two pictures of Simonis since his consecration, see his interview in the weekly *Vrij Nederland,* March 10, 1971, pp. 3–4, and the article "Bisschop Zijn in Nederland," *Internationale Katholieke Informatie,* VI, *14* (July 16–31, 1972), 3–6. Simonis' championing of his diocese's position on annulment is reported in *Internationale Katholiek Informatie,* VI, *6* (March 16–31, 1972), 4. See also Simonis' irenic letter in response to the diocesan pastoral council on the topic of ecumenism in *AK,* XXIX, *24* (November 26, 1974), columns 1100–1104. On the other hand, Simonis' ultimatum concerning the removal of a tenured professor from the Catholic Institute of Theology, Amsterdam, in September, 1974, is an indication that he retains strong conservative leanings.
7. Profile reported in *Internationale Katholieke Informatie,* V, *11* (June 1–15, 1971), 4.

On May 8, 1971, the Cathedral Chapter forwarded its list of three nominees—Dean Jochems of Heerlen, Dean Pelzer of Maastricht, and Dr. W. van Kempen of the diocesan curial staff, all considered moderates by the Cathedral Chapter—to Cardinal Alfrink for discussion by the Dutch episcopacy. On May 11, they sent the nomination list to the papal nuncio, Mgr. A. Felici. In the fall of 1970, Frans van Dooren, a conservative Catholic businessman in the Hague, wrote to several cloisters in Roermond to say that he considered Jan Gijsen the most capable to serve as the new bishop. Gijsen had given lectures for the Confrontatie and Katholiek Leven groups in the diocese on the topic of priesthood and the crisis in the church. These lectures, later printed in a brochure, suggested, in a remark widely interpreted by supporters and opponents of Gijsen as a disavowal of the Dutch bishops, that the pope was having difficulties because even some of the bishops were disobedient. In the judgment of the Cathedral Chapter, van Dooren's political activity on Gijsen's behalf was dangerous. They wrote the nuncio to tell him so. On July 6, 1971, van Dooren remarked that whatever the chapter might do, Gijsen was going to be the new bishop.[8]

When the Cathedral Chapter informed the nuncio on July 28, 1971, that in their opinion it would be disastrous if van Dooren were correct, the nuncio responded on August 7, 1971, that the remarks of van Dooren were the product of his own fantasy. The nuncio promised that the Cathedral Chapter would be informed and consulted if Rome decided to bypass its nominees.

Rome's long delay in naming a successor to Moors led to anxious reports and speculation about the person of the new bishop. Throughout the summer and fall of 1971, the Cathedral Chapter wrote to the Curia that the nomination of an explicit conservative would lead to "unholy polarization." Rome responded that no appointment had yet been definitely made.

On January 18, 1972, Dr. J. M. Gijsen, whose predominant pastoral experience was that of a chaplain for a group of retired nuns, was asked by the nuncio if he would accept the appointment as bishop. When he accepted, the appointment was made public on January 22. In response, the Dutch bishops released a laconic press communiqué: "There was some consultation on a number of points connected with the appointment. The bishops ask the faithful and

8. Documents helpful in following the events around Gijsen's appointment and consecration are available in *Internationale Katholieke Informatie*, VI, 3 (February 1–15, 1972), 3–4; 4 (February 16–29, 1972), 13–15; 5 (March 1–5, 1972), 27–29; and *AK*, XXVII, 10 (March 1972), columns 209–258. All citations until note 9 are taken from these sources.

administrators to accept the new bishop." The prevailing newspaper account of this cryptic comment about "some consultation connected with the appointment" was that the Dutch bishops were initially confronted with the appointment of Dean Joosten, the leader of the Katholiek Leven group. It was felt that the appointment of Joosten, an outspoken opponent of the bishops' policy, would be tantamount to a public repudiation by Rome of Alfrink and Dutch Catholicism. When the bishops refused to accept Joosten's nomination, Rome gave them an ultimatum to accept the lesser-known Gijsen.

The Cathedral Chapter of Roermond issued a press release to the effect that it "regretted that our careful advice was not followed, especially in our own time of growing openness and dialogue." The chapter further complained that the promised consultation between Rome and the chapter had not taken place. Nevertheless, the chapter asked all Catholics to give the new bishop a chance.

In the first weeks after his naming, most of the authorities in the diocese followed the bishops' advice to give Gijsen a chance to prove himself. Commenting on this response of the Dutch bishops, the national Catholic daily *De Volkskrant* said in an editorial, "No one should ever again say that the bishops of the Netherlands are not loyal to Rome." Most of the press remarks on the appointment commented less on the person of Gijsen than on what seemed Rome's complete disavowal of Alfrink and the bishops' policy. The appointment was front-page news in the Socialist, Protestant and Liberal papers. The leading weekly magazine of the Netherlands, *Elsevier's Magazine,* usually cautious in its church commentary, remarked: "One has to conclude that it is a humiliation of the rather prudent episcopacy, even if one grants fully the right of the pope to make an independent, final decision."

The pastoral council of the Roermond diocese met on January 29, 1972, to discuss their position on the new bishop. A motion to work supportively with Gijsen in the furtherance of diocesan policy was carried by a large majority. In a letter to all the faithful dated January 30, 1972, the retiring Bishop Moors requested that "all cooperate with my successor in faith and love for the good of all the diocese of Roermond."

In this relatively tense situation of the early weeks in February, the new bishop gave a flurry of press and television interviews in a somewhat cocksure style, stating that in his opinion there was need for greater clarity from the bishops. Against charges that he obtained the nomination by manipulation, Gijsen responded that he thought that the holy spirit could work through manipulations. On Sunday, February 6, 3,000 traditionalist Catholics organized a pilgrimage of Thanksgiving for "their" new bishop, carrying the statue of Mary, Star of the Sea, to a basilica in the city of Maastricht.

While the Dutch Catholics were making preparations for the consecration of Gijsen in Roermond, hoping that by the time it occurred discussions between the new nominee and the institutions of the diocese as well as the other Dutch bishops might lessen the emotional intensities involved, as they had in the Simonis case, Rome made a startling announcement: the pope had decided to consecrate Gijsen himself in St. Peters, along with many other bishops of the world, as a gesture of his concern and care for Dutch Catholics; and the pope had requested that Alfrink be present as co-consecrator. The pope's request was made known to the bishops on Monday, February 7, 1972. In a bishops' meeting the next day, the bishops informed the pope that they had decided not to accept his invitation, giving as their reason that they felt that a longer preparation of the Catholic community in Roermond was necessary to "come to the point of this consecration in all honesty." The new bishop needed time, they thought, to consult with the various institutions of the diocese. Finally, they feared that the consecration in Rome "would not be understood by many in the Netherlands for what the pope intended it to be, a visible sign of the unity between the church in the Netherlands with the pope and world church. They fear that, on the contrary, it can be the source of greater divisions in the community of faith." The Dutch bishops were plainly fearful that Gijsen would be championed by the traditionalist groups as "their" bishop, in a repudiation of the orthodoxy of the other bishops.

On February 9, Cardinal Villot sent a telegram to Alfrink saying that Gijsen had already accepted and that the pope earnestly requested Alfrink's presence as co-consecrator; the pope considered this gesture more important than the bishops' reasons against the Roman consecration. In an emergency meeting of the bishops to decide whether Alfrink should go to Rome as their representative, the bishops invited Gijsen for questioning. In their communiqué announcing their decision to honor the pope's request, the Dutch bishops stated that "it was apparent to the bishops that Mgr. Gijsen regrets the fact that his judgment of the bishops expressed in his brochure, 'The Priest and the Crisis in the Church,' was misunderstood as an accusation, because he did not mean it as such. Difference of opinion does not mean that he will not loyally cooperate with the bishops' conference. On the basis of this and for the sake of the unity within the church, the bishops have determined that Cardinal Alfrink will be present Sunday as co-consecrator.'' The bishops added that they hoped ''that no one will see in this decision a victory for their position at the cost of that of others.'' Even after the public humiliation of not being consulted by Rome in the appointment of the new bishop, the Dutch bishops continued to claim their rights. Thus, they responded to a papal decision to have Alfrink as co-consecrator by raising the question of whether Alfrink should go to Rome as *their* representative. They exacted a retraction of Gijsen's criticism of the bishops as a price for their cooperation.

On February 11, 1972, the bishops' decision was front-page news in most of the Dutch newspapers. The prevailing image was captured by the headline, recalling Pope Gregory VII's public humiliation of Emperor Henry IV, ''Alfrink Goes to Canossa.'' In an hour-long television interview the same day, Alfrink remarked, ''Rome did not listen a year ago to the warning at the consecration of Bishop Simonis in Rotterdam that a repetition of the same kind of nomination procedure must be avoided at all cost.'' When asked to comment on the role of the papal nuncio, Alfrink answered: ''The first line of information with the local hierarchy must not be discredited. I have tried now for twenty years to build up good communications with Rome. That is very difficult because so much other information about the church in the Netherlands goes to Rome without any control over its value by us.''

Since he has been bishop, Jan Gijsen has become one of the best-known and most controversial figures in Dutch society. Some people question his mental balance, while others see him as the savior of true doctrine and unity with Rome. Whether he agrees with the theology of Vatican II, or indeed whether he agrees with classic Catholic theology, whether he is a lonely and courageous champion of the proper role of the bishop, whether his authoritarian manner of acting betrays an authoritarian personality or mere courage in opposing a tide of compromise in the church, whether he is willing to accept dialogue and pluriformity and collegiality, and whether his opponents give him a chance to prove himself—these are all questions which are publicly discussed throughout the country. Individual Catholics and priests have claimed that this appointment has placed them before a dilemma of conscience, because to support him would seem to undermine the bishops' policy of a collegial church. Others see him as someone who is merely trying to right an exaggerated imbalance which has grown up since 1966.

An analysis of the stormy first hundred days of his reign, after which the diocese was left in a state of ecclesiastical civil war, leaves little doubt about Gijsen's initial position on a number of then controversial issues. In a flurry of public interviews and appearances, he compared himself to John the Baptist, with the mission of restoring the faith in the province of Limburg.[9]

On the question of his relation to the college of bishops, Gijsen pointed out in an open forum held in Geleen on April 10, 1972, that his appointment should not be seen as a complete disavowal of the policy of the Dutch bishops, but merely an indication that the bishops' policy was not strong and clear enough, a signal that the world church was increasingly unhappy with the freedom allowed to certain groups in the Netherlands. In his sermon on March 4, 1972, upon taking over the administration of the diocese (in the conspicuous absence of the body of the Dutch bishops) and in three documents—a letter to his priests, a letter to his faithful on Vocation Sunday, and a document prepared for discussion with diocesan bodies on his new policy entitled "Proof of a Vision for the Church in Roermond," as well as in public interviews held in *De Limburger* on April 7 and 8, 1972, and on national television on April 23, 1972—he never once alluded to the institution of a bishops' college.

In defining his self-understanding against a role definition of the bishop as a bridge-builder, who sets the rules for discussion and embodies in his person the unity between diverse groups within the church, himself above the polarized parties, Gijsen promised: "I will create great clarity. The polarization—the differences—are there already. You must not cloud them over." The new bishop signaled that his sympathies lay with those who opposed the Dutch reforms. Thus in his first sermon he remarked, "We know actually that not everyone is satisfied with the development of our church as that has become visible in the last years and that a not unimportant desire exists to change course, yes, even to reverse it." In order to create "clarity," the new bishop brought in his own team, men who agreed with his own vision, dismissing the two vicars-general of the diocese,

9. The documents cited in the text to follow the Gijsen controversy from March to May of 1972 are available in *AK*, XXVII, *20* and *21* (May 16–23, 1972), columns 449–491, and *24* and *25* (June 13–20, 1972), columns 555–583. Especially enlightening are his *De Limburger* interview and his television interview on "Brandpunt," April 23, 1972. Unless otherwise indicated all citations dealing with this period are from these sources.

Mgr. van Odijk and auxiliary Bishop H. Beel, without offering them further assignment, because "the bishop is of the opinion that the diocese must have a new administration in order to grant to its governance a clear profile and, as much as possible, *homogeneity* in thought and action."

In staking out a position on the priest as a collegial co-worker with the bishop, Gijsen continually stressed the language of duty. Everyone needed more humility, obedience, and acceptance of the cross of Jesus. In his "Proof for a Vision for the Church in Roermond," he summed up his view of the priest as "the hand and mouth of the bishop," whose most prominent characteristic should be obedience, self-abnegation, humility, and the acceptance of the cross of Jesus. In the *De Limburger* interview he stated that he saw priests as "the extension of the bishop." In a letter to all the faithful on Vocation Sunday, he devoted the major part of the letter to describing negative qualities in current priests.

The institutional arrangements which have guaranteed the concept of collegiality between bishop and priests in the Dutch dioceses, as we have seen, are four: a diocesan pastoral council with elected priest representatives; the Cathedral Chapter, whose members are appointed by the bishop in a body which has independent consultative powers; the council of all the deans of the diocese; and a role specialization by which a personnel officer or an appointment commission which enjoys the confidence of the lower clergy handles the assignment of priests in the diocese with an attempt to match the individual priest's needs, qualifications, and desires with the needs of pastoral teams or parishes. The new bishop decided to abolish the office of personnel officer and retain in his own hands the right to assign all priests.

In addressing himself to the role of public opinion in the church, Gijsen remarked: "I do not know whether it is so important whether the church is credible for public opinion or not. Christ was also not credible in his time. And then, what is public opinion? Does it exist?" The new bishop also staked out positions on the laity in the church. The laity has its own responsibility in the world under the norms set down by the church—that is, by the pope and the bishops. He tends to define the church in excessively clerical terms: the church is equated with bishops and priests.

In his efforts to create clarity for those who were confused by the Dutch bishops' policy, he espoused positions which differed markedly from the Dutch bishops' policy on church annulment and the thorny question of abortion. He stated in his interview in *De Limburger* that he considered abortion to be murder, and that any Catholic politician who cooperated with a law which legalized abortion could no longer be considered a Catholic. In so doing, the bishop neglected to make any reference to a much more subtle letter of the Dutch bishops on this question written the previous year, in which they distinguished between the morality of abortion as a private decision of conscience and the morality of laws which permitted abortion, a distinction between morality as such and the law obtaining in the Roman Catholic tradition at least since the time of Aquinas.[10]

Watching the long, painful, and embarrassing apprenticeship of Gijsen, who was reasserting the role of a bishop as a religious sovereign, as he came to grips with the genuine institutional realities of Dutch Catholicism, will help us to see those realities better. Dutch Catholicism is, in its structures, primarily a national unit, and furthermore since the mid-1960s it has been developing structural arrangements at the national and diocesan level which are supported by the majority of Dutch Catholics. Bishop Jan Gijsen, in setting out to reform these institutions, had declared himself to be, or was universally interpreted as, an opponent of the new structures. What happened to him in the process can allow us to see just how far the new structures have been consolidated.

When Bishop Gijsen attempted to substitute uniformity of staff by removing the previous two vicars, Vicar van Odijk, being interviewed on the KRO national broadcasting company on March 7, 1972, stated: "I must remark that Mgr. Gijsen is planning to bring about fundamental changes in the pastoral policy of the Netherlands Church Province and, in particular, in the policy of Mgr. Moors and his vicars. Because if it was only a question of certain small changes and nuances, then I assume that we as vicars could very well work with the bishop in mutual consultation and dialogue." The press communiqué of March 6, 1972, giving the bishop's reason for removing van Odijk and Bishop Beel from their posts, stated that Mgr. Gijsen wanted to avoid a situation in which the retiring vicars-general would be placed in a conflict of conscience by future policy decisions.

One of the central institutional facts of Dutch Catholicism is that even an authoritarian bishop does not control the flow of information in his church. Not all of the Dutch bishops together could control the flow of information produced by a vigorous Catholic daily press and

10. The episcopal letter on *abortus provocatus* in *AK*, XXVI, *11* (March 12, 1971), columns 223–238.

broadcasting company. The collective bishops of the Netherlands receive a sympathetic press presentation because they have long since learned that social authorities faced by a free media are better served by open, full information and by trust in responsible journalism.

The Cathedral Chapter, the central commission of the diocesan pastoral council, and the agenda commission of the deans of the diocese, as well as the chief officers of the curial service bureaucracy, rejected Mgr. Gijsen's "Proof of a Vision for the Church in Roermond" as a basis for cooperation. In a published response to Gijsen's document, these senior priests of the diocese stated that they could not, in conscience, work within his role definition of a bishop, which saw no room for the episcopal conference as a legitimate intervening institution between pope, world episcopacy, and local bishop. They published their response and their requests—collegiality between bishop, priests, and people, and pluriformity within the consultation and staffing of the diocese. The deans voted 23–1 against Gijsen, with only Dean J. Joosten of Echt voting for him.

On May 6, 1972, the diocesan pastoral council passed two resolutions which rejected the bishop's "Proof of a Vision" as "a very one-sided document," and requested that the deans of the diocese, the Cathedral Chapter, and the chief officers of the curial service bureaucracy continue in their posts and try to persuade the bishop to resolve the impasse. The majority of the council passed a motion (68 for, 7 against) to the effect that there was no longer any doubt about the existence of a complete break between the council and the bishop. The bishop, who had attended the council meeting, seemed stunned by the vote. "I feel that this is a rejection of my thought and efforts. I get the impression that the majority of the diocesan council is saying: you will be our bishop only when you think and proceed according to the line as we see it. If you do not do that, you are not our bishop."[11]

When Bishop Gijsen announced on May 15 that he was abolishing the office of a delegated personnel chief for the diocese, as well as the practice followed by all the other Dutch bishops of being represented in the National Commission on the Liturgy by representatives to whom the bishop delegated authority, emergency meetings were held by the Cathedral Chapter on May 16 and by the deans of the diocese on May 17. On May 19, the twelve service bureaucracies of the

11. For these citations, *De Tijd*, May 8, 1972, p. 3.

diocese, 23 of the 24 deans, and the central commission of the pastoral council published a communiqué in which they declared:

> The gathering of deans, the central commission of the Diocesan Pastoral Council, and the service bureaucracy must state in overwhelming majority that cooperation with the bishop at this time has become an impossibility. They do this with pain but think in the interest of the pastorate that they can no longer sit by and watch how the church in Limburg has turned into a chaos. They ask the bishop to restore the personnel service of the diocese. They see this as an absolute condition for coming to mutual cooperation. The readiness to cooperate remains present on their part so long as the bishop appears to grant some real meaning and content to consultation.

During these stormy months, as Gijsen progressively alienated himself from the overwhelming majority of his priests, the Cathedral Chapter had tried to avoid a complete impasse with the bishop in order to serve as a mediating body. Finally, on May 19, 1972, the chapter issued a press communication, stating: "the Cathedral Chapter must, to its great sorrow, admit that the policy execution of the bishop has led to an unholy situation for our diocese. In particular, the chapter desires to declare, emphatically, that the decision of the bishop in respect to the personnel service was taken without any consultation with the chapter, despite the promise made by the bishop to the chapter to consult the chapter before making concrete decisions." On May 24, 1972, the chapter announced to the press that it would appeal to the Holy See to mediate the impasse caused by the Holy See's recent appointment of Gijsen!

Polarization in the diocese became obvious when the daily Catholic newspapers in the province of Limburg carried, on May 19 and 20, an "Open Letter to the Priests of the Diocese of Roermond: We Support You," endorsed by 10,000 signatures of Catholic lay doctors, lawyers, mayors, and journalists. On May 20 a second paid advertisement without signatures stated, "Bishop Gijsen, go on with your policy. By our estimation 80 percent of the priests and *practicing* Catholics in Limburg support you." Partisan groups gathered signatures in support of their position.

Mgr. Gijsen's remarks on abortion were uttered in a touchy political context, because a bill to legalize abortion was then under discussion in the parliament. The Catholic KVP party had won majority support in the coalition government for a bill which would restrict abortion to cases where the mother's physical or psychological health was seriously in danger. Although previously to 1963 the KVP's electoral strength was such that it could effectively veto almost any bill in the parliament, electoral losses since the mid-1960s had reduced its power. The KVP leadership thought that the bill they supported allowing restricted legal abortion was more responsible than another bill allowing abortion on demand, which their two non-confessional coalition partners wanted to support. It seemed a foregone conclusion in the political climate of the Netherlands that a bill legalizing abortion was likely to pass. The KVP thought its position was acceptable within Catholic moral principles, enabling them to choose the lesser of two evils. It was this political context which formed the background for the nuanced position taken by the Dutch bishops condemning abortion in their 1971 letter. Some Catholics were unhappy with this episcopal lack of clarity.

When Bishop Gijsen declared that abortion is murder and that any Catholic who favored a bill which allowed abortion was no longer Catholic, he was slowly educated to some further institutional realities of Dutch Catholicism. Responding to Gijsen's interview, the chairman of the KVP parliamentary caucus, Mr. Frans Andriessen, issued a press statement in which he said that if certain church authorities found it necessary to speak out on the issue, they might at least wait until the definitive draft of the legislation was completed. Senator P. Steenkamp, the architect of the coalition compromise on abortion as the cabinet *formateur*, remarked to the press: "I do not feel personally touched in my integrity as a Catholic politician. That would be a very different matter, if Cardinal Alfrink, a man of great experience and feeling for diplomacy and tact, had taken such a stand." Catholic politicians were signalling their independence in the secular sphere.

In a press bulletin issued through the Dutch Catholic Press service on April 12, 1972, Gijsen corrected his first statement by distinguishing between a government minister who might execute the bill and a legislator who voted for it, confining his original strictures to the latter. Secondly, he retracted his first statement, leaving the judgment of Catholicity to the individual involved. "He must do some self-reflection. He should ask himself whether his conscience in this matter is sufficiently formed as that is expected of him." With these qualifications, Gijsen stood by his position.

On April 13, in a speech opening a Catholic hospital in Gelderop, Mgr. Bluyssen of Den Bosch, without mentioning any names, spoke of the problem of abortion in a widely publicized speech:

We are concerned here with a most delicate question that demands a nuanced judgment. *Abortus provocatus* is an evil because this operation occurs at the cost of what is developing into a human being. It is sad that in some circles this question is handled so easily and as if it were not a question of great importance. Only in very special cases can extreme situations of need make abortion unavoidable. Furthermore, we need to distinguish between the general rule and concrete situations of need. These last are always complicated in part because in a concrete situation several general rules can be involved. So, in the case when *abortus provocatus* might be considered, besides the general norm of protecting human life, the other general rule that a person in extreme need (for example, a pregnant woman whose health would be placed in grave danger by the birth of the child) has a right to optimum medical help also holds. *Abortus provocatus* could only be allowed as a last, extreme measure to save a life. . . . One ought also to see the distinction between punishments which the law exacts and a moral judgment. . . . Whatever happens, the proposal to change the law to legalize abortion in the circumscribed conditions shall not make abortion morally acceptable. Therefore, a different judgment will apply to the conscience. These are two different things which should be kept clearly distinct.[12]

The chairman of the KVP, Dr. D. De Zeeuw, announced on April 14 that he found Gijsen's remarks irresponsible. On April 17, he announced that he planned to meet with the bishop to discuss the issue. In a joint press communiqué stating the results of the talk, Gijsen's initial clarity ended up by his taking cover for the first time under the 1971 letter of the joint episcopacy. Their communiqué read:

This problem, which involves a question of conscience, must be handled with great prudence.

Bishop Gijsen and Mr. De Zeeuw are in agreement that everything must be done to make *abortus provocatus* unnecessary. Every energy must be employed to further the prevention (of unwanted pregnancies) and the mentality of acting with a sense of responsibility as well as a positive adoption policy.

Both recognize the proper responsibility of bishop and politician. Bishop Gijsen most emphatically supports the letter of the episcopacy as well as the interpretation of it given by Cardinal Alfrink. Mister de Zeeuw has, in his responsibility, explained . . . why Catholic politicians may have to cooperate in a legal regulation of *abortus provocatus* at this time in the Netherlands. . . .

12. Reported in *AK,* XXVII, *24* and *25* (June 13–20, 1972), column 553.

One of the institutional realities of Dutch Catholicism is that, by reason of the system of columnization, it has produced a large number of lay Catholic lawyers, doctors, politicians, scientists, and scholars who have been trained to take their Catholic responsibilities seriously. This combination of professional adult competence and strong Catholic identity—what the Dutch refer to as the emancipation of the Catholic laity—had been demonstrated years before, in the response to the bishops' Mandatory Letter of 1954, which showed that Dutch Catholics were not very well served by pure doses of duty language, and appeals to childlike obedience and responsibility. The priests who had championed this emancipation continued to join the laity in requests for new institutions which would mirror the consensus of the whole church. The considerable authority of the collective Dutch bishops has derived, in part, from their recognizing and leading the institutional revolution. That authority continues to grow and maintain itself because the Dutch bishops have developed multiple channels of communication to help them know rather well "the mind of their church." For some time, the Dutch bishops—with the exception of Mgr. Gijsen—have been cautious about making a final, considered episcopal pronouncement before consulting the prudent advice of Catholic theologians, labor leaders, politicians, doctors, educators, and catechists. As a result, almost any final decision by the collective episcopacy is guaranteed to enjoy a wide consensus.

Bishop Gijsen's whirlwind counter-revolution of one hundred days did not escape national attention or comment. The Council of Churches in North Brabant, Limburg, and Zeeland called upon all Dutch Christians not to give up working for ecumenical unity, which seemed endangered by Gijsen's appointment. The pastoral council of the diocese of Breda passed a resolution on May 17, 1972, stating that it considered the credibility of the church injured by Gijsen's decisions. The Catholic National Council on Church Missionary Activity wrote a letter to Gijsen on May 18, 1972, expressing its "concern for the credibility of the church, which you as bishop are so obviously doing violence to."

The Action Group Open Church was begun as a regional pressure group in the diocese of Roermond to preserve the new church from what they perceived as a threat in the person of Mgr. Gijsen. Within a month of the Gijsen consecration, the group was a national organization commanding the loyalties of key church elites. The National Industrial Apostolate for the Dutch episcopal conference sent a letter to the Dutch bishops dated March 1, 1972, calling the appointment of Gijsen a scandal.[13] It was unquestionable that a large group of Dutch Catholics were deeply insulted by the procedure by which Gijsen was appointed.

By the end of his stormy one hundred days in office, on May 24, 1972, when the Cathedral Chapter appealed to Rome to mediate the dispute, the break between Mgr. Gijsen and the priests of his diocese was almost complete. Table 20 reproduces the results of a survey of all the priests in Gijsen's diocese and the members of the diocesan pastoral council conducted in May 1972.[14] Gijsen had lost the loyalty of the overwhelming majority of priests and lay elites; only the retired diocesan priests tended to support him. The priests were asked to respond to the following question: "NN declares that he/she stands behind the overwhelming majority of the diocesan cadre; he/she does not stand behind the overwhelming majority of the diocesan cadre."

Of the 1038 active full-time church personnel, then, 686 had declared against Gijsen and only 115 for. It was unlikely that religious orders in the Netherlands would lend their collective support to pro-Gijsen moves. The Provincial Council for the Marist Fathers in the Netherlands disassociated the congregation from the appointment of one of its members as secretary of the bishop. When a Jesuit was appointed by Rome to act as mediator and later vicar-general for Gijsen, the Provincial of the Jesuits in the Netherlands made it clear that the appointment did not issue from his authority. None of the religious orders wanted to introduce unholy polarization within their own ranks to save Gijsen's shaky authority or to appear to be shoring him up at the expense of the other bishops.

Gijsen had made few attempts in his first one hundred days to take cover under the authority of the other bishops. Nor were the other bishops conspicuous in lending him any help. No other bishop made so much as a public reference to his name from the time of his conse-cration until the break with the Cathedral Chapter, although Mgr. Simonis stated in an interview held on March 21, 1972, on KRO radio that he regretted the way the bishop of Roermond was named, sug-gesting an alternative method of episcopal appointment by which the pope would pick an appointee from names forwarded by the episcopal conference.

Mgr. Gijsen traveled to Rome in July and was received by the pope in audience on July 15. On July 21, Gijsen issued a press com-muniqué from Rome suggesting that the Holy Father thought that

13. *AK*, XXVII, *20* and *21* (May 16–23, 1972), columns 452–453.
14. *AK*, XXVII, *35* (August 29, 1972), column 774.

TABLE 20.
Attitudes of Priests and Lay Elites of the Roermond
Diocese on the Conflict Between Bishop Gijsen
and the Diocesan Cadres

1. Diocesan Priests Active in the Ministry	(N = 600; 73% response rate)
Support the diocesan cadres	83%
Do not support the diocesan cadres	14%
Formula returned blank	3%
2. Diocesan Priests in Retirement	(N = 140; 49% response rate)
Support the diocesan cadres	25%
Do not support the diocesan cadres	68%
Formula returned blank	7%
3. Religious Order Priests Subject to Episcopal Appointment	(N = 230; 76.5% response rate)
Support the diocesan cadres	85%
Do not support the diocesan cadres	9.5%
Formula returned blank	5.5%
4. Religious Order Priests Not Subject to Episcopal Appointment	(N = 165; 100% response rate)
Support the diocesan cadres	76%
Do not support the diocesan cadres	22%
Formula returned blank	2%
5. Lay and Non-Priest Religious Members of the Diocesan Pastoral Council	(N = 66; 74% response rate)
Support the diocesan cadres	94%
Do not support the diocesan cadres	6%

the solution to the impasses in Roermond would only be possible when "clergy and people stand behind their bishop in heart and soul and trusting obedience." On July 19, 1972, the Cathedral Chapter received an answer from Cardinals Wright and Civardi in response to its appeal to the Holy See to mediate the dispute. In their letter the two cardinals stated that they could see no infringements of canon law in the way Gijsen had acted. Further, in a remark aimed at new Dutch collegial structures, the curial cardinals stated that, "the tendency to supplant the legitimate autonomy of the ordinary in his governance of his own diocese by appealing to interdiocesan institutions or other bishops goes against a fundamental requisite of the life and structure of the church.''[15]

The Cathedral Chapter declared, in response, its continued willingness to try to mediate the dispute—which rather obviously could not be so easily resolved as the Roman letter seemed to suggest in its naive appeals for solidarity. Upon his return from Rome, Gijsen appointed, on August 18, 1972, two temporary vicars-general, Father Heya van der Meer, S.J., and Pastor A. Meertens of Geleen, to facilitate the dialogue between the bishop and the various institutions of the diocese. He also requested that Dr. W. van Kempen and P. Korsten of the diocesan personnel service continue to handle the appointments of priests within the diocese, a retraction from the bishop's earlier intention to control all appointments himself.

Van der Meer's appointment came directly from the papacy, because according to the Jesuit constitutions, a Jesuit may not accept an office within the diocesan church unless expressly commanded to do so by the pope. Van der Meer had certain advantages as a mediator. His appointment was understood to be temporary. He was an outsider to Limburg, a man who had taken part in the Dutch Pastoral Council, was not branded as a member of any left-wing or right-wing pressure group, and was a holder of responsible governing positions within the Jesuit order as a member of the provincial's consultation staff and rector of the theological community in Amsterdam. As an elected delegate at the fifth session of the Pastoral Council, he had voted against resolutions to change the celibacy rule for priests. This fact enhanced his credibility with the conservatives. On the other hand, his outsider's role diminished somewhat his trustworthiness in the eyes of Limburg priests, who have been traditionally suspicious of Northerners. Furthermore, his reputation among Dutch Jesuits was that of a conservative moderate with a propensity to one-sided propagation of the traditional duty-and-humility rhetoric. Religious-order priests' fears that their open support for Gijsen would introduce polarization into their own ranks seemed confirmed when the leading Dutch liturgist, Bernard Huybers, resigned from the Jesuits in response to van der Meer's acceptance of a post under Gijsen.

Between August 18 and December 7, 1972, the impasse between the bishop, the diocesan pastoral council, and the deanery and curial

15. Letter of Cardinals Wright and Civardi in the name of the Congregation of the Clergy and the Congregation of the Bishops in *AK*, XXVII, 35 (August 29, 1972), columns 769–774.

staff continued, although on a less stormy basis than in the first hundred days. The bishop became strangely silent, giving no interviews or press communiqués. During this period, the Institute of Marketing and Research in Heerlen conducted a representative random-sample survey of Catholics in the diocese who were thirteen years and older. After almost nine months as bishop, Gijsen commanded the unqualified support of only 10 percent of the laity in the diocese. Twenty-seven percent declared that they were only partly in agreement with Gijsen's actions. Nineteen percent rejected his policy completely. Twenty-nine percent stated that they had no interest in the affair, while 15 percent stated no opinion.[16] Gijsen had very few supporters among the young. His strongest support came from traditional, older Catholics.

On December 7, Gijsen announced the permanent appointment of van der Meer and Meertens as vicars and of a new personnel chief for the diocese without consulting the Cathedral Chapter on the decision. Conflict broke out once again. Despite the fact that his move represented compromise on his earlier position that he would handle appointments directly, and personally attend the liturgical meetings instead of sending a delegate as the other Dutch bishops do, many of the Limburg priests complained that their trust had been betrayed by van der Meer, with whom they had spoken in confidence on the assumption that his appointment was temporary and mediatory. They felt that he had misrepresented his position. On December 8, the Solidarity Group Limburg, protesting the uncollegial methods of Gijsen, drew a hundred priests and laymen to a meeting in Sittard to protest the dismissal of van Kempen and Korsten as heads of the personnel service. They sent a telegram to the Dutch bishops asking for their intervention against "the dictatorial thrust of the bishop of Roermond."[17] The predicted polarization was evident on television newscasts which juxtaposed scenes of this meeting with film showing a traditionalist group outside the meeting praying the rosary in protest.

The Dutch bishops, who had taken a hands-off stance toward Gijsen, devoted their December 13, 1972, conference to the Roermond impasse. At the end of the meeting, the bishops issued a press communiqué: "The Dutch bishops can understand that many . . . Catholics are disappointed and feel that their trust has been betrayed by the latest events in the diocese of Roermond. On the other hand,

16. *De Volkskrant*, November 21, 1972, p. 6.
17. *AK*, XXVIII, *1* (January 9, 1973), column 36.

the bishops hope that the faithful . . . will continue to devote their energies to the church without allowing themselves to lose heart."[18]

In the aftermath of this crisis, Gijsen appeared more subdued and conciliatory. His vicar, van der Meer, coached him for hours to stage-manage his credibility for a television appearance on the "Brand-punt" television program in early January 1973, in which he answered interviewers' questions about the latest conflict in the diocese. He presented a revised version of his originally unacceptable "Proof for a Vision of the Church in Roermond" to the diocesan pastoral council. While the council members still found difficulties with the document, they did not reject it outright. They found a reasonable basis for dialogue within its conceptual scheme. Nevertheless, the conflict between Gijsen and his lower clergy over the issues of consultation, democratization, and pluriformity continued to smolder unresolved during the first half of 1973.

During the National Pastoral Dialogue held in Nordwijkerhout, January 26–28, 1973, the Saturday session gave rise to an emotional explosion, lasting several hours, as the critics of Bishop Gijsen sharply contested his dictatorial and authoritarian manner. The general theme of the three-day dialogue was "Achieving a Just Order in the World." In that connection, the delegates wanted a discussion of the situation in the diocese of Roermond on the premise that the church cannot bear witness to a just order in the world unless it shows credible signs of a just order in the church.

As soon as the criticism of Gijsen began, the papal nuncio immediately stalked out of the meeting in protest. Dr. Marga Klompe followed him and said, "It is, after all, an honest portrayal of the feelings to be found in the diocese of Roermond." The nuncio replied, "It is up to me to decide when I want to go away." The nuncio's somewhat mysterious and unexpected reappearance at the National Pastoral Dialogue the next morning was widely interpreted as a result of a reprimand from superior officers in Rome for his walk-out, and perhaps for his responsibility for getting Rome into the Gijsen mess in the first place. The nuncio refused to comment to the press about the National Pastoral Dialogue except to state that the church has remained untainted through the ages despite all schismatics and heretics. He also stated that he found the presence of delegate Joos Reuten "scandalous."[19] Reuten, one of the key members of the Septuagint group, had six months earlier retired from the

18. *De Volkskrant*, December 13, 1972, p. 2.
19. For Felici's remarks, cf., *De Tijd*, January 31, 1973, p. 6.

priesthood and sought permission to marry. He had been elected as a lay delegate from the diocese of Haarlem.

Bishop Gijsen sat glumly through several hours of criticism of his uncollegial manner. For the first time in almost a year, another bishop, albeit most guardedly, came to Gijsen's defense. Bishop Moller of Groningen stated:

> We cannot merely talk away the pain in Limburg. We bishops live most intensely with that pain. The bishop of Groningen and his colleagues lay under the same tensions and polarizations evident in Limburg. It is, at any rate, clear that the college of Dutch bishops is, itself, pluriform. Nevertheless, we can work together reasonably well and we want that cooperation to continue to grow. It is not a question of faith. . . . The bishops of the Netherlands have only one faith.[20]

In an emergency meeting on Sunday morning after the dramatic session devoted to the conflict, the other Dutch bishops tried to persuade Mgr. Gijsen to speak a few calming and conciliatory words to the congress. He refused. He was absent from the Sunday morning eucharist concelebrated by the other six Dutch bishops (curiously, he has never publicly concelebrated the eucharist with his fellow bishops), but he later reappeared for the discussion session. He left the Sunday afternoon sessions early.[21]

Between January and August 1973, a quiet truce seemed to reign in the diocese. Gijsen met with the deans of the diocese on February 15, 1973. He promised to engage in wider consultations with the grass-roots of the diocese and hoped, with the deans, to find a possibility for pluralism in the church, or, as he put it, "a way to reach a *both-and* mentality instead of an *either-or* one." The bishop began to say publicly that the differences and conflicts within the diocese were more complicated than he had first imagined. In the spring of 1973, he announced that he did not intend to found an alternate "ortho-dox" theological seminary, as many had feared, fulfilling a long-standing platform of the Confrontatie group. The bishop, however, made clear his intentions to form a separate communal living arrangement for students pursuing the priesthood.

Conflict between the bishop and his lower clergy broke out again in the summer of 1973 when eight students at the Institute of Theology and Pastorate in Heerlen, who were pursuing their pastoral appren-ticeship year before permanent assignment in the pastorate, wrote a

20. As cited in *De Tijd,* January 29, 1973, p. 6.
21. For the text of the pastoral dialogue, see *AK,* XVIII, 7 (April 3, 1973), columns 283–347.

rather impassioned letter to the Heerlen faculty council on May 19, 1973. The students were reacting to two recent actions: Gijsen's decision, without consulting the Heerlen faculty, to institute a communal living arrangement for students; and his refusal to ordain a graduating student who had been declared qualified for ordination by the school. Both were widely interpreted as displaying mistrust on the part of the bishop vis-à-vis the faculty and theological program of Heerlen. In their letter, the students wondered whether there would be any room for them in the pastorate, "in the church of Gijsen." The students were "anxious about the church because freedom, pluriformity, and dialogue are more and more being replaced by fear, lack of mutual trust, and persecution. The church has become for us less credible."[22] They asked the faculty of the school to join them in a dramatic *no* to the "church system of which Gijsen is the representative."

The students forwarded a copy of their letter to the agenda commission of the diocesan deans on June 12, 1973. On June 18, 1973, the director of the pastoral apprenticeship program of the school, A. Reijman, asked the deans to indicate their support for the training program being given at the school and to suggest that pastoral possibilities be made available for the school's graduates.

During the summer, the bishop became aware of these letters. On August 13, he wrote to the deans, the curatorium of the school, and the faculty council to demand that they make a clear choice: "I am asking you for an uncomplicated and very clear answer which will, in effect, choose either to agree with the position of the students as this was expressed in their letter of May 19, or to give an unconditional and absolute rejection of their position and the expressions which they used." The bishop refused to grant these three bodies any further information about the new community for seminarians, or about his refusal to ordain a student approved by the school, until these bodies made their unconditional surrender to his ultimatum. The deans were given until August 30 to reply.

The conflict became public on August 20 through a news item carried in the Catholic paper *De Limburger*. The following day, the bishop granted a newspaper interview, significantly to the non-Catholic, right-wing, *De Telegraaf*. "I take into consideration the most serious possibility that within a short time the schism will be a

---

22. For documents to follow the Heerlen dispute, see *AK*, XXVIII, *2* (October 2, 1973), columns 930–939 and (October 16, 1973), columns 979–985. All citations in the text related to this dispute are from these two sources.

fact. I am still hoping for a miracle but I do not expect it. We cannot allow a few rotten apples to spoil the whole box. If it is necessary, I will make known to the church in Limburg in which churches of the diocese Catholics can no longer worship and which priests and deans can no longer be considered as Roman Catholics.''

Local and national resources began to be mobilized against the bishop's one-sided ultimatum. Two protest groups, the Solidarity Group Limburg and the Action Group Open Church, protested the bishop's ukase. The Action Group Open Church statement commented: ''it appears from the dilemma which the bishop has placed before the deans that he equates the criticism of his practice and policy with a critique of the essence of the church and the very hierarchical structure thereof.''

On August 22, Professor Frans Haarsma of the Catholic University of Nijmegen wrote an article in *De Tijd,* in which he claimed that Gijsen's dilemma was as false as that of the students:

> The deans can only refuse to give the bishop the answer which he demands of them. Their contribution toward a resolution of the conflict can only lie in their refusal to be intimidated by ultimatums. The dilemma set before them is, after all, a false one. No church exists, however fallible, to which we have to say an unqualified no. To do that is to forget that each one of us is part of that very church. Hence, the question of the students to the faculty council and deans is not a proper question. Whoever wants to hold on to the gospel of Jesus Christ cannot avoid one or another concrete form of the church. In Limburg, the church is, concretely, that church in which Mgr Gijsen is the bishop. On the other hand, no concrete form of the church exists to which someone can give an unqualified yes. When measured against the norm of the gospel, the church must always undergo conversion, and I mean here *all* of the church and *all* of her members.

Following Haarsma's lead, the deans, in their August 25 meeting, voted 22–1 to reject the bishop's ultimatum, because ''your way of phrasing the question is unfair and was experienced by us as extremely painful. . . . We can neither understand nor accept the format of your letter, which places us before an unresolvable dilemma and leaves us with no room for another choice.'' The deans expressed their own position on the question of unity and pluriformity within the church:

> We want once again to make abundantly clear that we take our stand within the one Catholic church. We desire, therein, to experience and

preach the gospel of Jesus Christ, praying always for the spirit of God to direct us. It is our contention, however, that it is possible for us to stand within this one church with differences in our visions of the church. . . . We fear that a discussion of your questions, as they are formulated in your letter, shall lead to an unholy clash of conflicting positions which we consider disastrous for everyone in the diocese, for the laity, priests and, yes, also for you personally.

On August 30, the bishop met with the deans in a long and very difficult meeting. At the end of this meeting the bishop retracted his ultimatum. The press communiqué of the deans at the conclusion of this meeting stated: "There ought to be room for different visions, so that listening to the voice of the ordinary faithful and the understanding of the signs of the times also gain their proper place. On the basis of this formula, the sharp position of opposition is no longer necessary to the bishop and, therefore, he has retracted it."

Any hopes that Gijsen might become a collegial bishop seemed dashed by the end of his third year in office. He chose not to attend the National Pastoral Dialogue meetings of August 30 to September 1, 1974. His press release, which suggested that such dialogues between bishop, priest, and people were not wholesome for the church prompted the irenic Cardinal Alfrink in his opening address to the council to a public rebuttal:

The bishops find it extraordinarily regretful that our colleague from Roermond decided that he would not attend this pastoral dialogue. That is his prerogative, of course, and we do not cast doubt on his good intentions but we certainly want to make very clear here that we do not share any of the motives which were given to the publicity media as his reasons for staying away, inasmuch as they refer to the structure, organization, or the measure of competence of the National Pastoral Dialogue. We remain firm in our conviction that this dialogue can be wholesome for the church.[23]

In September 1974, Gijsen announced that he would no longer consider the theological school in Heerlen a suitable place for the instruction of future priests for his diocese. He opened an old-style seminary in Rolduc.[24] Despite his firm adherence to Roman directives, however, his authority remains shaky with his own lower clergy and the majority of Catholics in the diocese. He has not succeeded in being a bridge-builder beyond the traditionalists.[25] What Gijsen

23. See *AK*, XXIX, *21* (October 15, 1974), column 950.
24. See *AK*, XXIX, *20* (October 1, 1974), column 899.
25. For an account of a meeting of Roermond priests who were strongly critical of Gijsen, see *AK* XXIX, *5* (March 5, 1974), columns 229ff. The state of ecclesiastical civil war in his diocese

seems to have proved—in contradistinction to Bishop Simonis, whose term as bishop has been without such conflicts—is that no bishop in the Netherlands can try to function outside the new collegial structures without provoking serious conflict and paralysis within the diocese. It is apparent that the most important internal Dutch Catholic problem of the last ten years—the polarization of Catholic society into right-wing and left-wing camps—has been a great preoccupation of the national church since Gijsen drew the camps in his diocese into open ecclesiastical civil war.

It might be helpful to view the conflicts within Roermond and the other dioceses through the lens of Dutch political and industrial society, where the sense of proportionality of seats and state subsidies for each column or cubicle runs very deep. Some conservatives had been claiming that they did not have proportional representation in the Catholic institutional world—in the pastoral councils, deanships, and the faculty at Catholic theological centers, for example. Although the conservative charge of a cabal by a few radicals is hardly fair, the conservative voice, which was 10 percent by self-choice in the NIPO poll, did not have 10 percent of the jobs or seats in the years 1966–1970. They could make a credible case that the reformers' pluriformity was not perfectly proportional. I suspect that the moderate to progressive Catholics in the diocese of Roermond will continue to be as intransigent toward Gijsen as the Confrontatie group has been toward the Dutch bishops, until they get something like proportional representation in administrative posts—akin to the proportional allotment of ministerial posts in the Dutch coalition governments. Both the cries of "unfair play" against Gijsen and the pleas for pluriformity within the diocese gain national sympathy because they appeal to an ingrained Dutch sense of fair play. Any authority, inside or outside the Netherlands, which does not respect this sense of fair play and proportionality is bound to seem alien whatever its theological justification.

Asserting minority rights against democratic tyranny (the conservative Catholic case) is less credible in the 1970s than it was in the

---

continued through 1976. In February of 1975 he dismissed Father Nelen, C.S.S.R., from his post as mission director of the diocese of Roermond and replaced him with an elderly retired bishop. The diocesan missionary organizations as well as the national Dutch Catholic organizations refused to recognize Gijsen's new structures and pledged to continue working with Nelen. See *AK*, XXX, *3* (February 4, 1975), columns 127–140. For a dispute between Gijsen and the city-church in Maastricht in 1976 over Gijsen's relations with the theological school in Heerlen, see *AK*, XXXI, *11* (May 25, 1976), columns 500–501.

1960s, because the new methods for election to the National Pastoral Dialogue favor a more moderate representation. Moreover, if it means an authoritarian destruction of democratic institutions (the progressive case against Gijsen), it is likely to lead only to hopeless impasse, because a clear majority of Dutch Catholics favor democratization. The new institutions of the collegial church are not without their own problems. But given the stability of these institutions even against Roman and Dutch conservative attack, it seems likely that the new problems will be better addressed and solved within the institutions of collegiality than in battles to dismantle them.

JAN CARDINAL WILLEBRANDS

After the shock of the Simonis and Gijsen appointments, progressive groups feared the worst as they awaited a successor to Cardinal Alfrink as Archbishop of Utrecht. Alfrink, always a loyal player according to the rules, tendered his resignation upon reaching his seventy-fifth birthday. On December 20, 1975, Jan Cardinal Willebrands was appointed to succeed him. The choice seemed a brilliant one. His early career in the Netherlands marked him as a moderate progressive who opposed confessional separatism. Since 1960 he had served in the Secretariat for Christian Unity in Rome, having assumed directorship of the secretariat in 1969. He enjoyed an international reputation as a pioneer in ecumenical relations. He also knew the style and intrigues of Roman curial politics; indeed, he had often been mentioned as a possible pope. In Willebrands, loyalty to both church reform and Rome were guaranteed.

Willebrands' first gestures as Archbishop scored his sympathies with the new church. In a television interview carried on December 21, 1975, on the KRO network, Willebrands stressed his need to listen to his co-workers on the scene. He maintained Alfrink's curial staff of advisors. Moreover, Willebrands invoked the importance of the lay voice in the church and the need for pluriformity. He pledged to follow Alfrink's policy of being a bishop above parties.[26] Willebrands' appointment met wide and public approval from his fellow bishops, the Cathedral Chapter in Utrecht, and the Action Group Open Church, which celebrated the appointment as a sign that those in Rome responsible for the Simonis and Gijsen appointments had

26. See *AK*, XXI, *2* (January 20, 1976), columns 89–92.

lost influence.[27] In an important speech commemorating the twenty-fifth anniversary of Alfrink's episcopal consecration, Willebrands pointedly praised the structures of collegiality as Alfrink's greatest achievement.[28] Under his leadership, Dutch Catholicism successfully opposed a Roman move to dismiss married ex-priests from their teaching posts in the theological centers. His style, while different from Alfrink's—partly because he was away from the Netherlands during the stormy years of the 1960s—guarantees that the structural revolution which Alfrink championed will continue to be consolidated.

I have analyzed the reactions to and consequences of the appointments of Mgrs. Simonis and Gijsen and Cardinal Willebrands as a way to test my supposition that the new structures of collegiality have indeed been institutionalized. By his own accounting, Mgr. Simonis has been encapsulated by the new structures. Mgr. Gijsen has been blocked at every point in his efforts at counter-revolution by a massive coalition dedicated to protecting the collegial structures, a coalition which includes the other Dutch bishops, the majority of Gijsen's own lower clergy, the theologians, the Catholic mass media, and the elite lay groups. The lesson of his appointment is that in the Netherlands, bishops govern with the consent of the governed or they hardly govern at all. On the basis of the inability of two personalities, presumed to be unfavorable to the new collegial structures, to overturn their institutional embodiments, I have concluded that Dutch Catholicism is currently in stage seven of the process of structural differentiation (Table 2, Chapter One). Each year that passes, each new election that is held for parish, deanery, diocesan, or national pastoral councils, makes these structures more a solid part of the expected landscape for church decision-making in the Netherlands.

27. See *AK,* XI, *4* (February 17, 1976), column 184.
28. See *AK,* XXI, *17* (August, 1976), columns 795–796.

Chapter 9

Prognosis for the Future
of Dutch Catholicism

It has been my contention that changes in the Roman Catholic church since the 1960s are best seen as an adaptive reaction to structural differentiation. The crisis in Roman Catholicism does not indicate its eclipse or demise. It is a crisis of adaptation by which the church gives up the strategy of providing its own cradle-to-grave confessional organizations and turns to specialization in religious or pastoral tasks. Thus, as we have seen, while Dutch Catholicism had adopted a classic missionary strategy to bloc secularization, in the 1960s it switched to a cultural-pastoral strategy which looks to integrated autonomy of the church within the national society.

The church seems no less capable than other organizations—labor unions, school systems, political parties—of recognizing problems and thinking through and implementing solutions. I have followed a hypothesis which suggests seven stages in the process of problem-solving by which structural differentiation reduces the pressures due to dissatisfactions with the performance of incumbents of roles, and initial signs of disturbance are followed by a first attempt at a "holding action" on the part of the social authorities. In further stages, a period of experimenting with new ideas is followed by attempts to specify and institutionalize new structures. Finally, the new structures are consolidated as further problems begin to be defined and solved within the framework of the new structures.

The shift from a missionary to a cultural-pastoral strategy can be noted in several national settings for Roman Catholicism, so that the Dutch Catholics have shared the general direction of change with others. The rapidity and thoroughness with which Dutch Catholicism has instituted its new structures may be explained by a combination of unusual mobilization resources for change as the legacy of Dutch columnization, by social authorities open to change, and by an intense "founding experience" in an episode of collective effervescence connected with the Dutch Pastoral Council. New role definitions for bishop, priest, and laity not only helped to relieve inner Catholic tensions and the anomaly of a closed, somewhat authoritarian Catholic society within a wider, open democratic society but also relieved tensions within the wider society due to the inner contradictions of columnization.

The change from the missionary to the cultural-pastoral strategy has brought new coalition partners to Protestant and Socialist circles. This, in turn, has placed Catholic decision-makers in the dilemma of choosing between ties with these new partners and its bond with the international church. The moral authority of the church, especially as embodied in its episcopal voice, has expanded rather than diminished, so that the church joins other groups in articulating the Dutch civil religion not only for its own membership but for the whole society. Within the church community itself, there has been differentiation between the church as a moral and religious community of believers and the community as a separately organized political entity. The Dutch episcopacy has rather successfully served as a focal point of unity and consensus which maintains a loose coalition of radicals, progressives, moderates, and traditionalists in one church around a prudent, if open, Catholicism. The extreme right wing has challenged the legitimacy of the new pluriform and collegial church, turning to the Roman center as a coalition partner in its conflicts with the overwhelming majority of Dutch Catholics.

We need, however, to temper any undue optimism about the future because it is demonstrably the case that the church has suffered decline in some respects. On the other hand, the statistical evidence does not warrant a judgment that the institutional strength of the church has been weakened seriously as it faces the future.

A first index of the crisis of Dutch Catholicism is seen when we compare those who declared themselves to be Roman Catholic for the national census in 1960 and in 1970. In every census between 1920 and 1960, the Catholic population in the Netherlands increased both in absolute numbers and percentage of the whole population. In the 1970 census, however, Catholics showed a decrease in their percentage of the total population, although the absolute numbers of church members increased. In 1960 there were 4,634,478 registered

Catholics or 40 percent of the population; in 1970 there were 5,008,230 or 39.5 percent—a decrease of almost 1 percent.[1] How are we to account for this slight decline?

There are two major reasons. The first is that leakage from the church—persons who declared themselves Catholic in 1960 but not in 1970—totaled 300,000 or about 6 percent of the Catholic population. This is 200,000 more than the loss registered between 1947 and 1960. Considering that Dutch Catholicism moved in these years away from being "culture Christianity," where heavy pressures and sanctions were exerted against those who lapsed, and toward becoming a voluntary association based on free choice, this leakage seems remarkably low. Furthermore, the base population for deriving leakage statistics for the period 1960–1970, compared to the base for the period 1947–1960, was greater. Indeed, percentage of leakage remained relatively stable for the two periods. What did not remain stable was the high Catholic birthrate, which in earlier periods canceled out losses. The leakage figures, then, do not point to some new crisis.

In the period between 1960 and 1970 the number of conversions to Roman Catholicism in the Netherlands declined from 4,800 in 1960 to 1,500 in 1970. Most of the earlier conversions had been due to non-Catholics marrying Catholics and later converting. These were more than matched by leakage out of the church due to mixed marriages, a leakage which, as we have seen, has been partially arrested by new church laws allowing a more liberal mixed-marriage policy. The significant change in the Catholic growth rate in this decade, however, did not come from a decline in conversions. Indeed, any loss of influence due to decline in individual conversions seems more than compensated for by increased ecumenical cooperation.

The most significant cause for the relative decline in the Catholic percentage in the Dutch population is a dramatic drop in high Catholic birthrates due to the acceptance of birth control. In a survey of Dutch Catholics taken in June 1968, only 3 percent found birth control unacceptable. The papal encyclical *Humanae Vitae* had little impact on the Netherlands. Ninety-three percent of the

1. For comparisons of the 1960 and 1970 census, see P. van Leeuwen, "Toestand en Toekomst van de Kerken in Nederland," *AK,* XXVII, *24* and *25* (June 13–20, 1972), columns 542–550, and the report of the KASKI analysis in *Internationale Katholiek Informatie,* VI, *21* (November 1–15, 1972), pp. 3–4.

Dutch Catholics interviewed stated that their practice remained unaffected by the papal pronouncement.[2] This shift in attitude toward birth control is mirrored in the comparative percentages of Catholics by age distribution in the 1970 census: Dutch Catholics who were 8–14 years of age comprised 42.2 percent, whereas those who were 15–19 years accounted for 43.3 percent—a drop of over 1 percent, the same percentage by which the Catholic population as a whole declined. Abnormally high Catholic birthrates during the first half of this century had traditionally compensated for a constant 3 to 5 percent leakage per decade.

In the 1970 census, while the Gereformeerden percentages within the total population remained steady and the Catholics showed a slight decline, the Dutch Reformed Church exhibited a decline from 28.3 percent of the population in 1960 to 23.0 percent in 1970. The age distribution of the membership, furthermore, is very unfavorable for any chances of stabilizing the numbers or recouping losses. The percentage of Dutch citizens up to 44 years old who are members of the Dutch Reformed Church is below 23 percent. Only 19.3 percent of the Dutch population up to 14 years old, and 20.4 percent of those between 15 and 19 years old, are members of the Dutch Reformed Church. We can expect, therefore, that future censuses will display further decline for this group.

The Catholic age distribution in 1970, on the other hand, was extremely favorable for stable membership and even for future growth, since the Catholic percentage of the Dutch population under 44 years old is higher than the 39.5 percent overall national average. Table 21 shows the age distribution by percentages of the Dutch Catholic population under 44 years old.

The most noticeable deviation in the age distribution is the large drop in the age 20–24 category, showing that the largest defections from the church have come from this group. Whether this is a temporary phenomenon—a reaction to a formerly authoritarian church by youth reaching their majority—so that those presently in age categories up to 19 years will not necessarily follow the same pattern when they reach their majority, is impossible to predict, since there is no significant evidence of motivation for lapsing within this age group. The middle-level decision makers are very much aware of the youth as a special target group for the church, and are thus likely to support experimental pastoral programs which

2. See J. M. G. Thurlings, *De Wankele Zuil* (Amersfoort: De Hoorstink, 1971), pp. 160–161.

TABLE 21.

Percent of Dutch Population Which Is Catholic
by Age Distribution, 0–44 Years

Age	Percent
0–14	42.2
15–19	43.3
20–24	40.1
25–34	41.1
35–44	40.6

SOURCE: Netherlands Bureau of Statistics.

promise to maintain contact with them. During the Dutch Pastoral Council there were many calls for the church to focus its efforts on the youth: "Those who embody the future have the youth on their side." There were, indeed, pleas to choose for youth "even if it entails a radical reinterpretation of the meaning of what it is to be a church and a no less radical restructuring of the church community."[3] There seems very little reason, at present, to speak of a crisis in the membership stability or future of Dutch Catholicism taken as a whole.

Other kinds of statistics, however, give greater reason for alarm within the church. Between 1960 and 1970 there were dramatic declines in the number of priests in the Netherlands, owing to resignations from the priesthood and a decline in the numbers being ordained as well as to a marked decline in the percentage of Dutch Catholics attending weekly eucharist celebrations. Table 22 presents the figures for resignations from the priesthood, number of ordinations, and weekly mass attendance, 1960–1970.[4]

In 1969 Dutch Catholicism had 13,133 priests of whom 13.3 were over sixty-five years of age and one-third between 55 and 65. The estimates of the Catholic Sociological Bureau (KASKI) based on indices for predicting number of resignations, ordinations, and deaths, projected 12,094 priests for 1974 (18.5 percent of them over 65), and 11,111 for 1979 (26.7 percent of them over 65), and 8,764 in 1989.[5] How serious, in fact, is this crisis? Dramatic increases in resignations from the priesthood because of marriage during this

3. See the report, "Room for Youth in Becoming Adults," in *Pastoraal Concilie van de Nederlandse Kerkprovincie V*, (Amersfoort: Katholiek Archief, 1969), p. 98.
4. KASKI, memorandum No 183, pp. 14, 19, 20, 27.
5. Reported in KASKI, memorandum No. 197, January 1972, appendix 2.

TABLE 22.
Resignations from the Priesthood, Number of Ordinations,
and Weekly Mass Attendance, 1960–1970

Year	Resignations from the Priesthood (in absolute numbers)	Numbers of Ordinations (absolute numbers)	Weekly Mass Attendance, in Percent of Total Catholic Population
1960	11	318	
1961	15	306	
1962	14	279	
1963	16	301	
1964	18	271	
1965	45	237	
1966	74	227	64.4
1967	155	193	63.3
1968	202	143	56.0
1969	244	110	50.8
1970	243	48	47.2

same period can be documented for the church in France, Belgium, Germany, the United States, Spain, and Latin America. Although Dutch percentages are slightly higher than those for other national settings, the causes for the mass exodus of clergy do not seem to be peculiarly Dutch. The best explanations seem to lie in uncertainty about the role of the priest, new discussions about the value or meaning of the celibacy rule, and, seemingly most important, new possibilities of priests obtaining legitimacy for their "exit" in the form of approval for their laicization and subsequent right to marry.

Again, while the decline in the number of Dutch ordinands is particularly dramatic, the same pattern of reduced numbers of ordinations has emerged in the post-Vatican church in France, Spain, the United States, Belgium, and Germany. We must assume, therefore, that its causes are not peculiarly Dutch. On the other hand, the Dutch crisis is much less acute than it might at first appear. To begin with, the ratio of priests to laity according to projections for 1989 (one priest for every 1555 Catholics) will still compare favorably with the present ratio of priests to laity in almost every European and North American country. Dutch Catholicism had long produced a quota of priests for export; whereas Dutch Catholicism represents about 1 percent of world Catholicism, it has produced 10 percent of all missionary priests. In the late 1940s and 1950s Dutch Catholicism had excess priests to lend to Germany and France.

Despite the statistical realities, most Dutch Catholics believe that there is indeed a serious shortage of priests.

With the closing of many small and inefficient seminaries and the consolidation of theological studies in five centers, many priests have been freed from teaching for direct pastoral work. Indeed, whereas in 1950 almost 20 percent of the Dutch clergy were engaged in high school teaching, administration, or finances, by 1970 the percentage of Dutch priests in non-pastoral work was negligible. Their former jobs have been filled by laymen. Hence, there is better use of priestly specialization, which compensates for reduced numbers.

Finally, Dutch Catholicism has developed new forms of non-priestly ministry to make up for the declining number of priests. Hence, priests who resign from the ministry to marry, need not, as in almost every other national setting, be excluded from non-sacramental pastoral work. Again, new kinds of full-time lay "pastoral workers" have emerged. While the age distribution of the Dutch clergy is unfavorable, 63 percent of the 168 lay persons presently engaged in full-time pastoral work are younger than 36 years old. Further, by 1970 there were 195,500 Dutch lay Catholics, nearly 4 percent of all Catholics, involved in some form of active voluntary ministry—as choir members, liturgical readers, lay preachers, visitors for the sick of the parish, financial managers, and helpers in distributing communion or working on the liturgy.[6]

Similarly, while the number of ordinations for the celibate priesthood have declined, more than a thousand students are enrolled in theological centers, most of them in preparation for non-priestly pastoral work. Only an implicit identification of the church with the clergy can justify pessimism about the pastoral possibilities. Even the decline in numbers of the clergy, while real and symptomatic of an aging corps of priestly specialists, is less severe than is sometimes claimed. Optimism on this point, however, needs to be tempered by a recognition that most Dutch Catholics believe that a serious shortage of priests and the unfavorable age distribution of the priestly corps, coupled with resignations from the ministry on the part of the talented younger priests (most resignations fall in the age category 31–45), present a genuine morale problem for the remaining corps of priests. In 1971, 49 percent of Dutch priests were 56 years of age or older.

6. *De Weekeind Liturgie: Vormgeving, Spreiding, Organisatie en Ruimte,* KASKI report No. 323, February 1972, gives an overview of the number of lay liturgical leaders, communion distributors, and so on, as of October 1970.

The declining percentages of Dutch Catholics who attend weekly mass—a decline of 20 percent within a ten-year period—are an important and dramatic index of change which might point to a crisis of disorganization. Here, too, we need to view these statistics in some perspective. The decline is partially owing to a different interpretation of the meaning of missing mass since Vatican II. Prior to the council, Catholics believed that the deliberate missing of one weekly mass was a mortal sin. New theological interpretations of mortal sin and the relation between positive church law and the gospel, which stresses substantial rather than perfect observance as the norm, have altered this. Moreover, statistics show that of the non-weekly attenders, nearly 15 percent of the Catholic population over seven years of age attend mass one or two times a month.[7]

Dutch Catholic mass-attendance statistics look very similar to those of the United States or Germany, where declines of about 15 percent for a five-year period have also been registered.[8] Dutch statistics, like the American or German ones, also show a greater decline in attendance on the part of older Catholics (the 35 to 50 age group) than among the young.[9] In the absence of any systematic study of motivation for non-attendance, we can only speculate about the real reasons for the decline. I would expect that the declines will level off in the late 1970s around a steady statistic. Even with its dramatic declines, Dutch Catholic mass-attendance statistics still remain higher than those for Catholics in Germany, Belgium, and Switzerland, and more than double those for either Italy or France.

In the 1970s, other indicators of Catholic participation are generally favorable. Thus, 95 percent of all children born to Catholics are baptized. There is no noticeable decline in the percentage of Catholic children who attend Catholic schools—about 100 percent in primary and 80 percent in secondary schools. Almost all marriages between two Catholics are blessed in the church, and the percentage of mixed marriages blessed in a church has more than doubled since 1960. If we take into account predictable absences due to sickness, permanent shut-in status, or absence due to vaca-

---

7. See *AK*, XXX, *4* (February 18, 1975), column 156.
8. For the German statistics (a decline of 21 percent in weekly mass attendance between 1962 and 1974), see the *National Catholic Reporter*, vol. 11, no. 20, March 14, 1975, p. 20; for the American statistics (a decline of 22 percent in weekly mass attendance between 1961 and 1974), see Shirley Saldahna, William McCready, Kathleen McCourt, and Andrew M. Greeley, "American Catholics—Ten Years Later," in *The Critic*, XXXIII, *2* (January-February 1975), p. 15.
9. For the statistics, see *De Weekeind Liturgie*, report no. 323 of KASKI, p. 19.

tion, almost all Dutch Catholics over seven years of age attended Christmas services in 1972.[10] Again, contributions to church-related charities (the papal mission collection, Caritas, the Lenten mission collection) have all shown dramatic—in some cases a four-fold—increase since 1969.[11]

A balance sheet of gains and losses as revealed by the statistical evidence would not seem to justify viewing the crisis within Dutch Catholicism as one which seriously undermines the institutional strength of the church. The decreases in mass attendance are balanced by a more intense participation by about 4 percent of the lay population in active pastoral work. A decrease in the number of priests is more than matched by an increase in full-time or part-time lay ministry. It seems better to view the crisis of Dutch Catholicism as a rapid shift in modes of organizing the church around new strategies for influence than under the misleading and sweeping term "disorganization." If more pessimistic assessments of Dutch Catholicism remind us that the church faces new and serious problems in its declining priest corps and mass-attendance statistics, a sober reading of the statistical and structural record would seem to warrant a mildly optimistic view of the institutional strengths of the church as it faces the future, and an assertion that the new problems are probably less severe than the real and serious problems of the 1950s, stemming from the contradictions inherent in a structure of columnization.

What exactly is the content and extent of the much-discussed process of de-columnization and de-confessionalization of Dutch society in the 1960s? On balance, the evidence seems to point to the fact that de-columnization has taken place largely in the political arena. In all other activities, the Catholic column has remained stable or increased its percentage. Within the relatively stable structure of columnization, however, there have been three major shifts:

1. Attitudes favorable to columnization as a necessary adjunct of Catholic influence-strategies have declined much more sharply than actual columnization.

2. The Catholic organizations have adopted a more tolerant understanding of their Catholicism, seeing their identity within a context of a wider Christian ecumenical spirit as cooperative co-participants rather than antagonistic competitors in the pluralistic society.

10. For these statistics, see the KASKI report in *AK,* XXVII, *32* (August 8, 1972), columns 726–727; and *Internationale Katholieke Informatie,* VII, *1* (January 1–15, 1973), p. 5.
11. See *AK,* XXX, *4* (February 18, 1975), column 158.

3. The direct-control relation between the hierarchical church and the Catholic organizations has been severed. Appointments and policies for Catholic unions, parties, broadcasting, and schools belong within the competence of the lay staffs. The "official" church, for example, no longer has the right to appoint professors in the Catholic University or the president of the Catholic broadcasting company. Nor does it support columnization by applying a sanction system of excommunication or suggesting that Catholics who belong to non-Catholic organizations are somehow less Catholic. Again, within each of the Catholic organizations there have been movements toward democratization and collegial models of government similar to those within the church.

It will help to look at the evidence for decolumnization for several different activities between 1960 and 1970.[12]

POLITICS

Table 23 reproduces the percentage of the total vote gained by the Catholic KVP party, 1959–1972. While "practicing" Catholics (those who attend church every week) are more likely to vote KVP than "less practicing" Catholics, voting Catholic has become increasingly less an indicator of commitment. This becomes evident if we compare the percentage of "practicing" Catholics who voted KVP in three national elections: 77 percent in 1967; 70 percent in 1971; and 53 percent in 1972.[13]

The decline in the fortunes of the KVP seem to stem, then, from sources other than a loss of Catholic identity. Catholics now represent about one-fourth of all votes for the Socialist PVDA, the Liberal VVD, and the Moderate DS-70 and D-66 parties, and nearly half of the radical leftist PPR party, which is an ecumenically religious party based on gospel principles but opposed to columnization. In the five-party Socialist-confessional government formed in 1973, Catholics were represented as cabinet ministers and undersecretaries from the Socialist and PPR parties as well as the KVP. Non-Catholic parties have become less anti-religious as they aim at luring Catholics away from the KVP. While the KVP has sought to federate the three largest confessional parties into one centrist

12. For statistic on Catholic decolumnization, see the *KRO* brochure "Verzuiling en Ontzuiling" (Hilversum, 1960).
13. For the statistics on voting for the KVP, see *De Nederlandse Kiezer '72* (Alphen aan den Rijn: Samsom, 1973), p. 32.

TABLE 23.
KVP Percent of Total Vote

Year	Percent
1959	31.6
1963	31.9
1967	26.5
1971	22.3
1972	17.7

Christian Democratic party, its efforts have thus far proven unsuccessful. The KVP has also been unsuccessful in attracting non-Catholic voters. Voters for the KVP remain around 98 percent Catholic. However dramatic the process of de-confessionalization in Dutch politics in the 1960s—a process likely to continue in future elections—the confessional bloc which holds nearly one-third of all parliamentary seats is likely to occupy the central and controlling position in Dutch political life for some time to come.

LABOR UNIONS

The Catholic labor union showed a slight membership increase in the 1960s, from 411,785 members in 1961 to 428,346 in 1968. This growth, however, was less than the proportional growth of the Catholic population in the 1960s and lagged slightly behind the growth statistics for the larger Socialist NVV and the smaller Protestant CNV unions. Nevertheless, 80 percent of all Catholics organized into unions still belong to Catholic unions. The Catholic union has close working relations with the other two unions. The three have approved plans for a unitary federation, without, however, losing the separate identities of the three blocs. In place of an earlier arrangement for guaranteeing the Catholicity of the unions by appointing a priest-chaplain to every local union, the Catholic Union now has a think-tank, consisting mainly of lay leaders, whose task it is to make evident the consequences of the gospels for union activities. In the area of union activity, therefore, decolumnization entails more a defusing of ideological antagonism and the growth of cooperative federalism rather than any actual decline in the structure of columnization.

COMMUNICATIONS MEDIA

The same high percentage of Catholics (75 percent of all families) subscribe to a Catholic daily in the 1970s as in the 1950s. The actual number of subscriptions has increased from 818,000 in 1955 to 1,050,000 in 1968, with the regional and provincial Catholic dailies showing an especially high growth rate of 20 percent, from 602,000 subscriptions in 1955 to 770,000 in 1968. Although one of the national Catholic dailies, *De Volkskrant,* removed the title "Catholic" from its masthead in 1966 and has been successful in winning new non-Catholic subscribers, it continues to be considered Catholic since it has not noticeably lost Catholic subscribers or reduced the amount of space devoted to church news. Seventy-six percent of the readers of *De Volkskrant* in 1973 were Catholic, of which one-third were non-practicing.[14]

The KRO broadcasting company experienced some slippage in the 1960s but has begun to regain subscribers in the 1970s. The statistics for subscribers are: 604,243 in 1960, 545,262 in 1970, and 549,304 in 1972. Thus, the KRO has remained relatively stable, winning the support of about 55 percent of all Dutch Catholic families. The KRO is pursuing, in the 1970s, a policy of open, tolerant Catholicism and extensive internal democratization, which includes the election of its governing board of subscribers.[15]

The stability of the Catholic press and broadcasting's hold on the Catholic market indicates that Dutch Catholics will continue to be exposed to a greater percentage of church news, theology, and catechetics than their counterparts in other lands. This will both reinforce residual Catholic identities and guarantee the continuous critical eye of a free yet consciously Catholic press and communications media in the 1970s. This is a factor of great institutional strength for the continuance of open Catholicism in the Netherlands.

There have been no noticeable changes in the proportion of the Catholic column's hold on the school system, health services (Catholic hospitals, the Catholic White-Yellow Cross), and social work. Indeed, in the 1960s the Catholics gained further subsidies for higher education and auxiliary efforts in the social arena (for example, Formation Centers for continuing education).

What, then, besides political shifts in the direction of de-confes-

14. Information gained from the bureau of marketing research, *De Volkskrant.*
15. The KRO policy for the 1970s of supporting an open, tolerant Catholicism is presented in the brochure by I. B. M. Wust, "KRO: De Toekomst als Uitdaging" (Hilversum, 1969).

sionalization, is the content of de-columnization in other sectors of the Catholic column?

1. The attitudes of Catholics toward columnization have shifted so that only 42 percent of Catholics think that a Catholic newspaper is necessary, 38 percent underwrite the necessity of Catholic hospital systems, 37 percent that of a Catholic broadcasting company, and 34 percent that of Catholic unions. As many as 46 percent of the stable KVP voters think that party politics and religion should be separated. In the process of change in the 1960s, therefore, there exists a marked disproportionality between actual columnization, which is still very high, and a "columnization" mentality which has been noticeably reduced.[16]

2. Almost all of the Catholic organizations in the 1960s underwent a period of re-examining their identity by raising the question of the meaning and purpose of separate Catholic schools, unions, parties, broadcasting, and so on. Almost all of them, however, decided to retain and emphasize their Catholic identity so long as that identity was one of open, tolerant Catholicism based on a willingness to cooperate with non-Catholic sister organizations, instead of being an identity premised upon antagonism toward competing organizations from the other columns. Some Catholic groups, such as the Thijm fellowship or the Catholic Institute for Journalism, revised their statutes, in what proved to be largely symbolic acts, to state that they were ecumenically Christian rather than narrowly Catholic organizations.

3. A continuous extension of internal democratization has occurred within the Catholic organizations, most noticeably within the Catholic broadcasting company, school system, and—to a lesser extent—the Catholic unions. Like the church, the Catholic organizations have become less authoritarian in their bureaucratic structure.

With the reduction of the pressures of columnization caused by ideological antagonisms between the competing blocs, one should expect that the structure of columnization will maintain itself in the Catholic Netherlands for some time to come. The column's organizations will continue to receive state subsidy. Residual Catholic loyalties and the lack of more competitively attractive alternatives should generate continued adherence to the Catholic organizations, especially now that their authoritarian, elitist character has been considerably reduced. This means, then, that the enormous institutional

16. J. Thurlings, *De Wankele Zuil*, p. 144.

strengths of Dutch Catholicism will continue. The unique mobilization resources remain.

The extent of actual de-columnization is considerably less than the much used slogans of "de-confessionalization" would lead us to surmise, although the dramatic shift in attitudes should eventually lead to greater actual de-columnization. Except in the political arena, de-confessionalization chiefly entails a shift in the strategy of missionary separatism under clerical dominance to one of integrated autonomy and pluralist cooperation through the laity, who are seen as the key agents of Catholic influence in the wider society. Furthermore, the causal thrust of this change seems to have received its greatest stimulus from *within* the church rather than the reverse. As J. Thurlings has put it: "In the core of the church there has been more change than in the peripheral zones, and the movement toward de-confessionalization itself seems to have received its greatest stimulus from inside the church."[17]

PROGNOSIS FOR THE FUTURE

It is my judgment that the structural shifts of the 1960s within Dutch Catholicism have been consolidated, both in changes in Dutch Catholic attitudes and in structures. The problems faced by the church in the 1970s—polarization within the church of the left and right wings, intransigent refusal by the right wing to accept the legitimacy of the structural changes, a perceived shortage in the number of priests, and declines in church attendance—will be handled within the new structures. I do not foresee a successful dismantling of these structures or right-wing dominance of the church. With an institutionally free press and the structural realities of a Catholicism newly emerged out of columnization, new appointees as bishop, whatever their personalities or theological visions, will be forced to be more responsive to the interests and pressures of the entire Catholic community than bishops in other national settings with different, less democratic, structures for the church. To the extent that the real pressures of columnization have already been diffused and the basic structural contours of reform have been institutionalized, the atmosphere will, of course, be less emotionally charged or revolutionary than it was in the 1960s. I expect that the mood of the church will be one of quiet consolidation.

17. *Ibid.*, p. 151.

There are those in the Netherlands who read the evidence more pessimistically than I have. They point to the high personal costs to many of those involved in the reform of the 1960s and the fact that many of the first reformers (such as Mgr. Ruygers, Dr. C. Trimbos, and Daniel De Lange) have retired from active involvement in reform. The results of the reform were often more ambiguous than the reformers initially expected. It is evident that the new structures are not the kingdom of God on earth. Perhaps they have brought with them as many problems as those faced in earlier periods. But are not social structures always a delicate balance of pressures and tensions, entailing specific costs and advantages? The years 1958 to 1974 introduced more pain and dislocation for many people, and destroyed more traditions that they held sacred, than was foreseen in the years of enthusiastic rhetoric and euphoria. It would undoubtedly be small consolation to them that the model of structural differentiation could have warned them to expect just such conflict, pain, and dislocation as the price for successful reform.

The mood of many of the Dutch Catholics I interviewed was much more sober than in the 1960s. The collective effervescence has burned itself out. Nevertheless, Bishop Nierman was right when he commented in 1966, "one thing we know for sure: there is no turning back." Perhaps the record of Dutch Catholic reform is more ambiguous than my analysis has suggested. But even taking all the ambiguity into account, I am convinced that the structural revolution of Dutch Catholicism in the 1960s was by far the most significant sociological event within Dutch society in that period. I think, too, that when the religious history of the international Catholic church during the second half of the twentieth century is finally written, from a perspective of greater information and the advantage of a longer time interval, the Dutch structural revolution and the actors who brought it about will occupy a most prominent place in the account.

Index

Aalberse, P.J., 41–42
Abbink, G.A., 36n
Abortion, 278–279, 281–283
Action Group Open Church, 231, 239, 284–285, 292, 295
Action Group World Church, 231, 235, 238–239, 266–267
Adelbert Association, 95
Adolfs, Robert, 97n
Advanced Institute of Catechetics, 96
Advanced School of Economics, 77n
Aengenent, J.D., 41–42
Agricola, 25
Agterof, Andre, 134n
à Kempis, Thomas, 25
Alba, Duke of, 24
Alexander VII, 29
Alfrink, Bernard, 21, 112, 132–133; and John XXIII, 21–22, 147; defends Bishops' 1954 Mandatory Letter, 56, 88; on role of bishop, 88–89, 171–172, 188–189; and decolumnization, 90–91; and mixed marriages, 95; made cardinal, 97; and Vatican II, 97, 108–109; on laity's role in Vatican II preparations, 107–108; on Roman curia, 108, 109, 147; and contraception issue, 117; on free speech in Church, 123–124; and ecumenism, 127, 128–129; and conversion of Princess Irene, 129–130; and curial censorship, 139; and Paul VI, 147; on Dutch Catholic reform, 147–149; and Dutch Pastoral Council, 160, 171–172, 175, 192, 193; on "bishop in

council," 176, 177–178; on models of church, 181; on collegiality, 188–189, 269–270; as international figure, 190; and celibacy dispute, 192, 193, 195–196; as national hero, 201; and Sint Michael's Legion, 231–232; and Confrontatie, 233; and Septuagint, 241–242, 243; and *New Dutch Catechism*, 248, 249; on models of authority, 256; and Italian news media, 258–259; and Simonis appointment, 267, 268–269; and Gijsen affair, 273, 274, 275–276, 293; resignation of, 295; Willebrands on, 296
Algemeen Handelsblad, The, 33
Almond, G.A., 82
America, 258
Amsterdam City Church, 222–223
Amsterdam Student Church, 240, 243, 244
Andriessen, Frans, 282
Angell, Robert Cooley, 5n
Annual General Disputation for Catholic Students, 142
Annual St. Thomas Aquinas Dispute, 127
Anti-Catholicism, 32, 33, 37
Anti-Revolutionary Party (ARP), 36, 39–40, 41, 63, 72, 73 table
Apostolic vicars, 29–30, 32, 33
April Movement, 37
Aquinas, Saint Thomas, 213, 279
Archief van de Kerken, 219
Ariens, Alphonse, 41–42
Arminians, 26–28